SOURCES

Notable Selections in *Sociology*
THIRD EDITION

About the Editor

KURT FINSTERBUSCH received his bachelor's degree in history from Princeton University in 1957 and a bachelor of divinity degree from Grace Theological Seminary in 1960. His Ph.D. in sociology, from Columbia University, was conferred in 1969. He is the author of *Understanding Social Impacts* (Sage Publications, 1980); coauthor, with Jerald Hage, of *Organizational Change as a Development Strategy* (Lynne Rienner, 1987); and coauthor, with Annabelle Bender Motz, of *Social Research for Policy Decisions* (Wadsworth, 1980). He is currently a professor of sociology at the University of Maryland, College Park, and he is the academic editor of *Annual Editions: Sociology* and of *Taking Sides: Clashing Views on Controversial Social Issues* (now in its 10th edition), both published by Dushkin/McGraw-Hill.

SOURCES

Notable Selections in
Sociology

THIRD EDITION

Edited by
KURT FINSTERBUSCH
University of Maryland

Dushkin/McGraw-Hill

A Division of The McGraw-Hill Companies

I dedicate this book to Sophie, Jack, and Gus with the hope
that the wisdom it contains will help improve their world.

Third Edition

123456789FGRFGR321098

Library of Congress Cataloging-in-Publication Data
    Main entry under title:
    Sources: notable selections in sociology/edited by Kurt Finsterbusch.—3rd ed.
    Includes bibliographical references and index.
    1. Sociology. I. Finsterbusch, Kurt, *comp.*

                                                                            301
0-697-39140-X   95-74676

 Printed on Recycled Paper

Preface

The subject matter of sociology is ourselves—people interacting with one another in groups. Sociologists seek to understand in a systematic and scientific way the social behavior of human beings and human arrangements. Sociologists question seemingly familiar and commonplace aspects of our social lives, and offer novel and surprising answers. To study sociology is to explore society in new and dynamic ways.

Sociology is a form of scientific inquiry that gives us the intellectual tools for understanding our world more profoundly. As a discipline, sociology has evolved its own history of ideas and thinkers, research methods, and theories. In this volume, I have put directly into your hands those researchers and writers whose works have enduring value for the study of society.

Sources: Notable Selections in Sociology brings together 46 selections (classic articles, book excerpts, and case studies) that have shaped the study of society and our contemporary understanding of it. I have included the works of distinguished sociological observers, past and present, from Marx and Engels on class to Goffman on the presentation of self and Chirot on societal change. The selections also reflect the long-standing tradition in sociology of incorporating useful insights from related disciplines. Thus, the volume includes contributions by anthropologists, political scientists, psychologists, ecologists, and economists.

Each selection was chosen because, in my opinion, it has helped shape the sociological inquiry or is a profound description and analysis of a current sociological issue. For this third edition, I have replaced some of the classics that appeared in the second edition because profound social changes have reduced their applicability. In their place I have added recent selections that have not stood the test of time but that do represent a strand of current thinking that deserves consideration. In all, 16 of the 46 selections are new.

Each selection contains essential ideas used in the sociological enterprise or has served as some kind of a touchstone for other scholars. As a whole, *Sources* is designed to be an accessible, reasonably comprehensive introduction to sociological classics. I have tried to select readings across a broad spectrum, i.e., the ideas, insights, and themes presented in these selections are not necessarily limited to a particular society. Accordingly, they should enable students to analyze the behaviors and institutions of many nations.

Plan of the book.　　These selections are well suited to courses that attempt to convey the richness of the sociological perspective and require more than a superficial grasp of major sociological concepts and theories. The selections are organized topically around the major areas of study within sociology: the selections in Part 1 introduce the sociological perspective; Part 2, the individual and society; Part 3, stratification; Part 4, social institutions; and Part 5, social change and the future. Each selection is preceded by a headnote that establishes the relevance of the selection and provides biographical information on the author.

On the Internet.   Each part in this book is preceded by an *On the Internet* page. This page provides a list of Internet site addresses that are relevant to the part as well as a description of each site.

A word to the instructor.   An *Instructor's Manual With Test Questions* (multiple-choice and essay) is available through the publisher for the instructor using *Sources* in the classroom.

   Sources: Notable Selections in Sociology is only one title in the Sources series. If you are interested in seeing the table of contents for any of the other titles, please visit the Sources Web site at http://www.dushkin.com/sources/.

Acknowledgments.   I would like to extend my appreciation to the many professors across the United States and Canada who reviewed the second edition of *Sources*. Thanks go to those who responded with specific suggestions for this edition:

William F. Daddio
Georgetown University

Robert Dunne
Colorado College

Irene Fala
Baldwin Wallace College

Joseph Galaskiewicz
University of Minnesota

Albeno P. Garbin
University of Georgia

Anita Garey
University of New Hampshire

Dennis Malared
Grand Valley State University

Thomas Moore
Asbury College

Kenneth Morris
University of Georgia

Kelly Stelzer
Umpqua Community College

Richard Stempien
Mohawk Valley Community
   College

   I welcome your comments and observations about the selections in this volume and encourage you to write to me with suggestions for other selections to include or changes to consider. Please send your remarks to me in care of Dushkin/McGraw-Hill, Sluice Dock, Guilford, CT 06437.

Kurt Finsterbusch
University of Maryland

Contents

PART FOUR   *Social Institutions*   237

CHAPTER 10   The Political System   239

PART ONE

Introduction to Sociology

On the Internet . . .

Sites appropriate to Part One

The American Sociological Association (ASA), founded in 1905, is a nonprofit membership association dedicated to advancing sociology as a scientific discipline and profession serving the public good. With over 13,200 members, the ASA encompasses sociologists who are college and university faculty members, researchers, practitioners, and students.

```
http://www.asanet.org/default.htm
```

This page, created by Dr. Frank Elwell of Murray State University in Kentucky, is an undergraduate introduction to the works of C. Wright Mills. This site includes Mills's work on mass society, rationalization, industrialism, and the power elite.

```
http://msumusik.mursuky.edu/~felwell/
    http/mills/index.htm
```

The SocioWeb is an independent guide to the sociological resources that are available on the Internet and is founded in the belief that the Internet can help to unite the sociological community.

```
http://www.socioweb.com/~markbl/socioweb/
```

CHAPTER 1

The Sociological Perspective

1.1 PETER L. BERGER

Sociology as an Individual Pastime

What is sociology and what are the defining characteristics of a sociologist? Among the best answers to these questions are those given by Peter L. Berger. Berger (b. 1929) is director of the Institute for the Study of Economic Culture at Boston University and a prominent contemporary sociologist who is known for his pithy prose. In the following selection from his book *Invitation to Sociology: A Humanistic Perspective* (Anchor Books, 1963), Berger explains that sociology involves the passion to deeply understand the everyday social reality around us. The sociologist is a passionate questioner. Sociologists also desire to help people and improve society, but these characteristics are not unique to sociologists. They share these passions with many citizens and many other professions. According to Berger, sociologists are relatively unique in that they seek to understand society not as it is taught in Sunday school (i.e., not the way it should be) but as it actually is. Those who fear or are eager to avoid what Berger calls "shocking discoveries" should best stay away from sociology. *Invitation to Sociology* is considered one of the best statements on sociology and sociologists.

Key Concept: sociology as the passion to understand

*T*he sociologist ... is someone concerned with understanding society in a disciplined way. The nature of this discipline is scientific. This means that what the sociologist finds and says about the social phenomena he studies occurs within a certain rather strictly defined frame of reference. One of the main characteristics of this scientific frame of reference is that operations are bound by certain rules of evidence. As a scientist, the sociologist tries to be objective, to control his personal preferences and prejudices, to perceive clearly rather than to judge normatively. This restraint, of course, does not embrace the totality of the sociologist's existence as a human being, but is limited to his operations *qua* sociologist. Nor does the sociologist claim that his frame of reference is the only one within which society can be looked at. For that matter, very few scientists in any field would claim today that one should look at the world only scientifically. The botanist looking at a daffodil has no reason to dispute the right of the poet to look at the same object in a very different manner. There are many ways of playing. The point is not that one denies other people's games but that one is clear about the rules of one's own. The game of the sociologist, then, uses scientific rules. As a result, the sociologist must be clear in his own mind as to the meaning of these rules. That is, he must concern himself with methodological questions. Methodology does not constitute his goal. The latter, let us recall once more, is the attempt to understand society. Methodology helps in reaching this goal.... Finally, the interest of the sociologist is primarily theoretical. That is, he is interested in understanding for its own sake. He may be aware of or even concerned with the practical applicability and consequences of his findings, but at that point he leaves the sociological frame of reference as such and moves into realms of values, beliefs and ideas that he shares with other men who are not sociologists. ...

We would say then that the sociologist (that is, the one we would really like to invite to our game) is a person intensively, endlessly, shamelessly interested in the doings of men. His natural habitat is all the human gathering places of the world, wherever men come together. The sociologist may be interested in many other things. But his consuming interest remains in the world of men, their institutions, their history, their passions. And since he is interested in men, nothing that men do can be altogether tedious for him. He will naturally be interested in the events that engage men's ultimate beliefs, their moments of tragedy and grandeur and ecstasy. But he will also be fascinated by the commonplace, the everyday. He will know reverence, but this reverence will not prevent him from wanting to see and to understand. He may sometimes feel revulsion or contempt. But this also will not deter him from wanting to have his questions answered. The sociologist, in his quest for understanding, moves through the world of men without respect for the usual lines of demarcation. Nobility and degradation, power and obscurity, intelligence and folly—these are equally *interesting* to him, however unequal they may be in his personal values or tastes. Thus his questions may lead him to all possible levels of society, the best and the least known places, the most respected and the most despised. And, if he is a good sociologist, he will find himself in all these places because his own questions have so taken possession of him that he has little choice but to seek for answers. ...

The sociologist will occupy himself with matters that others regard as too sacred or as too distasteful for dispassionate investigation. He will find rewarding the company of priests or of prostitutes, depending not on his personal preferences but on the questions he happens to be asking at the moment. He will also concern himself with matters that others may find much too boring. He will be interested in the human interaction that goes with warfare or with great intellectual discoveries, but also in the relations between people employed in a restaurant or between a group of little girls playing with their dolls. His main focus of attention is not the ultimate significance of what men do, but the action in itself, as another example of the infinite richness of human conduct. So much for the image of our playmate.

In these journeys through the world of men the sociologist will inevitably encounter other professional Peeping Toms. Sometimes these will resent his presence, feeling that he is poaching on their preserves. In some places the sociologist will meet up with the economist, in others with the political scientist, in yet others with the psychologist or the ethnologist. Yet chances are that the questions that have brought him to these same places are different from the ones that propelled his fellow-trespassers. The sociologist's questions always remain essentially the same: "What are people doing with each other here?" "What are their relationships to each other?" "How are these relationships organized in institutions?" "What are the collective ideas that move men and institutions?" In trying to answer these questions in specific instances, the sociologist will, of course, have to deal with economic or political matters, but he will do so in a way rather different from that of the economist or the political scientist. . . .

The fascination of sociology lies in the fact that its perspective makes us see in a new light the very world in which we have lived all our lives. This also constitutes a transformation of consciousness. Moreover, this transformation is more relevant existentially than that of many other intellectual disciplines, because it is more difficult to segregate in some special compartment of the mind. The astronomer does not live in the remote galaxies, and the nuclear physicist can, outside his laboratory, eat and laugh and marry and vote without thinking about the insides of the atom. The geologist looks at rocks only at appropriate times, and the linguist speaks English with his wife. The sociologist lives in society, on the job and off it. His own life, inevitably, is part of his subject matter. Men being what they are, sociologists too manage to segregate their professional insights from their everyday affairs. But it is a rather difficult feat to perform in good faith.

The sociologist moves in the common world of men, close to what most of them would call real. The categories he employs in his analyses are only refinements of the categories by which other men live—power, class, status, race, ethnicity. As a result, there is a deceptive simplicity and obviousness about some sociological investigations. One reads them, nods at the familiar scene, remarks that one has heard all this before and don't people have better things to do than to waste their time on truisms—until one is suddenly brought up against an insight that radically questions everything one had previously assumed about this familiar scene. This is the point at which one begins to sense the excitement of sociology.

Let us take a specific example. Imagine a sociology class in a Southern college where almost all the students are white Southerners. Imagine a lecture on the subject of the racial system of the South. The lecturer is talking here of matters that have been familiar to his students from the time of their infancy. Indeed, it may be that they are much more familiar with the minutiae of this system than he is. They are quite bored as a result. It seems to them that he is only using more pretentious words to describe what they already know. Thus he may use the term "caste," one commonly used now by American sociologists to describe the Southern racial system. But in explaining the term he shifts to traditional Hindu society, to make it clearer. He then goes on to analyze the magical beliefs inherent in cast tabus, the social dynamics of commensalism and connubium [two types of relationship between two individuals], the economic interests concealed within the system, the way in which religious beliefs relate to the tabus, the effects of the caste system upon the industrial development of the society and vice versa—all in India. But suddenly India is not very far away at all. The lecture then goes back to its Southern theme. The familiar now seems not quite so familiar any more. Questions are raised that are new, perhaps raised angrily, but raised all the same. And at least some of the students have begun to understand that there are functions involved in this business of race that they have not read about in the newspapers (at least not those in their hometowns) and that their parents have not told them—partly, at least, because neither the newspapers nor the parents knew about them.

It can be said that the first wisdom of sociology is this—things are not what they seem. This too is a deceptively simple statement. It ceases to be simple after a while. Social reality turns out to have many layers of meaning. The discovery of each new layer changes the perception of the whole. . . .

People who like to avoid shocking discoveries, who prefer to believe that society is just what they were taught in Sunday School, who like the safety of the rules and the maxims of what Alfred Schutz [educator and author (1899–1959)] has called the "world-taken-for-granted," should stay away from sociology. People who feel no temptation before closed doors, who have no curiosity about human beings, who are content to admire scenery without wondering about the people who live in those houses on the other side of that river, should probably also stay away from sociology. They will find it unpleasant or, at any rate, unrewarding. People who are interested in human beings only if they can change, convert or reform them should also be warned, for they will find sociology much less useful than they hoped. And people whose interest is mainly in their own conceptual constructions will do just as well to turn to the study of little white mice. Sociology will be satisfying, in the long run, only to those who can think of nothing more entrancing than to watch men and to understand things human.

It may now be clear that we have, albeit deliberately, understated the case in the title of this chapter. To be sure, sociology is an individual pastime in the sense that it interests some men and bores others. Some like to observe human beings, others to experiment with mice. The world is big enough to hold all kinds and there is no logical priority for one interest as against another. But the word "pastime" is weak in describing what we mean. Sociology is more like a passion. The sociological perspective is more like a demon that possesses one, that drives one compellingly, again and again, to the questions that are its own. An introduction to sociology is, therefore, an invitation to a very special kind of passion. No passion is without its dangers. The sociologist who sells his wares should make sure that he clearly pronounces a *caveat emptor* quite early in the transaction.

Peter L. Berger

The Sociological Imagination

C. Wright Mills (1916–1962) was a leader of mid-twentieth-century American sociological thought who supported the idea that social scientists should play an active role in society, as opposed to merely observing and reporting on it. Outspoken and radical in his views, Mills was an inspiration to many young sociologists who followed in his footsteps in the 1960s. In the selection from his work reprinted here, Mills discusses what he calls the "sociological imagination." He notes that problems such as divorce and unemployment tend to be perceived as only the problems of individual men and women. However, if half of all marriages end in divorce, as is currently the case in the United States, for example, then divorce should also be considered a social problem, the result of numerous forces outside of the individual and sometimes beyond the control of the individual. Similarly, when unemployment is high, it is necessary to examine social, political, and economic factors that cause loss of employment, rather than to seek a purely personal explanation. Mills's book *The Sociological Imagination* (Oxford University Press, 1959), from which the following selection has been excerpted, helped illuminate the purposes of sociology. In it, Mills contends that it is the task of the sociologist to explain the distinction between the personal and the social and the relationship among the social forces that cause specific problems.

Key Concept: the sociological imagination

Nowadays men often feel that their private lives are a series of traps. They sense that within their everyday worlds, they cannot overcome their troubles, and in this feeling, they are often quite correct: What ordinary men are directly aware of and what they try to do are bounded by the private orbits in which they live; their visions and their powers are limited to close-up scenes of job, family, neighborhood; in other milieux, they move vicariously and remain spectators. And the more aware they become, however vaguely, of ambitions and of threats which transcend their immediate locales, the more trapped they seem to feel.

Underlying this sense of being trapped are seemingly impersonal changes in the very structure of continent-wide societies. The facts of contemporary history are also facts about the success and the failure of individual men and women. When a society is industrialized, a peasant becomes a worker; a feudal lord is liquidated or becomes a businessman. When classes rise or fall, a man is employed or unemployed; when the rate of investment goes up or down, a man takes new heart or goes broke. When wars happen, an insurance salesman becomes a rocket launcher; a store clerk, a radar man; a wife lives alone; a child grows up without a father. Neither the life of an individual nor the history of a society can be understood without understanding both.

Yet men do not usually define the troubles they endure in terms of historical change and institutional contradiction. The well-being they enjoy, they do not usually impute to the big ups and downs of the societies in which they live. Seldom aware of the intricate connection between the patterns of their own lives and the course of world history, ordinary men do not usually know what this connection means for the kinds of men they are becoming and for the kinds of history-making in which they might take part. They do not possess the quality of mind essential to grasp the interplay of man and society, of biography and history, of self and world. They cannot cope with their personal troubles in such ways as to control the structural transformations that usually lie behind them. . . .

It is not only information that they need—in this Age of Fact, information often dominates their attention and overwhelms their capacities to assimilate it. It is not only the skills of reason that they need—although their struggles to acquire these often exhaust their limited moral energy.

What they need, and what they feel they need, is a quality of mind that will help them to use information and to develop reason in order to achieve lucid summations of what is going on in the world and of what may be happening within themselves. It is this quality, I am going to contend, that journalists and scholars, artists and publics, scientists and editors are coming to expect of what may be called the sociological imagination.

The sociological imagination enables its possessor to understand the larger historical scene in terms of its meaning for the inner life and the external career of a variety of individuals. It enables him to take into account how individuals, in the welter of their daily experience, often become falsely conscious of their social positions. Within that welter, the framework of modern society is sought, and within that framework the psychologies of a variety of men and women are formulated. By such means the personal uneasiness of individuals is focused upon explicit troubles and the indifference of publics is transformed into involvement with public issues.

The first fruit of this imagination—and the first lesson of the social science that embodies it—is the idea that the individual can understand his own experience and gauge his own fate only by locating himself within his period, that he can know his own chances in life only by becoming aware of those of all individuals in his circumstances. In many ways it is a terrible lesson; in many ways a magnificent one. We do not know the limits of man's capacities for supreme effort or willing degradation, for agony or glee, for pleasurable brutality or the sweetness of reason. But in our time we have come to know that the limits of 'human nature' are frighteningly broad. We have come to know that every individual lives, from one generation to the next, in some society; that he lives out a biography, and that he lives it out within some historical sequence. By the fact of his living he contributes, however minutely, to the shaping of this society and to the course of its history, even as he is made by society and by its historical push and shove....

No social study that does not come back to the problems of biography, of history and of their intersections within a society has completed its intellectual journey. Whatever the specific problems of the classic social analysts, however limited or however broad the features of social reality they have examined, those who have been imaginatively aware of the promise of their work have consistently asked three sorts of questions:

1. What is the structure of this particular society as a whole? What are its essential components, and how are they related to one another? How does it differ from other varieties of social order? Within it, what is the meaning of any particular feature for its continuance and for its change?
2. Where does this society stand in human history? What are the mechanics by which it is changing? What is its place within and its meaning for the development of humanity as a whole? How does any particular feature we are examining affect, and how is it affected by, the historical period in which it moves? And this period—what are its essential features? How does it differ from other periods? What are its characteristic ways of history-making?
3. What varieties of men and women now prevail in this society and in this period? And what varieties are coming to prevail? In what ways are they selected and formed, liberated and repressed, made sensitive and blunted? What kinds of 'human nature' are revealed in the conduct and character we observe in this society in this period? And what is the meaning for 'human nature' of each and every feature of the society we are examining?

Whether the point of interest is a great power state or a minor literary mood, a family, a prison, a creed—these are the kinds of questions the best social analysts have asked. They are the intellectual pivots of classic studies of man in society—and they are the questions inevitably raised by any mind possessing the sociological imagination. For that imagination is the capacity to shift from one perspective to another—from the political to the psychological; from examination of a single family to comparative assessment of the national budgets of the world; from the theological school to the military establishment; from considerations of an oil industry to studies of contemporary poetry. It is the capacity to range from the most impersonal and remote transformations to the most intimate features of the human self—and to see the relations between the two. Back of its use there is always the urge to know the social and historical meaning of the individual in the society and in the period in which he has his quality and his being. . . .

C. Wright Mills

Perhaps the most fruitful distinction with which the sociological imagination works is between 'the personal troubles of milieu' and 'the public issues of social structure.' This distinction is an essential tool of the sociological imagination and a feature of all classic work in social science.

Troubles occur within the character of the individual and within the range of his immediate relations with others; they have to do with his self and with those limited areas of social life of which he is directly and personally aware. Accordingly, the statement and the resolution of troubles properly lie within the individual as a biographical entity and within the scope of his immediate milieu—the social setting that is directly open to his personal experience and to some extent his willful activity. A trouble is a private matter: values cherished by an individual are felt by him to be threatened.

Issues have to do with matters that transcend these local environments of the individual and the range of his inner life. They have to do with the organization of many such milieux into the institutions of an historical society as a whole, with the ways in which various milieux overlap and interpenetrate to form the larger structure of social and historical life. An issue is a public matter: some value cherished by publics is felt to be threatened. Often there is a debate about what that value really is and about what it is that really threatens it. This debate is often without focus if only because it is the very nature of an issue, unlike even widespread trouble, that it cannot very well be defined in terms of the immediate and everyday environments of ordinary men. An issue, in fact, often involves a crisis in institutional arrangements, and often too it involves what Marxists call 'contradictions' or 'antagonisms.'

In these terms, consider unemployment. When, in a city of 100,000, only one man is unemployed, that is his personal trouble, and for its relief we properly look to the character of the man, his skills, and his immediate opportunities. But when in a nation of 50 million employees, 15 million men are unemployed, that is an issue, and we may not hope to find its solution within the range of opportunities open to any one individual. The very structure of opportunities has collapsed. Both the correct statement of the problem and the range of possible solutions require us to consider the economic and political institutions of the society, and not merely the personal situation and character of a scatter of individuals.

Consider war. The personal problem of war, when it occurs, may be how to survive it or how to die in it with honor; how to make money out of it; how to climb into the higher safety of the military apparatus; or how to contribute to the war's termination. In short, according to one's values, to find a set of milieux and within it to survive the war or make one's death in it meaningful. But the structural issues of war have to do with its causes; with what types of men it throws up into command; with its effects upon economic and political, family and religious institutions, with the unorganized irresponsibility of a world of nation-states.

Consider marriage. Inside a marriage a man and a woman may experience personal troubles, but when the divorce rate during the first four years of marriage is 250 out of every 1,000 attempts, this is an indication of a structural issue having to do with the institutions of marriage and the family and other institutions that bear upon them.

Or consider the metropolis—the horrible, beautiful, ugly, magnificent sprawl of the great city. For many upper-class people, the personal solution to 'the problem of the city' is to have an apartment with private garage under it in the heart of the city, and forty miles out, a house by Henry Hill, garden by Garrett Eckbo, on a hundred acres of private land. In these two controlled environments—with a small staff at each end and a private helicopter connection—most people could solve many of the problems of personal milieux caused by the facts of the city. But all this, however splendid, does not solve the public issues that the structural fact of the city poses. What should be done with this wonderful monstrosity? Break it all up into scattered units, combining residence and work? Refurbish it as it stands? Or, after evacuation, dynamite it and build new cities according to new plans in new places? What should those plans be? And who is to decide and to accomplish whatever choice is made? These are structural issues; to confront them and to solve them requires us to consider political and economic issues that affect innumerable milieux.

In so far as an economy is so arranged that slumps occur, the problem of unemployment becomes incapable of personal solution. In so far as war is inherent in the nation-state system and in the uneven industrialization of the world, the ordinary individual in his restricted milieu will be powerless—with or without psychiatric aid—to solve the troubles this system or lack of system imposes upon him. In so far as the family as an institution turns women into darling little slaves and men into their chief providers and unweaned dependents, the problem of a satisfactory marriage remains incapable of purely private solution. In so far as the overdeveloped megalopolis and the overdeveloped automobile are built-in features of the overdeveloped society, the issues of urban living will not be solved by personal ingenuity and private wealth.

What we experience in various and specific milieux, I have noted, is often caused by structural changes. Accordingly, to understand the changes of many personal milieux we are required to look beyond them. And the number and variety of such structural changes increase as the institutions within which we live become more embracing and more intricately connected with one another. To be aware of the idea of social structure and to use it with sensibility is to be capable of tracing such linkages among a great variety of milieux. To be able to do that is to possess the sociological imagination.

PART TWO

The Individual and Society

On the Internet . . .

Sites appropriate to Part Two

Anthro TECH focuses on providing Web services that enhance the discipline of anthropology. This site contains an extensive database of categorized, cross-referenced, and searchable anthropological resources. The database is geared toward both seasoned anthropologists and students.

    http://www.anthrotech.com/

This site provides indexes of culture and ethnic studies, criminology, population and demographics, and statistical sources.

    http://www.library.upenn.edu/resources/
        social/sociology/sociology.html

Atlantic Unbound is *The Atlantic Monthly*'s home on the Web. This site features numerous articles on culture, politics, and society.

    http://www.theatlantic.com/index-js.htm

This is a document repository, developed at Brock University's Department of Sociology, for the work of George Herbert Mead. Here you can find information about Mead's research and his contributions to social psychology.

    http://paradigm.soci.brocku.ca/~lward/
        frame2.html

CHAPTER 2 Culture

2.1 CLYDE KLUCKHOHN

The Meaning of Culture

Culture is a key concept in sociology and basic to understanding all social behavior. For sociologists, *culture* does not mean good manners, fine wine, or the behavior of individuals who are perceived as cultured. Rather, *culture* refers to the total way of life commonly followed by the members of a society. It includes values, beliefs, customs, technology, religion, and the roles people play. In the following selection from *Mirror for Man: The Relation of Anthropology to Modern Life* (McGraw-Hill, 1949), anthropologist Clyde Kluckhohn explains how knowledge of a society's culture can lead to an understanding of human behavior. He points out that culture is learned and that each society transmits informally and formally the required rules that regulate behavior in small and large ways.

Culture explains why people act so differently, and, in what is considered to be one of the best explanations of culture, Kluckhohn adeptly uses these differences to teach the significance of culture. Kluckhohn (1905–1960) was a long-time professor of anthropology at Harvard University and was best known for his demographic studies of the Navaho Indian. Widely respected as a cultural anthropologist, he brought to his studies of cultural patterns rich psychological insights and a systematic method of analyzing values, religion, and ritual.

Key Concept: culture defined as the total way of life of a society's people

Why do the Chinese dislike milk and milk products? Why would the Japanese die willingly in a Banzai charge that seemed senseless to Americans? Why do some nations trace descent through the father, others through the mother, still others through both parents? Not because different peoples have

15

different instincts, not because they were destined by God or Fate to different habits, not because the weather is different in China and Japan and the United States. Sometimes shrewd common sense has an answer that is close to that of the anthropologist: "because they were brought up that way." By "culture" anthropology means the total life way of a people, the social legacy the individual acquires from his group. Or culture can be regarded as that part of the environment that is the creation of man....

One of the interesting things about human beings is that they try to understand themselves and their own behavior. While this has been particularly true of Europeans in recent times, there is no group which has not developed a scheme or schemes to explain man's actions. To the insistent human query "why?" the most exciting illumination anthropology has to offer is that of the concept of culture. Its explanatory importance is comparable to categories such as evolution in biology, gravity in physics, disease in medicine. A good deal of human behavior can be understood, and indeed predicted, if we know a people's design for living. Many acts are neither accidental nor due to personal peculiarities nor caused by supernatural forces nor simply mysterious. Even those of us who pride ourselves on our individualism follow most of the time a pattern not of our own making. We brush our teeth on arising. We put on pants —not a loincloth or a grass skirt. We eat three meals a day—not four or five or two. We sleep in a bed—not in a hammock or on a sheep pelt. I do not have to know the individual and his life history to be able to predict these and countless other regularities, including many in the thinking process, of all Americans who are not incarcerated in jails or hospitals for the insane.

To the American woman a system of plural wives seem "instinctively" abhorrent. She cannot understand how any woman can fail to be jealous and uncomfortable if she must share her husband with other women. She feels it "unnatural" to accept such a situation. On the other hand, a Koryak woman of Siberia, for example, would find it hard to understand how a woman could be so selfish and so undesirous of feminine companionship in the home as to wish to restrict her husband to one mate.

Some years ago I met in New York City a young man who did not speak a word of English and was obviously bewildered by American ways. By "blood" he was as American as you or I, for his parents had gone from Indiana to China as missionaries. Orphaned in infancy, he was reared by a Chinese family in a remote village. All who met him found him more Chinese than American. The facts of his blue eyes and light hair were less impressive than a Chinese style of gait, Chinese arm and hand movements, Chinese facial expression, and Chinese modes of thought. The biological heritage was American, but the cultural training had been Chinese. He returned to China.

Another example of another kind: I once knew a trader's wife in Arizona who took a somewhat devilish interest in producing a cultural reaction. Guests who came her way were often served delicious sandwiches filled with a meat that seemed to be neither chicken nor tuna fish yet was reminiscent of both. To queries she gave no reply until each had eaten his fill. She then explained that what they had eaten was not chicken, not tuna fish, but the rich, white flesh of freshly killed rattlesnakes. The response was instantaneous—vomiting, often violent vomiting. A biological process is caught in a cultural web....

Culture arises out of human nature, and its forms are restricted both by man's biology and by natural laws. It is equally true that culture channels biological processes—vomiting, weeping, fainting, sneezing, the daily habits of food intake and waste elimination. When a man eats, he is reacting to an internal "drive," namely, hunger contractions consequent upon the lowering of blood sugar, but his precise reaction to these internal stimuli cannot be predicted by physiological knowledge alone. Whether a healthy adult feels hungry twice, three times, or four times a day and the hours at which this feeling recurs is a question of culture. *What* he eats is of course limited by availability, but is also partly regulated by culture. It is a biological fact that some types of berries are poisonous; it is a cultural fact that, a few generations ago, most Americans considered tomatoes to be poisonous and refused to eat them. Such selective, discriminative use of the environment is characteristically cultural. In a still more general sense, too, the process of eating is channeled by culture. Whether a man eats to live, lives to eat, or merely eats and lives is only in part an individual matter, for there are also cultural trends. Emotions are physiological events. Certain situations will evoke fear in people from any culture. But sensations of pleasure, anger, and lust may be stimulated by cultural cues that would leave unmoved someone who has been reared in a different social tradition.

Except in the case of newborn babies and of individuals born with clear-cut structural or functional abnormalities we can observe innate endowments only as modified by cultural training. In a hospital in New Mexico where Zuñi Indian, Navaho Indian, and white American babies are born, it is possible to classify the newly arrived infants as unusually active, average, and quiet. Some babies from each "racial" group will fall into each category, though a higher proportion of the white babies will fall into the unusually active class. But if a Navaho baby, a Zuñi baby, and a white baby—all classified as unusually active at birth—are again observed at the age of two years, the Zuñi baby will no longer seem given to quick and restless activity—*as compared with the white child* —though he may seem so as compared with the other Zuñis of the same age. The Navaho child is likely to fall in between as contrasted with the Zuñi and the white, though he will probably still seem more active than the average Navaho youngster....

Culture is a *way* of thinking, feeling, believing. It is the group's knowledge stored up (in memories of men; in books and objects) for future use. We study the products of this "mental" activity: the overt behavior, the speech and gestures and activities of people, and the tangible results of these things such as tools, houses, cornfields, and what not....

Since culture is an abstraction, it is important not to confuse culture with society. A "society" refers to a group of people who interact more with each other than they do with other individuals—who cooperate with each other for the attainment of certain ends. You can see and indeed count the individuals who make up a society. A "culture" refers to the distinctive ways of life of such a group of people. Not all social events are culturally patterned. New types of circumstances arise for which no cultural solutions have as yet been devised.

A culture constitutes a storehouse of the pooled learning of the group. A rabbit starts life with some innate responses. He can learn from his own experience and perhaps from observing other rabbits. A human infant is born with fewer instincts and greater plasticity. His main task is to learn the answers that persons he will never see, persons long dead, have worked out. Once he has learned the formulas supplied by the culture of his group, most of his behavior becomes almost as automatic and unthinking as if it were instinctive. There is a tremendous amount of intelligence behind the making of a radio, but not much is required to learn to turn it on.

The members of all human societies face some of the same unavoidable dilemmas, posed by biology and other facts of the human situation. This is why the basic categories of all cultures are so similar. Human culture without language is unthinkable. No culture fails to provide for aesthetic expression and aesthetic delight. Every culture supplies standardized orientations toward the deeper problems, such as death. Every culture is designed to perpetuate the group and its solidarity, to meet the demands of individuals for an orderly way of life and for satisfaction of biological needs.

However, the variations on these basic themes are numberless. Some languages are built up out of twenty basic sounds, others out of forty. Nose plugs were considered beautiful by predynastic Egyptians but are not by the modern French. Puberty is a biological fact. But one culture ignores it, another prescribes informal instructions about sex but no ceremony, a third has impressive rites for girls only, a fourth for boys and girls. In this culture, the first menstruation is welcomed as a happy, natural event; in that culture the atmosphere is full of dread and supernatural threat. Each culture dissects nature according to its own system of categories. . . .

Every culture must deal with the sexual instinct. Some, however, seek to deny all sexual expression before marriage, whereas a Polynesian adolescent who was not promiscuous would be distinctly abnormal. Some cultures enforce lifelong monogamy, others, like our own, tolerate serial monogamy; in still other cultures, two or more women may be joined to one man or several men to a single woman. Homosexuality has been a permitted pattern in the Greco-Roman world, in parts of Islam, and in various primitive tribes. Large portions of the population of Tibet, and of Christendom at some places and periods, have practiced complete celibacy. To us marriage is first and foremost an arrangement between two individuals. In many more societies marriage is merely one facet of a complicated set of reciprocities, economic and otherwise, between two families or clans.

The essence of the cultural process is selectivity. The selection is only exceptionally conscious and rational. Cultures are like Topsy. They just grew. Once, however, a way of handling a situation becomes institutionalized, there is ordinarily great resistance to change or deviation. When we speak of "our sacred beliefs," we mean of course that they are beyond criticism and that the person who suggests modification or abandonment must be punished. No person is emotionally indifferent to his culture. Certain cultural premises may become totally out of accord with a new factual situation. Leaders may recognize this and reject the old ways in theory. Yet their emotional loyalty continues in the face of reason because of the intimate conditionings of early childhood.

A culture is learned by individuals as the result of belonging to some particular group, and it constitutes that part of learned behavior which is shared with others. It is our social legacy, as contrasted with our organic heredity. It is one of the important factors which permits us to live together in an organized society, giving us ready-made solutions to our problems, helping us to predict the behavior of others, and permitting others to know what to expect of us.

Culture regulates our lives at every turn. From the moment we are born until we die there is, whether we are conscious of it or not, constant pressure upon us to follow certain types of behavior that other men have created for us. Some paths we follow willingly, others we follow because we know no other way, still others we deviate from or go back to most unwillingly. Mothers of small children know how unnaturally most of this comes to us—how little regard we have, until we are "culturalized," for the "proper" place, time and manner for certain acts such as eating, excreting, sleeping, getting dirty, and making loud noises. But by more or less adhering to a system of related designs for carrying out all the acts of living, a group of men and women feel themselves linked together by a powerful chain of sentiments. [American anthropologist] Ruth Benedict gave an almost complete definition of the concept when she said, "Culture is that which binds men together."

It is true any culture is a set of techniques for adjusting both to the external environment and to other men. However, cultures create problems as well as solve them. If the lore of a people states that frogs are dangerous creatures, or that it is not safe to go about at night because of witches or ghosts, threats are posed which do not arise out of the inexorable facts of the external world. Cultures produce needs as well as provide a means of fulfilling them. There exists for every group culturally defined, acquired drives that may be more powerful in ordinary daily life than the biologically inborn drives. Many Americans, for example, will work harder for "success" than they will for sexual satisfaction.

Most groups elaborate certain aspects of their culture far beyond maximum utility or survival value. In other words, not all culture promotes physical survival. At times, indeed, it does exactly the opposite. Aspects of culture which once were adaptive may persist long after they have ceased to be useful. An analysis of any culture will disclose many features which cannot possibly be construed as adaptations to the total environment in which the group now finds itself. However, it is altogether likely that these apparently useless features represent survivals, with modifications through time, of cultural forms which were adaptive in one or another previous situation.

Any cultural practice must be functional or it will disappear before long. That is, it must somehow contribute to the survival of the society or to the adjustment of the individual. However, many cultural functions are not manifest but latent. A cowboy will walk three miles to catch a horse which he then rides one mile to the store. From the point of view of manifest function this is positively irrational. But the act has the latent function of maintaining the cowboy's prestige in the terms of his own subculture. One can instance the buttons on the sleeve of a man's coat, our absurd English spelling, the use of capital letters, and a host of other apparently nonfunctional customs. They serve mainly the latent function of assisting individuals to maintain their security by preserving continuity with the past and by making certain sectors of life familiar and predictable.

Every culture is a precipitate of history. In more than one sense history is a sieve. Each culture embraces those aspects of the past which, usually in altered form and with altered meanings, live on in the present. Discoveries and inventions, both material and ideological, are constantly being made available to a group through its historical contacts with other peoples or being created by its own members. However, only those that fit the total immediate situation in meeting the group's needs for survival or in promoting the psychological adjustment of individuals will become part of the culture. The process of culture building may be regarded as an addition to man's innate biological capacities, an addition providing instruments which enlarge, or may even substitute for, biological functions, and to a degree, compensating for biological limitations— as in ensuring that death does not always result in the loss of humanity of what the deceased has learned.

Culture is like a map. Just as a map isn't the territory but an abstract representation of a particular area, so also a culture is an abstract description of trends toward uniformity in the words, deeds, and artifacts of a human group. If a map is accurate and you can read it, you won't get lost; if you know a culture, you will know your way around in the life of a society....

Every group's way of life, then, is a structure—not a haphazard collection of all the different physically possible and functionally effective patterns of belief and action. A culture is an interdependent system based upon linked premises and categories whose influence is greater, rather than less, because they are seldom put in words. Some degree of internal coherence which is felt rather than rationally constructed seems to be demanded by most of the participants in any culture. As [philosopher Alfred North] Whitehead has remarked, "Human life is driven forward by its dim apprehension of notions too general for its existing language."

In sum, the distinctive way of life that is handed down as the social heritage of a people does more than supply a set of skills for making a living and a set of blueprints for human relations. Each different way of life makes its own assumptions about the ends and purposes of human existence, about what human beings have a right to expect from each other and the gods, about what constitutes a fulfillment or frustration. Some of these assumptions are made explicit in the lore of the folk; others are tacit premises which the observer must infer by finding consistent trends in word and deed.

2.2 HORACE MINER

Body Ritual Among the Nacirema

For decades, leading Western anthropologists have focused their cultural research on so-called primitive societies, journeying to foreign lands to study
new and exotic societies and cultures. Horace Miner (b. 1912), who is a professor emeritus of sociology and anthropology at the University of Michigan,
devoted his research to the social structure of preindustrial cities and the urbanization and modernization of peasants. In the following selection, Miner
holds a mirror to the exotic Nacirema. He systematically examines their cultural patterns—their preoccupation with cleanliness, how they handle their
physical and mental health, the various aspects of their economic behavior,
and so on. The rituals of the Nacirema, elegantly depicted by Miner, give
shape to a culture that at first could appear quite foreign to most Americans;
however, on closer examination, there is something familiar sounding to all
this! "Body Ritual Among the Nacirema," first published in *American Anthropologist* in June 1956, is an enlightening and popular account of how
an anthropologist looks at one society's culture.

Key Concept: the diversity of human behavior and how it can be studied

*T*he anthropologist has become so familiar with the diversity of ways
in which different peoples behave in similar situations that he is not apt to be
surprised by even the most exotic customs. In fact, if all of the logically possible
combinations of behavior have not been found somewhere in the world, he is
apt to suspect that they must be present in some yet undescribed tribe. This
point has, in fact, been expressed with respect to clan organization by Murdock
(1949:71). In this light, the magical beliefs and practices of the Nacirema present
such unusual aspects that it seems desirable to describe them as an example of
the extremes to which human behavior can go.

Professor Linton first brought the ritual of the Nacirema to the attention
of anthropologists twenty years ago (1936:326), but the culture of this people
is still very poorly understood. They are a North American group living in the
territory between the Canadian Cree, the Yaqui and Tarahumare of Mexico, and
the Carib and Arawak of the Antilles. Little is known of their origin, though
tradition states that they came from the east. According to Nacirema mythology,

their nation was originated by a culture hero, Notgnishaw, who is otherwise known for two great feats of strength—the throwing of a piece of wampum across the river Pa-To-Mac and the chopping down of a cherry tree in which the Spirit of Truth resided.

Nacirema culture is characterized by a highly developed market economy which has evolved in a rich natural habitat. While much of the people's time is devoted to economic pursuits, a large part of the fruits of these labors and a considerable portion of the day are spent in ritual activity. The focus of this activity is the human body, the appearance and health of which loom as a dominant concern in the ethos of the people. While such a concern is certainly not unusual, its ceremonial aspects and associated philosophy are unique.

The fundamental belief underlying the whole system appears to be that the human body is ugly and that its natural tendency is to debility and disease. Incarcerated in such a body, man's only hope is to avert these characteristics through the use of the powerful influences of ritual and ceremony. Every household has one or more shrines devoted to this purpose. The more powerful individuals in the society have several shrines in their houses and, in fact, the opulence of a house is often referred to in terms of the number of such ritual centers it possesses. Most houses are of wattle and daub construction [woven rods and twigs plastered with clay], but the shrine rooms of the more wealthy are walled with stone. Poorer families imitate the rich by applying pottery plaques to their shrine walls.

While each family has at least one such shrine, the rituals associated with it are not family ceremonies but are private and secret. The rites are normally only discussed with children, and then only during the period when they are being initiated into these mysteries. I was able, however, to establish sufficient rapport with the natives to examine these shrines and to have the rituals described to me.

The focal point of the shrine is a box or chest which is built into the wall. In this chest are kept the many charms and magical potions without which no native believes he could live. These preparations are secured from a variety of specialized practitioners. The most powerful of these are the medicine men, whose assistance must be rewarded with substantial gifts. However, the medicine men do not provide the curative potions for their clients, but decide what the ingredients should be and then write them down in an ancient and secret language. This writing is understood only by the medicine men and by the herbalists who, for another gift, provide the required charm.

The charm is not disposed of after it has served its purpose, but is placed in the charm-box of the household shrine. As these magical materials are specific for certain ills, and the real or imagined maladies of the people are many, the charm-box is usually full to overflowing. The magical packets are so numerous that people forget what their purposes were and fear to use them again. While the natives are very vague on this point, we can only assume that the idea in retaining all the old magical materials is that their presence in the charm-box, before which the body rituals are conducted, will in some way protect the worshipper.

Beneath the charm-box is a small font. Each day every member of the family, in succession, enters the shrine room, bows his head before the charm-box, mingles different sorts of holy water in the font, and proceeds with a brief rite of ablution. The holy waters are secured from the Water Temple of the community, where the priests conduct elaborate ceremonies to make the liquid ritually pure.

In the hierarchy of magical practitioners, and below the medicine men in prestige, are specialists whose designation is best translated "holy-mouth-men." The Nacirema have an almost pathological horror and fascination with the mouth, the condition of which is believed to have a supernatural influence on all social relationships. Were it not for the rituals of the mouth, they believe that their teeth would fall out, their gums bleed, their jaws shrink, their friends desert them, and their lovers reject them. . . .

[T]he people seek out a holy-mouth-man once or twice a year. These practitioners have an impressive set of paraphernalia, consisting of a variety of augers, awls, probes, and prods. The use of these objects in the exorcism of the evils of the mouth involves almost unbelievable ritual torture of the client. The holy-mouth-man opens the client's mouth and, using the above mentioned tools, enlarges any holes which decay may have created in the teeth. Magical materials are put into these holes. . . .

It is to be hoped that, when a thorough study of the Nacirema is made, there will be a careful inquiry into the personality structure of these people. One has but to watch the gleam in the eye of a holy-mouth-man, as he jabs an awl into an exposed nerve, to suspect that a certain amount of sadism is involved. If this can be established, a very interesting pattern emerges, for most of the population shows definite masochistic tendencies. It was to these that Professor Linton referred in discussing a distinctive part of the daily body ritual which is performed only by men. This part of the rite involves scraping and lacerating the surface of the face with a sharp instrument. Special women's rites are performed only four times during each lunar month, but what they lack in frequency is made up in barbarity. As part of this ceremony, women bake their heads in small ovens for about an hour. The theoretically interesting point is that what seems to be a preponderantly masochistic people have developed sadistic specialists.

The medicine men have an imposing temple, or *latipso*, in every community of any size. The more elaborate ceremonies required to treat very sick patients can only be performed at this temple. These ceremonies involve not only the thaumaturge but a permanent group of vestal maidens who move sedately about the temple chambers in distinctive costume and headdress.

The *latipso* ceremonies are so harsh that it is phenomenal that a fair proportion of the really sick natives who enter the temple ever recover. Small children whose indoctrination is still incomplete have been known to resist attempts to take them to the temple because "that is where you go to die." Despite this fact, sick adults are not only willing but eager to undergo the protracted ritual purification, if they can afford to do so. No matter how ill the supplicant or how grave the emergency, the guardians of many temples will not admit a client if he cannot give a rich gift to the custodian. Even after one has gained admission and survived the ceremonies, the guardians will not permit the neophyte to leave until he makes still another gift.

The supplicant entering the temple is first stripped of all his or her clothes. In every-day life the Nacirema avoids exposure of his body and its natural functions. Bathing and excretory acts are performed only in the secrecy of the household shrine, where they are ritualized as part of the body-rites. Psychological shock results from the fact that body secrecy is suddenly lost upon entry into the *latipso*. A man, whose own wife has never seen him in an excretory act, suddenly finds himself naked and assisted by a vestal maiden while he performs his natural functions into a sacred vessel. This sort of ceremonial treatment is necessitated by the fact that the excreta are used by a diviner to ascertain the course and nature of the client's sickness. Female clients, on the other hand, find their naked bodies are subjected to the scrutiny, manipulation and prodding of the medicine men.

Few supplicants in the temple are well enough to do anything but lie on their hard beds. The daily ceremonies, like the rites of the holy-mouth-men, involve discomfort and torture. With ritual precision, the vestals awaken their miserable charges each dawn and roll them about on their beds of pain while performing ablutions, in the formal movements of which the maidens are highly trained. At other times they insert magic wands in the supplicant's mouth or force him to eat substances which are supposed to be healing. From time to time the medicine men come to their clients and jab magically treated needles into their flesh. The fact that these temple ceremonies may not cure, and may even kill the neophyte, in no way decreases the people's faith in the medicine men.

There remains one other kind of practitioner, known as a "listener." This witch-doctor has the power to exorcise the devils that lodge in the heads of people who have been bewitched. The Nacirema believe that parents bewitch their own children. Mothers are particularly suspected of putting a curse on children while teaching them the secret body rituals. The counter-magic of the witch-doctor is unusual in its lack of ritual. The patient simply tells the "listener" all his troubles and fears, beginning with the earliest difficulties he can remember. The memory displayed by the Nacirema in these exorcism sessions is truly remarkable. It is not uncommon for the patient to bemoan the rejection he felt upon being weaned as a babe, and a few individuals even see their troubles going back to the traumatic effects of their own birth.

In conclusion, mention must be made of certain practices which have their base in native esthetics but which depend upon the pervasive aversion to the natural body and its functions. There are ritual fasts to make fat people thin and ceremonial feasts to make thin people fat. Still other rites are used to make women's breasts large if they are small, and smaller if they are large. General dissatisfaction with breast shape is symbolized in the fact that the ideal form is virtually outside the range of human variation. A few women afflicted with almost inhuman hypermammary development are so idolized that they make a handsome living by simply going from village to village and permitting the natives to stare at them for a fee.

Reference has already been made to the fact that excretory functions are ritualized, routinized, and relegated to secrecy. Natural reproductive functions are similarly distorted. Intercourse is taboo as a topic and scheduled as an act. Efforts are made to avoid pregnancy by the use of magical materials or by limiting intercourse to certain phases of the moon. Conception is actually very infrequent. When pregnant, women dress so as to hide their condition. Parturition takes place in secret, without friends or relatives to assist, and the majority of women do not nurse their infants.

Our review of the ritual life of the Nacirema has certainly shown them to be a magic-ridden people. It is hard to understand how they have managed to exist so long under the burdens which they have imposed upon themselves. But even such exotic customs as these take on real meaning when they are viewed with the insight provided by Malinowski when he wrote (1948:70):

> Looking from far and above, from our high places of safety in the developed civilization, it is easy to see all the crudity and irrelevance of magic. But without its power and guidance early man could not have mastered his practical difficulties as he has done, nor could man have advanced to the higher stages of civilization.

REFERENCES

Linton, Ralph. 1936. *The Study of Man.* New York, D. Appleton-Century Co.
Malinowski, Bronislaw. 1948. *Magic, Science, and Religion.* Glencoe, The Free Press.
Murdock, George P. 1949. *Social Structure.* New York, The Macmillan Co.

The Mountain People

Anthropologists who study the culture of people in less-developed societies invariably find social organizations and institutions that are responsible for the survival and continuity of the group. In the following excerpt, Colin M. Turnbull describes the Ik tribe of Northern Uganda, who appear to lack a social organization and who, for various reasons, have failed to develop a minimum of institutional arrangements that would enable them to develop a humanity and provide continuity for the group.

Many positive aspects of relatively integrated societies are taken for granted and overlooked by their members. The unique case of the Ik—a minimally organized, integrated, and functioning society—reveals, by contrast, the value of relatively integrated societies, such as those in North America. Turnbull, however, argues that the industrial world is in considerable danger of suffering some of the evils of excessive individualism that the Ik suffer.

Turnbull (b. 1924) is an anthropologist who has intensively studied several tribes in Africa and whose interests lie in exploring deteriorating human interpersonal and intergroup relationships. A former consultant to the U.S. State Department, his best-known publications include *The Forest People* (Simon & Schuster, 1961) and *The Mountain People* (Simon & Schuster, 1972), from which the following selection has been excerpted.

Key Concept: survival by diligent attention to one's own needs while ignoring the needs of others

*I*n what follows, there will be much to shock, and the reader will be tempted to say, "how primitive, how savage, how disgusting," and, above all, "how inhuman." The first judgments are typical of the kind of ethno- and egocentricism from which we can never quite escape. But "how inhuman" is of a different order and supposes that there are certain values inherent in humanity itself, from which the people described here seem to depart in a most drastic manner. In living the experience, however, and perhaps in reading it, one finds that it is oneself one is looking at and questioning; it is a voyage in quest of the basic human and a discovery of his potential for inhumanity, a potential that lies within us all.

Just before World War II the Ik tribe had been encouraged to settle in northern Uganda, in the mountainous northeast corner bordering on Kenya to the east and Sudan to the north. Until then they had roamed in nomadic bands, as hunters and gatherers, through a vast region in all three countries. The Kidepo Valley below Mount Morungole was their major hunting territory. After they were confined to a part of their former area, Kidepo was made a national park and they were forbidden to hunt or gather there.

The concept of family in a nomadic society is a broad one; what really counts most in everyday life is community of residence, and those who live close to each other are likely to see each other as effectively related, whether there is any kinship bond or not. Full brothers, on the other hand, who live in different parts of the camp may have little concern for each other.

It is not possible, then, to think of the family as a simple, basic unit. A child is brought up to regard any adult living in the same camp as a parent, and age-mate as a brother or sister. The Ik had this essentially social attitude toward kinship, and it readily lent itself to the rapid and disastrous changes that took place following the restriction of their movement and hunting activities. The family simply ceased to exist.

It is a mistake to think of small-scale societies as "primitive" or "simple." Hunters and gatherers, most of all, appear simple and straightforward in terms of their social organization, yet that is far from true. If we can learn about the nature of society from a study of small-scale societies, we can also learn about human relationships. The smaller the society, the less emphasis there is on the formal system and the more there is on interpersonal and intergroup relations. Security is seen in terms of these relationships, and so is survival. The result, which appears so deceptively simple, is that hunters frequently display those characteristics that we find so admirable in man: kindness, generosity, consideration, affection, honesty, hospitality, compassion, charity. For them, in their tiny, close-knit society, these are necessities for survival. In our society anyone possessing even half these qualities would find it hard to survive, yet we think these virtues are inherent in man. I took it for granted that the Ik would possess these same qualities. But they were as unfriendly, uncharitable, inhospitable and generally mean as any people can be. For those positive qualities we value so highly are no longer functional for them; even more than in our own society they spell ruin and disaster. It seems that, far from being basic human qualities, they are luxuries we can afford in times of plenty or are mere mechanisms for survival and security. Given the situation in which the Ik found themselves, man has no time for such luxuries, and a much more basic man appears, using more basic survival tactics. . . .

Atum ["the senior of all the Ik on Morungole"] was waiting for me. He said that he had told all the Ik that Iciebam [friend of the Ik] had arrived to live with them and that I had given the workers a "holiday" so they could greet me. They were waiting in the villages. They were very hungry, he added, and many were dying. That was probably one of the few true statements he ever made, and I never even considered believing it. . . .

After [touring the Ik villages] Atum said we should start back and called over his shoulder to his village. A muffled sound came from within, and he said, "That's my wife, she is very sick—and hungry." I offered to go and see her, but he shook his head. Back at the Land Rover I gave Atum some food and some aspirin, not knowing what else to give him to help his wife....

While the Ik were working, their heads kept turning as though they were expecting something to happen. Every now and again one would stand up and peer into the distance and then take off into the bush for an hour or so. On one such occasion, after the person had been gone two hours, the others started drifting off. By then I knew them better; I looked for a wisp of smoke and followed it to where the road team was cooking a goat. Smoke was a giveaway, though, so they economized on cooking and ate most food nearly raw. It is a curious hangover from what must once have been a moral code that Ik will offer food if surprised in the act of eating, though they now go to enormous pains not to be so surprised.

I was always up before dawn, but by the time I got up to the villages they were always deserted. One morning I followed the little *oror* [gulley] up from *oror a pirre'i* [Ravine of Pirre] while it was still quite dark, and I met Lomeja on his way down. He took me on my first illicit hunt in Kidepo. He told me that if he got anything he would share it with me and with anyone else who managed to join us but that he certainly would not take anything back to his family. "Each one of them is out seeing what he can get for himself, and do you think they will bring any back for me?"

Lomeja was one of the very few Ik who seemed glad to volunteer information. Unlike many of the others, he did not get up and leave as I approached. Apart from him, I spent most of my time, those days, with Losike, the potter. She told me that Nangoli, the old lady in the adjoining compound, and her husband, Amuarkuar, were rather peculiar. They helped each other get food and water, and they brought it back to their compound to eat together.

I still do not know how much real hunger there was at that time, for most of the younger people seemed fairly well fed, and the few skinny old people seemed healthy and active. But my laboriously extracted genealogies showed that there were quite a number of old people still alive and allegedly in these villages, though they were never to be seen. Then Atum's wife died.

Atum told me nothing about it but kept up his demands for food and medicine. After a while the beady-eyed Lomongin told me that Atum was selling the medicine I was giving him for his wife. I was not unduly surprised and merely remarked that that was too bad for his wife. "Oh no," said Lomongin, "she has been dead for weeks."...

Kauar [one of the Ik workers] always played and joked with the children when they came back from foraging. He used to volunteer to make the two-day walk into Kaabong and the even more tiring two-day climb back to get mail for me or to buy a few things for others. He always asked if he had made the trip more quickly than the last time.

Then one day Kauar went to Kaabong and did not come back. He was found on the last peak of the trail, cold and dead. Those who found him took the things he had been carrying and pushed his body into the bush. I still see his open, laughing face, see him giving precious tidbits to the children, comforting some child who was crying, and watching me read the letters he carried so lovingly for me. And I still think of him probably running up that viciously steep mountainside so he could break his time record and falling dead in his pathetic prime because he was starving. . . .

Anyone falling down was good for a laugh, but I never saw anyone actually trip anyone else. The adults were content to let things happen and then enjoy them; it was probably conservation of energy. The children, however, sought their pleasures with vigor. The best game of all, at this time, was teasing poor little Adupa. She was not so little—in fact she should have been an adult, for she was nearly 13 years old—but Adupa was a little mad. Or you might say she was the only sane one, depending on your point of view. Adupa did not jump on other people's play houses, and she lavished enormous care on hers and would curl up inside it. That made it all the more jump-on-able. The other children beat her viciously.

Children are not allowed to sleep in the house after they are "put out," which is at about three years old, four at the latest. From then on they sleep in the open courtyard, taking what shelter they can against the stockade. They may ask for permission to sit in the doorway of their parents' house but may not lie down or sleep there. "The same thing applies to old people," said Atum, "if they can't build a house of their own and, of course, *if* their children let them stay in their compounds."

I saw a few old people, most of whom had taken over abandoned huts. For the first time I realized that there really was starvation and saw why I had never known it before: it was confined to the aged. Down in Giriko's village the old ritual priest, Lolim, confidentially told me that he was sheltering an old man who had been refused shelter by his son. But Lolim did not have enough food for himself, let alone his guest; could I . . . I liked old Lolim, so, not believing that Lolim had a visitor at all, I brought him a double ration that evening. There was a rustling in the back of the hut, and Lolim helped ancient Lomeraniang to the entrance. They shook with delight at the sight of the food.

When the two old men had finished eating, I left; I found a hungry-looking and disapproving little crowd clustered outside. They muttered to each other about wasting food. From then on I brought food daily, but in a very short time Lomeraniang was dead, and his son refused to come down from the village above to bury him. Lolim scratched a hole and covered the body with a pile of stones he carried himself, one by one.

Hunger was indeed more severe than I knew, and, after the old people, the children were the next to go. It was all quite impersonal—even to me, in most cases, since I had been immunized by the Ik themselves against sorrow on their behalf. But Adupa was an exception. Her madness was such that she did not know just how vicious humans could be. Even worse, she thought that parents were for loving, for giving as well as receiving. Her parents were not given to fantasies. When she came for shelter, they drove her out; and when she came because she was hungry, they laughed the Icien laugh, as if she had made them happy.

Adupa's reactions became slower and slower. When she managed to find food—fruit peels, skins, bits of bone, half-eaten berries—she held it in her hand and looked at it with wonder and delight. Her playmates caught on quickly; they put tidbits in her way and watched her simple drawn little face wrinkle in a smile. Then as she raised her hand to her mouth, they set on her with cries of excitement, fun and laughter, beating her savagely over the head. But that is not how she died. I took to feeding her, which is probably the cruelest thing I could have done, a gross selfishness on my part to try to salve my own rapidly disappearing conscience. I had to protect her, physically, as I fed her. But the others would beat her anyway, and Adupa cried, not because of the pain in her body but because of the pain she felt at the great, vast, empty wasteland where love should have been.

It was *that* that killed her. She demanded that her parents love her. Finally they took her in, and Adupa was happy and stopped crying. She stopped crying forever because her parents went away and closed the door tight behind them, so tight that weak little Adupa could never have moved it.

The Ik seem to tell us that the family is not such a fundamental unit as we usually suppose, that it is not essential to social life. In the crisis of survival facing the Ik, the family was one of the first institutions to go, and the Ik as a society have survived.

The other quality of life that we hold to be necessary for survival—love—the Ik dismiss as idiotic and highly dangerous. But we need to see more of the Ik before their absolute lovelessness becomes truly apparent.

In this curious society there is one common value to which all Ik hold tenaciously. It is *ngag*, "food." That is the one standard by which they measure right and wrong, goodness and badness. The very word for "good" is defined in terms of food. "Goodness" is "the possession of food," or the "*individual* possession of food." If you try to discover their concept of a "good man," you get the truly Icien answer: one who has a full stomach.

We should not be surprised, then, when the mother throws her child out at three years old. At that age a series of *rites de passage* begins. In this environment a child has no chance of survival on his own until he is about 13, so children form age bands. The junior band consists of children between three and seven, the senior of eight- to twelve-year-olds. Within the band each child seeks another close to him in age for defense against the older children. These friendships are temporary, however, and inevitably there comes a time when each turns on the one that up to then had been the closest to him; that is the *rite de passage,* the destruction of that fragile bond called friendship. When this has happened three or four times, the child is ready for the world.

The weakest are soon thinned out, and the strongest survive to achieve leadership of the band. Such a leader is eventually driven out, turned against by his fellow band members. Then the process starts all over again; he joins the senior age band as its most junior member.

The final *rite de passage* is into adulthood, at the age of 12 or 13. By then the candidate has learned the wisdom of acting on his own, for his own good, while acknowledging that on occasion it is profitable to associate temporarily with others. . . .

There seemed to be increasingly little among the Ik that could by any stretch of the imagination be called social life, let alone social organization. The family does not hold itself together; economic interest is centered on as many stomachs as there are people; and cooperation is merely a device for furthering an interest that is consciously selfish. We often do the same thing in our so-called "altruistic" practices, but we tell ourselves it is for the good of others.

The Ik have dispensed with the myth of altruism. Though they have no centralized leadership or means of physical coercion, they do hold together with remarkable tenacity.

In our world, where the family has also lost much of its value as a social unit and where religious belief no longer binds us into communities, we maintain order only through coercive power that is ready to uphold a rigid law and through an equally rigid penal system. The Ik, however, have learned to do without coercion, either spiritual or physical. It seems that they have come to a recognition of what they accept as man's basic selfishness, of his natural determination to survive as an individual before all else. This they consider to be man's basic right, and they allow others to pursue that right without recrimination. . . .

[The oldest and greatest Icien ritual priest] Lolim became ill and had to be protected while eating the food I gave him. Then the children began openly ridiculing him and teasing him, dancing in front of him and kneeling down so that he would trip over them. His grandson used to creep up behind him and with a pair of hard sticks drum a lively tattoo on the old man's bald head.

I fed him whenever I could, but often he did not want more than a bite. Once I found him rolled up in his protective ball, crying. He had had nothing to eat for four days and no water for two. He had asked his children, who all told him not to come near them.

The next day I saw him leaving Atum's village, where his son Longoli lived. Longoli swore that he had been giving his father food and was looking after him. Lolim was not shuffling away; it was almost a run, the run of a drunken man, staggering from side to side. I called to him, but he made no reply, just a kind of long, continuous and horrible moan. He had been to Longoli to beg him to let him into his compound because he knew he was going to die in a few hours, Longoli calmly told me afterward. Obviously Longoli could not do a thing like that: a man of Lolim's importance would have called for an enormous funeral feast. So he refused. Lolim begged Longoli then to open up Nangoli's *asak* for him so that he could die in *her* compound. But Longoli drove him out, and he died alone. . . .

If there was such a thing as an Icien morality, I had not yet perceived it, though traces of a moral past remained. But it still remained a possibility, as did the existence of an unspoken, unmanifest belief that might yet reveal itself and provide a basis for the reintegration of society. I was somewhat encouraged in this hope by the unexpected flight of old Nangoli, widow of Amuarkuar.

When Nangoli returned and found her husband dead, she did an odd thing: she grieved. She tore down what was left of their home, uprooted the stockade, tore up whatever was growing in her little field. Then she fled with a few belongings.

Some weeks later I heard that she and her children had gone over to the Sudan and built a village there. This migration was so unusual that I decided to see whether this runaway village was different.

Lojieri led the way, and Atum came along. One long day's trek got us there. Lojieri pulled part of the brush fence aside, and we went in and wandered around. He and Atum looked inside all the huts, and Lojieri helped himself to tobacco from one and water from another. Surprises were coming thick and fast.

That households should be left open and untended with such wealth inside . . . That there should have been such wealth, for as well as tobacco and jars of water there were baskets of food, and meat was drying on racks. There were half a dozen or so compounds, but they were separated from each other only by a short line of sticks and brush. It was a village, and these were homes, the first and last I was to see.

The dusk had already fallen, and Nangoli came in with her children and grandchildren. They had heard us and came in with warm welcomes. There was no hunger here, and in a very short time each kitchen hearth had a pot of food cooking. Then we sat around the central fire and talked until late, and it was another universe.

There was no talk of "how much better it is here than there"; talk revolved around what had happened on the hunt that day. Loron was lying on the ground in front of the fire as his mother made gentle fun of him. His wife, Kinimei, whom I had never seen even speak to him at Pirre, put a bowl of fresh-cooked berries and fruit in front of him. It was all like a nightmare rather than a fantasy, for it made the reality of Pirre seem all the more frightening. . . .

[Back at Pirre, t]he days of drought wore on into weeks and months and, like everyone else, I became rather bored with sickness and death. I survived rather as did the young adults, by diligent attention to my own needs while ignoring those of others.

More and more it was only the young who could go far from the village as hunger became starvation. Famine relief had been initiated down at Kasile, and those fit enough to make the trip set off. When they came back, the contrast between them and the others was that between life and death. Villages were villages of the dead and dying, and there was little difference between the two. People crawled rather than walked. After a few feet some would lie down to rest, but they could not be sure of ever being able to sit up again, so they mostly stayed upright until they reached their destination. They were going nowhere, these semianimate bags of skin and bone; they just wanted to be with others, and they stopped whenever they met. Perhaps it was the most important demonstration of sociality I ever saw among the Ik. Once they met, they neither spoke nor did anything together.

Early one morning, before dawn, the village moved. In the midst of a hive of activity were the aged and crippled, soon to be abandoned, in danger of being trampled but seemingly unaware of it. Lolim's widow, Lo'ono, whom I had never seen before, also had been abandoned and had tried to make her way down the mountainside. But she was totally blind and had tripped and rolled to the bottom of the *oror a pirre'i;* there she lay on her back, her legs and arms thrashing feebly, while a little crowd laughed.

At this time a colleague was with me. He kept the others away while I ran to get medicine and food and water, for Lo'ono was obviously near dead from hunger and thirst as well as from the fall. We treated her and fed her and asked her to come back with us. But she asked us to point her in the direction of her son's new village. I said I did not think she would get much of a welcome there, and she replied that she knew it but wanted to be near him when she died. So we gave her more food, put her stick in her hand and pointed her the right way. She suddenly cried. She was crying, she said, because we had reminded her that there had been a time when people had helped each other, when people had been kind and good. Still crying, she set off.

The Ik up to this point had been tolerant of my activities, but all this was too much. They said that what we were doing was wrong. Food and medicine were for the living, not the dead. I thought of Lo'ono. And I thought of other old people who had joined in the merriment when they had been teased or had a precious morsel of food taken from their mouths. They knew that it was silly of them to expect to go on living, and, having watched others, they knew that the spectacle really was quite funny. So they joined in the laughter. Perhaps if we had left Lo'ono, she would have died laughing. But we prolonged her misery for no more than a few brief days. Even worse, we reminded her of when things had been different, of days when children had cared for parents and parents for children. She was already dead, and we made her unhappy as well. At the time I was sure we were right, doing the only "human" thing. In a way we *were*—we were making life more comfortable for ourselves. But now I wonder if the Ik way was not right, if I too should not have laughed as Lo'ono flapped about, then left her to die. . . .

And now that all the old are dead, what is left? Every Ik who is old today was thrown out at three and has survived, and in consequence has thrown his own children out and knows that they will not help him in his old age any more than he helped his parents. The system has turned one full cycle and is now self-perpetuating; it has eradicated what we know as "humanity" and has turned the world into a chilly void where man does not seem to care even for himself, but survives. Yet into this hideous world Nangoli and her family quietly returned because they could not bear to be alone.

For the moment abandoning the very old and the very young, the Ik as a whole must be searched for one last lingering trace of humanity. They appear to have disposed of virtually all the qualities that we normally think of as differentiating us from other primates, yet they survive without seeming to be greatly different from ourselves in terms of behavior. Their behavior is more extreme, for we do not start throwing our children out until kindergarten. We have shifted responsibility from family to state, the Ik have shifted it to the individual.

It has been claimed that human beings are capable of love and, indeed, are dependent upon it for survival and sanity. The Ik offer us an opportunity for testing this cherished notion that love is essential to survival. If it is, the Ik should have it.

Love in human relationships implies mutuality, a willingness to sacrifice the self that springs from a consciousness of identity. This seems to bring us back to the Ik, for it implies that love is self-oriented, that even the supreme sacrifice of one's life is no more than selfishness, for the victim feels amply rewarded by the pleasure he feels in making the sacrifice. The Ik, however, do not value emotion above survival, and they are without love. . . .

When the rains failed for the second year running, I knew that the Ik as a society were almost certainly finished and that the monster they had created in its place, that passionless, feelingless association of individuals, would spread like a fungus, contaminating all it touched. When I left, I too had been contaminated. . . .

I departed with a kind of forced gaiety, feeling that I should be glad to be gone but having forgotten how to be glad. I certainly was not thinking of returning within a year, but I did. The following spring I heard that rain had come at last and that the fields of the Ik had never looked so prosperous, nor the country so green and fertile. A few months away had refreshed me, and I wondered if my conclusions had not been excessively pessimistic. So early that summer, I set off to be present for the first harvests in three years.

I was not surprised too much when two days after my arrival and installation at the police post I found Logwara, the blind man, lying on the roadside bleeding, while a hundred yards up other Ik were squabbling over the body of a hyena. Logwara had tried to get there ahead of the others to grab the meat and had been trampled on.

First I looked at the villages. The lush outer covering concealed an inner decay. All the villages were like this to some extent, except for Lokelea's. There the tomatoes and pumpkins were so carefully pruned and cleaned, so that the fruits were larger and healthier. In what had been my own compound the shade trees had been cut down for firewood, and the lovely hanging nests of the weaver birds were gone.

The fields were even more desolate. Every field without exception had yielded in abundance, and it was a new sensation to have vision cut off by thick crops. But every crop was rotting from sheer neglect.

The Ik said that they had no need to bother guarding the fields. There was so much food they could never eat it all, so why not let the birds and baboons take some? The Ik had full bellies; they were good. The *di* at Atum's village was much the same as usual, people sitting or lying about. People were still stealing from each other's fields, and nobody thought of saving for the future.

It was obvious that nothing had really changed due to the sudden glut of food except that interpersonal relationships had deteriorated still further and that Icien individualism had heightened beyond what I thought even Ik to be capable of.

The Ik had faced a conscious choice between being humans and being parasites and had chosen the latter. When they saw their fields come alive, they were confronted with a problem. If they reaped the harvest, they would have to store grain for eating and planting, and every Ik knew that trying to store anything was a waste of time. Further, if they made their fields look too promising, the government would stop famine relief. So the Ik let their fields rot and continued to draw famine relief.

The Ik were not starving any longer; the old and infirm had all died the previous year, and the younger survivors were doing quite well. But the famine relief was administered in a way that was little short of criminal. As before, only the young and well were able to get down from Pirre to collect the relief; they were given relief for those who could not come and told to take it back. But they never did—they ate it themselves.

The facts are there, though those that can be read here form but a fraction of what one person was able to gather in under two years. There can be no mistaking the direction in which those facts point, and that is the most important thing of all, for it may affect the rest of mankind as it has affected the Ik. The Ik have "progressed," one might say, since the change that has come to them came with the advent of civilization to Africa. They have made of a world that was alive a world that is dead—a cold, dispassionate world that is without ugliness because it is without beauty, without hate because it is without love, and without any realization of truth even, because it simply is. And the symptoms of change in our own society indicate that we are heading in the same direction.

Those values we cherish so highly may indeed be basic to human society but not to humanity, and that means that the Ik show that society itself is not indispensable for man's survival and that man is capable of associating for purposes of survival without being social. The Ik have replaced human society with a mere survival system that does not take human emotion into account. . . .

Such interaction as there is within this system is one of mutual exploitation. That is how it already is with the Ik. In our own world the mainstays of a society based on a truly social sense of mutuality are breaking down, indicating that perhaps society as we know it has outworn its usefulness and that by clinging to an outworn system we are bringing about our own destruction. Family, economy, government and religion, the basic categories of social activity and behavior, no longer create any sense of social unity involving a shared and mutual responsibility among all members of our society. At best they enable the individual to survive as an individual. It is the world of the individual, as is the world of the Ik. . . .

The Ik teach us that our much vaunted human values are not inherent in humanity at all but are associated only with a particular form of survival called society and that all, even society itself, are luxuries that can be dispensed with. That does not make them any less wonderful, and if man has any greatness, it is surely in his ability to maintain these values, even shortening an already pitifully short life rather than sacrifice his humanity. But that too involves choice, and the Ik teach us that man can lose the will to make it. That is the point at which there is an end to truth, to goodness and to beauty, an end to the struggle for their achievement, which gives life to the individual and strength and meaning to society. The Ik have relinquished all luxury in the name of individual survival, and they live on as a people without life, without passion, beyond humanity. We pursue those trivial, idiotic technological encumbrances, and all the time we are losing our potential for social rather than individual survival, for hating as well as loving, losing perhaps our last chance to enjoy life with all the passion that is our nature.

The Code of the Streets

A recent newspaper article told of a 14-year-old honor student who was shot by a 15-year-old boy who felt that he was being "dissed" (or shown disrespect) by prolonged eye contact. We might think "this is crazy," when in fact, it might be logical. It follows the logic of what Elijah Anderson, in the following selection from "The Code of the Streets," *The Atlantic Monthly* (May 1994), describes as the *code of the streets,* or the culture that governs many people in today's urban ghettos. The rules of the street culture prescribe proper attire; many types of behavior, including appropriate responses to being challenged; the use of violence; and, perhaps most importantly, respect and deference. To an outsider, including children of families who espouse traditional values, the rules may be repugnant. Failing to observe them (even by those who are not part of the street culture), however, is perceived as provocative and disrespectful, and it invites violence. Anderson points out that there are no boundaries between young people of the street and other young people. Those of the street demand conformity to their code, and frequently hard-working families must encourage their children to be familiar with street rules in order to survive.

Anderson is a professor of sociology at the University of Pennsylvania. He has written *A Place on the Corner* (University of Chicago Press, 1978) and *Streetwise: Race, Class, and Change in an Urban Community* (University of Chicago Press, 1990).

Key Concept: code of the streets

Of all the problems besetting the poor inner-city black community, none is more pressing than that of interpersonal violence and aggression. It wreaks havoc daily with the lives of community residents and increasingly spills over into downtown and residential middle-class areas. Muggings, burglaries, carjackings, and drug-related shootings, all of which may leave their victims or innocent bystanders dead, are now common enough to concern all urban and many suburban residents. The inclination to violence springs from the circumstances of life among the ghetto poor—the lack of jobs that pay a living wage, the stigma of race, the fallout from rampant drug use and drug trafficking, and the resulting alienation and lack of hope for the future.

Simply living in such an environment places young people at special risk of falling victim to aggressive behavior. Although there are often forces in the community which can counteract the negative influences, by far the most powerful being a strong, loving, "decent" (as inner-city residents put it) family committed to middle-class values, the despair is pervasive enough to have spawned an oppositional culture, that of "the streets," whose norms are often consciously opposed to those of mainstream society. These two orientations—decent and street—socially organize the community, and their coexistence has important consequences for residents, particularly children growing up in the inner city. Above all, this environment means that even youngsters whose home lives reflect mainstream values—and the majority of homes in the community do— must be able to handle themselves in a street-oriented environment.

This is because the street culture has evolved what may be called a code of the streets, which amounts to a set of informal rules governing interpersonal public behavior, including violence. The rules prescribe both a proper comportment and a proper way to respond if challenged. They regulate the use of violence and so allow those who are inclined to aggression to precipitate violent encounters in an approved way. The rules have been established and are enforced mainly by the street-oriented, but on the streets the distinction between street and decent is often irrelevant; everybody knows that if the rules are violated, there are penalties. Knowledge of the code is thus largely defensive; it is literally necessary for operating in public. Therefore, even though families with a decency orientation are usually opposed to the values of the code, they often reluctantly encourage their children's familiarity with it to enable them to negotiate the inner-city environment.

At the heart of the code is the issue of respect—loosely defined as being treated "right," or granted the deference one deserves. However, in the troublesome public environment of the inner city, as people increasingly feel buffeted by forces beyond their control, what one deserves in the way of respect becomes more and more problematic and uncertain. This in turn further opens the issue of respect to sometimes intense interpersonal negotiation. In the street culture, especially among young people, respect is viewed as almost an external entity that is hard-won but easily lost, and so must constantly be guarded. The rules of the code in fact provide a framework for negotiating respect. The person whose very appearance—including his clothing, demeanor, and way of moving—deters transgressions feels that he possesses, and may be considered by others to possess, a measure of respect. With the right amount of respect, for instance, he can avoid "being bothered" in public. If he is bothered, not only may he be in physical danger but he has been disgraced or "dissed" (disrespected). Many of the forms that dissing can take might seem petty to middle-class people (maintaining eye contact for too long, for example), but to those invested in the street code, these actions become serious indications of the other person's intentions. Consequently, such people become very sensitive to advances and slights, which could well serve as warnings of imminent physical confrontation.

This hard reality can be traced to the profound sense of alienation from mainstream society and its institutions felt by many poor inner-city black people, particularly the young. The code of the streets is actually a cultural adaptation to a profound lack of faith in the police and the judicial system. The police are most often seen as representing the dominant white society and not caring to protect inner-city residents. When called, they may not respond, which is one reason many residents feel they must be prepared to take extraordinary measures to defend themselves and their loved ones against those who are inclined to aggression. Lack of police accountability has in fact been incorporated into the status system: the person who is believed capable of "taking care of himself" is accorded a certain deference, which translates into a sense of physical and psychological control. Thus the street code emerges where the influence of the police ends and personal responsibility for one's safety is felt to begin. Exacerbated by the proliferation of drugs and easy access to guns, this volatile situation results in the ability of the street-oriented minority (or those who effectively "go for bad") to dominate the public spaces.

DECENT AND STREET FAMILIES

Although almost everyone in poor inner-city neighborhoods is struggling financially and therefore feels a certain distance from the rest of America, the decent and the street family in a real sense represent two poles of value orientation, two contrasting conceptual categories. The labels "decent" and "street," which the residents themselves use, amount to evaluative judgments that confer status on local residents. The labeling is often the result of a social contest among individuals and families of the neighborhood. Individuals of the two orientations often coexist in the same extended family. Decent residents judge themselves to be so while judging others to be of the street, and street individuals often present themselves as decent, drawing distinctions between themselves and other people. In addition, there is quite a bit of circumstantial behavior—that is, one person may at different times exhibit both decent and street orientations, depending on the circumstances. Although these designations result from so much social jockeying, there do exist concrete features that define each conceptual category.

Generally, so-called decent families tend to accept mainstream values more fully and attempt to instill them in their children. Whether married couples with children or single-parent (usually female) households, they are generally "working poor" and so tend to be better off financially than their street-oriented neighbors. They value hard work and self-reliance and are willing to sacrifice for their children. Because they have a certain amount of faith in mainstream society, they harbor hopes for a better future for their children, if not for themselves. Many of them go to church and take a strong interest in their children's schooling. Rather than dwelling on the real hardships and inequities facing them, many such decent people, particularly the increasing number of grandmothers raising grandchildren, see their difficult situation as a test from God and derive great support from their faith and from the church community.

Extremely aware of the problematic and often dangerous environment in which they reside, decent parents tend to be strict in their child-rearing practices, encouraging children to respect authority and walk a straight moral line. They have an almost obsessive concern about trouble of any kind and remind their children to be on the lookout for people and situations that might lead to it. At the same time, they are themselves polite and considerate of others, and teach their children to be the same way. At home, at work, and in church, they strive hard to maintain a positive mental attitude and a spirit of cooperation.

So-called street parents, in contrast, often show a lack of consideration for other people and have a rather superficial sense of family and community. Though they may love their children, many of them are unable to cope with the physical and emotional demands of parenthood, and find it difficult to reconcile their needs with those of their children. These families, who are more fully invested in the code of the streets than the decent people are, may aggressively socialize their children into it in a normative way. They believe in the code and judge themselves and others according to its values.

In fact the overwhelming majority of families in the inner-city community try to approximate the decent-family model, but there are many others who clearly represent the worst fears of the decent family. Not only are their financial resources extremely limited, but what little they have may easily be misused. The lives of the street-oriented are often marked by disorganization. In the most desperate circumstances people frequently have a limited understanding of priorities and consequences, and so frustrations mount over bills, food, and, at times, drink, cigarettes, and drugs. Some tend toward self-destructive behavior; many street-oriented women are crack-addicted ("on the pipe"), alcoholic, or involved in complicated relationships with men who abuse them. In addition, the seeming intractability of their situation, caused in large part by the lack of well-paying jobs and the persistence of racial discrimination, has engendered deep-seated bitterness and anger in many of the most desperate and poorest blacks, especially young people. The need both to exercise a measure of control and to lash out at somebody is often reflected in the adults' relations with their children. At the least, the frustrations of persistent poverty shorten the fuse in such people—contributing to a lack of patience with anyone, child or adult, who irritates them.

In these circumstances a woman—or a man, although men are less consistently present in children's lives—can be quite aggressive with children, yelling at and striking them for the least little infraction of the rules she has set down. Often little if any serious explanation follows the verbal and physical punishment. This response teaches children a particular lesson. They learn that to solve any kind of interpersonal problem one must quickly resort to hitting or other violent behavior. Actual peace and quiet, and also the appearance of calm, respectful children conveyed to her neighbors and friends, are often what the young mother most desires, but at times she will be very aggressive in trying to get them. Thus she may be quick to beat her children, especially if they defy her law, not because she hates them but because this is the way she knows to control them. In fact, many street-oriented women love their children dearly. Many mothers in the community subscribe to the notion that there is a "devil in the boy" that must be beaten out of him or that socially "fast girls need to be whupped." Thus much of what borders on child abuse in the view of social authorities is acceptable parental punishment in the view of these mothers.

Many street-oriented women are sporadic mothers whose children learn to fend for themselves when necessary, foraging for food and money any way they can get it. The children are sometimes employed by drug dealers or become addicted themselves. These children of the street, growing up with little supervision, are said to "come up hard." They often learn to fight at an early age, sometimes using short-tempered adults around them as role models. The street-oriented home may be fraught with anger, verbal disputes, physical aggression, and even mayhem. The children observe these goings-on, learning the lesson that might makes right. They quickly learn to hit those who cross them, and the dog-eat-dog mentality prevails. In order to survive, to protect oneself, it is necessary to marshal inner resources and be ready to deal with adversity in a hands-on way. In these circumstances physical prowess takes on great significance.

In some of the most desperate cases, a street-oriented mother may simply leave her young children alone and unattended while she goes out. The most irresponsible women can be found at local bars and crack houses, getting high and socializing with other adults. Sometimes a troubled woman will leave very young children alone for days at a time. Reports of crack addicts abandoning their children have become common in drug-infested inner-city communities. Neighbors or relatives discover the abandoned children, often hungry and distraught over the absence of their mother. After repeated absences, a friend or relative, particularly a grandmother, will often step in to care for the young children, sometimes petitioning the authorities to send her, as guardian of the children, the mother's welfare check, if the mother gets one. By this time, however, the children may well have learned the first lesson of the streets: survival itself, let alone respect, cannot be taken for granted; you have to fight for your place in the world.

CAMPAIGNING FOR RESPECT

These realities of inner-city life are largely absorbed on the streets. At an early age, often even before they start school, children from street-oriented homes gravitate to the streets, where they "hang"—socialize with their peers. Children from these generally permissive homes have a great deal of latitude and are allowed to "rip and run" up and down the street. They often come home from school, put their books down, and go right back out the door. On school nights eight- and nine-year-olds remain out until nine or ten o'clock (and teenagers typically come in whenever they want to). On the streets they play in groups that often become the source of their primary social bonds. Children from decent homes tend to be more carefully supervised and are thus likely to have curfews and to be taught how to stay out of trouble.

When decent and street kids come together, a kind of social shuffle occurs in which children have a chance to go either way. Tension builds as a child comes to realize that he must choose an orientation. The kind of home he comes from influences but does not determine the way he will ultimately turn out —although it is unlikely that a child from a thoroughly street-oriented family will easily absorb decent values on the streets. Youths who emerge from street-oriented families but develop a decency orientation almost always learn those values in another setting—in school, in a youth group, in church. Often it is the result of their involvement with a caring "old head" (adult role model).

In the street, through their play, children pour their individual life experiences into a common knowledge pool, affirming, confirming, and elaborating on what they have observed in the home and matching their skills against those of others. And they learn to fight. Even small children test one another, pushing and shoving, and are ready to hit other children over circumstances not to their liking. In turn, they are readily hit by other children, and the child who is toughest prevails. Thus the violent resolution of disputes, the hitting and cursing, gains social reinforcement. The child in effect is initiated into a system that is really a way of campaigning for respect....

Those street-oriented adults with whom children come in contact—including mothers, fathers, brothers, sisters, boyfriends, cousins, neighbors, and friends—help them along in forming this understanding by verbalizing the messages they are getting through experience: "Watch your back." "Protect yourself." "Don't punk out." "If somebody messes with you, you got to pay them back." "If someone disses you, you got to straighten them out." Many parents actually impose sanctions if a child is not sufficiently aggressive. For example, if a child loses a fight and comes home upset, the parent might respond, "Don't you come in here crying that somebody beat you up; you better get back out there and whup his ass. I didn't raise no punks! Get back out there and whup his ass. If you don't whup his ass, I'll whup your ass when you come home." Thus the child obtains reinforcement for being tough and showing nerve....

SELF-IMAGE BASED ON "JUICE"

By the time they are teenagers, most youths have either internalized the code of the streets or at least learned the need to comport themselves in accordance with its rules, which chiefly have to do with interpersonal communication. The code revolves around the presentation of self. Its basic requirement is the display of a certain predisposition to violence. Accordingly, one's bearing must send the unmistakable if sometimes subtle message to "the next person" in public that one is capable of violence and mayhem when the situation requires it, that one can take care of oneself. The nature of this communication is largely determined by the demands of the circumstances but can include facial expressions, gait, and verbal expressions—all of which are geared mainly to deterring aggression. Physical appearance, including clothes, jewelry, and grooming, also plays an important part in how a person is viewed; to be respected, it is important to have the right look.

Even so, there are no guarantees against challenges, because there are always people around looking for a fight to increase their share of respect—or "juice," as it is sometimes called on the street. Moreover, if a person is assaulted, it is important, not only in the eyes of his opponent but also in the eyes of his "running buddies," for him to avenge himself. Otherwise he risks being "tried" (challenged) or "moved on" by any number of others. To maintain his honor he must show he is not someone to be "messed with" or "dissed." In general, the person must "keep himself straight" by managing his position of respect among others; this involves in part his self-image, which is shaped by what he thinks others are thinking of him in relation to his peers.

Objects play an important and complicated role in establishing self-image. Jackets, sneakers, gold jewelry, reflect not just a person's taste, which tends to be tightly regulated among adolescents of all social classes, but also a willingness to possess things that may require defending. A boy wearing a fashionable, expensive jacket, for example, is vulnerable to attack by another who covets the jacket and either cannot afford to buy one or wants the added satisfaction of depriving someone else of his. However, if the boy forgoes the desirable jacket and wears one that isn't "hip," he runs the risk of being teased and possibly even assaulted as an unworthy person. To be allowed to hang with certain prestigious crowds, a boy must wear a different set of expensive clothes—sneakers and athletic suit—every day. Not to be able to do so might make him appear socially deficient. The youth comes to covet such items—especially when he sees easy prey wearing them.

In acquiring valued things, therefore, a person shores up his identity—but since it is an identity based on having things, it is highly precarious. This very precariousness gives a heightened sense of urgency to staying even with peers, with whom the person is actually competing. Young men and women who are able to command respect through their presentation of self—by allowing their possessions and their body language to speak for them—may not have to campaign for regard but may, rather, gain it by the force of their manner. Those who are unable to command respect in this way must actively campaign for it—and are thus particularly alive to slights.

One way of campaigning for status is by taking the possessions of others. In this context, seemingly ordinary objects can become trophies imbued with symbolic value that far exceeds that monetary worth. Possession of the trophy can symbolize the ability to violate somebody—to "get in his face," to take something of value from him, to "dis" him, and thus to enhance one's own worth by stealing someone else's. The trophy does not have to be something material. It can be another person's sense of honor, snatched away with a derogatory remark. It can be the outcome of a fight. It can be the imposition of a certain standard, such as a girl's getting herself recognized as the most beautiful. Material things, however, fit easily into the pattern. Sneakers, a pistol, even somebody else's girlfriend, can become a trophy. When a person can take something from another and then flaunt it, he gains a certain regard by being the owner, or the controller, of that thing. But this display of ownership can then provoke other people to challenge him. This game of who controls what is thus constantly being played out on inner-city streets, and the trophy—extrinsic or intrinsic, tangible or intangible—identifies the current winner.

An important aspect of this often violent give-and-take is its zero-sum quality. That is, the extent to which one person can raise himself up depends on his ability to put another person down. This underscores the alienation that permeates the inner-city ghetto community. There is a generalized sense that very little respect is to be had, and therefore everyone competes to get what affirmation he can of the little that is available. The craving for respect that results gives people thin skins. Shows of deference by others can be highly soothing, contributing to a sense of security, comfort, self-confidence, and self-respect. Transgressions by others which go unanswered diminish these feelings and are believed to encourage further transgressions. Hence one must be ever vigilant against the transgressions of others or even *appearing* as if transgressions will be tolerated. Among young people, whose sense of self-esteem is particularly vulnerable, there is an especially heightened concern with being disrespected. Many inner-city young men in particular crave respect to such a degree that they will risk their lives to attain and maintain it....

BY TRIAL OF MANHOOD

On the street, among males these concerns about things and identity have come to be expressed in the concept of "manhood." Manhood in the inner city means taking the prerogatives of men with respect to strangers, other men, and women —being distinguished as a man. It implies physicality and a certain ruthlessness. Regard and respect are associated with this concept in large part because of its practical application: if others have little or no regard for a person's manhood, his very life and those of his loved ones could be in jeopardy. But there is a chicken-and-egg aspect to this situation: one's physical safety is more likely to be jeopardized in public *because* manhood is associated with respect. In other words, an existential link has been created between the idea of manhood and one's self-esteem, so that it has become hard to say which is primary. For many inner-city youths, manhood and respect are flip sides of the same coin; physical and psychological well-being are inseparable, and both require a sense of control, of being in charge.

The operating assumption is that a man, especially a real man, knows what other men know—the code of the streets. And if one is not a real man, one is somehow diminished as a person, and there are certain valued things one simply does not deserve. There is thus believed to be a certain justice to the code, since it is considered that everyone has the opportunity to know it....

So when a person ventures outside, he must adopt the code—a kind of shield, really—to prevent others from "messing with" him.... [F]or those who are invested in the code, the clear object of their demeanor is to discourage strangers from even thinking about testing their manhood. And the sense of power that attends the ability to deter others can be alluring even to those who know the code without being heavily invested in it—the decent inner-city youths. Thus a boy who has been leading a basically decent life can, in trying circumstances, suddenly resort to deadly force.

Central to the issue of manhood is the widespread belief that one of the most effective ways of gaining respect is to manifest "nerve." Nerve is shown when one takes another person's possessions (the more valuable the better), "messes with" someone's woman, throws the first punch, "gets in someone's face," or pulls a trigger. Its proper display helps on the spot to check others who would violate one's person and also helps to build a reputation that works to prevent future challenges. But since such a show of nerve is a forceful expression of disrespect toward the person on the receiving end, the victim may be greatly offended and seek to retaliate with equal or greater force. A display of nerve, therefore, can easily provoke a life-threatening response, and the background knowledge of that possibility has often been incorporated into the concept of nerve.

True nerve exposes a lack of fear of dying. Many feel that it is acceptable to risk dying over the principle of respect. In fact, among the hard-core street-oriented, the clear risk of violent death may be preferable to being "dissed" by another. The youths who have internalized this attitude and convincingly display it in their public bearing are among the most threatening people of all, for it is commonly assumed that they fear no man. As the people of the community say, "They are the baddest dudes on the street." . . . The difference between the decent and the street-oriented youth is often that the decent youth makes a conscious decision to appear tough and manly; in another setting—with teachers, say, or at his part-time job—he can be polite and deferential. The street-oriented youth, on the other hand, has made the concept of manhood a part of his very identity—he has difficulty manipulating it—it often controls him. . . .

AN OPPOSITIONAL CULTURE

The attitudes of the wider society are deeply implicated in the code of the streets. Most people in inner-city communities are not totally invested in the code, but the significant minority of hard-core street youths who are have to maintain the code in order to establish reputations because they have—or feel they have—few other ways to assert themselves. For these young people the standards of the street code are the only game in town. The extent to which some children—particularly those who through upbringing have become most alienated and those lacking in strong and conventional social support—experience, feel, and internalize racist rejection and contempt from mainstream society may strongly encourage them to express contempt for the more conventional society in turn. In dealing with this contempt and rejection, some youngsters will consciously invest themselves and their considerable mental resources in what amounts to an oppositional culture to preserve themselves and their self-respect. Once they do, any respect they might be able to garner in the wider system pales in comparison with the respect available in the local system; thus they often lose interest in even attempting to negotiate the mainstream system.

At the same time, many less alienated young blacks have assumed a street-oriented demeanor as a way of expressing their blackness while really embracing a much more moderate way of life; they, too, want a nonviolent setting in which to live and raise a family. These decent people are trying hard to be part of the mainstream culture, but the racism, real and perceived, that they encounter helps to legitimate the oppositional culture. And so on occasion they adopt street behavior. In fact, depending on the demands of the situation, many people in the community slip back and forth between decent and street behavior.

A vicious cycle has thus been formed. The hopelessness and alienation many young inner-city black men and women feel, largely as a result of endemic joblessness and persistent racism, fuels the violence they engage in. This violence serves to confirm the negative feelings many whites and some middle-class blacks harbor toward the ghetto poor, further legitimating the oppositional culture and the code of the streets in the eyes of many poor young blacks. Unless this cycle is broken, attitudes on both sides will become increasingly entrenched, and the violence, which claims victims black and white, poor and affluent, will only escalate.

Different Words, Different Worlds

In the following selection, Deborah Tannen analyzes inter- and intragender relationships. She postulates that a major reason why frictions arise between men and women is because boys and girls grow up in different cultures. When they reach adulthood their conversations are, in essence, cross-cultural. Tannen shows the contrast between the female and male cultures by comparing her and her husband's reactions to comments made by their friends and acquaintances about their commuting marriage. Tannen perceived the comments as supportive, while her husband perceived the comments as denigrating. To Tannen, life for men is a competition to avoid failure and to succeed more than others. Women are also very concerned with status or success, but they focus more on *intimacy,* whereas men focus more on *independence.* Tannen expands on this point with a discussion of the different conceptions of decision making held by women and men.

Tannen is a professor of linguistics at Georgetown University. Her books, which focus on the communication differences between men and women, include *That's Not What I Meant!* (William Morrow, 1986), *Conversation Style* (Ablex Publishing, 1984), *Gender and Discourse* (Oxford University Press, 1994), *Talking from 9 to 5* (William Morrow, 1994), and *You Just Don't Understand: Women and Men in Conversation* (William Morrow, 1990), from which the following selection has been excerpted. Her latest book is *The Argument Culture: Moving from Debate to Dialogue* (Random House, 1998).

Key Concept: gender clashes in adult relationships

Many years ago I was married to a man who shouted at me, "I do not give you the right to raise your voice to me, because you are a woman and I am a man." This was frustrating, because I knew it was unfair. But I also knew just what was going on. I ascribed his unfairness to his having grown up in a country where few people thought women and men might have equal rights.

Now I am married to a man who is a partner and friend. We come from similar backgrounds and share values and interests. It is a continual source of pleasure to talk to him. It is wonderful to have someone I can tell everything to, someone who understands. But he doesn't always see things as I do, doesn't always react to things as I expect him to. And I often don't understand why he says what he does.

At the time I began working on this book, we had jobs in different cities. People frequently expressed sympathy by making comments like "That must be rough," and "How do you stand it?" I was inclined to accept their sympathy and say things like "We fly a lot." Sometimes I would reinforce their concern: "The worst part is having to pack and unpack all the time." But my husband reacted differently, often with irritation. He might respond by de-emphasizing the inconvenience: As academics, we had four-day weekends together, as well as long vacations throughout the year and four months in the summer. We even benefited from the intervening days of uninterrupted time for work. I once overheard him telling a dubious man that we were lucky, since studies have shown that married couples who live together spend less than half an hour a week talking to each other; he was implying that our situation had advantages.

I didn't object to the way my husband responded—everything he said was true—but I was surprised by it. I didn't understand why he reacted as he did. He explained that he sensed condescension in some expressions of concern, as if the questioner were implying, "Yours is not a real marriage; your ill-chosen profession has resulted in an unfortunate arrangement. I pity you, and look down at you from the height of complacence, since my wife and I have avoided your misfortune." It had not occurred to me that there might be an element of one-upmanship in these expressions of concern, though I could recognize it when it was pointed out. Even after I saw the point, though, I was inclined to regard my husband's response as slightly odd, a personal quirk. He frequently seemed to see others as adversaries when I didn't.

... I now see that my husband was simply engaging the world in a way that many men do: as an individual in a hierarchical social order in which he was either one-up or one-down. In this world, conversations are negotiations in which people try to achieve and maintain the upper hand if they can, and protect themselves from others' attempts to put them down and push them around. Life, then, is a contest, a struggle to preserve independence and avoid failure.

I, on the other hand, was approaching the world as many women do: as an individual in a network of connections. In this world, conversations are negotiations for closeness in which people try to see and give confirmation and support, and to reach consensus. They try to protect themselves from others' attempts to push them away. Life, then, is a community, a struggle to preserve intimacy and avoid isolation. Though there are hierarchies in this world too, they are hierarchies more of friendship than of power and accomplishment.

Women are also concerned with achieving status and avoiding failure, but these are not the goals they are *focused* on all the time, and they tend to pursue them in the guise of connection. And men are also concerned with achieving involvement and avoiding isolation, but they are not *focused* on these goals, and they tend to pursue them in the guise of opposition.

Discussing our differences from this point of view, my husband pointed out to me a distinction I had missed: He reacted the way I just described only if expressions of concern came from men in whom he sensed an awareness of hierarchy. And there were times when I too disliked people's expressing sympathy about our commuting marriage. I recall being offended by one man who seemed to have a leering look in his eye when he asked, "How do you manage this long-distance romance?" Another time I was annoyed when a woman who knew me only by reputation approached us during the intermission of a play, discovered our situation by asking my husband where he worked, and kept the conversation going by asking us all about it. In these cases, I didn't feel put down; I felt intruded upon. If my husband was offended by what he perceived as claims to superior status, I felt these sympathizers were claiming inappropriate intimacy.

INTIMACY AND INDEPENDENCE

Intimacy is key in a world of connection where individuals negotiate complex networks of friendship, minimize differences, try to reach consensus, and avoid the appearance of superiority, which would highlight differences. In a world of status, *independence* is key, because a primary means of establishing status is to tell others what to do, and taking orders is a marker of low status. Though all humans need both intimacy and independence, women tend to focus on the first and men on the second. It is as if their lifeblood ran in different directions.

These differences can give women and men differing views of the same situation, as they did in the case of a couple I will call Linda and Josh. When Josh's old high-school chum called him at work and announced he'd be in town on business the following month, Josh invited him to stay for the weekend. That evening he informed Linda that they were going to have a houseguest, and that he and his chum would go out together the first night to shoot the breeze like old times. Linda was upset. She was going to be away on business the week before, and the Friday night when Josh would be out with his chum would be her first night home. But what upset her the most was that Josh had made these plans on his own and informed her of them, rather than discussing them with her before extending the invitation.

Linda would never make plans, for a weekend or an evening, without first checking with Josh. She can't understand why he doesn't show her the same courtesy and consideration that she shows him. But when she protests, Josh says, "I can't say to my friend, 'I have to ask my wife for permission'!"

To Josh, checking with his wife means seeking permission, which implies that he is not independent, not free to act on his own. It would make him feel like a child or an underling. To Linda, checking with her husband has nothing to do with permission. She assumes that spouses discuss their plans with each other because their lives are intertwined, so the actions of one have consequences for the other. Not only does Linda not mind telling someone, "I have to check with Josh"; quite the contrary—she likes it. It makes her feel good to know and show that she is involved with someone, that her life is bound up with someone else's.

Linda and Josh both felt more upset by this incident, and others like it, than seemed warranted, because it cut to the core of their primary concerns.

Linda was hurt because she sensed a failure of closeness in their relationship: He didn't care about her as much as she cared about him. And he was hurt because he felt she was trying to control him and limit his freedom.

A similar conflict exists between Louise and Howie, another couple, about spending money. Louise would never buy anything costing more than a hundred dollars without discussing it with Howie, but he goes out and buys whatever he wants and feels they can afford, like a table saw or a new power mower. Louise is disturbed, not because she disapproves of the purchases, but because she feels he is acting as if she were not in the picture.

Many women feel it is natural to consult with their partners at every turn, while many men automatically make more decisions without consulting their partners. This may reflect a broad difference in conceptions of decision making. Women expect decisions to be discussed first and made by consensus. They appreciate the discussion itself as evidence of involvement and communication. But many men feel oppressed by lengthy discussions about what they see as minor decisions, and they feel hemmed in if they can't just act without talking first. When women try to initiate a freewheeling discussion by asking, "What do you think?" men often think they are being asked to decide....

MIXED JUDGMENTS AND MISJUDGMENTS

Because men and women are regarding the landscape from contrasting vantage points, the same scene can appear very different to them, and they often have opposite interpretations of the same action.

A colleague mentioned that he got a letter from a production editor working on his new book, instructing him to let her know if he planned to be away from his permanent address at any time in the next six months, when his book would be in production. He commented that he hadn't realized how like a parole officer a production editor could be. His response to this letter surprised me, because I have received similar letters from publishers, and my response is totally different: I like them, because it makes me feel important to know that my whereabouts matter. When I mentioned this difference to my colleague, he was puzzled and amused, as I was by his reaction. Though he could understand my point of view intellectually, emotionally he could not imagine how one could not feel framed as both controlled and inferior in rank by being told to report one's movements to someone. And though I could understand his perspective intellectually, it simply held no emotional resonance for me.

In a similar spirit, my colleague remarked that he had read a journal article written by a woman who thanked her husband in the acknowledgments section of her paper for helpful discussion of the topic. When my colleague first read this acknowledgment, he thought the author must be incompetent, or at least insecure: Why did she have to consult her husband about her own work? Why couldn't she stand on her own two feet? After hearing my explanation that women value evidence of connection, he reframed the acknowledgment and concluded that the author probably valued her husband's involvement in her work and made reference to it with the pride that comes of believing one has evidence of a balanced relationship.

If my colleague's reaction is typical, imagine how often women who think they are displaying a positive quality—connection—are misjudged by men who perceive them as revealing a lack of independence, which the men regard as synonymous with incompetence and insecurity....

MALE-FEMALE CONVERSATION IS CROSS-CULTURAL COMMUNICATION

If women speak and hear a language of connection and intimacy, while men speak and hear a language of status and independence, then communication between men and women can be like cross-cultural communication, prey to a clash of conversational styles. Instead of different dialects, it has been said they speak different genderlects.

The claim that men and women grow up in different worlds may at first seem patently absurd. Brothers and sisters grow up in the same families, children to parents of both genders. Where, then, do women and men learn different ways of speaking and hearing?

IT BEGINS AT THE BEGINNING

Even if they grow up in the same neighborhood, on the same block, or in the same house, girls and boys grow up in different worlds of words. Others talk to them differently and expect and accept different ways of talking from them. Most important, children learn how to talk, how to have conversations, not only from their parents but from their peers. After all, if their parents have a foreign or regional accent, children do not emulate it; they learn to speak with the pronunciation of the region where they grow up. Anthropologists Daniel Maltz and Ruth Borker summarize research showing that boys and girls have very different ways of talking to their friends. Although they often play together, boys and girls spend most of their time playing in same-sex groups. And, although some of the activities they play at are similar, their favorite games are different, and their ways of using language in their games are separated by a world of difference.

Boys tend to play outside, in large groups that are hierarchically structured. Their groups have a leader who tells others what to do and how to do it, and resists doing what other boys propose. It is by giving orders and making them stick that high status is negotiated. Another way boys achieve status is to take center stage by telling stories and jokes, and by sidetracking or challenging the stories and jokes of others. Boys' games have winners and losers and elaborate systems of rules that are frequently the subjects of arguments. Finally, boys are frequently heard to boast of their skill and argue about who is best at what.

Girls, on the other hand, play in small groups or in pairs; the center of a girl's social life is a best friend. Within the group, intimacy is key: Differentiation is measured by relative closeness. In their most frequent games, such as jump rope and hopscotch, everyone gets a turn. Many of their activities (such as playing house) do not have winners or losers. Though some girls are certainly more skilled than others, girls are expected not to boast about it, or show that they think they are better than the others. Girls don't give orders; they express their preferences as suggestions, and suggestions are likely to be accepted. Whereas boys say, "Gimme that!" and "Get outta here!" girls say, "Let's do this," and "How about doing that?" Anything else is put down as "bossy." They don't grab center stage—they don't want it—so they don't challenge each other directly. And much of the time, they simply sit together and talk. Girls are not accustomed to jockeying for status in an obvious way; they are more concerned that they be liked.

Gender differences in ways of talking have been described by researchers observing children as young as three. Amy Sheldon videotaped three- to four-year-old boys and girls playing in threesomes at a day-care center. She compared two groups of three—one of boys, one of girls—that got into fights about the same play item: a plastic pickle. Though both groups fought over the same thing, the dynamics by which they negotiated their conflicts were different. . . .

In comparing the boys' and girls' pickle fights, Sheldon points out that, for the most part, the girls mitigated the conflict and preserved harmony by compromise and evasion. Conflict was more prolonged among the boys, who used more insistence, appeals to rules, and threats of physical violence. However, to say that these little girls and boys used *more* of one strategy or another is not to say that they didn't use the other strategies at all. . . .

This study suggests that boys and girls both want to get their way, but they tend to do so differently. Though social norms encourage boys to be openly competitive and girls to be openly cooperative, different situations and activities can result in different ways of behaving. Marjorie Harness Goodwin compared boys and girls engaged in two task-oriented activities: The boys were making slingshots in preparation for a fight, and the girls were making rings. She found that the boys' group was heirarchical: The leader told the others what to do and how to do it. The girls' group was egalitarian: Everyone made suggestions and tended to accept the suggestions of others. But observing the girls in a different activity—playing house—Goodwin found that they too adopted hierarchical structures: The girls who played mothers issued orders to the girls playing children, who in turn sought permission from their play-mothers. Moreover, a girl who was a play-mother was also a kind of manager of the game. This study shows that girls know how to issue orders and operate in a hierarchical structure, but they don't find that mode of behavior appropriate when they engage in task activities with their peers. They do find it appropriate in parent-child relationships, which they enjoy practicing in the form of play.

These worlds of play shed light on the world views of women and men in relationships. The boys' play illuminates why men would be on the lookout for signs they are being put down or told what to do. The chief commodity that is bartered in the boys' hierarchical world is status, and the way to achieve and maintain status is to give orders and get others to follow them. A boy in a low-status position finds himself being pushed around. So boys monitor their relations for subtle shifts in status by keeping track of who's giving orders and who's taking them.

These dynamics are not the ones that drive girls' play. The chief commodity that is bartered in the girls' community is intimacy. Girls monitor their friendships for subtle shifts in alliance, and they seek to be friends with popular girls. Popularity is a kind of status, but it is founded on connection. It also places popular girls in a bind. By doing field work in a junior high school, Donna Eder found that popular girls were paradoxically—and inevitably—disliked. Many girls want to befriend popular girls, but girls' friendships must necessarily be limited, since they entail intimacy rather than large group activities. So a popular girl must reject the overtures of most of the girls who seek her out—with the result that she is branded "stuck up."

THE KEY IS UNDERSTANDING

If adults learn their ways of speaking as children growing up in separate social worlds of peers, then conversation between women and men is cross-cultural communication. Although each style is valid on its own terms, misunderstandings arise because the styles are different. Taking a cross-cultural approach to male-female conversations makes it possible to explain why dissatisfactions are justified without accusing anyone of being wrong or crazy.

CHAPTER 3 Socialization, Personality Development, and the Social Construction of Society

3.1 GEORGE HERBERT MEAD

The Development of the Self in Social Interaction

Unless they are socialized, people lack language, culture, abstract thought, and a concept of the self. How does this socialization take place and allow the human animal to attain complexity of thought, motivations, and actions? George Herbert Mead provided a truly brilliant answer to this question in the 1920s.

Mead (1863–1931) was a sociologist and social philosopher at the University of Chicago in the 1920s. Together with his colleagues Charles H. Cooley, W. I. Thomas, and others, he developed the field of symbolic interactionism, which holds that social interactions develop through symbols,

54

*Chapter 3
Socialization,
Personality
Development,
and the Social
Construction
of Society*

language, signs, and gestures. He helped change the way we think about ourselves and about the way we develop through interaction with relatives and the larger society.

In the following excerpt from *Mind, Self and Society* (University of Chicago Press, 1934), Mead discusses his theory on the development of the self through social interaction. He elaborates on the process of socialization and the concepts of role-taking, the significant other, and the generalized other.

Key Concept: the self

*I*n our statement of the development of intelligence we have already suggested that the language process is essential for the development of the self. The self has a character which is different from that of the physiological organism proper. The self is something which has a development; it is not initially there, at birth, but arises in the process of social experience and activity, that is, develops in the given individual as a result of his relations to that process as a whole and to other individuals within that process....

It is the characteristic of the self as an object to itself that I want to bring out. This characteristic is represented in the word "self," which is a reflexive, and indicates that which can be both subject and object. This type of object is essentially different from other objects, and in the past it has been distinguished as conscious, a term which indicates an experience with, an experience of, one's self. It was assumed that consciousness in some way carried this capacity of being an object to itself. In giving a behavioristic statement of consciousness we have to look for some sort of experience in which the physical organism can become an object to itself.

... How can an individual get outside himself (experientially) in such a way as to become an object to himself? This is the essential psychological problem of selfhood or of self-consciousness; and its solution is to be found by referring to the process of social conduct or activity in which the given person or individual is implicated. The apparatus of reason would not be complete unless it swept itself into its own analysis of the field of experience; or unless the individual brought himself into the same experiential field as that of the other individual selves in relation to whom he acts in any given social situation. Reason cannot become impersonal unless it takes an objective, non-affective attitude toward itself; otherwise we have just consciousness, not *self*-consciousness. And it is necessary to rational conduct that the individual should thus take an objective, impersonal attitude toward himself, that he should become an object to himself. For the individual organism is obviously an essential and important fact or constituent element of the empirical situation in which it acts; and without taking objective account of itself as such, it cannot act intelligently, or rationally.

The individual experiences himself as such, not directly, but only indirectly, from the particular standpoints of other individual members of the same social group, or from the generalized standpoint of the social group as a whole to which he belongs. For he enters his own experience as a self or individual, not directly or immediately, not by becoming a subject to himself, but only in so far as he first becomes an object to himself just as other individuals are objects to him or in his experience; and he becomes an object to himself only by taking the attitudes of other individuals toward himself within a social environment or context of experience and behavior in which both he and they are involved....

The self, as that which can be an object to itself, is essentially a social structure, and it arises in social experience. After a self has arisen, it in a certain sense provides for itself its social experiences, and so we can conceive of an absolutely solitary self. But it is impossible to conceive of a self arising outside of social experience. When it has arisen we can think of a person in solitary confinement for the rest of his life, but who still has himself as a companion, and is able to think and to converse with himself as he had communicated with others. That process to which I have just referred, of responding to one's self as another responds to it, taking part in one's own conversation with others, being aware of what one is saying and using that awareness of what one is saying to determine what one is going to say thereafter—that is a process with which we are all familiar. We are continually following up our own address to other persons by an understanding of what we are saying, and using that understanding in the direction of our continued speech. We are finding out what we are going to say, what we are going to do, by saying and doing, and in the process we are continually controlling the process itself. In the conversation of gestures what we say calls out a certain response in another and that in turn changes our own action, so that we shift from what we started to do because of the reply the other makes. The conversation of gestures is the beginning of communication. The individual comes to carry on a conversation of gestures with himself. He says something, and that calls out a certain reply in himself which makes him change what he was going to say. One starts to say something, we will presume an unpleasant something, but when he starts to say it he realizes it is cruel. The effect on himself of what he is saying checks him; there is here a conversation of gestures between the individual and himself. We mean by significant speech that the action is one that affects the individual himself, and that the effect upon the individual himself is part of the intelligent carrying-out of the conversation with others. Now we, so to speak, amputate that social phase and dispense with it for the time being, so that one is talking to one's self as one would talk to another person....

We realize in everyday conduct and experience that an individual does not mean a great deal of what he is doing and saying. We frequently say that such an individual is not himself. We come away from an interview with a realization that we have left out important things, that there are parts of the self that did not get into what was said. What determines the amount of the self that gets into communication is the social experience itself. Of course, a good deal of the self does not need to get expression. We carry on a whole series of different relationships to different people. We are one thing to one man and another thing to another. There are parts of the self which exist only for the self in relationship to itself. We divide ourselves up in all sorts of different selves with reference

56

*Chapter 3
Socialization,
Personality
Development,
and the Social
Construction
of Society*

to our acquaintances. We discuss politics with one and religion with another. There are all sorts of different selves answering to all sorts of different social reactions. It is the social process itself that is responsible for the appearance of the self; it is not there as a self apart from this type of experience....

We find in children something that answers to this double, namely, the invisible, imaginary companions which a good many children produce in their own experience. They organize in this way the responses which they call out in other persons and call out also in themselves. Of course, this playing with an imaginary companion is only a peculiarly interesting phase of ordinary play. Play in this sense, especially the stage which precedes the organized games, is a play at something. A child plays at being a mother, at being a teacher, at being a policeman; that is, it is taking different rôles, as we say. We have something that suggests this in what we call the play of animals: a cat will play with her kittens, and dogs play with each other. Two dogs playing with each other will attack and defend, in a process which if carried through would amount to an actual fight. There is a combination of responses which checks the depth of the bite. But we do not have in such a situation the dogs taking a definite rôle in the sense that a child deliberately takes the rôle of another. This tendency on the part of the children is what we are working with in the kindergarten where the rôles which the children assume are made the basis for training. When a child does assume a rôle he has in himself the stimuli which call out that particular response or group of responses. He may, of course, run away when he is chased, as the dog does, or he may turn around and strike back just as the dog does in his play. But that is not the same as playing at something. Children get together to "play Indian." This means that the child has a certain set of stimuli which call out in itself the responses that they would call out in others, and which answer to an Indian. In the play period the child utilizes his own responses to these stimuli which he makes use of in building a self. The response which he has a tendency to make to these stimuli organizes them. He plays that he is, for instance, offering himself something, and he buys it; he gives a letter to himself and takes it away; he addresses himself as a parent, as a teacher; he arrests himself as a policeman. He has a set of stimuli which call out in himself the sort of responses they call out in others. He takes this group of responses and organizes them into a certain whole. Such is the simplest form of being another to one's self. It involves a temporal situation. The child says something in one character and responds in another character, and then his responding in another character is a stimulus to himself in the first character, and so the conversation goes on. A certain organized structure arises in him and in his other which replies to it, and these carry on the conversation of gestures between themselves.

If we contrast play with the situation in an organized game, we note the essential difference that the child who plays in a game must be ready to take the attitude of everyone else involved in that game, and that these different rôles must have a definite relationship to each other. Taking a very simple game such as hide-and-seek, everyone with the exception of the one who is hiding is a person who is hunting. A child does not require more than the person who is hunted and the one who is hunting. If a child is playing in the first sense he just goes on playing, but there is no basic organization gained. In that early stage he passes from one rôle to another just as a whim takes him. But in a game where a number of individuals are involved, then the child taking one rôle must be ready to take the rôle of everyone else. If he gets in a baseball nine he must have the responses of each position involved in his own position. He must know what everyone else is going to do in order to carry out his own play. He has to take all of these rôles. They do not all have to be present in consciousness at the same time, but at some moments he has to have three or four individuals present in his own attitude, such as the one who is going to throw the ball, the one who is going to catch it, and so on. These responses must be, in some degree, present in his own make-up. In the game, then, there is a set of responses of such others so organized that the attitude of one calls out the appropriate attitudes of the other.

This organization is put in the form of the rules of the game. Children take a great interest in rules. They make rules on the spot in order to help them-selves out of difficulties. Part of the enjoyment of the game is to get these rules. Now, the rules are the set of responses which a particular attitude calls out. You can demand a certain response in others if you take a certain attitude. These responses are all in yourself as well. There you get an organized set of such responses as that to which I have referred, which is something more elaborate than the rôles found in play. Here there is just a set of responses that follow on each other indefinitely. At such a stage we speak of a child as not yet having a fully developed self. The child responds in a fairly intelligent fashion to the immediate stimuli that come to him, but they are not organized. He does not organize his life as we would like to have him do, namely, as a whole. There is just a set of responses to the type of play. The child reacts to a certain stimulus, and the reaction is in himself that is called out in others, but he is not a whole self. In his game he has to have an organization of these rôles; otherwise he cannot play the game. The game represents the passage in the life of the child from taking the rôle of others in play to the organized part that is essential to self-consciousness in the full sense of the term. . . .

The fundamental difference between the game and play is that in the latter the child must have the attitude of all the others involved in that game. The attitudes of the other players which the participant assumes organize into a sort of unit, and it is that organization which controls the response of the individual. The illustration used was of a person playing baseball. Each one of his own acts is determined by his assumption of the action of the others who are playing the game. What he does is controlled by his being everyone else on that team, at least in so far as those attitudes affect his own particular response. We get then an "other" which is an organization of the attitudes of those involved in the same process.

The organized community or social group which gives to the individual his unity of self may be called "the generalized other." The attitude of the gen-eralized other is the attitude of the whole community. Thus, for example, in the case of such a social group as a ball team, the team is the generalized other in so far as it enters—as an organized process or social activity—into the experience of any one of the individual members of it. . . .

*Chapter 3
Socialization,
Personality
Development,
and the Social
Construction
of Society*

It is in the form of the generalized other that the social process influences the behavior of the individuals involved in it and carrying it on, i.e., that the community exercises control over the conduct of its individual members; for it is in this form that the social process or community enters as a determining factor into the individual's thinking. In abstract thought the individual takes the attitude of the generalized other toward himself, without reference to its expression in any particular other individuals; and in concrete thought he takes that attitude in so far as it is expressed in the attitudes toward his behavior of those other individuals with whom he is involved in the given social situation or act. But only by taking the attitude of the generalized other toward himself, in one or another of these ways, can he think at all; for only thus can thinking—or the internalized conversation of gestures which constitutes thinking—occur. And only through the taking by individuals of the attitude or attitudes of the generalized other toward themselves is the existence of a universe of discourse, as that system of common or social meanings which thinking presupposes at its context, rendered possible.

The self-conscious human individual, then, takes or assumes the organized social attitudes of the given social group or community (or of some one section thereof) to which he belongs, toward the social problems of various kinds which confront that group or community at any given time, and which arise in connection with the correspondingly different social projects of organized co-operative enterprises in which that group or community as such is engaged; and as an individual participant in these social projects or co-operative enterprises, he governs his own conduct accordingly. In politics, for example, the individual identifies himself with an entire political party and takes the organized attitudes of that entire party toward the rest of the given social community and toward the problems which confront the party within the given social situation; and he consequently reacts or responds in terms of the organized attitudes of the party as a whole. He thus enters into a special set of social relations with all the other individuals who belong to that political party; and in the same way he enters into various other special sets of social relations, with various other classes of individuals respectively, the individuals of each of these classes being the other members of some one of the particular organized subgroups (determined in socially functional terms) of which he himself is a member within the entire given society or social community. . . .

Such is the process by which a personality arises. I have spoken of this as a process in which a child takes the rôle of the other, and said that it takes place essentially through the use of language. Language is predominantly based on the vocal gesture by means of which co-operative activities in a community are carried out. Language in its significant sense is that vocal gesture which tends to arouse in the individual the attitude which it arouses in others, and it is this perfecting of the self by the gesture which mediates the social activities that gives rise to the process of taking the rôle of the other. . . .

What goes to make up the organized self is the organization of the attitudes which are common to the group. A person is a personality because he belongs to a community, because he takes over the institutions of that community into his own conduct. He takes its language as a medium by which he gets his personality, and then through a process of taking the different rôles that all the others furnish he comes to get the attitude of the members of the community. Such, in a certain sense, is the structure of a man's personality. There are certain common responses which each individual has toward certain common things, and in so far as those common responses are awakened in the individual when he is affecting other persons he arouses his own self. The structure, then, on which the self is built is this response which is common to all, for one has to be a member of a community to be a self. Such responses are abstract attitudes, but they constitute just what we term a man's character. They give him what we term his principles, the acknowledged attitudes of all members of the community toward what are the values of that community. He is putting himself in the place of the generalized other, which represents the organized responses of all the members of the group. It is that which guides conduct controlled by principles, and a person who has such an organized group of responses is a man whom we say has character, in the moral sense. . . .

There is one other matter which I wish briefly to refer to now. The only way in which we can react against the disapproval of the entire community is by setting up a higher sort of community which in a certain sense out-votes the one we find. A person may reach a point of going against the whole world about him; he may stand out by himself over against it. But to do that he has to speak with the voice of reason to himself. He has to comprehend the voices of the past and of the future. That is the only way in which the self can get a voice which is more than the voice of the community. As a rule we assume that this general voice of the community is identical with the larger community of the past and the future; we assume that an organized custom represents what we call morality. The things one cannot do are those which everybody would condemn. If we take the attitude of the community over against our own responses, that is a true statement, but we must not forget this other capacity, that of replying to the community and insisting on the gesture of the community changing. We can reform the order of things; we can insist on making the community standards better standards. We are not simply bound by the community. We are engaged in a conversation in which what we say is listened to by the community and its response is one which is affected by what we have to say. This is especially true in critical situations. A man rises up and defends himself for what he does; he has his "day in court"; he can present his views. He can perhaps change the attitude of the community toward himself. The process of conversation is one in which the individual has not only the right but the duty of talking to the community of which he is a part, and bringing about those changes which take place through the interaction of individuals. That is the way, of course, in which society gets ahead, by just such interactions as those in which some person thinks a thing out. We are continually changing our social system in some respects, and we are able to do that intelligently because we can think.

The Social Construction of Gender

Gender socialization is the process by which girls and boys learn behavior that is considered appropriate to their gender. According to Margaret L. Andersen, the fact that we learn much gender-specific behavior means that gender is socially constructed. The process of socialization begins on the day of birth when the infant is identified as female or male through pink or blue attire. What is appropriate for a girl or boy is communicated by numerous agents of socialization—in infancy from the immediate caregiver, and in adolescence from peers, teachers, the media, etc. It is expressed in many ways, from the toys offered to children to the games children play—the boy climbs trees; the girl skips rope. Not everyone conforms to the gender models that culture prescribes, and this deviation is often not accepted socially. The girl who climbs trees is called a tomboy and will probably face increasing pressure to become more feminine as a teenager. The boy who does not play rough games will probably be censured by his peers.

Andersen argues that the pressure to adopt gender-appropriate behavior is evidence that socialization controls us by giving us a definition of who we are and our place in the world. Moreover, it encourages and discourages the acquisition of certain skills by gender. But more women today are acquiring skills that contradict gender models, such as the skills of an electrician, plumber, engineer, or astronaut. Andersen believes that these changes will weaken and blur the gender models.

Andersen is a professor of sociology at the University of Delaware. She is the author of *Thinking About Women: Sociological Perspectives on Sex and Gender*, 4th ed. (Allyn & Bacon, 1997), a foremost textbook for gender roles courses and the source from which the following selection has been excerpted.

Key Concept: socialization and gender roles

SOCIALIZATION AND THE FORMATION
OF GENDER IDENTITY

The fact that gender is a social, not a natural, phenomenon means that it is learned. Although rooted in institutions, gender is passed on through social learning and is enacted through what sociologists call gender roles. Gender roles are the patterns of behavior in which women and men engage, based on the cultural expectations associated with their gender. Gender roles are learned through the process of *socialization*. It is through the socialization process that individuals acquire an identity based on gender. *Gender identity* is an individual's specific definition of self, based on that person's understanding of what it means to be a man or a woman. In other words, it is through the socialization process that gender is socially constructed.

Sanctions and Expectations

Through gender socialization, different behaviors and attitudes are encouraged and discouraged in men and women. That is, social expectations about what is properly masculine and feminine are communicated to us through the socialization process. Our family, peers, and teachers, as well as the media and religious groups, act as agents of the socialization process. Although probably none of us becomes exactly what the cultural ideal prescribes, our roles in social institutions are conditioned by the gender relations we learn in our social development.

Some persons become more perfectly socialized than others, and sociologists have warned against the idea of seeing humans as totally passive, overly socialized creatures (Wrong, 1961). To some extent, we probably all resist the expectations society has of us. Our uniqueness as individuals stems in part from this resistance, as well as from variations in the social experiences we have. Studying patterns of gender socialization does not deny individual differences, but it does point to the common experiences shared by girls as they become women and boys as they become men. However much we may believe that we were raised in a gender-neutral environment, research and careful observation show how pervasive and generally effective the process of gender-role socialization is. Although some of us conform more than others, socialization acts as a powerful system of social control.

Peter Berger (1963) describes social control as something like a series of concentric circles. At the center is the individual, who is surrounded by different levels of control, ranging from the subtle—such as learned roles, peer pressure, and ridicule—to the overt—such as violence, physical threat, and imprisonment. According to Berger, it is usually not necessary for powerful agents in the society to resort to extreme sanctions because what we think and believe about ourselves usually keeps us in line. In this sense, socialization acts as a powerful system of social control.

The conflicts we encounter when we try to cross or deny the boundaries between the sexes are good evidence of the strength of gendered expectations in our culture. . . .

Chapter 3
Socialization,
Personality
Development,
and the Social
Construction
of Society

The pressure to adopt gender-appropriate behavior is evidence that the socialization process controls us in several ways. First, it gives us a definition of ourselves. Second, it defines the external world and our place within it. Third, it provides our definition of others and our relationships with them. Fourth, the socialization process encourages and discourages the acquisition of certain skills by gender.

Conformity to traditional roles takes its toll on both men and women, and research shows that those who conform most fully to gender-role expectations experience a range of negative consequences. Higher male mortality rates can be attributed to the stress in masculine roles; among women, those with the most traditionally feminine identities are more likely to be depressed (Tinsley, Sullivan-Guest, and McGuire, 1984). Women who score as very feminine on personality tests also tend to be dissatisfied and anxious and to have lower self-esteem than do less traditionally feminine women (Thornton and Leo, 1992). Research also indicates that depression is related to traditional gender roles. Housewives, generally speaking, report more depression than do women employed outside the home, although this is mitigated by a number of factors. Employed women with lower incomes and who have young children have higher rates of depression than do women who work only in the home; not surprisingly, this indicates the effect that stress has on mental health. At the same time, housewives whose gender expectations for themselves are in conflict with those of their husbands for them report higher rates of depression than do housewives whose expectations are congruent with their husbands' (Krause, 1982; Cleary and Mechanic, 1983)....

Men and women with more androgynous gender orientations—that is to say, those having a balance of masculine and feminine personality characteristics—show signs of greater mental health and more positive self-images. For example, research among middle-aged professional men shows that those who are the most androgynous perceive themselves to be more healthy than do more traditional men of their age and status (Downey, 1984). Personality tests given to male and female college students also show that those who score high on both masculine and feminine traits (and, therefore, are defined as more androgynous) have higher self-esteem than students who score higher on one gender type or another (Spence, Helmreich, and Stampp, 1975). Finally, research also shows that, in spite of the strains experienced by women with multiple roles, those with multiple roles report more gratification, status security, and enrichment in their lives (Gerson, 1985)....

SOCIALIZATION ACROSS THE LIFE COURSE

Socialization begins at birth, and it continues throughout adulthood, even though gender roles are established very early. When we encounter new social experiences, we are socialized to adopt new roles through the expectations others have of us. Socialization patterns can be observed in many individual and group experiences and in the context of all of the institutions of society.

This section examines the processes and consequences of gender socialization as it occurs throughout the life course.

63

*Margaret L.
Andersen*

Infancy

Beginning in infancy, boys and girls are treated differently. Research on infant socialization shows, in fact, how quickly gender expectations become part of our experience. One innovative study asked first-time parents to describe their babies only twenty-four hours after birth. Although physical examination revealed no objective differences between male and female infants, the parents of girls reported their babies to be softer, smaller, and less attentive than did the parents of boys. More than mothers did, fathers described their sons as larger, better coordinated, more alert, and stronger than girls; also more than did mothers, fathers described their daughters as delicate, weak, and inattentive (Rubin, Provenzano, and Hull, 1974). In an interesting twist of this classic study, researchers have more recently found that young children describe infants in more gender-stereotyped ways than do adults (Stern and Karraker, 1989).

Research continues to show that parents treat their infants differently, depending on the infant's sex. How parents act may even be unintentional or subtle, but it has an effect on later life, nonetheless. In one fascinating series of studies, researchers observed fathers and mothers (in couples) walking young children through public places. Both fathers and mothers were more likely to let boy toddlers walk alone than they were to allow girls to do so. These same observers found that even when the child was out of the stroller, mothers were far more likely to push the empty stroller than were the fathers, demonstrating the attachment of mothers to child care roles. (Mitchell et al., 1992). Despite the fact that mothers are much more likely than fathers to engage in and manage child care, research also finds that fathers are more likely to gender-type their children (Mitchell et al., 1992). Parents living in nontraditional households, however, do tend to gender-stereotype their children less than parents do in traditional families (Weisner et al., 1994).

Parents are not the only agents of gender socialization, however. Other children have just as important an impact on learning gender roles. Children of all ages notice the sex of infants and use it as a basis for responding to the child. As children grow, their engagement in gender stereotyping also increases, especially between the ages of 3 and 14 (Vogel et al., 1991). Peers develop expectations and definitions of gender-appropriate behaviors and use those expectations as the basis for their interaction with others.

Childhood Play and Games

Research in child development emphasizes the importance of play and games in the maturation of children. Through play, children learn the skills of social interaction, develop cognitive and analytical abilities, and are taught the values and attitudes of their culture. The games that children play have great

64

*Chapter 3
Socialization,
Personality
Development,
and the Social
Construction
of Society*

significance for the children's intellectual, moral, personal, and social development—and for their gender identity.

George Herbert Mead, a social psychologist and major sociological theorist in the early twentieth century, described three stages in which socialization occurs: imitation, play, and game. In the imitation stage, infants simply copy the behavior of significant persons in their environment. In the play stage, the child begins "taking the role of the other"—seeing himself or herself from the perspective of another person. Mead argues that taking the role of the other is a cognitive process that permits the child to develop a self-concept. Self-concepts emerge through interacting with other people and from learning to perceive how others see us. The other people most emotionally important to the child (who may be parents, siblings, or other primary caretakers) are, in Mead's term, significant others. In the play stage, children learn to take the role of significant others, primarily by practicing others' social roles—for example, "playing Mommy" or "playing Daddy."

In the game stage, children are able to do more. Rather than seeing themselves from the perspective of only one significant other at a time, they can play games requiring them to understand how several other people (including more than just significant others) view them simultaneously. Playing baseball, to use Mead's example, involves the roles and expectations of many more people than does "playing Mommy." Eventually, children in the game stage learn to orient themselves not just to significant others but to a generalized other, as well. The generalized other represents the cultural expectations of the whole social community....

Research reveals the pervasiveness of gender stereotyping as it is learned in early childhood play. The toys and play activities that parents select for children are a significant source of gender socialization....

Researchers have observed that, compared with girls' rooms, boys' rooms contain toys of more different classes (educational, sports, animals, spatial-temporal objects, depots, military equipment, machines, and vehicles) and that boys' toys tend to encourage activities outside of the home. Girls' toys, on the other hand, both are less varied in type and encourage play within the home....

Children's literature is also an important source of their learned images of women's and men's places in the world. Although since the 1960s there has been substantial improvement in the inclusion of women in children's literature, girls and women are still depicted as less adventurous, in need of rescue, and in fewer occupations than men. One study comparing nonsexist picture books with conventional children's books did find that females are shown as more independent and men as less aggressive in the nonsexist books; however, females in the non-sexist books are also shown as more nurturing, more emotional and less physically active than they are in the conventional books. Whenever women are shown in children's books as exhibiting power and leadership, they tend to be mythical figures—superheroines or fairy godmothers (Davis, 1984; Purcell and Stewart, 1990; Weitzman, et al., 1972). Female characters are also more likely to be depicted using household artifacts, whereas men use nondomestic objects (Crabb and Bielawski, 1994). Books written by African Americans are also more likely to show girls and women as less dependent and more competitive but also as more nurturing than do books written by White authors (Clark, Lennon, and Morris, 1993).

Detailed observations of children's play and games reveal the significance that they have for learning gender roles. In a classic study, Lever (1978) observed fifth-grade children (most of whom in her study are White and middle-class) and measured the complexity of boys' and girls' activities.... She distinguished play from games by noting that play does not involve explicit goals, whereas games tend to have a recognized goal or end point. Games also tend to be structured by teams that work together toward a common goal; play, although it involves cooperative interaction, is not structured in team relationships.

Lever's findings reveal several patterns in the gender differences of children's play. Girls tend to play, whereas boys interact through games. Girls' games have fewer rules than boys games, and, for girls, the largest category of activity is play involving a single role. Girls' games focus on a single central person (e.g., tag), whereas boys play in larger groups and with more complex role differentiation. Girls are also more cooperative, whereas boys are more competitive; boys' play and games often include face-to-face competition, whereas girls' competition is more indirect. Girls are more likely to play games involving repeated ritual (such as jumping rope), whereas boys will follow more elaborate rules. According to Lever, ritualistic play does not exercise physical and mental skills to the extent that rules do, because it is repetitive and more passive. Finally, when girls play games with rules, they tend to ignore the rules, whereas boys more rigidly adhere to established principles of play.

Lever concludes that through play and games, boys learn involvement with the generalized order; girls, on the other hand, are more involved with "particular others." Such differences are significant because the dimensions of complexity that characterize children's play also describe the organization of modern industrial societies. Complex societies involve an elaborate division of labor and elaborate differentiation of roles; these societies also are heterogeneous and are organized according to rationalized rules and social structures. Lever concludes that boys' games better prepare them for leadership and organizational skills that are useful both in childhood and in adult life. Her implication is that the socialization girls get through games leaves them inadequately prepared to succeed in the complex organization of modern society. Her speculation has been borne out by a recent study finding that professional business women were more likely than other employed women to have played competitive sports as children; they also had more male playmates (Coats and Overman, 1992)....

Socialization and the Schools

Socialization takes place not only in the home, but also through other institutions and relationships. Although we tend to think of the family as the primary source of social values and identity, peers, teachers, the media, and other significant others are important agents of the socialization process. Schools, in particular, exercise much influence on the creation of gendered attitudes and

Chapter 3
Socialization,
Personality
Development,
and the Social
Construction
of Society

behavior, so much so that some researchers call learning gender the "second curriculum" in the schools (Best, 1983). In the schools, curriculum materials, teachers' expectations, educational tracking, and peer relations encourage girls and boys to learn gender-related skills and self-concepts.

Within schools, teachers and older children display expectations that encourage children to behave and think in particular ways; moreover, these expectations are strongly influenced by gender. Teachers, for example, respond more often to boys in the classroom. Even when they do so in response to boys' misbehaving, they are calling more attention to the boys (Sadker and Sadker, 1994). Differences between boys and girls become exaggerated through practices that divide them into two distinct human groups (Thorne, 1993). In schools, children are often seated in separate gender groups or sorted into play groups based on gender; these practices heighten gender differences, making them even more significant in the children's interactions. In school, boys tend to be the center of attention, even when they are getting attention for disruptive behavior; girls are, in general, less visible and more typically praised for passive and acquiescent behavior (Sadker and Sadker, 1994; American Association of University Women Educational Foundation, 1991)....

Adult Socialization and the Aging Process

As we encounter new experiences throughout our lives, we learn the role expectations associated with our new statuses. Although our gender identity is established relatively early in life, changes in our status in society—for example, graduation, marriage, or a new job—bring new expectations for our behavior and beliefs.

Aging is perhaps the one thing about our lives that is inevitable; yet, as a social experience, it has different consequences for men and women. Cross-cultural evidence shows that aging is less stressful for women in societies where there is a strong tie to family and kin, not just to a husband; where there are extended, not nuclear, family systems; where there is a positive role for mothers-in-law (rather than the degrading status attached to it in our society); and where there are strong mother-child relationships throughout life. Even within our own society, racial and ethnic groups attach more value to older persons, thereby easing the transition to later life. Although the elderly in African American and Latino communities experience even greater difficulties with poverty and health than do the White elderly (Jones, 1985), their valued role in the extended family seems to alleviate some of the stress associated with growing old.

Gender differences in the social process of aging can be attributed greatly to the emphasis on youth found in this culture and, in particular, to the association of youth and sexuality in women. Cultural stereotypes portray older men as distinguished, older women as barren. As a woman ages, unlike a man, she will generally experience a loss of prestige; men gain prestige as they become more established in their careers. The consequences for both are great. Because men draw their self-esteem and their connections to others largely from their jobs, they may find retirement to be an especially stressful period. Sociologists also point out that because men have learned to be task oriented rather than person oriented, they may have difficulty establishing new relationships in retirement or widowhood (Hess and Markson, 1991)....

Margaret L. Andersen

LIMITATIONS OF THE SOCIALIZATION PERSPECTIVE

... Individual experience reflects the larger society; reexamining the events in our lives that created our gender identity is a fundamental step in recognizing how we came to be who we are and how we can change. There are, though, limitations in seeing gender relations as emerging primarily through socialization. Although the socialization process shows how individuals become gendered persons, it does not explain the social structural origins of gender inequality. Understanding socialization helps us to see that gender expectations have their origins outside the individual, but socialization theories do not explain the institutional bases of those origins, and, therefore, they are not causal theories of women's status in society.

Society as Symbolic Interaction

In introductory sociology textbooks, sociology is typically portrayed as having three major theoretical perspectives: functionalism, conflict theory, and symbolic interaction. These labels do not describe today's sociologists very well, but they were major positions 30 to 40 years ago. Robert K. Merton was a leader in the functionalist perspective, while Karl Marx was a strong representative of the conflict theory. Herbert Blumer is well known for the symbolic interaction perspective.

In the selection that follows, which is from "Society as Symbolic Interaction," in Arnold M. Rose, ed., *Human Behavior and Social Processes* (Houghton Mifflin, 1962), Blumer coins the term *symbolic interaction* and gives definition to this perspective. Blumer draws substantially from George Herbert Mead, one of his teachers, and considers both society and the self as the outcome of many interactions involving communication through symbols (mainly language). In contrast to functionalism and conflict theory—which describe mainly the macro level of the society, the nation, the institution, or the organization—the symbolic interaction perspective describes the micro level of the ordinary life of individuals interacting at home, work, or play. It focuses on how people interpret the symbolic and behavioral actions of others and respond to them. Blumer objects to the relatively unexamined assumption of most sociologists that people's behavior is largely explained by the environmental pressures that are upon them. Blumer instead explains a person's behavior as arising "from how he interprets and handles [environmental pressures] in the action which he is constructing." Blumer thus gives agency back to the individual. The process of symbolic interaction leads people to be students, politicians, criminals, heroes, and ministers, and to create families, businesses, crowds, movements, universities, societies, and so on. Blumer argues that these created social structures are not actors in themselves. Only individuals act, and their actions create and continually recreate these macro social constructions.

Key Concept: symbolic interaction

A view of human society as symbolic interaction has been followed more than it has been formulated. Partial, usually fragmentary, statements of it are to be found in the writings of a number of eminent scholars.... What I have to present should be regarded as my personal version. My aim is to present the basic premises of the point of view and to develop their methodological consequences for the study of human group life.

The term "symbolic interaction" refers, of course, to the peculiar and distinctive character of interaction as it takes place between human beings. The peculiarity consists in the fact that human beings interpret or "define" each other's actions instead of merely reacting to each other's actions. Their "response" is not made directly to the actions of one another but instead is based on the meaning which they attach to such actions. Thus, human interaction is mediated by the use of symbols, by interpretation, or by ascertaining the meaning of one another's actions. This mediation is equivalent to inserting a process of interpretation between stimulus and response in the case of human behavior.

The simple recognition that human beings interpret each other's actions as the means of acting toward one another has permeated the thought and writings of many scholars of human conduct and of human group life. Yet few of them have endeavored to analyze what such interpretation implies about the nature of the human being or about the nature of human association. They are usually content with a mere recognition that "interpretation" should be caught by the student, or with a simple realization that symbols, such as cultural norms or values, must be introduced into their analyses. Only G. H. Mead, in my judgment, has sought to think through what the act of interpretation implies for an understanding of the human being, human action, and human association. The essentials of his analysis are so penetrating and profound and so important for an understanding of human group life that I wish to spell them out, even though briefly.

The key feature in Mead's analysis is that the human being has a self. This idea should not be cast aside as esoteric or glossed over as something that is obvious and hence not worthy of attention. In declaring that the human being has a self, Mead had in mind chiefly that the human being can be the object of his own actions. He can act toward himself as he might act toward others. Each of us is familiar with actions of this sort in which the human being gets angry with himself, rebuffs himself, takes pride in himself, argues with himself, tries to bolster his own courage, tells himself that he should "do this" or not "do that," sets goals for himself, makes compromises with himself, and plans what he is going to do. That the human being acts toward himself in these and countless other ways is a matter of easy empirical observation. To recognize that the human being can act toward himself is no mystical conjuration.

Mead regards this ability of the human being to act toward himself as the central mechanism with which the human being faces and deals with his world. This mechanism enables the human being to make indications to himself of things in his surroundings and thus to guide his actions by what he notes. Anything of which a human being is conscious is something which he is indicating to himself—the ticking of a clock, a knock at the door, the appearance of a friend, the remark made by a companion, a recognition that he has a task to perform, or the realization that he has a cold. Conversely, anything of which he is not conscious is, *ipso facto*, something which he is not indicating to himself. The conscious life of the human being, from the time that he awakens until

70

*Chapter 3
Socialization,
Personality
Development,
and the Social
Construction
of Society*

he falls asleep, is a continual flow of self-indications—notations of the things with which he deals and takes into account. We are given, then, a picture of the human being as an organism which confronts its world with a mechanism for making indications to itself. This is the mechanism that is involved in interpreting the actions of others. To interpret the actions of another is to point out to oneself that the action has this or that meaning or character.

Now, according to Mead, the significance of making indications to oneself is of paramount importance. The importance lies along two lines. First, to indicate something is to extricate it from its setting, to hold it apart, to give it a meaning or, in Mead's language, to make it into an object. An object—that is to say, anything that an individual indicates to himself—is different from a stimulus; instead of having an intrinsic character which acts on the individual and which can be identified apart from the individual, its character or meaning is conferred on it by the individual. The object is a product of the individual's disposition to act instead of being an antecedent stimulus which evokes the act. Instead of the individual being surrounded by an environment of pre-existing objects which play upon him and call forth his behavior, the proper picture is that he constructs his objects on the basis of his on-going activity. In any of his countless acts—whether minor, like dressing himself, or major, like organizing himself for a professional career—the individual is designating different objects to himself, giving them meaning, judging their suitability to his action, and making decisions on the basis of the judgment. This is what is meant by interpretation or acting on the basis of symbols.

The second important implication of the fact that the human being makes indications to himself is that his action is constructed or built up instead of being a mere release. Whatever the action in which he is engaged, the human individual proceeds by pointing out to himself the divergent things which have to be taken into account in the course of his action. He has to note what he wants to do and how he is to do it; he has to point out to himself the various conditions which may be instrumental to his action and those which may obstruct his action; he has to take account of the demands, the expectations, the prohibitions, and the threats as they may arise in the situation in which he is acting. His action is built up step by step through a process of such self-indication. The human individual pieces together and guides his action by taking account of different things and interpreting their significance for his prospective action. There is no instance of conscious action of which this is not true.

The process of constructing action through making indications to oneself cannot be swallowed up in any of the conventional psychological categories. This process is distinct from and different from what is spoken of as the "ego" —just as it is different from any other conception which conceives of the self in terms of composition or organization. Self-indication is a moving communicative process in which the individual notes things, assesses them, gives them a meaning, and decides to act on the basis of the meaning. The human being stands over against the world, or against "alters," with such a process and not with a mere ego. Further, the process of self-indication cannot be subsumed under the forces, whether from the outside or inside, which are presumed to play upon the individual to produce his behavior. Environmental pressures, external stimuli, organic drives, wishes, attitudes, feelings, ideas, and their like do not cover or explain the process of self-indication. The process of self-indication stands over against them in that the individual points out to himself and interprets the appearance or expression of such things, noting a given social demand that is made on him, recognizing a command, observing that he is hungry, realizing that he wishes to buy something, aware that he has a given feeling, conscious that he dislikes eating with someone he despises, or aware that he is thinking of doing some given thing. By virtue of indicating such things to himself, he places himself over against them and is able to act back against them, accepting them, rejecting them, or transforming them in accordance with how he defines or interprets them. His behavior, accordingly, is not a result of such things as environmental pressures, stimuli, motives, attitudes, and ideas but arises instead from how he interprets and handles these things in the action which he is constructing. The process of self-indication by means of which human action is formed cannot be accounted for by factors which precede the act. The process of self-indication exists in its own right and must be accepted and studied as such. It is through this process that the human being constructs his conscious action.

Now Mead recognizes that the formation of action by the individual through a process of self-indication always takes place in a social context. Since this matter is so vital to an understanding of symbolic interaction it needs to be explained carefully. Fundamentally, group action takes the form of a fitting together of individual lines of action. Each individual aligns his action to the action of others by ascertaining what they are doing or what they intend to do—that is, by getting the meaning of their acts. For Mead, this is done by the individual "taking the role" of others—either the role of a specific person or the role of a group (Mead's "generalized other"). In taking such roles the individual seeks to ascertain the intention or direction of the acts of others. He forms and aligns his own action on the basis of such interpretation of the acts of others. This is the fundamental way in which group action takes place in human society.

The foregoing are the essential features, as I see them, in Mead's analysis of the bases of symbolic interaction. They presuppose the following: that human society is made up of individuals who have selves (that is, make indications to themselves); that individual action is a construction and not a release, being built up by the individual through noting and interpreting features of the situations in which he acts; that group or collective action consists of the aligning of individual actions, brought about by the individuals' interpreting or taking into account each other's actions. Since my purpose is to present and not to defend the position of symbolic interaction I shall not endeavor in this essay to advance support for the three premises which I have just indicated. I wish merely to say that the three premises can be easily verified empirically. I know of no instance of human group action to which the three premises do not apply. The reader is challenged to find or think of a single instance which they do not fit.

I wish now to point out that sociological views of human society are, in general, markedly at variance with the premises which I have indicated as underlying symbolic interaction. Indeed, the predominant number of such views, especially those in vogue at the present time, do not see or treat human society

72

*Chapter 3
Socialization,
Personality
Development,
and the Social
Construction
of Society*

as symbolic interaction. Wedded, as they tend to be, to some form of sociological determinism, they adopt images of human society, of individuals in it, and of group action which do not square with the premises of symbolic interaction. I wish to say a few words about the major lines of variance.

Sociological thought rarely recognizes or treats human societies as composed of individuals who have selves. Instead, they assume human beings to be merely organisms with some kind of organization, responding to forces which play upon them. Generally, although not exclusively, these forces are lodged in the make-up of the society, as in the case of "social system," "social structure," "culture," "status position," "social role," "custom," "institution," "collective representation," "social situation," "social norm," and "values." The assumption is that the behavior of people as members *of a society* is an expression of the play on them of these kinds of factors or forces. This, of course, is the logical position which is necessarily taken when the scholar explains their behavior or phases of their behavior in terms of one or another of such social factors. The individuals who compose a human society are treated as the media through which such factors operate, and the social action of such individuals is regarded as an expression of such factors. This approach or point of view denies, or at least ignores, that human beings have selves—that they act by making indications to themselves. Incidentally, the "self" is not brought into the picture by introducing such items as organic drives, motives, attitudes, feelings, internalized social factors, or psychological components. Such psychological factors have the same status as the social factors mentioned: they are regarded as factors which play on the individual to produce his action. They do not constitute the process of self-indication. The process of self-indication stands over against them, just as it stands over against the social factors which play on the human being. Practically all sociological conceptions of human society fail to recognize that the individuals who compose it have selves in the sense spoken of.

Correspondingly, such sociological conceptions do not regard the social actions of individuals in human society as being constructed by them through a process of interpretation. Instead, action is treated as a product of factors which play on and through individuals. The social behavior of people is not seen as built up by them through an interpretation of objects, situations, or the actions of others. If a place is given to "interpretation," the interpretation is regarded as merely an expression of other factors (such as motives) which precede the act, and accordingly disappears as a factor in its own right. Hence, the social action of people is treated as an outward flow or expression of forces playing on them rather than as acts which are built up by people through their interpretation of the situations in which they are placed.

These remarks suggest another significant line of difference between general sociological views and the position of symbolic interaction. These two sets of views differ in where they lodge social action. Under the perspective of symbolic interaction, social action is lodged in acting individuals who fit their respective lines of action to one another through a process of interpretation; group action is the collective action of such individuals. As opposed to this view, sociological conceptions generally lodge social action in the action of society or in some unit of society. Examples of this are legion. Let me cite a few. Some conceptions, in treating societies or human groups as "social systems," regard group action as an expression of a system, either in a state of balance or seeking to achieve balance. Or group action is conceived as an expression of the "functions" of a society or of a group. Or group action is regarded as the outward expression of elements lodged in society or the group, such as cultural demands, societal purposes, social values, or institutional stresses. These typical conceptions ignore or blot out a view of group life or of group action as consisting of the collective or concerted actions of individuals seeking to meet their life situations. If recognized at all, the efforts of people to develop collective acts to meet their situations are subsumed under the play of underlying or transcending forces which are lodged in society or its parts. The individuals composing the society or the group become "carriers," or media for the expression of such forces; and the interpretative behavior by means of which people form their actions is merely a coerced link in the play of such forces.

The indication of the foregoing lines of variance should help to put the position of symbolic interaction in better perspective. In the remaining discussion I wish to sketch somewhat more fully how human society appears in terms of symbolic interaction. . . .

Human society is to be seen as consisting of acting people, and the life of the society is to be seen as consisting of their actions. The acting units may be separate individuals, collectivities whose members are acting together on a common quest, or organizations acting on behalf of a constituency. . . .

Corresponding respect must be shown to the conditions under which such units act. One primary condition is that action takes place in and with regard to a situation. Whatever be the acting unit—an individual, a family, a school, a church, a business firm, a labor union, a legislature, and so on—any particular action is formed in the light of the situation in which it takes place. This leads to the recognition of a second major condition, namely, that the action is formed or constructed by interpreting the situation. The acting unit necessarily has to identify the things which it has to take into account—tasks, opportunities, obstacles, means, demands, discomforts, dangers, and the like; it has to assess them in some fashion and it has to make decisions on the basis of the assessment. Such interpretative behavior may take place in the individual guiding his own action, in a collectivity of individuals acting in concert, or in "agents" acting on behalf of a group or organization. Group life consists of acting units developing acts to meet the situations in which they are placed.

Usually, most of the situations encountered by people in a given society are defined or "structured" by them in the same way. Through previous interaction they develop and acquire common understandings or definitions of how to act in this or that situation. These common definitions enable people to act alike. The common repetitive behavior of people in such situations should not mislead the student into believing that no process of interpretation is in play; on the contrary, even though fixed, the actions of the participating people are constructed by them through a process of interpretation. Since ready-made and commonly accepted definitions are at hand, little strain is placed on people in guiding and organizing their acts. However, many other situations may not be defined in a single way by the participating people. In the event, their lines of action do not fit together readily and collective action is blocked. Interpretations have to be developed and effective accommodation of the participants to

74

*Chapter 3
Socialization,
Personality
Development,
and the Social
Construction
of Society*

one another has to be worked out. In the case of such "undefined" situations, it is necessary to trace and study the emerging process of definition which is brought into play....

From the standpoint of symbolic interaction, social organization is a framework inside of which acting units develop their actions. Structural features, such as "culture," "social systems," "social stratification," or "social roles," set conditions for their action but do not determine their action. People—that is, acting units—do not act toward culture, social structure or the like; they act toward situations. Social organization enters into action only to the extent to which it shapes situations in which people act, and to the extent to which it supplies fixed sets of symbols which people use in interpreting their situations. These two forms of influence of social organization are important. In the case of settled and stabilized societies, such as isolated primitive tribes and peasant communities, the influence is certain to be profound. In the case of human societies, particularly modern societies, in which streams of new situations arise and old situations become unstable, the influence of organization decreases. One should bear in mind that the most important element confronting an acting unit in situations is the actions of other acting units. In modern society, with its increasing criss-crossing of lines of action, it is common for situations to arise in which the actions of participants are not previously regularized and standardized. To this extent, existing social organization does not shape the situations. Correspondingly, the symbols or tools of interpretation used by acting units in such situations may vary and shift considerably. For these reasons, social action may go beyond, or depart from, existing organization in any of its structural dimensions.

CHAPTER 4 Social Roles and the Presentation of Self

4.1 PETER L. BERGER

Sociological Perspective—Society in Man

One of the most elementary concepts in sociology is that of role. It is borrowed from the language of the theater and captures the simple fact that people behave most of the time in accordance with the dictates of society's script for the roles that they play. In the following excerpt from his book *Invitation to Sociology: A Humanistic Perspective* (Anchor Books, 1963), Peter L. Berger elaborates on the concept of role and shows how important it is for understanding social phenomena.

Although the basic insight that we "play" social roles is relatively obvious, Berger explains several surprising aspects of roles. First, roles not only prescribe certain actions but also the emotions and attitudes that belong to these actions. We learn not only what to do but also what to feel. Second, in the process of learning a role, one takes on the identity of that role and is identified by others with that role. Finally, role theory contradicts the view that the self is relatively fixed and consistent. Rather, the self is relatively fluid and is continuously created and re-created in each role or social situation. This last point of Berger's theory contradicts commonly held views of

76

Chapter 4
Social
Roles and the
Presenta-
tion of Self

the self. Berger, however, supports role-playing as a natural, unconscious aspect of socialization and role theory as an accurate way to evaluate human behavior.

Berger (b. 1929) is director of the Institute for the Study of Economic Culture at Boston University. He supports what he calls "methodological atheism," which argues for explanations of society and social life that are based on scientific study.

Key Concept: role theory

*R*ole theory has been almost entirely an American intellectual development. Some of its germinal insights go back to William James, while its direct parents are two other American thinkers, Charles Cooley and George Herbert Mead. It cannot be our purpose here to give a historical introduction to this quite fascinating portion of intellectual history. Rather than try this even in outline, we shall start more systematically by beginning our consideration of the import of role theory with [a] look at [sociologist William Isaac] Thomas' concept of the definition of the situation.

The reader will recall Thomas' understanding of the social situation as a sort of reality agreed upon *ad hoc* by those who participate in it, or, more exactly, those who do the defining of the situation. From the viewpoint of the individual participant this means that each situation he enters confronts him with specific expectations and demands of him specific responses to these expectations.... [P]owerful pressures exist in just about any social situation to ensure that the proper responses are indeed forthcoming. Society can exist by virtue of the fact that most of the time most people's definitions of the most important situations at least coincide approximately. The motives of the publisher and the writers of these lines may be rather different, but the ways the two define the situation in which this book is being produced are sufficiently similar for the joint venture to be possible. In similar fashion there may be quite divergent interests present in a classroom of students, some of them having little connection with the educational activity that is supposedly going on, but in most cases these interests (say, that one student came to study the subject being taught, while another simply registers for every course taken by a certain redhead he is pursuing) can coexist in the situation without destroying it. In other words, there is a certain amount of leeway in the extent to which response must meet expectation for a situation to remain sociologically viable. Of course, if the definitions of the situation are too widely discrepant, some form of social conflict or disorganization will inevitably result—say, if some students interpret the classroom meeting as a party, or if an author has no intention of producing a book but is using his contract with one publisher to put pressure on another.

While an average individual meets up with very different expectations in different areas of his life in society, the situations that produce these expectations fall into certain clusters. A student may take two courses from two different professors in two different departments, with considerable variations in the expectations met with in the two situations (say, as between formality or informality in the relations between professor and students). Nevertheless, the situations will be sufficiently similar to each other and to other classroom situations previously experienced to enable the student to carry into both situations essentially the same overall response. In other words, in both cases, with but a few modifications, he will be able to *play the role* of student. A role, then, may be defined as a typified response to a typified expectation. Society has predefined the fundamental typology. To use the language of the theater, from which the concept of role is derived, we can say that society provides the script for all the *dramatis personae*. The individual actors, therefore, need but slip into the roles already assigned to them before the curtain goes up. As long as they play their roles as provided for in this script, the social play can proceed as planned.

The role provides the pattern according to which the individual is to act in the particular situation. Roles, in society as in the theater, will vary in the exactness with which they lay down instructions for the actor. Taking occupational roles for an instance, a fairly minimal pattern goes into the role of garbage collector, while physicians or clergymen or officers have to acquire all kinds of distinctive mannerisms, speech and motor habits, such as military bearing, sanctimonious diction or bedside cheer. It would, however, be missing an essential aspect of the role if one regarded it merely as a regulatory pattern for externally visible actions. One feels more ardent by kissing, more humble by kneeling and more angry by shaking one's fist. That is, the kiss not only expresses ardor but manufactures it. Roles carry with them both certain actions and the emotions and attitudes that belong to these actions. The professor putting on an act that pretends to wisdom comes to feel wise. The preacher finds himself believing what he preaches. The soldier discovers martial stirrings in his breast as he puts on his uniform. In each case, while the emotion or attitude may have been present before the role was taken on, the latter inevitably strengthens what was there before. In many instances there is every reason to suppose that nothing at all anteceded the playing of the role in the actor's consciousness. In other words, one becomes wise by being appointed a professor, believing by engaging in activities that presuppose belief, and ready for battle by marching in formation.

Let us take an example. A man recently commissioned as an officer, especially if he came up through the ranks, will at first be at least slightly embarrassed by the salutes he now receives from the enlisted men he meets on his way. Probably he will respond to them in a friendly, almost apologetic manner. The new insignia on his uniform are at that point still something that he has merely put on, almost like a disguise. Indeed, the new officer may even tell himself and others that underneath he is still the same person, that he simply has new responsibilities (among which... is the duty to accept the salutes of enlisted men). This attitude is not likely to last very long. In order to carry out his new role of officer, our man must maintain a certain bearing. This bearing has quite definite implications. Despite all the double-talk in this area that is customary in so-called democratic armies, such as the American one, one of the fundamental implications is that an officer is a superior somebody, entitled to obedience and respect on the basis of this superiority. Every military salute given by an inferior in rank is an act of obeisance, received as a matter of course by the one who returns it. Thus, with every salute given and accepted (along,

78

*Chapter 4
Social
Roles and the
Presenta-
tion of Self*

of course, with a hundred other ceremonial acts that enhance his new status) our man is fortified in his new bearing—and in its, as it were, ontological presuppositions. He not only acts like an officer, he feels like one. Gone are the embarrassment, the apologetic attitude, the I'm-just-another-guy-really grin. If on some occasion an enlisted man should fail to salute with the appropriate amount of enthusiasm or even commit the unthinkable act of failing to salute at all, our officer is not merely going to punish a violation of military regulations. He will be driven with every fiber of his being to redress an offence against the appointed order of his cosmos.

It is important to stress in this illustration that only very rarely is such a process deliberate or based on reflection. Our man has not sat down and figured out all the things that ought to go into his new role, including the things that he ought to feel and believe. The strength of the process comes precisely from its unconscious, unreflecting character. He has become an officer almost as effortlessly as he grew into a person with blue eyes, brown hair and a height of six feet....

Every role in society has attached to it a certain identity.... [S]ome of these identities are trivial and temporary ones, as in some occupations that demand little modification in the being of their practitioners. It is not difficult to change from garbage collector to night watchman. It is considerably more difficult to change from clergyman to officer. It is very, very difficult to change from Negro to white. And it is almost impossible to change from man to woman. These differences in the ease of role changing ought not to blind us to the fact that even identities that we consider to be our essential selves have been socially assigned. Just as there are racial roles to be acquired and identified with, so there are sexual roles. To say "I am a man" is just as much a proclamation of role as to say "I am a colonel in the U.S. Army." We are well aware of the fact that one is born a male, while not even the most humorless martinet imagines himself to have been born with a golden eagle sitting on his umbilical cord. But to be biologically male is a far cry from the specific, socially defined (and, of course, socially relative) role that goes with the statement "I am a man." A male child does not have to learn to have an erection. But he must learn to be aggressive, to have ambitions, to compete with others, and to be suspicious of too much gentleness in himself. The male role in our society, however, requires all these things that one must learn, as does a male identity. To have an erection is not enough—if it were, regiments of psychotherapists would be out of work.

This significance of role theory could be summarized by saying that, in a sociological perspective, identity is socially bestowed, socially sustained and socially transformed. The example of the man in process of becoming an officer may suffice to illustrate the way in which identities are bestowed in adult life. However, even roles that are much more fundamentally part of what psychologists would call our personality than those associated with a particular adult activity are bestowed in very similar manner through a social process. This has been demonstrated over and over again in studies of so-called socialization— the process by which a child learns to be a participant member of society.

Probably the most penetrating theoretical account of this process is the one given by Mead, in which the genesis of the self is interpreted as being one and the same event as the discovery of society. The child finds out who he is as he learns what society is. He learns to play roles properly belonging to him by learning, as Mead puts it, "to take the role of the other"—which, incidentally, is the crucial sociopsychological function of play, in which children masquerade with a variety of social roles and in doing so discover the significance of those being assigned to them. All this learning occurs, and can only occur, in interaction with other human beings, be it the parents or whoever else raises the child. The child first takes on roles *vis-à-vis* what Mead calls his "significant others," that is, those persons who deal with him intimately and whose attitudes are decisive for the formation of his conception of himself. Later, the child learns that the roles he plays are not only relevant to this intimate circle. but relate to the expectations directed toward him by society at large. This higher level of abstraction in the social response Mead calls the discovery of the "generalized other." That is, not only the child's mother expects him to be good, clean and truthful, society in general does so as well. Only when this general conception of society emerges is the child capable of forming a clear conception of himself. "Self" and "society," in the child's experience, are the two sides of the same coin.

In other words, identity is not something "given," but is bestowed in acts of social recognition. We become that as which we are addressed. The same idea is expressed in Cooley's well-known description of the self as a reflection in a looking glass. This does not mean, of course, that there are not certain characteristics an individual is born with, that are carried by his genetic heritage regardless of the social environment in which the latter will have to unfold itself. Our knowledge of man's biology does not as yet allow us a very clear picture of the extent to which this may be true. We do know, however, that the room for social formation within those genetic limits is very large indeed. Even with the biological questions left largely unsettled, we can say that to be human is to be recognized as human, just as to be a certain kind of man is to be recognized as such. The child deprived of human affection and attention becomes dehumanized. The child who is given respect comes to respect himself. A little boy considered to be a *schlemiel* [or a bungler] becomes one, just as a grown-up treated as an awe-inspiring young god of war begins to think of himself and act as is appropriate to such a figure—and, indeed, merges his identity with the one he is presented with in these expectations.

Identities are socially bestowed. They must also be socially sustained, and fairly steadily so. One cannot be human all by oneself and, apparently, one cannot hold on to any particular identity all by oneself. The self-image of the officer as an officer can be maintained only in a social context in which others are willing to recognize him in this identity. If this recognition is suddenly withdrawn, it usually does not take very long before the self-image collapses. . . .

Role theory, when pursued to its logical conclusions, does far more than provide us with a convenient shorthand for the description of various social activities. It gives us a sociological anthropology, that is, a view of man based on his existence in society. This view tells us that man plays dramatic parts in the grand play of society, and that, speaking sociologically, he *is* the masks that he must wear to do so. The human person also appears now in a dramatic context, true to its theatrical etymology (*persona*, the technical term given to the actors' masks in classical theater). The person is perceived as a repertoire of

80

*Chapter 4
Social
Roles and the
Presenta-
tion of Self*

roles, each one properly equipped with a certain identity. The range of an individual person can be measured by the number of roles he is capable of playing. The person's biography now appears to us as an uninterrupted sequence of stage performances, played to different audiences, sometimes involving drastic changes of costume, always demanding that the actor *be* what he is playing.

Such a sociological view of personality is far more radical in its challenge to the way that we commonly think of ourselves than most psychological theories. It challenges radically one of the fondest presuppositions about the self—its continuity. Looked at sociologically, the self is no longer a solid, given entity that moves from one situation to another. It is rather a process, continuously created and re-created in each social situation that one enters, held together by the slender thread of memory.... Nor is it possible within this framework of understanding to take refuge in the unconscious as containing the "real" contents of the self, because the presumed unconscious self is just as subject to social production as is the so-called conscious one.... In other words, man is not *also* a social being, but he is social in every aspect of his being that is open to empirical investigation. Still speaking sociologically then, if one wants to ask who an individual "really" is in this kaleidoscope of roles and identities, one can answer only by enumerating the situations in which he is one thing and those in which he is another.

Now, it is clear that such transformations cannot occur *ad infinitum* and that some are easier than others. An individual becomes so habituated to certain identities that, even when his social situation changes, he has difficulty keeping up with the expectations newly directed toward him. The difficulties that healthy and previously highly active individuals have when they are forced to retire from their occupation show this very clearly. The transformability of the self depends not *only* on its social context, but also on the degree of its habituation to previous identities and perhaps also on certain genetically given traits. While these modifications in our model are necessary to avoid a radicalization of our position, they do not detract appreciably from the discontinuity of the self as revealed by sociological analysis....

One might obtain the impression from all of this that there is really no essential difference between most people and those afflicted with what psychiatry calls "multiple personality." If someone wanted to harp on the word "essential" here, the sociologist might agree with the statement. The actual difference, however, is that for "normal" people (that is, those so recognized by their society) there are strong pressures toward consistency in the various roles they play and the identities that go with these roles. These pressures are both external and internal. Externally the others with whom one must play one's social games, and on whose recognition one's own parts depend, demand that one present at least a relatively consistent picture to the world. A certain degree of role discrepancy may be permitted, but if certain tolerance limits are passed society will withdraw its recognition of the individual in question, defining him as a moral or psychological aberration....

There are also internal pressures toward consistency, possibly based on very profound psychological needs to perceive oneself as a totality. Even the contemporary urban masquerader, who plays mutually irreconcilable roles in different areas of his life, may feel internal tensions though he can successfully control external ones by carefully segregating his several *mises en scène* [environments or settings] from each other. To avoid such anxieties people commonly segregate their consciousness as well as their conduct. By this we do not mean that they "repress" their discrepant identities into some "unconscious," for within our model we have every reason to be suspicious of such concepts. We rather mean that they focus their attention only on that particular identity that, so to speak, they require at the moment. Other identities are forgotten for the duration of this particular act. The way in which socially disapproved sexual acts or morally questionable acts of any kind are segregated in consciousness may serve to illustrate this process. The man who engages in, say, homosexual masochism has a carefully constructed identity set aside for just these occasions. When any given occasion is over, he checks that identity again at the gate, so to speak, and returns home as affectionate father, responsible husband, perhaps even ardent lover of his wife. In the same way, the judge who sentences a man to death segregates the identity in which he does this from the rest of his consciousness, in which he is a kindly, tolerant and sensitive human being. The Nazi concentration-camp commander who writes sentimental letters to his children is but an extreme case of something that occurs in society all the time.

It would be a complete misunderstanding of what has just been said if the reader now thought that we are presenting a picture of society in which everybody schemes, plots and deliberately puts on disguises to fool his fellow men. On the contrary, role-playing and identity-building processes are generally unreflected and unplanned, almost automatic. The psychological needs for consistency of self-image just mentioned ensure this. Deliberate deception requires a degree of psychological self-control that few people are capable of. That is why insincerity is rather a rare phenomenon. Most people are sincere, because this is the easiest course to take psychologically.

The Presentation of Self in Everyday Life

During any one day we engage in a variety of social interactions in which we perform a number of specific social roles, such as mother, friend, customer, student, and so on.

Prominent sociologist Erving Goffman (1922–1982) studied and defined rules that govern social behavior and social interaction. One theory he developed is called the "dramaturgical" approach, in which social behavior is viewed as a staged performance and each actor intentionally conveys specific impressions to the others. This approach is explored in Goffman's most famous book *The Presentation of Self in Everyday Life* (Anchor Books, 1959), from which the following selection is taken. In it, Goffman provides various examples that demonstrate how one tries to control the conduct of others by influencing "the definition of the situation" through the staging of one's behavior according to how one wants to be treated and valued.

Goffman's analysis might raise some perplexing questions about the authenticity of most human behavior. He seems to say that people are always acting or staging their behavior, which suggests that their actions are not authentic expressions of the self but are carefully planned maneuvers designed to create the desired perceptions in others. This interpretation, however, is too simple. Goffman argues that by staging a specific behavior one claims or owns this behavior and demands treatment accordingly.

Key Concept: presentation of self

When an individual enters the presence of others, they commonly seek to acquire information about him or to bring into play information about him already possessed. They will be interested in his general socioeconomic status, his conception of self, his attitude toward them, his competence, his trustworthiness, etc. Although some of this information seems to be sought almost as an end in itself, there are usually quite practical reasons for acquiring it. Information about the individual helps to define the situation, enabling others to know in advance what he will expect of them and what they may expect of him. Informed in these ways, the others will know how best to act in order to call forth a desired response from him.

For those present, many sources of information become accessible and many carriers (or "sign-vehicles") become available for conveying this information. If unacquainted with the individual, observers can glean clues from his conduct and appearance which allow them to apply their previous experience with individuals roughly similar to the one before them or, more important, to apply untested stereotypes to him. They can also assume from past experience that only individuals of a particular kind are likely to be found in a given social setting. They can rely on what the individual says about himself or on documentary evidence he provides as to who and what he is. If they know, or know of, the individual by virtue of experience prior to the interaction, they can rely on assumptions as to the persistence and generality of psychological traits as a means of predicting his present and future behavior.

However, during the period in which the individual is in the immediate presence of the others, few events may occur which directly provide the others with the conclusive information they will need if they are to direct wisely their own activity. Many crucial facts lie beyond the time and place of interaction or lie concealed within it. For example, the "true" or "real" attitudes, beliefs, and emotions of the individual can be ascertained only indirectly, through his avowals or through what appears to be involuntary expressive behavior.... They will be forced to accept some events as conventional or natural signs of something not directly available to the senses. In Ichheiser's terms,[1] the individual will have to act so that he intentionally or unintentionally *expresses* himself, and the others will in turn have to be *impressed* in some way by him.

The expressiveness of the individual (and therefore his capacity to give impressions) appears to involve two radically different kinds of sign activity: the expression that he *gives*, and the expression that he *gives off*. The first involves verbal symbols or their substitutes which he uses admittedly and solely to convey the information that he and the others are known to attach to these symbols. This is communication in the traditional and narrow sense. The second involves a wide range of action that others can treat as symptomatic of the actor, the expectation being that the action was performed for reasons other than the information conveyed in this way. As we shall have to see, this distinction has an only initial validity. The individual does of course intentionally convey misinformation by means of both of these types of communication, the first involving deceit, the second feigning.

Taking communication in both its narrow and broad sense, one finds that when the individual is in the immediate presence of others, his activity will have a promissory character. The others are likely to find that they must accept the individual on faith, offering him a just return while he is present before them in exchange for something whose true value will not be established until after he has left their presence. (Of course, the others also live by inference in their dealings with the physical world, but it is only in the world of social interaction that the objects about which they make inferences will purposely facilitate and hinder this inferential process.) The security that they justifiably feel in making inferences about the individual will vary, of course, depending on such factors as the amount of information they already possess about him, but no amount of such past evidence can entirely obviate the necessity of acting on the basis of inferences....

84

*Chapter 4
Social
Roles and the
Presenta-
tion of Self*

Let us now turn from the others to the point of view of the individual who presents himself before them. He may wish them to think highly of him, or to think that he thinks highly of them, or to perceive how in fact he feels toward them, or to obtain no clear-cut impression; he may wish to ensure sufficient harmony so that the interaction can be sustained, or to defraud, get rid of, confuse, mislead, antagonize, or insult them. Regardless of the particular objective which the individual has in mind and of his motive for having this objective, it will be in his interests to control the conduct of the others, especially their responsive treatment of him. This control is achieved largely by influencing the definition of the situation which the others come to formulate, and he can influence this definition by expressing himself in such a way as to give them the kind of impression that will lead them to act voluntarily in accordance with his own plan. Thus, when an individual appears in the presence of others, there will usually be some reason for him to mobilize his activity so that it will convey an impression to others which it is in his interests to convey. Since a girl's dormitory mates will glean evidence of her popularity from the calls she receives on the phone, we can suspect that some girls will arrange for calls to be made, and Willard Waller's finding can be anticipated:

> It has been reported by many observers that a girl who is called to the telephone in the dormitories will often allow herself to be called several times, in order to give all the other girls ample opportunity to hear her paged.[2]

Of the two kinds of communication—expressions given and expressions given off—this report will be primarily concerned with the latter, with the more theatrical and contextual kind, the nonverbal, presumably unintentional kind, whether this communication be purposely engineered or not. As an example of what we must try to examine, I would like to cite at length a novelistic incident in which Preedy, a vacationing Englishman, makes his first appearance on the beach of his summer hotel in Spain:

> But in any case he took care to avoid catching anyone's eye. First of all, he had to make it clear to those potential companions of his holiday that they were of no concern to him whatsoever. He stared through them, round them, over them —eyes lost in space. The beach might have been empty. If by chance a ball was thrown his way, he looked surprised; then let a smile of amusement lighten his face (Kindly Preedy), looked around dazed to see that there *were* people on the beach, tossed it back with a smile to himself and not a smile *at* the people, and then resumed carelessly his nonchalant survey of space.
>
> But it was time to institute a little parade, the parade of the Ideal Preedy. By devious handlings he gave any who wanted to look a chance to see the title of his book—a Spanish translation of Homer, classic thus, but not daring, cosmopolitan too—and then gathered together his beachwrap and bag into a neat sand-resistant pile (Methodical and Sensible Preedy), rose slowly to stretch at ease his huge frame (Big-Cat Preedy), and tossed aside his sandals (Carefree Preedy, after all).
>
> The marriage of Preedy and the sea! There were alternative rituals. The first involved the stroll that turns into a run and a dive straight into the water, thereafter smoothing into a strong splashless crawl towards the horizon. But of course not really to the horizon. Quite suddenly he would turn on to his back and thrash

great white splashes with his legs, somehow thus showing that he could have swum further had he wanted to, and then would stand up a quarter out of water for all to see who it was.

The alternative course was simpler, it avoided the cold-water shock and it avoided the risk of appearing too high-spirited. The point was to appear to be so used to the sea, the Mediterranean, and this particular beach, that one might as well be in the sea as out of it. It involved a slow stroll down and into the edge of the water—not even noticing his toes were wet, land and water all the same to *him!*—with his eyes up at the sky gravely surveying portents, invisible to others, of the weather (Local Fisherman Preedy).[3]

The novelist means us to see that Preedy is improperly concerned with the extensive impressions he feels his sheer bodily action is giving off to those around him. We can malign Preedy further by assuming that he has acted merely in order to give a particular impression, that this is a false impression, and that the others present receive either no impression at all, or, worse still, the impression that Preedy is affectedly trying to cause them to receive this particular impression. But the important point for us here is that the kind of impression Preedy thinks he is making is in fact the kind of impression that others correctly and incorrectly glean from someone in their midst.

I have said that when an individual appears before others his actions will influence the definition of the situation which they come to have. Sometimes the individual will act in a thoroughly calculating manner, expressing himself in a given way solely in order to give the kind of impression to others that is likely to evoke from them a specific response he is concerned to obtain. Sometimes the individual will be calculating in his activity but be relatively unaware that this is the case. Sometimes he will intentionally and consciously express himself in a particular way, but chiefly because the tradition of his group or social status require this kind of expression and not because of any particular response (other than vague acceptance or approval) that is likely to be evoked from those impressed by the expression. Sometimes the traditions of an individual's role will lead him to give a well-designed impression of a particular kind and yet he may be neither consciously nor unconsciously disposed to create such an impression. The others, in their turn, may be suitably impressed by the individual's efforts to convey something, or may misunderstand the situation and come to conclusions that are warranted neither by the individual's intent nor by the facts. In any case, insofar as the others act *as if* the individual had conveyed a particular impression, we may take a functional or pragmatic view and say that the individual has "effectively" projected a given definition of the situation and "effectively" fostered the understanding that a given state of affairs obtains.

There is one aspect of the others' response that bears special comment here. Knowing that the individual is likely to present himself in a light that is favorable to him, the others may divide what they witness into two parts: a part that is relatively easy for the individual to manipulate at will, being chiefly his verbal assertions, and a part in regard to which he seems to have little concern or control, being chiefly derived from the expressions he gives off. The others may then use what are considered to be the ungovernable aspects of his

86

*Chapter 4
Social
Roles and the
Presenta-
tion of Self*

expressive behavior as a check upon the validity of what is conveyed by the governable aspects. In this a fundamental asymmetry is demonstrated in the communication process, the individual presumably being aware of only one stream of his communication, the witnesses of this stream and one other. For example, in Shetland Isle one crofter's [or farmer's] wife, in serving native dishes to a visitor from the mainland of Britain, would listen with a polite smile to his polite claims of liking what he was eating; at the same time she would take note of the rapidity with which the visitor lifted his fork or spoon to his mouth, the eagerness with which he passed food into his mouth, and the gusto expressed in chewing the food, using these signs as a check on the stated feelings of the eater. . . .

Now given the fact that others are likely to check up on the more controllable aspects of behavior by means of the less controllable, one can expect that sometimes the individual will try to exploit this very possibility, guiding the impression he makes through behavior felt to be reliably informing. For example, in gaining admission to a tight social circle, the participant observer may not only wear an accepting look while listening to an informant, but may also be careful to wear the same look when observing the informant talking to others; observers of the observer will then not as easily discover where he actually stands. . . .

This kind of control upon the part of the individual reinstates the symmetry of the communication process, and sets the stage for a kind of information game—a potentially infinite cycle of concealment, discovery, false revelation, and rediscovery. It should be added that since the others are likely to be relatively unsuspicious of the presumably unguided aspect of the individual's conduct, he can gain much by controlling it. The others of course may sense that the individual is manipulating the presumably spontaneous aspects of his behavior, and seek in this very act of manipulation some shading of conduct that the individual has not managed to control. This again provides a check upon the individual's behavior, this time his presumably uncalculated behavior, thus re-establishing the asymmetry of the communication process. . . .

When we allow that the individual projects a definition of the situation when he appears before others, we must also see that the others, however passive their role may seem to be, will themselves effectively project a definition of the situation by virtue of their response to the individual and by virtue of any lines of action they initiate to him. Ordinarily the definitions of the situation projected by the several different participants are sufficiently attuned to one another so that open contradiction will not occur. I do not mean that there will be the kind of consensus that arises when each individual present candidly expresses what he really feels and honestly agrees with the expressed feeling of the others present. This kind of harmony is an optimistic ideal and in any case not necessary for the smooth working of society. Rather, each participant is expected to suppress his immediate heartfelt feelings, conveying a view of the situation which he feels the others will be able to find at least temporarily acceptable. The maintenance of this surface of agreement, this veneer of consensus, is facilitated by each participant concealing [his] wants behind statements while asserting values to which everyone present feels obliged to give lip service. Further, there is usually a kind of division of definitional labor.

Each participant is allowed to establish the tentative official ruling regarding matters which are vital to him but not immediately important to others, e.g., the rationalizations and justifications by which he accounts for his past activity. In exchange for this courtesy he remains silent or non-committal on matters important to others but not immediately important to him. We have then a kind of interactional *modus vivendi* [manner of living]. Together, the participants contribute to a single over-all definition of the situation which involves not so much a real argument as to what exists but rather a real agreement as to whose claims concerning what issues will be temporarily honored. Real agreement will also exist concerning the desirability of avoiding an open conflict of definitions of the situation. I will refer to this level of agreement as a "working consensus." It is to be understood that the working consensus established in one interaction setting will be quite different in content from the working consensus established in a different type of setting. Thus, between two friends at lunch, a reciprocal show of affection, respect, and concern for the other is maintained. In service occupations, on the other hand, the specialist often maintains an image of disinterested involvement in the problem of the client, while the client responds with a show of respect for the competence and integrity of the specialist. Regardless of such differences in content, however, the general form of these working arrangements is the same.

In noting the tendency for a participant to accept the definitional claims made by the others present, we can appreciate the crucial importance of the information that the individual *initially* possesses or acquires concerning his fellow participants, for it is on the basis of this initial information that the individual starts to define the situation and starts to build up lines of responsive action. The individual's initial projection commits him to what he is proposing to be and requires him to drop all pretenses of being other things. As the interaction among the participants progresses, additions and modifications in this initial informational state will of course occur, but it is essential that these later developments be related without contradiction to, and even built up from, the initial positions taken by the several participants. It would seem that an individual can more easily make a choice as to what line of treatment to demand from and extend to the others present at the beginning of an encounter than he can alter the line of treatment that is being pursued once the interaction is underway.

In everyday life, of course, there is a clear understanding that first impressions are important. Thus, the work adjustment of those in service occupations will often hinge upon a capacity to seize and hold the initiative in the service relations, a capacity that will require subtle aggressiveness on the part of the server when he is of lower socioeconomic status than his client. W. F. Whyte suggests the waitress as an example:

> The first point that stands out is that the waitress who bears up under pressure does not simply respond to her customers. She acts with some skill to control her behavior. The first question to ask when we look at the customer relationship is, "Does the waitress get the jump on the customer, or does the customer get the jump on the waitress?" The skilled waitress realizes the crucial nature of this question. . . .

88

*Chapter 4
Social
Roles and the
Presenta-
tion of Self*

The skilled waitress tackles the customer with confidence and without hesitation. For example, she may find that a new customer has seated himself before she could clear off the dirty dishes and change the cloth. He is now leaning on the table studying the menu. She greets him, says, "May I change the cover, please?" and, without waiting for an answer, takes his menu away from him so that he moves back from the table, and she goes about her work. The relationship is handled politely but firmly, and there is never any question as to who is in charge.[4]

When the interaction that is initiated by "first impressions" is itself merely the initial interaction in an extended series of interactions involving the same participants, we speak of "getting off on the right foot" and feel that it is crucial that we do so. Thus, one learns that some teachers take the following view:

> You can't ever let them get the upper hand on you or you're through. So I start out tough. The first day I get a new class in, I let them know who's boss.... You've got to start off tough, then you can ease up as you go along. If you start out easy-going, when you try to be tough, they'll just look at you and laugh.[5]

Similarly, attendants in mental institutions may feel that if the new patient is sharply put in his place the first day on the ward and made to see who is boss, much future difficulty will be prevented.

Given the fact that the individual effectively projects a definition of the situation when he enters the presence of others, we can assume that events may occur within the interaction which contradict, discredit, or otherwise throw doubt upon this projection. When these disruptive events occur, the interaction itself may come to a confused and embarrassed halt. Some of the assumptions upon which the responses of the participants had been predicated become untenable, and the participants find themselves lodged in an interaction for which the situation has been wrongly defined and is now no longer defined. At such moments the individual whose presentation has been discredited may feel ashamed while the others present may feel hostile, and all the participants may come to feel ill at ease, nonplussed, out of countenance, embarrassed, experiencing the kind of anomy that is generated when the minute social system of face-to-face interaction breaks down.

In stressing the fact that the initial definition of the situation projected by an individual tends to provide a plan for the cooperative activity that follows—in stressing this action point of view—we must not overlook the crucial fact that any projected definition of the situation also has a distinctive moral character. It is this moral character of projections that will chiefly concern us in this report. Society is organized on the principle that any individual who possesses certain social characteristics has a moral right to expect that others will value and treat him in an appropriate way. Connected with this principle is a second, namely that an individual who implicitly or explicitly signifies that he has certain social characteristics ought in fact to be what he claims he is. In consequence, when an individual projects a definition of the situation and thereby makes an implicit or explicit claim to be a person of a particular kind, he automatically exerts a moral demand upon the others, obliging them to value and treat him in the manner that persons of his kind have a right to expect. He also implicitly forgoes all claims to be things he does not appear to be and hence forgoes the treatment that would be appropriate for such individuals. The others find, then, that the individual has informed them as to what is and as to what they *ought* to see as the "is."

One cannot judge the importance of definitional disruptions by the frequency with which they occur, for apparently they would occur more frequently were not constant precautions taken. We find that preventive practices are constantly employed to avoid these embarrassments and that corrective practices are constantly employed to compensate for discrediting occurrences that have not been successfully avoided. When the individual employs these strategies and tactics to protect his own projections, we may refer to them as "defensive practices"; when a participant employs them to save the definition of the situation projected by another, we speak of "protective practices" or "tact." Together, defensive and protective practices comprise the techniques employed to safeguard the impression fostered by an individual during his presence before others. It should be added that while we may be ready to see that no fostered impression would survive if defensive practices were not employed, we are less ready perhaps to see that few impressions could survive if those who received the impression did not exert tact in their reception of it.

In addition to the fact that precautions are taken to prevent disruption of projected definitions, we may also note that an intense interest in these disruptions comes to play a significant role in the social life of the group. Practical jokes and social games are played in which embarrassments which are to be taken unseriously are purposely engineered. Fantasies are created in which devastating exposures occur. Anecdotes from the past—real, embroidered, or fictitious—are told and retold, detailing disruptions which occurred, almost occurred, or occurred and were admirably resolved. There seems to be no grouping which does not have a ready supply of these games, reveries, and cautionary tales, to be used as a source of humor, a catharsis for anxieties, and a sanction for inducing individuals to be modest in their claims and reasonable in their projected expectations.... Journalists tell of times when an all-too-meaningful misprint occurred, and the paper's assumption of objectivity or decorum was humorously discredited. Public servants tell of times a client ridiculously misunderstood form instructions, giving answers which implied an unanticipated and bizarre definition of the situation.[6] ...

To summarize, then, I assume that when an individual appears before others he will have many motives for trying to control the impression they receive of the situation.

NOTES

1. Gustav Ichheiser, "Misunderstandings in Human Relations," Supplement to *The American Journal of Sociology,* 55 (September 1949): 6–7.

2. Willard Waller, "The Rating and Dating Complex," *American Sociological Review,* 2: 730.

3. William Sansom, *A Contest of Ladies* (London: Hogarth, 1956), pp. 230–32.

90

*Chapter 4
Social
Roles and the
Presenta-
tion of Self*

4. W. F. Whyte, "When Workers and Customers Meet," Chap. VII, *Industry and Society*, ed. W. F. Whyte (New York: McGraw-Hill, 1946), pp. 132–33.

5. Teacher interview quoted by Howard S. Becker, "Social Class Variations in the Teacher-Pupil Relationship" *Journal of Educational Sociology*, 25: 459.

6. Peter Blau, *Dynamics of Bureaucracy: A Study of Interpersonal Relationships in Two Government Agencies*, 2nd ed. (Chicago: University of Chicago Press, 1963).

CHAPTER 5 # Deviance, Crime, and Social Control

5.1 DANIEL PATRICK MOYNIHAN

Defining Deviancy Down

Daniel Patrick Moynihan, the senior U.S. senator from New York and a sociological scholar, explores a concept in the work of the nineteenth-century French sociologist Emile Durkheim that deviancy may be fairly constant in organized societies. If the people of a society obey the laws and norms of society more perfectly, then once-tolerable infractions will become intolerable; thus the amount of intolerable behavior remains relatively constant. For example, in the restricted society of a monastery, the slightest miscues are treated as serious offenses, thus discouraging future intolerable behavior from occurring. Moynihan also provides some insight into the opposite direction of change; that is, when deviancy becomes much more prevalent. He argues that society will then lower its standards so that the role of deviancy remains fairly stable. Therefore, notes Moynihan, the definition of deviant behavior is dynamic. In applying this theory today, he suggests that deviant behavior has increased beyond the level we can afford to recognize. In the past, society was far less tolerant of deviance. Now society has become more tolerant even though there is apparent widespread moral outrage when deviancy occurs.

Moynihan remains active as a scholar even as he currently serves as a U.S. senator. He has authored many books and articles on public policies, including *The Negro Family: The Case for National Action* (U.S. Department of Labor, 1965), *The Maximum Feasible Misunderstanding* (Free Press, 1969), and *Politics of a Guaranteed Income* (Random House, 1973). The following selection is from "Defining Deviancy Down," *The American Scholar* (Winter 1993).

Key Concept: deviancy and tolerance in organized societies

*I*n one of the founding texts of sociology, *The Rules of Sociological Method (1895)*, Emile Durkheim set it down that "crime is normal." "It is," he wrote, "completely impossible for any society entirely free of it to exist." By defining what is deviant, we are enabled to know what is not, and hence to live by shared standards....

[S]eventy years later... , in 1965, Kai T. Erikson published *Wayward Puritans*, a study of "crime rates" in the Massachusetts Bay Colony. The plan behind the book, as Erikson put it, was "to test [Durkheim's] notion that the number of deviant offenders a community can afford to recognize is likely to remain stable over time." The notion proved out very well indeed. Despite occasional crime waves, as when itinerant Quakers refused to take off their hats in the presence of magistrates, the amount of deviance in this corner of seventeenth-century New England fitted nicely with the supply of stocks and whipping posts. Erikson remarks:

> ... A community's capacity for handling deviance, let us say, can be roughly estimated by counting its prison cells and hospital beds, its policemen and psychiatrists, its courts and clinics. Most communities, it would seem, operate with the expectation that a relatively constant number of control agents is necessary to cope with a relatively constant number of offenders. The amount of men, money, and material assigned by society to "do something" about deviant behavior does not vary appreciably over time, and the implicit logic which governs the community's efforts to man a police force or maintain suitable facilities for the mentally ill seems to be that there is a fairly stable quota of trouble which should be anticipated.
>
> In this sense, the agencies of control often seem to define their job as that of keeping deviance within bounds rather than that of obliterating it altogether. Many judges, for example, assume that severe punishments are a greater deterrent to crime than moderate ones, and so it is important to note that many of them are apt to impose harder penalties when crime seems to be on the increase and more lenient ones when it does not, almost as if the power of the bench were being used to keep the crime rate from getting out of hand.

Erikson was taking issue with what he described as "a dominant strain in sociological thinking" that took for granted that a well-structured society "is somehow designed to prevent deviant behavior form occurring." In both authors, Durkheim and Erikson, there is an undertone that suggests that, with deviancy, as with most social goods, there is the continuing problem of demand exceeding supply. Durkheim invites us to

> imagine a society of saints, a perfect cloister of exemplary individuals. Crimes, properly so called, will there be unknown; but faults which appear venial to the layman will create there the same scandal that the ordinary offense does in ordinary consciousness. If, then, this society has the power to judge and punish, it will define these acts as criminal and will treat them as such.

[Durkheim commented] that there need be no cause for congratulations should the amount of crime drop "too noticeably below the normal level." It would not appear that Durkheim anywhere contemplates the possibility of too much crime. Clearly his theory would have required him to deplore such a development, but the possibility seems never to have occurred to him.

Erikson, writing much later in the twentieth century, contemplates both possibilities. "Deviant persons can be said to supply needed services to society." There is no doubt a tendency for the supply of any needed thing to run short. But he is consistent. There can, he believes, be *too much* of a good thing. Hence "the number of deviant offenders a community *can afford* to recognize is likely to remain stable over time." [My emphasis]

Social scientists are said to be on the lookout for poor fellows getting a bum rap. But here is a theory that clearly implies that there are circumstances in which society will choose *not* to notice behavior that would be otherwise controlled, or disapproved, or even punished.

It appears to me that this is in fact what we in the United States have been doing of late. I proffer the thesis that, over the past generation, since the time Erikson wrote, the amount of deviant behavior in American society has increased beyond the levels the community can "afford to recognize" and that, accordingly, we have been re-defining deviancy so as to exempt much conduct previously stigmatized, and also quietly raising the "normal" level in categories where behavior is now abnormal by any earlier standard. . . .

Let me, then, offer three categories of redefinition in these regards: the *altruistic,* the *opportunistic,* and the *normalizing.*

The first category, the *altruistic,* may be illustrated by the deinstitutionalization movement within the mental health profession that appeared in the 1950s. The second category, the opportunistic, is seen in the interest group rewards derived from the acceptance of "alternative" family structures. The third category, the normalizing, is to be observed in the growing acceptance of unprecedented levels of violent crime.

It happens that I was present at the beginning of the deinstitutionalization movement. Early in 1955 Averell Harriman, then the new governor of New York, met with his new commissioner of mental hygiene, Dr. Paul Hoch, who described the development, at one of the state mental hospitals, of a tranquilizer derived from rauwolfia. The medication had been clinically tested and appeared to be an effective treatment for many severely psychotic patients, thus increasing the percentage of patients discharged. Dr. Hoch recommended that it be used systemwide; Harriman found the money. That same year Congress created a Joint Commission on Mental Health and Illness whose mission was to formulate "comprehensive and realistic recommendations" in this area, which was then a matter of considerable public concern. Year after year, the population of mental institutions grew. Year after year, new facilities had to be built.... (In *Spanning the Century: The Life of W. Averell Harriman*, Rudy Abramson writes: "New York's mental hospitals in 1955 were overflowing warehouses, and new patients were being admitted faster than space could be found for them. When Harriman was inaugurated, 94,000 New Yorkers were confined to state hospitals. Admissions were running at more than 2,500 a year and rising, making the Department of Mental Hygiene the fastest-growing, most-expensive, most-hopeless department of state government.")

The discovery of tranquilizers was adventitious. Physicians were seeking cures for disorders that were just beginning to be understood. Even a limited success made it possible to believe that the incidence of this particular range of disorders, which had seemingly required persons to be confined against their will or even awareness, could be greatly reduced. The Congressional Commission submitted its report in 1961; it proposed a nationwide program of deinstitutionalization.

Late in 1961, President Kennedy appointed an interagency committee to prepare legislative recommendations based upon the report.... This included the recommendation of the National Institute of Mental Health that 2,000 community mental health centers (one per 100,000 of population) be built by 1980. A buoyant Presidential Message to Congress followed early in 1963. "If we apply our medical knowledge and social insights fully," President Kennedy pronounced, "all but a small portion of the mentally ill can eventually achieve a wholesome and a constructive social adjustment." A "concerted national attack on mental disorders [was] now possible and practical." The President signed the Community Mental Health Centers Construction Act on October 31, 1963, his last public bill-signing ceremony. He gave me a pen.

The mental hospitals emptied out. At the time Governor Harriman met with Dr. Hoch in 1955, there were 93,314 adult residents of mental institutions maintained by New York State. As of August 1992, there were 11,363. This occurred across the nation. However, the number of community mental health centers never came near the goal of the 2,000 proposed community centers. Only some 482 received federal construction funds between 1963 and 1980. The next year, 1981, the program was folded into the Alcohol and Other Drug Abuse block grant and disappeared from view. Even when centers were built, the results were hardly as hoped for. David F. Musto of Yale writes that the planners had bet on improving national mental health "by improving the quality of general community life through expert knowledge, not merely by more effective treatment of the already ill." There was no such knowledge....

Our second, or *opportunistic* mode of re-definition, reveals at most a nominal intent to do good. The true object is to do well, a long-established motivation among mortals. In this pattern, a growth in deviancy makes possible a transfer of resources, including prestige, to those who control the deviant population. This control would be jeopardized if any serious effort were made to reduce the deviancy in question. This leads to assorted strategies for re-defining the behavior in question as not all that deviant, really.

In the years from 1963 to 1965, the Policy Planning Staff of the U.S. Department of Labor picked up the first tremors of what Samuel H. Preston, in the 1984 Presidential Address to the Population Association of America, would call "the earthquake that shuddered through the American family in the past twenty years." *The New York Times* ... provided a succinct accounting of Preston's point:

> Thirty years ago, 1 in every 40 white children was born to an unmarried mother; today it is 1 in 5, according to Federal data. Among blacks, 2 of 3 children are born to an unmarried mother; 30 years ago the figure was 1 in 5.

In 1991, Paul Offner and I published longitudinal data showing that, of children born in the years 1967–69, some 22.1 percent were dependent on welfare—that is to say, Aid to Families with Dependent Children—before reaching age 18. This broke down as 15.7 percent for white children, 72.3 percent for black children. Projections for children born in 1980 gave rates of 22.2 percent and 82.9 percent respectively. A year later, a *New York Times* series on welfare and poverty called this a "startling finding ... a symptom of vast social calamity."

And yet there is little evidence that these facts are regarded as a calamity in municipal government. To the contrary, there is general acceptance of the situation as normal. Political candidates raise the subject, often to the point of dwelling on it. But while there is a good deal of demand for symbolic change, there is none of the marshaling of resources that is associated with significant social action. Nor is there any lack of evidence that there is a serious social problem here.

Richard T. Gill writes of "an accumulation of data showing that intact biological parent families offer children very large advantages compared to any other family or non-family structure one can imagine." Correspondingly, the disadvantages associated with single-parent families spill over into other areas of social policy that now attract great public concern....

To cite another example, there is at present no more vexing problem of social policy in the United States than that posed by education.... The 1966 report *Equality of Educational Opportunity* by James S. Coleman and his associates established that the family background of students played a much stronger role in student achievement relative to variations in the ten (and still standard) measures of school quality.

In a 1992 study entitled *America's Smallest School: The Family,* Paul Barton came up with the elegant and persuasive concept of the parent-pupil ratio as a measure of school quality. Barton, who was on the policy planning staff in the Department of Labor in 1965, noted the great increase in the proportion of children living in single-parent families since then. He further noted that the proportion "varies widely among the states" and is related to "variation in achievement" among them. The correlation between the percentage of eighth graders living in two-parent families and average mathematics proficiency is a solid .74. North Dakota, highest on the math test, is second highest on the family compositions scale—that is, it is second in the percentage of kids coming from two-parent homes. The District of Columbia, lowest on the family scale, is second lowest in the test score.

... No demand for change comes from that community—or as near to no demand as makes no matter. *For there is good money to be made out of bad schools.* This is a statement that will no doubt please many a hard heart, and displease many genuinely concerned to bring about change. To the latter, a group in which I would like to include myself, I would only say that we are obliged to ask why things do not change.

For a period there was some speculation that, if family structure got bad enough, this mode of deviancy would have less punishing effects on children. In 1991 Deborah A. Dawson, of the National Institutes of Health, examined the thesis that "the psychological effects of divorce and single parenthood on children were strongly influenced by a sense of shame in being 'different' from the norm." If this were so, the effect should have fallen off in the 1980s, when being from a single-parent home became much more common. It did not. "The problems associated with task overload among single parents are more constant in nature," Dawson wrote, adding that since the adverse effects had not diminished, they were "not based on stigmatization but rather on inherent problems in alternative family structures"—*alternative* here meaning other than two-parent families. We should take note of such candor. Writing in the *Journal of Marriage and the Family* in 1989, Sara McLanahan and Karen Booth noted: "Whereas a decade ago the prevailing view was that single motherhood had no harmful effects on children, recent research is less optimistic."

The year 1990 saw more of this lesson. In a paper prepared for the Progressive Policy Institute, Elaine Ciulla Kamarck and William A. Galston wrote that "if the economic effects of family breakdown are clear, the psychological effects are just now coming into focus."

" ... As for juvenile crime, they cite Douglas Smith and G. Roger Jarjoura: "Neighborhoods with larger percentages of youth (those aged 12 to 20) and areas with higher percentages of single-parent households also have higher rates of violent crime." ...

Our *normalizing* category most directly corresponds to Erikson's proposition that "the number of deviant offenders a community can afford to recognize is likely to remain stable over time." Here we are dealing with the popular psychological notion of "denial." In 1965, having reached the conclusion that there would be a dramatic increase in single-parent families, I reached the further conclusion that this would in turn lead to a dramatic increase in crime. In an article in *America,* I wrote:

> From the wild Irish slums of the 19th century Eastern seaboard to the riot-torn suburbs of Los Angeles, there is one unmistakable lesson in American history: a community that allows a large number of young men to grow up in broken families, dominated by women, never acquiring any stable relationship to male authority, never acquiring any set of rational expectations about the future—that

community asks for and gets chaos. Crime, violence, unrest, unrestrained lashing out at the whole social structure—that is not only to be expected; it is very near to inevitable.

The inevitable, as we now know, has come to pass, but here again our response is curiously passive. Crime is a more or less continuous subject of political pronouncement, and from time to time it will be at or near the top of opinion polls as a matter of public concern. But it never gets much further than that. In the words spoken from the bench, Judge Edwin Torres of the New York State Supreme Court, Twelfth Judicial District, described how "the slaughter of the innocent marches unabated: subway riders, bodega owners, cab drivers, babies; in laundromats, at cash machines, on elevators, in hallways." In personal communication, he writes: "This numbness, this near narcoleptic state can diminish the human condition to the level of combat infantrymen, who, in protracted campaigns, can eat their battlefield rations seated on the bodies of the fallen, friend and foe alike. A society that loses its sense of outrage is doomed to extinction." There is no expectation that this will change, nor any efficacious public insistence that it do so. The crime level has been *normalized.*

Consider the St. Valentine's Day Massacre. In 1929 in Chicago during Prohibition, four gangsters killed seven gangsters on February 14. The nation was shocked. The event became legend. It merits not one but two entries in the *World Book Encyclopedia.* I leave it to others to judge, but it would appear that the society in the 1920s was simply not willing to put up with this degree of deviancy. In the end, the Constitution was amended, and Prohibition, which lay behind so much gangster violence, ended.

In recent years, again in the context of illegal traffic in controlled substances, this form of murder has returned. But it has done so at a level that induces denial. James Q. Wilson comments that Los Angeles has the equivalent of a St. Valentine's Day Massacre every weekend. Even the most ghastly re-enactments of such human slaughter produce only moderate responses....

A Kai Erikson of the future will surely need to know that the Department of Justice in 1990 found that Americans reported only about 38 percent of all crimes and 48 percent of violent crimes. This, too, can be seen as a means of *normalizing* crime. In much the same way, the vocabulary of crime reporting can be seen to move toward the normal-seeming. A teacher is shot on her way to class. The *Times* subhead reads: "Struck in the Shoulder in the Year's First Shooting Inside a School." First of the season....

The hope—if there be such—of this essay has been twofold. It is, first, to suggest that the Durkheim constant, as I put it, is maintained by a dynamic process which adjusts upwards and *downwards.* Liberals have traditionally been alert for upward redefining that does injustice to individuals. Conservatives have been correspondingly sensitive to downward redefining that weakens societal standards. Might it not help if we could all agree that there is a dynamic at work here? It is not revealed truth, nor yet a scientifically derived formula. It is simply a pattern we observe in ourselves. Nor is it rigid. There may once have been an unchanging supply of jail cells which more or less determined the number of prisoners. No longer. We are building new prisons at a prodigious rate. Similarly, the executioner is back. There is something of a competition in Congress to think up new offenses for which the death penalty is seemed the only available deterrent. Possibly also modes of execution, as in "fry the kingpins." Even so, we are getting used to a lot of behavior that is not good for us.

As noted earlier, Durkheim states that there is "nothing desirable" about pain. Surely what he meant was that there is nothing pleasurable. Pain, even so, is an indispensable warning signal. But societies under stress, much like individuals, will turn to pain killers of various kinds that end up concealing real damage. There is surely nothing desirable about *this*. If our analysis wins general acceptance, if, for example, more of us came to share Judge Torres's genuine alarm at "the trivialization of the lunatic crime rate" in his city (and mine), we might surprise ourselves how well we respond to the manifest decline of the American civic order. Might.

5.2 STANLEY MILGRAM

Some Conditions of Obedience and Disobedience to Authority

In the aftermath of World War II, civilized people around the world recoiled when they learned the full extent of Nazi Germany's policy of torturing and killing millions of innocent people. Most of the people who participated in the rounding up, transporting, guarding, and killing of the victims of this policy did not want to be instruments of death and torture, but they obeyed the orders of those in authority.

Many social scientists attributed this kind of behavior to the structured obedience of subjects in an authoritarian society. There was the assumption that this phenomenon was unique to authoritarian societies and that it was something that could not happen in a free and democratic society—America, for example. In totalitarian states, people do what they are told to do, no questions asked, or they suffer terrible consequences. Force, and fear of it, explains their obedient behavior.

But the research of experimental social psychologist Stanley Milgram in the 1960s showed that people in democratic countries will also inflict great pain on others in obedience to authority. In the following selection from "Some Conditions of Obedience and Disobedience to Authority," *Human Relations* (vol. 18, no. 1, 1965), Milgram describes his now-famous and controversial series of experiments in which he tested a cross section of American men to determine the extent to which they would administer various levels of electric shock to another person when ordered to do so by what is perceived as a legitimate authority.

Milgram (1933–1984) was a professor of psychology at Yale University for many years and also taught at City University of New York. He is especially well-known for his investigations into obedience and group norms. His work sparked much controversy and even protest when it was first published, but his *Obedience to Authority: An Experimental View* (Harper & Row, 1975) is considered by many sociologists and psychologists to have revealed a provocative truth.

Key Concept: obedience to authority

*T*he situation in which one agent commands another to hurt a third turns up time and again as a significant theme in human relations.... We describe an experimental program, recently concluded at Yale University, in which a particular expression of this conflict is studied by experimental means.

In its most general form the problem may be defined thus: if X tells Y to hurt Z, under what conditions will Y carry out the command of X and under what conditions will he refuse. In the more limited form possible in laboratory research, the question becomes: if an experimenter tells a subject to hurt another person, under what conditions will the subject go along with this instruction, and under what conditions will he refuse to obey. The laboratory problem is not so much a dilution of the general statement as one concrete expression of the many particular forms this question may assume.

One aim of the research was to study behavior in a strong situation of deep consequence to the participants, for the psychological forces operative in powerful and lifelike forms of the conflict may not be brought into play under diluted conditions....

TERMINOLOGY

If Y follows the command of X we shall say that he has obeyed X; if he fails to carry out the command of X, we shall say that he has disobeyed X. The terms to *obey* and to *disobey*, as used here, refer to the subject's overt action only, and carry no implication for the motive or experiential states accompanying the action....

A subject who complies with the entire series of experimental commands will be termed an *obedient* subject; one who at any point in the command series defies the experimenter will be called a *disobedient* or *defiant* subject. As used in this report, the terms refer only to the subject's performance in the experiment, and do not necessarily imply a general personality disposition to submit to or reject authority.

SUBJECT POPULATION

The subjects used in all experimental conditions were male adults, residing in the greater New Haven and Bridgeport [Connecticut] areas, aged 20 to 50 years, and engaged in a wide variety of occupations. Each experimental condition described in this report employed 40 fresh subjects and was carefully balanced for age and occupational types. The occupational composition for each experiment was: workers, skilled and unskilled: 40 per cent; white collar, sales, business: 40 per cent; professionals: 20 per cent. The occupations were intersected with three age categories (subjects in 20s, 30s, and 40s, assigned to each condition in the proportions of 20, 40, and 40 per cent respectively).

The focus of the study concerns the amount of electric shock a subject is willing to administer to another person when ordered by an experimenter to give the 'victim' increasingly more severe punishment. The act of administering shock is set in the context of a learning experiment, ostensibly designed to study the effect of punishment on memory. Aside from the experimenter, one naïve subject and one accomplice perform in each session. On arrival each subject is paid $4.50. After a general talk by the experimenter, telling how little scientists know about the effect of punishment on memory, subjects are informed that one member of the pair will serve as teacher and one as learner. A rigged drawing is held so that the naïve subject is always the teacher, and the accomplice becomes the learner. The learner is taken to an adjacent room and strapped into an 'electric chair'.

The naïve subject is told that it is his task to teach the learner a list of paired associates, to test him on the list, and to administer punishment whenever the learner errs in the test. Punishment takes the form of electric shock, delivered to the learner by means of a shock generator controlled by the naïve subject. The teacher is instructed to increase the intensity of electric shock one step on the generator on each error. The learner, according to plan, provides many wrong answers, so that before long the naïve subject must give him the strongest shock on the generator. Increases in shock level are met by increasingly insistent demands from the learner that the experiment be stopped because of the growing discomfort to him. However, in clear terms the experimenter orders the teacher to continue with the procedure in disregard of the learner's protests. *Thus, the naïve subject must resolve a conflict between two mutually incompatible demands from the social field. He may continue to follow the orders of the experimenter and shock the learner with increasing severity, or he may refuse to follow the orders of the experimenter and heed the learner's pleas. The experimenter's authority operates not in a free field, but against ever-mounting countervailing pressures from the person being punished.*

A few technical points need to be considered before the findings of the study are described. For the purpose of delivering shock, a simulated shock generator is used, with 30 clearly marked voltage levels that range from 15 to 450 volts (and each activated by one of 30 individual lever switches set in a horizontal line). The naïve subject is given a sample shock of 45 volts to convince him of the authenticity of the instrument. The generator bears verbal designations that range from 'Slight Shock' to 'Danger: Severe Shock'.

The responses of the victim are standardized on tape, and each protest is coordinated to a particular voltage level on the shock generator. Starting with 75 volts the learner begins to grunt and moan. At 150 volts he demands to be let out of the experiment. At 180 volts he cries out that he can no longer stand the pain. At 300 volts he refuses to provide any more answers to the memory test, insisting that he is no longer a participant in the experiment and must be freed. In response to this last tactic, the experimenter instructs the naïve subject to treat the absence of an answer as equivalent to a wrong answer, and to follow the usual shock procedure. The experimenter reinforces his demand with the statement: 'You have no other choice, you must go on!' (This imperative is used whenever the naïve subject tries to break off the experiment.) If the subject refuses to give the next higher level of shock, the experiment is considered at an end. A quantitative value is assigned to the subject's performance based on the maximum intensity shock he administered before breaking off. Thus any subject's score may range from zero (for a subject unwilling to administer the first shock level) to 30 (for a subject who proceeds to the highest voltage level on the board). For any particular subject and for any particular experimental condition the degree to which participants have followed the experimenter's orders may be specified with a numerical value, corresponding to the metric on the shock generator. . . .

IMMEDIACY OF THE VICTIM

This series consisted of four experimental conditions. In each condition the victim was brought 'psychologically' closer to the subject giving him shocks.

In the first condition (Remote Feedback) the victim was placed in another room and could not be heard or seen by the subject, except that, at 300 volts, he pounded on the wall in protest. After 315 volts he no longer answered or was heard from.

The second condition (Voice Feedback) was identical to the first except that voice protests were introduced. As in the first condition the victim was placed in an adjacent room, but his complaints could be heard clearly through a door left slightly ajar, and through the walls of the laboratory.

The third experimental condition (Proximity) was similar to the second, except that the victim was now placed in the same room as the subject, and 1 1/2 feet from him. Thus he was visible as well as audible, and voice cues were provided.

The fourth, and final, condition of this series (Touch-Proximity) was identical to the third, with this exception: the victim received a shock only when his hand rested on a shockplate. At the 150-volt level the victim again demanded to be let free and, in this condition, refused to place his hand on the shockplate. The experimenter ordered the naïve subject to force the victim's hand onto the plate. Thus obedience in this condition required that the subject have physical contact with the victim in order to give him punishment beyond the 150-volt level.

Forty adult subjects were studied in each condition. The data revealed that obedience was significantly reduced as the victim was rendered more immediate to the subject. The mean maximum shock for the conditions is shown in *Figure 1*.

Expressed in terms of the proportion of obedient to defiant subjects, the findings are that 34 per cent of the subjects defied the experimenter in the Remote condition, 37.5 per cent in Voice Feedback, 60 per cent in Proximity, and 70 per cent in Touch-Proximity.

How are we to account for this effect? A first conjecture might be that as the victim was brought closer the subject became more aware of the intensity of his suffering and regulated his behavior accordingly. This makes sense, but

FIGURE 1

103

Mean Maxima in Proximity Series

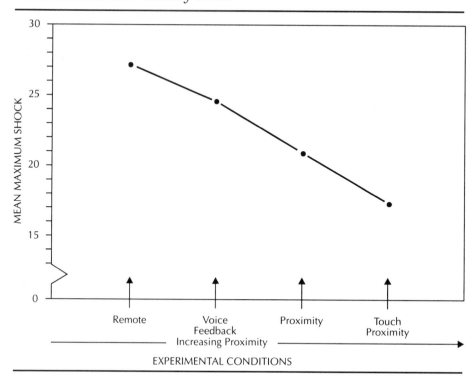

our evidence does not support the interpretation. There are no consistent differences in the attributed level of pain across the four conditions (i.e. the amount of pain experienced by the victim as estimated by the subject and expressed on a 14-point scale). But it is easy to speculate about alternative mechanisms:

> *Empathic cues.* In the Remote and to a lesser extent the Voice Feedback condition, the victim's suffering possesses an abstract, remote quality for the subject. He is aware, but only in a conceptual sense, that his actions cause pain to another person; the fact is apprehended, but not felt. The phenomenon is common enough. The bombardier can reasonably suppose that his weapons will inflict suffering and death, yet this knowledge is divested of affect, and does not move him to a felt, emotional response to the suffering resulting from his actions....
>
> *Denial and narrowing of the cognitive field.* The Remote condition allows a narrowing of the cognitive field so that the victim is put out of mind. The subject no longer considers the act of depressing a lever relevant to moral judgement, for it is no longer associated with the victim's suffering. When the victim is close it is more difficult to exclude him phenomenologically.... The mechanism of denial can no longer be brought into play. One subject in the Remote condition said: 'It's funny how you really begin to forget that there's a guy out there, even though you can hear him. For a long time I just concentrated on pressing the switches and reading the words.'

Reciprocal fields. If in the Proximity condition the subject is in an improved position to observe the victim, the reverse is also true. The actions of the subject now come under proximal scrutiny by the victim. Possibly, it is easier to harm a person when he is unable to observe our actions than when he can see what we are doing. His surveillance of the action directed against him may give rise to shame, or guilt, which may then serve to curtail the action. . . .

Phenomenal unity of act. In the Remote conditions it is more difficult for the subject to gain a sense of *relatedness* between his own actions and the consequences of these actions for the victim. There is a physical and spatial separation of the act and its consequences. The subject depresses a lever in one room, and protests and cries are heard from another. The two events are in correlation, yet they lack a compelling phenomenological unity. . . .

Incipient group formation. Placing the victim in another room not only takes him further from the subject, but the subject and the experimenter are drawn relatively closer. There is incipient group formation between the experimenter and the subject, from which the victim is excluded. The wall between the victim and the others deprives him of an intimacy which the experimenter and subject feel. In the Remote condition, the victim is truly an outsider, who stands alone, physically and psychologically.

When the victim is placed close to the subject, it becomes easier to form an alliance with him against the experimenter. Subjects no longer have to face the experimenter alone. They have an ally who is close at hand and eager to collaborate in a revolt against the experimenter. Thus, the changing set of spatial relations leads to a potentially shifting set of alliances over the several experimental conditions.

Acquired behavior dispositions. It is commonly observed that laboratory mice will rarely fight with their litter mates. . . . [T]he organism learns that it is safer to be aggressive toward others at a distance, and precarious to be so when the parties are within arm's reach. Through a pattern of rewards and punishments, he acquires a disposition to avoid aggression at close quarters, a disposition which does not extend to harming others at a distance. And this may account for experimental findings in the remote and proximal experiments. . . .

CLOSENESS OF AUTHORITY

If the spatial relationship of the subject and victim is relevant to the degree of obedience, would not the relationship of subject to experimenter also play a part?

There are reasons to feel that, on arrival, the subject is oriented primarily to the experimenter rather than to the victim. He has come to the laboratory to fit into the structure that the experimenter—not the victim—would provide. He has come less to understand his behavior than to *reveal* that behavior to a competent scientist, and he is willing to display himself as the scientist's purposes require. Most subjects seem quite concerned about the appearance they are making before the experimenter, and one could argue that this preoccupation in a relatively new and strange setting makes the subject somewhat insensitive to the triadic nature of the social situation. . . .

In a series of experiments we varied the physical closeness and degree of surveillance of the experimenter. In one condition the experimenter sat just a few feet away from the subject. In a second condition, after giving initial instructions the experimenter left the laboratory and gave his orders by telephone; in still a third condition the experimenter was never seen, providing instructions by means of a tape recording activated when the subjects entered the laboratory.

Obedience dropped sharply as the experimenter was physically removed from the laboratory. The number of obedient subjects in the first condition (Experimenter Present) was almost three times as great as in the second, where the experimenter gave his orders by telephone. Twenty-six subjects were fully obedient in the first condition, and only 9 in the second.... Subjects seemed able to take a far stronger stand against the experimenter when they did not have to encounter him face to face, and the experimenter's power over the subject was severely curtailed.

Moreover, when the experimenter was absent, subjects displayed an interesting form of behavior that had not occurred under his surveillance. Though continuing with the experiment, several subjects administered lower shocks than were required and never informed the experimenter of their deviation from the correct procedure.... Indeed, in telephone conversations some subjects specifically assured the experimenter that they were raising the shock level according to instruction, whereas in fact they were repeatedly using the lowest shock on the board. This form of behavior is particularly interesting: although these subjects acted in a way that clearly undermined the avowed purposes of the experiment, they found it easier to handle the conflict in this manner than to precipitate an open break with authority....

Experiments in this series show that the physical *presence* of an authority is an important force contributing to the subject's obedience or defiance. Taken together with the first experimental series on the proximity of the victim, it would appear that something akin to fields of force, diminishing in effectiveness with increasing psychological distance from their source, have a controlling effect on the subject's performance. As the victim is brought closer, the subject finds it harder to administer shocks to him. When the victim's position is held constant relative to the subject, and the authority is made more remote, the subject finds it easier to break off the experiment. This effect is substantial in both cases, but manipulation of the experimenter's position yielded the more powerful results. Obedience to destructive commands is highly dependent on the proximal relations between authority and subject.

TENSIONS

The description of final scores does not fully convey the character of the subjects' performance, and it would be useful to interrupt our reporting of quantitative relationships to remark on the subjects' general reaction to the situation.

One might suppose that a subject would simply break off or continue as his conscience and temperament dictated. Yet this is very far from what happened. There were powerful reactions of tension and emotional strain in a substantial proportion of the participants. Persons were observed to sweat, tremble, stutter, bite their lips, and groan as they found themselves increasingly implicated in the experimental conflict. Some sense of the subjects' mood can be gotten from a transcript of their remarks at break-off point. Here are the remarks of two defiant subjects:

> Is he banging?... Is he hurt out there? Well, I don't want to be responsible for anything that happens to him. No, I can't go on with it. I don't know whether he's all right or not. I mean he may have a heart condition or something; I wouldn't feel right doing it. He's banging for help. He's evidently in trouble or he wouldn't bang... I don't see any sense to this—to knocking him out or something. I just can't see it.
> *(Subject refuses to administer shocks)* [Subject 0108]

> The man is banging. He wants to get out... I'm sorry. If the man wants to get out I'd just as soon stop... I don't want to administer any more [extremely excited]... I will gladly refund the check, but I will not harm this man... I'm sorry, I will not give him any more if he obviously wants to get out. There is no money in the world that will make me hurt another individual. [Subject 010X]

And here is a transcript from an obedient subject. He began the experiment calmly, but became increasingly tense as the experiment proceeded. After administering the 150-volt shock, he began to address the experimenter in agitated tones:

> *150 volts delivered.* You want me to keep going?
> *165 volts delivered.* That guy is hollering in there. There's a lot of them here. He's liable to have heart condition. You want me to go?
> *180 volts delivered.* He can't stand it! I'm not going to kill that man in there! You hear him hollering? He's hollering. He can't stand it. What if something happens to him?... I'm not going to get that man sick in there. He's hollering in there. You know what I mean? I mean I refuse to take responsibility. He's getting hurt in there. He's in there hollering. Too many left here. Geez, if he gets them wrong. There's too many of them left. I mean who is going to take responsibility if anything happens to that gentleman?
> *[The experimenter accepts responsibility.]* All right.
> *195 volts delivered.* You see he's hollering. Hear that. Gee, I don't know. *[The experimenter says: 'The experiment requires that you go on.']*—I know it does sir, but I mean —hugh—he don't know what he's in for. He's up to 195 volts.
> *210 volts delivered*
> *225 volts delivered*
> *240 volts delivered.* Aw, no. You mean I've got to keep going up with the scale? No sir. I'm not going to kill that man! I'm not going to give him 450 volts! *[The experimenter says: 'The experiment requires that you go on.']*—I know it does, but that man is hollering in there, sir....

Despite his numerous, agitated objections, which were constant accompaniments to his actions, the subject unfailingly obeyed the experimenter, proceeding to the highest shock level on the generator. He displayed a curious dissociation between word and action. Although at the verbal level he had resolved not to go on, his actions were fully in accord with the experimenter's commands. This subject did not want to shock the victim, and he found it an extremely disagreeable task, but he was unable to invent a response that would free him from E's authority. Many subjects cannot find the specific verbal formula that would enable them to reject the role assigned to them by the experimenter. Perhaps our culture does not provide adequate models for disobedience....

BACKGROUND AUTHORITY

In psychophysics, animal learning, and other branches of psychology, the fact that measures are obtained at one institution rather than another is irrelevant to the interpretation of the findings, so long as the technical facilities for measurement are adequate and the operations are carried out with competence.

But it cannot be assumed that this holds true for the present study. The effectiveness of the experimenter's commands may depend in an important way on the larger institutional context in which they are issued. The experiments described thus far were conducted at Yale University, an organization which most subjects regarded with respect and sometimes awe. In post-experimental interviews several participants remarked that the locale and sponsorship of the study gave them confidence in the integrity, competence, and benign purposes of the personnel; many indicated that they would not have shocked the learner if the experiments had been done elsewhere.

This issue of background authority seemed to us important for an interpretation of the results that had been obtained thus far; moreover it is highly relevant to any comprehensive theory of human obedience. Consider, for example, how closely our compliance with the imperatives of others is tied to particular institutions and locales in our day-to-day activities. On request, we expose our throats to a man with a razor blade in the barber shop, but would not do so in a shoe store; in the latter setting we willingly follow the clerk's request to stand in our stockinged feet, but resist the command in a bank. In the laboratory of a great university, subjects may comply with a set of commands that would be resisted if given elsewhere. *One must always question the relationship of obedience to a person's sense of the context in which he is operating.*

To explore the problem we moved our apparatus to an office building in industrial Bridgeport and replicated experimental conditions, without any visible tie to the university.

Bridgeport subjects were invited to the experiment through a mail circular similar to the one used in the Yale study, with appropriate changes in letterhead, etc. As in the earlier study, subjects were paid $4.50 for coming to the laboratory. The same age and occupational distributions used at Yale, and the identical personnel, were employed.

The purpose in relocating in Bridgeport was to assure a complete dissociation from Yale, and in this regard we were fully successful. On the surface, the study appeared to be conducted by RESEARCH ASSOCIATES OF BRIDGEPORT, an organization of unknown character (the title had been concocted exclusively for use in this study).

The experiments were conducted in a three-room office suite in a somewhat run-down commercial building located in the downtown shopping area. The laboratory was sparsely furnished, though clean, and marginally respectable in appearance. When subjects inquired about professional affiliations, they were informed only that we were a private firm conducting research for industry....

There was no noticeable reduction in tension for the Bridgeport subjects. And the subjects' estimation of the amount of pain felt by the victim was slightly, though not significantly, higher than in the Yale study.

A failure to obtain complete obedience in Bridgeport would indicate that the extreme compliance found in New Haven subjects was tied closely to the background authority of Yale University; if a large proportion of the subjects remained fully obedient, very different conclusions would be called for.

As it turned out, the level of obedience in Bridgeport, although somewhat reduced, was not significantly lower than that obtained at Yale. A large proportion of the Bridgeport subjects were fully obedient to the experimenter's commands (48 per cent of the Bridgeport subjects delivered the maximum shock *vs.* 65 per cent in the corresponding condition at Yale)....

LEVELS OF OBEDIENCE AND DEFIANCE

One general finding that merits attention is the high level of obedience manifested in the experimental situation. Subjects often expressed deep disapproval of shocking a man in the face of his objections, and others denounced it as senseless and stupid. Yet many subjects complied even while they protested. The proportion of obedient subjects greatly exceeded the expectations of the experimenter and his colleagues. At the outset, we had conjectured that subjects would not, in general, go above the level of 'Strong Shock'. In practice, many subjects were willing to administer the most extreme shocks available when commanded by the experimenter. For some subjects the experiment provides an occasion for aggressive release. And for others it demonstrates the extent to which obedient dispositions are deeply ingrained, and are engaged irrespective of their consequences for others. Yet this is not the whole story. Somehow, the subject becomes implicated in a situation from which he cannot disengage himself....

Many people, not knowing much about the experiment, claim that subjects who go to the end of the board are sadistic. Nothing could be more foolish as an overall characterization of these persons. It is like saying that a person thrown into a swift-flowing stream is necessarily a fast swimmer, or that he has great stamina because he moves so rapidly relative to the bank. The context of action must always be considered. The individual, upon entering the laboratory, becomes integrated into a situation that carries its own momentum. The subject's problem then is how to become disengaged from a situation which is moving in an altogether ugly direction.

The fact that disengagement is so difficult testifies to the potency of the forces that keep the subject at the control board. Are these forces to be conceptualized as individual motives and expressed in the language of personality dynamics, or are they to be seen as the effects of social structure and pressures arising from the situational field?

A full understanding of the subject's action will, I feel, require that both perspectives be adopted. The person brings to the laboratory enduring dispositions toward authority and aggression, and at the same time he becomes enmeshed in a social structure that is no less an objective fact of the case....

POSTSCRIPT

Almost a thousand adults were individually studied in the obedience research, and there were many specific conclusions regarding the variables that control obedience and disobedience to authority. Some of these have been discussed briefly in the preceding sections, and more detailed reports will be released subsequently.

There are now some other generalizations I should like to make, which do not derive in any strictly logical fashion from the experiments as carried out, but which, I feel, ought to be made. They are formulations of an intuitive sort that have been forced on me by observation of many subjects responding to the pressures of authority. The assertions represent a painful alteration in my own thinking; and since they were acquired only under the repeated impact of direct observation, I have no illusion that they will be generally accepted by persons who have not had the same experience.

With numbing regularity good people were seen to knuckle under the demands of authority and perform actions that were callous and severe. Men who are in everyday life responsible and decent were seduced by the trappings of authority, by the control of their perceptions, and by the uncritical acceptance of the experimenter's definition of the situation, into performing harsh acts.

What is the limit of such obedience? At many points we attempted to establish a boundary. Cries from the victim were inserted; not good enough. The victim claimed heart trouble; subjects still shocked him on command. The victim pleaded that he be let free, and his answers no longer registered on the signal box; subjects continued to shock him. At the outset we had not conceived that such drastic procedures would be needed to generate disobedience, and each step was added only as the ineffectiveness of the earlier techniques became clear. The final effort to establish a limit was the Touch-Proximity condition. But the very first subject in this condition subdued the victim on command, and proceeded to the highest shock level. A quarter of the subjects in this condition performed similarly.

The results, as seen and felt in the laboratory, are to this author disturbing. They raise the possibility that human nature, or—more specifically—the kind of character produced in American democratic society, cannot be counted on to insulate its citizens from brutality and inhumane treatment at the direction of malevolent authority. A substantial proportion of people do what they are told to do, irrespective of the content of the act and without limitations of conscience, so long as they perceive that the command comes from a legitimate authority. If in this study an anonymous experimenter could successfully command adults to subdue a fifty-year-old man, and force on him painful electric shocks against his protests, one can only wonder what government, with its vastly greater authority and prestige, can command of its subjects. There is, of course, the extremely important question of whether malevolent political institutions could or would arise in American society. The present research contributes nothing to this issue.

5.3 HERBERT C. KELMAN
AND V. LEE HAMILTON

The My Lai Massacre: A Military Crime of Obedience

"How could this happen?" is what we often say to each other when an event shocks us. Who can explain why two young boys shot and killed some of their schoolmates in Jonesboro, Arkansas; why the Unabomber maimed and killed people he barely knew with mail bombs; why Hitler tried to exterminate the Jews in Europe (and why his death camp personnel carried out his orders); and why American troops massacred innocent villagers at My Lai during the Vietnam War?

Some explanation for why the My Lai massacre occurred is provided by social psychologists Herbert C. Kelman and V. Lee Hamilton in the following selection from their book *Crimes of Obedience: Toward a Social Psychology of Authority and Responsibility* (Yale University Press, 1989). Kelman and Hamilton mention the confusing orders that led some to believe that the authorities were ordering the massacre, the nearly genocidal policy undergirding the American strategy in Vietnam, the routinization of the episode ("all in a day's work"), and the dehumanization of the victims. These processes were clearly operating, and their identification helps to make this episode more understandable. But in the end, no explanation is adequate.

At times it is appropriate to recognize the mystery of life. The natural sciences have come to realize that there are limits to scientific knowledge. The social sciences face greater limits and uncertainties. They applaud explanations that work most of the time. More causes are operating on most social phenomena than can be captured either theoretically or empirically. In addition, social phenomena are based on human interactions, and humans are wonderfully complicated beings who behave in terms of their imperfect perceptions and interpretations. Deviance and crime are particularly interesting and challenging phenomena to understand. Kelman and Hamilton's explication of this crime of obedience extends the boundaries of the subject.

111

Kelman has served as the Richard Clarke Cabot Professor of Social Ethics at Harvard University since 1968. He also serves as director of the Program on International Conflict Analysis and Resolution at Harvard's Center for International Affairs. He has held positions at the National Institute of Mental Health and at Johns Hopkins University, and he was the winner of the Grawemeyer Award for Ideas Improving World Order in 1997. Hamilton is currently chair of the Department of Sociology at the University of Maryland, College Park.

Key Concept: crime of obedience

*T*he My Lai massacre was investigated and charges were brought in 1969 and 1970. Trials and disciplinary actions lasted into 1971. Entire books have been written about the army's year-long cover-up of the massacre, and the cover-up was a major focus of the army's own investigation of the incident. Our central concern here is the massacre itself—a crime of obedience—and public reactions to such crimes, rather than the lengths to which many went to deny the event. Therefore, this account concentrates on one day: March 16, 1968.

Many verbal testimonials to the horrors that occurred at My Lai were available. More unusual was the fact that an army photographer, Ronald Haeberle, was assigned the task of documenting the anticipated military engagement at My Lai—and documented a massacre instead. Later, as the story of the massacre emerged, his photographs were widely distributed and seared the public conscience. What might have been dismissed as unreal or exaggerated was depicted in photographs of demonstrable authenticity. The dominant image appeared on the cover of *Life:* piles of bodies jumbled together in a ditch along a trail—the dead all apparently unarmed. All were Oriental, and all appeared to be children, women, or old men. Clearly there had been a mass execution, one whose image would not quickly fade.

So many bodies (over twenty in the cover photo alone) are hard to imagine as the handiwork of one killer. These were not. They were the product of what we call a crime of obedience. Crimes of obedience begin with orders. But orders are often vague and rarely survive with any clarity the transition from one authority down a chain of subordinates to the ultimate actors. The operation at Son My was no exception. . . .

The Son My operation was planned by Lieutenant Colonel Barker and his staff as a search-and-destroy mission with the objective of rooting out the Forty-eighth Viet Cong Battalion from their base area of Son My village. Apparently no written orders were ever issued. Barker's superior, Col. Oran Henderson, arrived at the staging point the day before. Among the issues he reviewed with the assembled officers were some of the weaknesses of prior operations by their units, including their failure to be appropriately aggressive in pursuit of the enemy. Later briefings by Lieutenant Colonel Barker and his staff asserted that no one except Viet Cong was expected to be in the village after 7 A.M. on the following day. The "innocent" would all be at the market. Those present at the briefings gave conflicting accounts of Barker's exact orders, but he conveyed at least a strong suggestion that the Son My area was to be obliterated. As the army's inquiry reported: "While there is some conflict in the testimony as to whether LTC Barker ordered the destruction of houses, dwellings, livestock, and other foodstuffs in the Son My area, the preponderance of the evidence indicates that such destruction was implied, if not specifically directed, by his orders of 15 March" (Peers Report, in Goldstein et al., 1976, p. 94).

Evidence that Barker ordered the killing of civilians is even more murky. What does seem clear, however, is that—having asserted that civilians would be away at the market—he did not specify what was to be done with any who might nevertheless be found on the scene. The Peers Report therefore considered it "reasonable to conclude that LTC Barker's minimal or nonexistent instructions concerning the handling of noncombatants created the potential for grave misunderstandings as to his intentions and for interpretation of his orders as authority to fire, without restriction, on all persons found in target area" (Goldstein et al., 1976, p. 95). Since Barker was killed in action in June 1968, his own formal version of the truth was never available.

Charlie Company's Captain Medina was briefed for the operation by Barker and his staff. He then transmitted the already vague orders to his own men.... It is apparent that Medina relayed to the men at least some of Barker's general message—to expect Viet Cong resistance, to burn, and to kill livestock. It is not clear that he ordered the slaughter of the inhabitants, but some of the men who heard him thought he had. One of those who claimed to have heard such orders was Lt. William Calley....

The action for Company C began at 7:30 as their first wave of helicopters touched down near the subhamlet of My Lai 4. By 7:47 all of Company C was present and set to fight. But instead of the Viet Cong Forty-eighth Battalion, My Lai was filled with the old men, women, and children who were supposed to have gone to market. By this time, in their version of the war, and with whatever orders they thought they had heard, the men from Company C were nevertheless ready to find Viet Cong everywhere. By nightfall, the official tally was 128 VC killed and three weapons captured, although later unofficial body counts ran as high as 500. The operation at Son My was over. And by nightfall, as Hersh reported: "the Viet Cong were back in My Lai 4, helping the survivors bury the dead. It took five days. Most of the funeral speeches were made by the Communist guerrillas. Nguyen Bat was not a Communist at the time of the massacre, but the incident changed his mind. 'After the shooting,' he said, 'all the villagers became Communists'" (1970, p. 74). To this day, the memory of the massacre is kept alive by markers and plaques designating the spots where groups of villagers were killed, by a large statue, and by the My Lai Museum, established in 1975.

But what could have happened to leave American troops reporting a victory over Viet Cong when in fact they had killed hundreds of noncombatants? It is not hard to explain the report of victory; that is the essence of a cover-up. It is harder to understand how the killings came to be committed in the first place, making a cover-up necessary.

MASS EXECUTIONS AND THE
DEFENSE OF SUPERIOR ORDERS

Some of the atrocities of March 16, 1968, were evidently unofficial, spontaneous acts: rapes, tortures, killings. For example, Hersh (1970) describes Charlie Company's Second Platoon as entering "My Lai 4 with guns blazing" (p. 50); more graphically, Lieutenant "Brooks and his men in the second platoon to the north had begun to systematically ransack the hamlet and slaughter the people, kill the livestock, and destroy the crops. Men poured rifle and machine-gun fire into huts without knowing—or seemingly caring—who was inside" (pp. 49–50)....

But a substantial amount of the killing was *organized* and traceable to one authority: the First Platoon's Lt. William Calley. Calley was originally charged with 109 killings, almost all of them mass executions at the trail and other locations. He stood trial for 102 of these killings, was convicted of 22 in 1971, and at first received a life sentence. Though others—both superior and subordinate to Calley—were brought to trial, he was the only one convicted for the My Lai crimes. Thus, the only actions of My Lai for which *anyone* was ever convicted were mass executions, ordered and committed....

The day's quiet beginning has already been noted. Troops landed and swept unopposed into the village. The three weapons eventually reported as the haul from the operation were picked up from three apparent Viet Cong who fled the village when the troops arrived and were pursued and killed by helicopter gunships. Obviously the Viet Cong did frequent the area. But it appears that by about 8:00 A.M. no one who met the troops was aggressive, and no one was armed. By the laws of war Charlie Company had no argument with such people.

As they moved into the village, the soldiers began to gather its inhabitants together. Shortly after 8:00 A.M. Lieutenant Calley told Pfc. Paul Meadlo that "you know what to do with" a group of villagers Meadlo was guarding. Estimates of the numbers in the group ranged as high as eighty women, children, and old men, and Meadlo's own estimate under oath was thirty to fifty people. As Meadlo later testified, Calley returned after ten or fifteen minutes: "He [Calley] said, 'How come they're not dead?' I said, 'I didn't know we were supposed to kill them.' He said, 'I want them dead.' He backed off twenty or thirty feet and started shooting into the people—the Viet Cong—shooting automatic. He was beside me. He burned four or five magazines. I burned off a few, about three. I helped shoot 'em" (Hammer, 1971, p. 155). Meadlo himself and others testified that Meadlo cried as he fired; others reported him later to be sobbing and "all broke up." It would appear that to Lieutenant Calley's subordinates something was unusual, and stressful, in these orders.

At the trial, the first specification in the murder charge against Calley was for this incident; he was accused of premeditated murder of "an unknown number, not less than 30, Oriental human beings, males and females of various ages, whose names are unknown, occupants of the village of My Lai 4, by means of shooting them with a rifle" (Goldstein et al., 1976, p. 497).

Among the helicopters flying reconnaissance above Son My was that of CWO Hugh Thompson. By 9:00 or soon after Thompson had noticed some horrifying events from his perch. As he spotted wounded civilians, he sent down smoke markers so that soldiers on the ground could treat them. They killed them instead. He reported to headquarters, trying to persuade someone to stop what was going on. Barker, hearing the message, called down to Captain Medina. Medina, in turn, later claimed to have told Calley that it was "enough for today." But it was not yet enough.

At Calley's orders, his men began gathering the remaining villagers—roughly seventy-five individuals, mostly women and children—and herding them toward a drainage ditch. Accompanied by three or four enlisted men, Lieutenant Calley executed several batches of civilians who had been gathered into ditches....

It is noteworthy that during these executions more than one enlisted man avoided carrying out Calley's orders, and more than one, by sworn oath, directly refused to obey them. For example, Pfc. James Joseph Dursi testified, when asked if he fired when Lieutenant Calley ordered him to: "No. I just stood there. Meadlo turned to me after a couple of minutes and said 'Shoot! Why don't you shoot! Why don't you fire!' He was crying and yelling. I said, 'I can't! I won't!' And the people were screaming and crying and yelling. They kept firing for a couple of minutes, mostly automatic and semi-automatic" (Hammer, 1971, p. 143)....

The most unusual instance of resistance to authority came from the skies. CWO Hugh Thompson, who had protested the apparent carnage of civilians, was Calley's inferior in rank but was not in his line of command. He was also watching the ditch from his helicopter and noticed some people moving after the first round of slaughter—chiefly children who had been shielded by their mothers' bodies. Landing to rescue the wounded, he also found some villagers hiding in a nearby bunker. Protecting the Vietnamese with his own body, Thompson ordered his men to train their guns on the Americans and to open fire if the Americans fired on the Vietnamese. He then radioed for additional rescue helicopters and stood between the Vietnamese and the Americans under Calley's command until the Vietnamese could be evacuated. He later returned to the ditch to unearth a child buried, unharmed, beneath layers of bodies. In October 1969, Thompson was awarded the Distinguished Flying Cross for heroism at My Lai, specifically (albeit inaccurately) for the rescue of children hiding in a bunker "between Viet Cong forces and advancing friendly forces" and for the rescue of a wounded child "caught in the intense crossfire" (Hersh, 1970, p. 119). Four months earlier, at the Pentagon, Thompson had identified Calley as having been at the ditch....

William Calley was not the only man tried for the events at My Lai. The actions of over thirty soldiers and civilians were scrutinized by investigators; over half of these had to face charges or disciplinary action of some sort. Targets of investigation included Captain Medina, who was tried, and various higher-ups, including General Koster. But Lieutenant Calley was the only person convicted, the only person to serve time.

The core of Lieutenant Calley's defense was superior orders. What this meant to him—in contrast to what it meant to the judge and jury—can be gleaned from his responses to a series of questions from his defense attorney,

George Latimer, in which Calley sketched out his understanding of the laws of war and the actions that constitute doing one's duty within those laws:

> **Latimer:** Did you receive any training... which had to do with the obedience to orders?
>
> **Calley:** Yes, sir.
>
> **Latimer:** ... what were you informed [were] the principles involved in that field?
>
> **Calley:** That all orders were to be assumed legal, that the soldier's job was to carry out any order given him to the best of his ability.
>
> **Latimer:** ... what might occur if you disobeyed an order by a senior officer?
>
> **Calley:** You could be court-martialed for refusing an order and refusing an order in the face of the enemy, you could be sent to death, sir.
>
> **Latimer:** [I am asking] whether you were required in any way, shape or form to make a determination of the legality or illegality of an order?
>
> **Calley:** No, sir. I was never told that I had the choice, sir.
>
> **Latimer:** If you had a doubt about the order, what were you supposed to do?
>
> **Calley:** ... I was supposed to carry the order out and then come back and make my complaint. (Hammer, 1971, pp. 240–241)

Lieutenant Calley steadfastly maintained that his actions within My Lai had constituted, in his mind, carrying out orders from Captain Medina. Both his own actions and the orders he gave to others (such as the instruction to Meadlo to "waste 'em") were entirely in response to superior orders. He denied any intent to kill individuals and any but the most passing awareness of distinctions among the individuals: "I was ordered to go in there and destroy the enemy. That was my job on that day. That was the mission I was given. I did not sit down and think in terms of men, women, and children. They were all classified the same, and that was the classification that we dealt with, just as enemy soldiers." When Latimer asked if in his own opinion Calley had acted "rightly and according to your understanding of your directions and orders," Calley replied, "I felt then and I still do that I acted as I was directed, and I carried out the orders that I was given, and I do not feel wrong in doing so, sir" (Hammer, 1971, p. 257).

His court-martial did not accept Calley's defense of superior orders and clearly did not share his interpretation of his duty. The jury evidently reasoned that, even if there had been orders to destroy everything in sight and to "waste the Vietnamese," any reasonable person would have realized that such orders were illegal and should have refused to carry them out. The defense of superior orders under such conditions is inadmissible under international and military law. The U.S. Army's *Law of Land Warfare* (Dept. of the Army, 1956), for example, states that "the fact that the law of war has been violated pursuant to an order of a superior authority, whether military or civil, does not deprive the act in question of its character of a war crime, nor does it constitute a defense in the trial of an accused individual, unless he did not know and could not reasonably have been expected to know that the act was unlawful" and that "members of the armed forces are bound to obey only lawful orders" (in Falk et al., 1971, pp. 71–72)....

Lieutenant Calley was initially sentenced to life imprisonment. That sentence was reduced: first to twenty years, eventually to ten (the latter by Secretary of Defense Callaway in 1974). Calley served three years before being released on bond. The time was spent under house arrest in his apartment, where he was able to receive visits from his girlfriend. He was granted parole on September 10, 1975.

SANCTIONED MASSACRES

The slaughter at My Lai is an instance of a class of violent acts that can be described as sanctioned massacres: acts of indiscriminate, ruthless, and often systematic mass violence, carried out by military or paramilitary personnel while engaged in officially sanctioned campaigns, the victims of which are defenseless and unresisting civilians, including old men, women, and children. Sanctioned massacres have occurred throughout history. Within American history, My Lai had its precursors in the Philippine war around the turn of the century and in the massacres of American Indians. Elsewhere in the world, one recalls the Nazis' "final solution" for European Jews, the massacres and deportations of Armenians by Turks, the liquidation of the kulaks and the great purges in the Soviet Union, and more recently the massacres in Indonesia and Bangladesh, in Biafra and Burundi, in South Africa and Mozambique, in Cambodia and Afghanistan, in Syria and Lebanon. . . .

[T]he occurrence of sanctioned massacres cannot be adequately explained by the existence of psychological forces—whether these be characterological dispositions to engage in murderous violence or profound hostility against the target—so powerful that they must find expression in violent acts unhampered by moral restraints. Instead, the major instigators for this class of violence derive from the policy process. The question that really calls for psychological analysis is why so many people are willing to formulate, participate in, and condone policies that call for the mass killings of defenseless civilians. Thus it is more instructive to look not at the motives for violence but at the conditions under which the usual moral inhibitions against violence become weakened. Three social processes that tend to create such conditions can be identified: authorization, routinization, and dehumanization. Through authorization, the situation becomes so defined that the individual is absolved of the responsibility to make personal moral choices. Through routinization, the action becomes so organized that there is no opportunity for raising moral questions. Through dehumanization, the actors' attitudes toward the target and toward themselves become so structured that it is neither necessary nor possible for them to view the relationship in moral terms.

Authorization

Sanctioned massacres by definition occur in the context of an authority situation, a situation in which, at least for many of the participants, the moral principles that generally govern human relationships do not apply. Thus, when acts of violence are explicitly ordered, implicitly encouraged, tacitly approved, or at least permitted by legitimate authorities, people's readiness to commit or condone them is enhanced. That such acts are authorized seems to carry automatic justification for them. Behaviorally, authorization obviates the necessity of making judgments or choices. Not only do normal moral principles become inoperative, but—particularly when the actions are explicitly ordered—a different kind of morality, linked to the duty to obey superior orders, tends to take over.

In an authority situation, individuals characteristically feel obligated to obey the orders of the authorities, whether or not these correspond with their personal preferences. They see themselves as having no choice as long as they accept the legitimacy of the orders and of the authorities who give them. Individuals differ considerably in the degree to which—and the conditions under which—they are prepared to challenge the legitimacy of an order on the grounds that the order itself is illegal, or that those giving it have overstepped their authority, or that it stems from a policy that violates fundamental societal values. Regardless of such individual differences, however, the basic structure of a situation of legitimate authority requires subordinates to respond in terms of their role obligations rather than their personal preferences; they can openly disobey only by challenging the legitimacy of the authority. Often people obey without question even though the behavior they engage in may entail great personal sacrifice or great harm to others. . . .

Routinization

Authorization processes create a situation in which people become involved in an action without considering its implications and without really making a decision. Once they have taken the initial step, they are in a new psychological and social situation in which the pressures to continue are powerful. As Lewin (1947) has pointed out, many forces that might originally have kept people out of a situation reverse direction once they have made a commitment (once they have gone through the "gate region") and now serve to keep them in the situation. For example, concern about the criminal nature of an action, which might originally have inhibited a person from becoming involved, may now lead to deeper involvement in efforts to justify the action and to avoid negative consequences.

Despite these forces, however, given the nature of the actions involved in sanctioned massacres, one might still expect moral scruples to intervene; but the likelihood of moral resistance is greatly reduced by transforming the action into routine, mechanical, highly programmed operations. Routinization fulfills two functions. First, it reduces the necessity of making decisions, thus minimizing the occasions in which moral questions may arise. Second, it makes it easier to avoid the implications of the action, since the actor focuses on the details of the job rather than on its meaning. The latter effect is more readily achieved among those who participate in sanctioned massacres from a distance—from their desks or even from the cockpits of their bombers. . . .

*Herbert C.
Kelman and V.
Lee Hamilton*

Authorization processes override standard moral considerations; routinization processes reduce the likelihood that such considerations will arise. Still, the inhibitions against murdering one's fellow human beings are generally so strong that the victims must also be stripped of their human status if they are to be subjected to systematic killing. Insofar as they are dehumanized, the usual principles of morality no longer apply to them.

Sanctioned massacres become possible to the extent that the victims are deprived in the perpetrators' eyes of the two qualities essential to being perceived as fully human and included in the moral compact that governs human relationships: *identity*—standing as independent, distinctive individuals, capable of making choices and entitled to live their own lives—and *community*—fellow membership in an interconnected network of individuals who care for each other and respect each other's individuality and rights. Thus, when a group of people is defined entirely in terms of a category to which they belong, and when this category is excluded from the human family, moral restraints against killing them are more readily overcome.

Dehumanization of the enemy is a common phenomenon in any war situation. Sanctioned massacres, however, presuppose a more extreme degree of dehumanization, insofar as the killing is not in direct response to the target's threats or provocations. It is not what they have done that marks such victims for death but who they are—the category to which they happen to belong. They are the victims of policies that regard their systematic destruction as a desirable end or an acceptable means. Such extreme dehumanization becomes possible when the target group can readily be identified as a separate category of people who have historically been stigmatized and excluded by the victimizers; often the victims belong to a distinct racial, religious, ethnic, or political group regarded as inferior or sinister.

REFERENCES

Department of the Army. (1956). *The law of land warfare* (Field Manual, No. 27-10). Washington, D.C.: U.S. Government Printing Office.

Falk, R. A.; Kolko, G.; & Lifton, R. J. (Eds.). (1971). *Crimes of war.* New York: Vintage Books.

Goldstein, J.; Marshall, B.; & Schwartz, J. (Eds.). (1976). *The My Lai massacre and its coverup: Beyond the reach of law?* (The Peers report with a supplement and introductory essay on the limits of law). New York: Free Press.

Hammer, R. (1971). *The court-martial of Lt. Calley.* New York: Coward, McCann, & Geoghegan.

Hersh, S. (1970). *My Lai 4: A report on the massacre and its aftermath.* New York: Vintage Books.

———. (1972). *Coverup.* New York: Random House.

Lewin, K. (1947). Group decison and social change. In T. M. Newcomb & E. L. Hartley (Eds.), *Readings in social psychology.* New York: Holt.

What to Do About Crime

According to James Q. Wilson, the United States has two crime problems: the high rate of property crime and the high level of juvenile violence. In the following selection from "What to Do About Crime," *Commentary* (September 1994), Wilson discusses primarily the latter problem. The violence of the young is in large measure a part of the gang life of an alienated and self-destructive underclass. Studies of youth in the United States and abroad show that 6 percent of boys of a given age are responsible for 50 percent of all crimes. These boys tend to come from unstable families in poor communities. They tend to have criminal records and low verbal intelligence, and they frequently abuse alcohol and drugs. They are usually poor students, and they are impulsive and emotionally cold.

Various methods for controlling juvenile violence have been suggested, such as establishing curfews for teenagers and having police return truants to school. Although these methods may be helpful, for prevention to be effective it must be massive in scope and begin when the child is two or three years old, according to Wilson. The critical years are ages one to ten, when boys are most affected by weak parental attachment, poor supervision, drug and alcohol abuse, and an unstable environment.

Wilson calls for a series of changes, including welfare support to teenage mothers if they live in a two-parent home that would provide effective supervision to the young mother, or group homes to teach parenting. Illegitimacy, Wilson argues, is a curse, not an alternative lifestyle, and it should be stigmatized.

Wilson is the James Collins Professor of Management and Public Policy at the University of California, Los Angeles. He has authored or coauthored many books on crime and public policy, including *Thinking About Crime* (Vintage Books, 1977), *Crime and Human Nature,* with Richard J. Herrnstein (Simon & Schuster, 1985), and *The Moral Sense* (Free Press, 1993).

Key Concept: crime and juvenile violence

When the United States experienced the great increase in crime that began in the early 1960's and continued through the 1970's, most Americans were inclined to attribute it to conditions unique to this country....

Now, 30 years later, any serious discussion of crime must begin with the fact that, except for homicide, most industrialized nations have crime rates that resemble those in the United States. All the world is coming to look like America. In 1981, the burglary rate in Great Britain was much less than that in the United States; within six years the two rates were the same; today, British homes are more likely to be burgled than American ones. In 1980, the rate at which automobiles were stolen was lower in France than in the United States; today, the reverse is true. By 1984, the burglary rate in the Netherlands was nearly twice that in the United States. In Australia and Sweden certain forms of theft are more common than they are here. While property-crime rates were declining during most of the 1980's in the United States, they were rising elsewhere.

America, it is true, continues to lead the industrialized world in murders. There can be little doubt that part of this lead is to be explained by the greater availability of handguns here. Arguments that once might have been settled with insults or punches are today more likely to be settled by shootings. But guns are not the whole story. Big American cities have had more homicides than comparable European ones for almost as long as anyone can find records. New York and Philadelphia have been more murderous than London since the early part of the 19th century. This country has had a violent history; with respect to murder, that seems likely to remain the case.

But except for homicide, things have been getting better in the United States for over a decade. Since 1980, robbery rates (as reported in victim surveys) have declined by 15 percent. And even with regard to homicide, there is relatively good news: in 1990, the rate at which adults killed one another was no higher than it was in 1980, and in many cities it was considerably lower.

This is as it was supposed to be. Starting around 1980, two things happened that ought to have reduced most forms of crime. The first was the passing into middle age of the postwar baby boom. By 1990, there were 1.5 million fewer boys between the ages of fifteen and nineteen than there had been in 1980, a drop that meant that this youthful fraction of the population fell from 9.3 percent to 7.2 percent of the total.

In addition, the great increase in the size of the prison population, caused in part by the growing willingness of judges to send offenders to jail, meant that the dramatic reductions in the costs of crime to the criminal that occurred in the 1960's and 1970's were slowly (and very partially) being reversed. Until around 1985, this reversal involved almost exclusively real criminals and parole violators; it was not until after 1985 that more than a small part of the growth in prison populations was made up of drug offenders.

Because of the combined effect of fewer young people on the street and more offenders in prison, many scholars, myself included, predicted a continuing drop in crime rates throughout the 1980's and into the early 1990's. We were almost right: crime rates did decline. But suddenly, starting around 1985, even as adult homicide rates were remaining stable or dropping, *youthful* homicide rates shot up.

Alfred Blumstein of Carnegie-Mellon University has estimated that the rate at which young males, ages fourteen to seventeen, kill people has gone up significantly for whites and incredibly for blacks. Between 1985 and 1992, the homicide rate for young white males went up by about 50 percent but for young black males it *tripled.* . . .

The United States, then, does not have *a* crime problem, it has at least two. Our high (though now slightly declining) rates of property crime reflect a profound, worldwide cultural change: prosperity, freedom, and mobility have emancipated people almost everywhere from those ancient bonds of custom, family, and village that once held in check both some of our better and many of our worst impulses. The power of the state has been weakened, the status of children elevated, and the opportunity for adventure expanded; as a consequence, we have experienced an explosion of artistic creativity, entrepreneurial zeal, political experimentation—and criminal activity. A global economy has integrated the markets for clothes, music, automobiles—and drugs.

There are only two restraints on behavior—morality, enforced by individual conscience or social rebuke, and law, enforced by the police and the courts. If society is to maintain a behavioral equilibrium, any decline in the former must be matched by a rise in the latter (or vice versa). If familial and traditional restraints on wrongful behavior are eroded, it becomes necessary to increase the legal restraints. But the enlarged spirit of freedom and the heightened suspicion of the state have made it difficult or impossible to use the criminal-justice system to achieve what custom and morality once produced....

Our other crime problem has to do with the kind of felonies we have: high levels of violence, especially youthful violence, often occurring as part of urban gang life, produced disproportionately by a large, alienated, and self-destructive underclass. This part of the crime problem, though not uniquely American, is more important here than in any other industrialized nation....

Criminology has learned a great deal about who these people are. In studies both here and abroad it has been established that about 6 percent of the boys of a given age will commit half or more of all the serious crime produced by all boys of that age. Allowing for measurement errors, it is remarkable how consistent this formula is—6 percent causes 50 percent. It is roughly true in places as different as Philadelphia, London, Copenhagen, and Orange County, California.

We also have learned a lot about the characteristics of the 6 percent. They tend to have criminal parents, to live in cold or discordant families (or pseudo-families), to have a low verbal-intelligence quotient and to do poorly in school, to be emotionally cold and temperamentally impulsive, to abuse alcohol and drugs at the earliest opportunity, and to reside in poor, disorderly communities. They begin their misconduct at an early age, often by the time they are in the third grade....

Here a puzzle arises: if 6 percent of the males causes so large a fraction of our collective misery, and if young males are less numerous than once was the case, why are crime rates high and rising? The answer, I conjecture, is that the traits of the 6 percent put them at high risk for whatever criminogenic forces operate in society. As the costs of crime decline or the benefits increase; as drugs and guns become more available; as the glorification of violence becomes more commonplace; as families and neighborhoods lose some of their restraining power—as all these things happen, almost all of us will change our ways to some degree. For the most law-abiding among us, the change will be quite modest: a few more tools stolen from our employer, a few more traffic lights run when no police officer is watching, a few more experiments with fashionable drugs, and a few more business deals on which we cheat. But for the least law-abiding among us, the change will be dramatic: they will get drunk daily instead of just on Saturday night, try PCP or crack instead of marijuana, join gangs instead of marauding in pairs, and buy automatic weapons instead of making zip guns....

Much is said these days about preventing or deterring crime, but it is important to understand exactly what we are up against when we try. Prevention, if it can be made to work at all, must start very early in life, perhaps as early as the first two or three years, and given the odds it faces—childhood impulsivity, low verbal facility, incompetent parenting, disorderly neighborhoods—it must also be massive in scope. Deterrence, if it can be made to work better (for surely it already works to some degree), must be applied close to the moment of the wrongful act or else the present-orientedness of the youthful would-be offender will discount the threat so much that the promise of even a small gain will outweigh its large but deferred costs.

In this country, however, and in most Western nations, we have profound misgivings about doing anything that would give prevention or deterrence a chance to make a large difference. The family is sacrosanct; the family-preservation movement is strong; the state is a clumsy alternative. "Crime-prevention" programs, therefore, usually take the form of creating summer jobs for adolescents, worrying about the unemployment rate, or (as in the proposed 1994 crime bill) funding midnight basketball leagues. There may be something to be said for all these efforts, but crime prevention is not one of them. The typical high-rate offender is well launched on his career before he becomes a teenager or has ever encountered the labor market; he may like basketball, but who pays for the lights and the ball is a matter of supreme indifference to him.

Prompt deterrence has much to recommend it: the folk wisdom that swift and certain punishment is more effective than severe penalties is almost surely correct. But the greater the swiftness and certainty, the less attention paid to the procedural safeguards essential to establishing guilt. As a result, despite their good instincts for the right answers, most Americans, frustrated by the restraints (many wise, some foolish) on swiftness and certainty, vote for proposals to increase severity: if the penalty is 10 years, let us make it 20 or 30; if the penalty is life imprisonment, let us make it death; if the penalty is jail, let us make it caning.

Yet the more draconian the sentence, the less (on the average) the chance of its being imposed; plea bargains see to that. And the most draconian sentences will, of necessity, tend to fall on adult offenders nearing the end of their criminal careers and not on the young ones who are in their criminally most productive years. (The peak ages of criminality are between sixteen and eighteen; the average age of prison inmates is ten years older.) I say "of necessity" because almost every judge will give first-, second-, or even third-time offenders a break, reserving the heaviest sentences for those men who have finally exhausted judicial patience or optimism.

Laws that say "three strikes and you're out" are an effort to change this, but they suffer from an inherent contradiction. If they are carefully drawn so as to target only the most serious offenders, they will probably have minimal impact on the crime rate: but if they are broadly drawn so as to make a big impact on the crime rate, they will catch many petty repeat offenders who few of us think really deserve life imprisonment.

Prevention and deterrence, albeit hard to augment, at least are plausible strategies. Not so with many of the other favorite nostrums, like reducing the amount of violence on television. Televised violence may have some impact on criminality, but I know of few scholars who think the effect is very large....

As for rehabilitating juvenile offenders, it has some merit, but there are rather few success stories. Individually, the best (and best evaluated) programs have minimal, if any, effects: collectively, the best estimate of the crime reduction value of these programs is quite modest, something on the order of 5 to 10 percent.

What, then, is to be done? Let us begin with policing.... [M]any leaders and students of law enforcement now urge the police to be "proactive": to identify, with the aid of citizen groups, problems that can be solved so as to prevent criminality, and not only to respond to it. This is often called community-based policing; it seems to entail something more than feel-good meetings with honest citizens, but something less than allowing neighborhoods to assume control of the police function.

The new strategy might better be called problem-oriented policing. It requires the police to engage in *directed*, not random, patrol. The goal of that direction should be to reduce, in a manner consistent with fundamental liberties, the opportunity for high-risk persons to do those things that increase the likelihood of their victimizing others.

For example, the police might stop and pat down persons whom they reasonably suspect may be carrying illegal guns. The Supreme Court has upheld such frisks when an officer observes " unusual conduct" leading him to conclude that "criminal activity may be afoot" on the part of a person who may be "armed and dangerous."...

The same directed-patrol strategy might help keep known offenders drug-free. Most persons jailed in big cities are found to have been using illegal drugs within the day or two preceding their arrest. When convicted, some are given probation on condition that they enter drug-treatment programs; others are sent to prisons where (if they are lucky) drug-treatment programs operate. But in many cities the enforcement of such probation conditions is casual or nonexistent; in many states, parolees are released back into drug-infested communities with little effort to ensure that they participate in whatever treatment programs are to be found there.

Almost everyone agrees that more treatment programs should exist. But what many advocates overlook is that the key to success is steadfast participation and many, probably most, offenders have no incentive to be steadfast. To cope with this, patrol officers could enforce random drug tests on probationers and parolees on their beats; failing to take a test when ordered, or failing the test when taken, should be grounds for immediate revocation of probation or parole, at least for a brief period of confinement....

Another promising tactic is to enforce truancy and curfew laws. This arises from the fact that much crime is opportunistic: idle boys, usually in small groups, sometimes find irresistible the opportunity to steal or the challenge to fight. Deterring present-oriented youngsters who want to appear fearless in the eyes of their comrades while indulging their thrill-seeking natures is a tall order. While it is possible to deter the crimes they commit by a credible threat of prompt sanctions, it is easier to reduce the chances for risky group idleness in the first place.

In Charleston, South Carolina, for example, chief Reuben Greenberg instructed his officers to return all school-age children to the schools from which they were truant and to return all youngsters violating an evening-curfew agreement to their parents. As a result, groups of school-age children were no longer to be found hanging out in the shopping malls or wandering the streets late at night....

All these tactics have in common putting the police, as the criminologist Lawrence Sherman of the University of Maryland phrases it, where the "hot spots" are. Most people need no police attention except for a response to their calls for help. A small fraction of people (and places) need constant attention. Thus, in Minneapolis, *all* of the robberies during one year occurred at just 2 percent of the city's addresses. To capitalize on this fact, the Minneapolis police began devoting extra patrol attention, in brief but frequent bursts of activity, to those locations known to be trouble spots. Robbery rates evidently fell by as much as 20 percent and public disturbances by even more.

Some of the worst hot spots are outdoor drug markets. Because of either limited resources, a fear of potential corruption, or a desire to catch only the drug kingpins, the police in some cities (including, from time to time, New York) neglect street-corner dealing. By doing so, they get the worst of all worlds.

The public, seeing the police ignore drug dealing that is in plain view, assumes that they are corrupt whether or not they are. The drug kingpins, who are hard to catch and are easily replaced by rival smugglers, find that their essential retail distribution system remains intact. Casual or first-time drug users, who might not use at all if access to supplies were difficult, find access to be effortless and so increase their consumption. People who might remain in treatment programs if drugs were hard to get drop out upon learning that they are easy to get. Interdicting without merely displacing drug markets is difficult but not impossible, though it requires motivation which some departments lack and resources which many do not have.

The sheer number of police on the streets of a city probably has only a weak, if any, relationship with the crime rate; what the police do is more important than how many there are, at least above some minimum level. Nevertheless, patrols directed at hot spots, loitering truants, late-night wanderers, probationers, parolees, and possible gun carriers, all in addition to routine investigative activities, will require more officers in many cities. Between 1977 and 1987, the number of police officers declined in a third of the 50 largest cities and fell relative to population in many more. Just how far behind police resources have lagged can be gauged from this fact: in 1950 there was one violent crime reported for every police officer; in 1980 there were three violent crimes reported for every officer. . . .

Of late, drugs have changed American penal practice. In 1982, only about 8 percent of state-prison inmates were serving time on drug convictions. In 1987, that started to increase sharply; by 1994, over 60 percent of all federal and about 25 percent of all state prisoners were there on drug charges. In some states, such as New York, the percentage was even higher.

This change can be attributed largely to the advent of crack cocaine, Whereas snorted cocaine powder was expensive, crack was cheap; whereas the former was distributed though networks catering to elite tastes, the latter was mass-marketed on street corners. People were rightly fearful of what crack was doing to their children and demanded action; as a result, crack dealers started going to prison in record numbers.

Unfortunately, these penalties do not have the same incapacitative effect as sentences for robbery. A robber taken off the street is not replaced by a new robber who has suddenly found a market niche, but a drug dealer sent away is replaced by a new one because an opportunity has opened up.

We are left, then, with the problem of reducing the demand for drugs, and that in turn requires either prevention programs on a scale heretofore unimagined or treatment programs with a level of effectiveness heretofore unachieved. . . .

[I]t is necessary either to build much more prison space, find some other way of disciplining drug offenders, or both. There is very little to be gained, I think, from shortening the terms of existing non-drug inmates in order to free up more prison space. Except for a few elderly, nonviolent offenders serving very long terms, there are real risks associated with shortening the terms of the typical inmate.

Scholars disagree about the magnitude of those risks, but the best studies, such as the one of Wisconsin inmates done by John DiIulio of Princeton, suggest that the annual costs to society in crime committed by an offender on the street and probably twice the costs of putting him in a cell. . . .

But I caution the reader to understand that there are no easy prison solutions to crime, even if we build the additional space. The state-prison population more than doubled between 1980 and 1990, yet the victimization rate for robbery fell by only 23 percent. Even if we assign all of that gain to the increased deterrent and incapacitative effect of prison, which is implausible, the improvement is not vast. . . .

Recall my discussion of the decline in the costs of crime to the criminal, measured by the number of days in prison that result, on average, from the commission of a given crime. That cost is vastly lower today than in the 1950's. But much of the decline (and since 1974, nearly all of it) is the result of a drop in the probability of being arrested for a crime, not in the probability of being imprisoned once arrested.

Anyone who has followed my writings on crime knows that I have defended the use of prison both to deter crime and incapacitate criminals. I continue to defend it. But we must recognize two facts. First, even modest additional reductions in crime, comparable to the ones achieved in the early 1980's, will require vast increases in correctional costs and encounter bitter judicial resistance to mandatory sentencing laws. Second, America's most troubling crime problem—the increasingly violent behavior of disaffected and impulsive youth—may be especially hard to control by means of marginal and delayed increases in the probability of punishment....

For as long as I can remember, the debate over crime has been between those who wished to rely on the criminal-justice system and those who wished to attack the root causes of crime. I have always been in the former group because what its opponents depicted as "root causes"—unemployment, racism, poor housing, too little schooling, a lack of self-esteem—turned out, on close examination, not to be major causes of crime at all.

Of late, however, there has been a shift in the debate. Increasingly those who want to attack root causes have begun to point to real ones—temperament, early family experiences, and neighborhood effects. The sketch I gave earlier of the typical high-rate young offender suggests that these factors are indeed at the root of crime. The problem now is to decide whether any can be changed by plan and at an acceptable price in money and personal freedom.

If we are to do this, we must confront the fact that the critical years of a child's life are ages one to ten, with perhaps the most important being the earliest years. During those years, some children are put gravely at risk by some combination of heritable traits, prenatal insults (maternal drug and alcohol abuse or poor diet), weak parent-child attachment, poor supervision, and disorderly family environment....

In this country we tend to separate programs designed to help children from those that benefit their parents. The former are called "child development," the latter "welfare reform." This is a great mistake. Everything we know about long-term welfare recipients indicates that their children are at risk for the very problems that child-helping programs later try to correct.

The evidence from a variety of studies is quite clear: even if we hold income and ethnicity constant, children (and especially boys) raised by a single mother are more likely than those raised by two parents to have difficulty in school, get in trouble with the law, and experience emotional and physical problems. Producing illegitimate children is not an "alternative life-style" or simply an imprudent action; it is a curse. Making mothers work will not end the curse; under current proposals, it will not even save money.

The absurdity of divorcing the welfare problem from the child-development problem becomes evident as soon as we think seriously about what we want to achieve. Smaller welfare expenditures? Well, yes, but not if it hurts children. More young mothers working? Probably not; young mothers ought to raise their young children, and work interferes with that unless *two* parents can solve some difficult and expensive problems.

What we really want is *fewer illegitimate children*, because such children, by being born out of wedlock are, except in unusual cases, being given early admission to the underclass. And failing that, we want the children born to single (and typically young and poor) mothers to have a chance at a decent life.

Letting teenage girls set up their own households at public expense neither discourages illegitimacy nor serves the child's best interests. If they do set up their own homes, then to reach those with the fewest parenting skills and the most difficult children will require the kind of expensive and intensive home visits and family support-programs....

One alternative is to tell a girl who applies for welfare that she can only receive it on condition that she live either in the home of *two* competent parents (her own if she comes from an intact family) or in a group home where competent supervision and parent training will be provided by adults unrelated to her. Such homes would be privately managed but publicly funded by pooling welfare checks, food stamps, and housing allowances....

Group homes funded by pooled welfare benefits would make the task of parent training much easier and provide the kind of structured, consistent, and nurturant environment that children need. A few cases might be too difficult for these homes, and for such children, boarding schools—once common in American cities for disadvantaged children, but now almost extinct—might be revived....

My focus on changing behavior will annoy some readers. For them the problem is poverty and the worst feature of single-parent families is that they are inordinately poor. Even to refer to a behavioral or cultural problem is to "stigmatize" people.

Indeed it is. Wrong behavior—neglectful, immature, or incompetent parenting; the production of out-of-wedlock babies—*ought* to be stigmatized. There are many poor men of all races who do not abandon the women they have impregnated, and many poor women of all races who avoid drugs and do a good job of raising their children. If we fail to stigmatize those who give way to temptation, we withdraw the rewards from those who resist them. This becomes all the more important when entire communities, and not just isolated households, are dominated by a culture of fatherless boys preying on innocent persons and exploiting immature girls.

We need not merely stigmatize, however. We can try harder to move children out of those communities, either by drawing them into safe group homes or facilitating (through rent supplements and housing vouchers) the relocation of them and their parents to neighborhoods with intact social structures and an ethos of family values....

I seriously doubt that this country has the will to address either of its two crime problems, save by acts of individual self-protection. We could in theory make justice swifter and more certain, but we will not accept the restrictions on liberty and the weakening of procedural safeguards that this would entail. We could vastly improve the way in which our streets are policed, but some of us will not pay for it and the rest of us will not tolerate it. We could alter the way in which at-risk children experience the first few years of life, but the opponents of this —welfare-rights activists, family preservationists, budget cutters, and assorted ideologues—are numerous and the bureaucratic problems enormous.

Unable or unwilling to do such things, we take refuge in substitutes: we debate the death penalty, we wring our hands over television, we lobby to keep prisons from being built in our neighborhoods, and we fall briefly in love with trendy nostrums that seem to cost little and promise much. . . .

Meanwhile, just beyond the horizon, there lurks a cloud that the winds will soon bring over us. The population will start getting younger again. By the end of this decade there will be a million more people between the ages of fourteen and seventeen than there are now. Half of this extra million will be male. Six percent of them will become high-rate, repeat offenders—30,000 more muggers, killers, and thieves than we have now.

Get ready.

CHAPTER 6 Social Organization: Groups, Associations, Communities, and Rational Organizations

6.1 CHARLES HORTON COOLEY

Primary Groups

Charles Horton Cooley (1864–1929) was a sociologist and social psychologist who developed the school of social behaviorism during his teaching career at the University of Michigan. In his studies of society, he integrated sociopsychological and structural phenomena, as reflected in his three major publications: *Human Nature and Social Order* (1902), *Social Organization* (1909), and *Social Process* (1918).

In the following excerpt from *Social Organization,* Cooley discusses primary groups and shows that they are "fundamental in forming the social nature and ideals of the individual." The foremost primary group in all societies (preindustrial or modern) is the family, with play groups and friendship groups also being important in the formative years. Relationships in such groups are face-to-face, emotional, enduring, and involve the whole person.

Primary groups are the major source for the socialization of children, and they teach children their basic skills, such as language, walking, the values they cherish, the customs that guide their lives, and even their initial sense of themselves.

Key Concept: primary group and secondary group

*B*y primary groups I mean those characterized by intimate face-to-face association and coöperation. They are primary in several senses, but chiefly in that they are fundamental in forming the social nature and ideals of the individual. The result of intimate association, psychologically, is a certain fusion of individualities in a common whole, so that one's very self, for many purposes at least, is the common life and purpose of the group. Perhaps the simplest way of describing this wholeness is by saying that it is a "we"; it involves the sort of sympathy and mutual identification for which "we" is the natural expression. One lives in the feeling of the whole and finds the chief aims of his will in that feeling.

It is not to be supposed that the unity of the primary group is one of mere harmony and love. It is always a differentiated and usually a competitive unity, admitting of self-assertion and various appropriative passions; but these passions are socialized by sympathy, and come, or tend to come, under the discipline of a common spirit. The individual will be ambitious, but the chief object of his ambition will be some desired place in the thought of the others, and he will feel allegiance to common standards of service and fair play. So the boy will dispute with his fellows a place on the team, but above such disputes will place the common glory of his class and school.

The most important spheres of this intimate association and coöperation—though by no means the only ones—are the family, the play-group of children, and the neighborhood or community group of elders. These are practically universal, belonging to all times and all stages of development; and are accordingly a chief basis of what is universal in human nature and human ideals. The best comparative studies of the family, such as those of Westermarck[1] or Howard,[2] show it to us as not only a universal institution, but as more alike the world over than the exaggeration of exceptional customs by an earlier school had led us to suppose. Nor can any one doubt the general prevalence of play-groups among children or of informal assemblies of various kinds among their elders. Such association is clearly the nursery of human nature in the world about us, and there is no apparent reason to suppose that the case has anywhere or at any time been essentially different.

As regards play, I might, were it not a matter of common observation, multiply illustrations of the universality and spontaneity of the group discussion and coöperation to which it gives rise. The general fact is that children, especially boys after about their twelfth year, live in fellowships in which their sympathy, ambition and honor are engaged even more, often, than they are in the family. Most of us can recall examples of the endurance by boys of injustice and even cruelty, rather than appeal from their fellows to parents or teachers—

as, for instance, in the hazing so prevalent at schools, and so difficult, for this very reason, to suppress. And how elaborate the discussion, how cogent the public opinion, how hot the ambitions in these fellowships.

Nor is this facility of juvenile association, as is sometimes supposed, a trait peculiar to English and American boys; since experience among our immigrant population seems to show that the offspring of the more restrictive civilizations of the continent of Europe form self-governing play-groups with almost equal readiness. Thus Miss Jane Addams, after pointing out that the "gang" is almost universal, speaks of the interminable discussion which every detail of the gang's activity receives, remarking that "in these social folkmotes, so to speak, the young citizen learns to act upon his own determination."[3]

Of the neighborhood group it may be said, in general, that from the time men formed permanent settlements upon the land, down, at least, to the rise of modern industrial cities, it has played a main part of the primary, heart-to-heart life of the people. Among our Teutonic forefathers the village community was apparently the chief sphere of sympathy and mutual aid for the commons all through the "dark" and middle ages, and for many purposes it remains so in rural districts at the present day. In some countries we still find it with all its ancient vitality, notably in Russia, where the mir, or self-governing village group, is the main theatre of life, along with the family, for perhaps fifty millions of peasants.

In our own life the intimacy of the neighborhood has been broken up by the growth of an intricate mesh of wider contacts which leaves us strangers to people who live in the same house. And even in the country the same principle is at work, though less obviously, diminishing our economic and spiritual community with our neighbors. How far this change is a healthy development, and how far a disease, is perhaps still uncertain.

Besides these almost universal kinds of primary association, there are many others whose form depends upon the particular state of civilization; the only essential thing, as I have said, being a certain intimacy and fusion of personalities. In our own society, being little bound by place, people easily form clubs, fraternal societies and the like, based on congeniality, which may give rise to real intimacy. Many such relations are formed at school and college, and among men and women brought together in the first instance by their occupations—as workmen in the same trade, or the like. Where there is a little common interest and activity, kindness grows like weeds by the roadside.

But the fact that the family and neighborhood groups are ascendant in the open and plastic time of childhood makes them even now incomparably more influential than all the rest.

Primary groups are primary in the sense that they give the individual his earliest and completest experience of social unity, and also in the sense that they do not change in the same degree as more elaborate relations, but form a comparatively permanent source out of which the latter are ever springing. Of course they are not independent of the larger society, but to some extent reflect its spirit; as the German family and the German school bear somewhat distinctly the print of German militarism. But this, after all, is like the tide setting back into creeks, and does not commonly go very far. Among the German, and still more among the Russian, peasantry are found habits of free coöperation and discussion almost uninfluenced by the character of the state; and it is a familiar and well-supported view that the village commune, self-governing as regards local affairs and habituated to discussion, is a very widespread institution in settled communities, and the continuator of a similar autonomy previously existing in the clan. "It is man who makes monarchies and establishes republics, but the commune seems to come directly from the hand of God."[4]

In our own cities the crowded tenements and the general economic and social confusion have sorely wounded the family and the neighborhood, but it is remarkable, in view of these conditions, what vitality they show; and there is nothing upon which the conscience of the time is more determined than upon restoring them to health.

These groups, then, are springs of life, not only for the individual but for social institutions. They are only in part moulded by special traditions, and, in larger degree, express a universal nature. The religion or government of other civilizations may seem alien to us, but the children or the family group wear the common life, and with them we can always make ourselves at home.

NOTES

1. *The History of Human Marriage.*
2. *A History of Matrimonial Institutions.*
3. *Newer Ideals of Peace,* 177.
4. De Tocqueville, *Democracy in America,* vol. i, chap. 5.

The Prosperous Community: Social Capital and Public Life

Americans living today benefit from what sociologists have termed *social capital*—aspects of social organization that are beneficial to all—which was created by their ancestors and handed down through institutions and culture. Existing social capital makes people's actions, both individually and collectively, more productive today. In fact, one of the greatest differences between rich and poor countries is their varied stocks of social capital, and this discovery is one of the principle contributions of sociology. Over the past quarter-century, however, this idea has receded while the social sciences have emphasized physical capital and competition among workers and businesses.

In recent years Robert D. Putnam has rediscovered the importance of social capital. His study of Italian regional governments demonstrates how social capital in the form of voluntary cooperative actions and relationships make effective governments possible. In the following selection from "The Prosperous Community: Social Capital and Public Life," *The American Prospect* (Spring 1993), Putnam argues that the lack of or decline in social capital contributes to a wide array of social problems and the weakening of many social institutions.

Putnam is the Dillion Professor of International Affairs and director of the Center for International Studies at Harvard University. His research on Italian regional governments is reported in *Making Democracy Work: Civic Traditions in Modern Italy* (Princeton University Press, 1993).

Key Concept: social capital

Your corn is ripe today; mine will be so tomorrow. 'Tis profitable for us both, that I should labour with you today, and that you should aid me tomorrow. I have no kindness for you, and know you have as little for me. I will not, therefore, take any pains upon your account; and should I labour with you upon my own account, in expectation of a return, I know I should be disappointed, and that I should in vain depend upon your gratitude. Here then I leave you to labour alone; you treat me in the same manner. The seasons change; and both of us lose our harvests for want of mutual confidence and security.

—David Hume

The predicament of the farmers in Hume's parable is all too familiar in communities and nations around the world:

- Parents in communities everywhere want better educational opportunities for their children, but collaborative efforts to improve public schools falter.
- Residents of American ghettos share an interest in safer streets, but collective action to control crime fails.
- Poor farmers in the Third World need more effective irrigation and marketing schemes, but cooperation to these ends proves fragile.
- Global warming threatens livelihoods from Manhattan to Mauritius, but joint action to forestall this shared risk founders.

Failure to cooperate for mutual benefit does not necessarily signal ignorance or irrationality or even malevolence, as philosophers since Hobbes have underscored. Hume's farmers were not dumb, or crazy, or evil; they were trapped. Social scientists have lately analyzed this fundamental predicament in a variety of guises: the tragedy of the commons; the logic of collective action; public goods; the prisoners' dilemma. In all these situations, as in Hume's rustic anecdote, everyone would be better off if everyone could cooperate. In the absence of coordination and credible mutual commitment, however, everyone defects, ruefully but rationally, confirming one another's melancholy expectations.

How can such dilemmas of collective action be overcome, short of creating some Hobbesian Leviathan? Social scientists in several disciplines have recently suggested a novel diagnosis of this problem, a diagnosis resting on the concept of *social capital*. By analogy with notions of physical capital and human capital—tools and training that enhance individual productivity—"social capital" refers to features of social organization, such as networks, norms, and trust, that facilitate coordination and cooperation for mutual benefit. Social capital enhances the benefits of investment in physical and human capital.

Working together is easier in a community blessed with a substantial stock of social capital. This insight turns out to have powerful practical implications for many issues on the American national agenda—for how we might overcome the poverty and violence of South Central Los Angeles, or revitalize industry in the Rust Belt, or nurture the fledgling democracies of the former Soviet empire and the erstwhile Third World. Before spelling out these implications, however, let me illustrate the importance of social capital by recounting an investigation that several colleagues and I have conducted over the last two decades on the seemingly arcane subject of regional government in Italy.

LESSONS FROM AN ITALIAN EXPERIMENT

Beginning in 1970, Italians established a nationwide set of potentially powerful regional governments. These 20 new institutions were virtually identical in form, but the social, economic, political, and cultural contexts in which they were implanted differed dramatically, ranging from the preindustrial to the postindustrial, from the devoutly Catholic to the ardently Communist, from the inertly feudal to the frenetically modern. Just as a botanist might investigate plant development by measuring the growth of genetically identical seeds sown in different plots, we sought to understand government performance by studying how these new institutions evolved in their diverse settings.

As we expected, some of the new governments proved to be dismal failures—inefficient, lethargic, and corrupt. Others have been remarkably successful, however, creating innovative day care programs and job-training centers, promoting investment and economic development, pioneering environmental standards and family clinics—managing the public's business efficiently and satisfying their constituents.

What could account for these stark differences in quality of government? Some seemingly obvious answers turned out to be irrelevant. Government organization is too similar from region to region for that to explain the contrasts in performance. Party politics or ideology makes little difference. Affluence and prosperity have no direct effect. Social stability or political harmony or population movements are not the key. None of these factors is correlated with good government as we had anticipated. Instead, the best predictor is one that Alexis de Tocqueville might have expected. Strong traditions of civic engagement— voter turnout, newspaper readership, membership in choral societies and literary circles, Lions Clubs, and soccer clubs—are the hallmarks of a successful region.

Some regions of Italy, such as Emilia-Romagna and Tuscany, have many active community organizations. Citizens in these regions are engaged by public issues, not by patronage. They trust one another to act fairly and obey the law. Leaders in these communities are relatively honest and committed to equality. Social and political networks are organized horizontally, not hierarchically. These "civic communities" value solidarity, civic participation, and integrity. And here democracy works.

At the other pole are "uncivic" regions, like Calabria and Sicily, aptly characterized by the French term *incivisme*. The very concept of citizenship is stunted there. Engagement in social and cultural associations is meager. From the point of view of the inhabitants, public affairs is somebody else's business— *i notabili*, "the bosses," "the politicians"—but not theirs. Laws, almost everyone agrees, are made to be broken, but fearing others' lawlessness, everyone demands sterner discipline. Trapped in these interlocking vicious circles, nearly everyone feels powerless, exploited, and unhappy. It is hardly surprising that representative government here is less effective than in more civic communities.

The historical roots of the civic community are astonishingly deep. Enduring traditions of civic involvement and social solidarity can be traced back nearly a millennium to the eleventh century, when communal republics were established in places like Florence, Bologna, and Genoa, exactly the communities that today enjoy civic engagement and successful government. At the core of this civic heritage are rich networks of organized reciprocity and civic solidarity—guilds, religious fraternities, and tower societies for self-defense in the medieval communes; cooperatives, mutual aid societies, neighborhood associations, and choral societies in the twentieth century.

These communities did not become civic simply because they were rich. The historical record strongly suggests precisely the opposite: They have become rich because they were civic. The social capital embodied in norms and networks of civic engagement seems to be a precondition for economic development, as well as for effective government. Development economists take note: Civics matters.

How does social capital undergird good government and economic progress? First, networks of civic engagement foster sturdy norms of generalized reciprocity: I'll do this for you now, in the expectation that down the road you or someone else will return the favor. "Social capital is akin to what Tom Wolfe called the 'favor bank' in his novel, *The Bonfire of the Vanities*," notes economist Robert Frank. A society that relies on generalized reciprocity is more efficient than a distrustful society, for the same reason that money is more efficient than barter. Trust lubricates social life.

Networks of civic engagement also facilitate coordination and communication and amplify information about the trustworthiness of other individuals. Students of prisoners' dilemmas and related games report that cooperation is most easily sustained through repeat play. When economic and political dealing is embedded in dense networks of social interaction, incentives for opportunism and malfeasance are reduced. This is why the diamond trade, with its extreme possibilities for fraud, is concentrated within close-knit ethnic enclaves. Dense social ties facilitate gossip and other valuable ways of cultivating reputation—an essential foundation for trust in a complex society.

Finally, networks of civic engagement embody past success at collaboration, which can serve as a cultural template for future collaboration. The civic traditions of north-central Italy provide a historical repertoire of forms of cooperation that, having proved their worth in the past, are available to citizens for addressing new problems of collective action.

Sociologist James Coleman concludes, "Like other forms of capital, social capital is productive, making possible the achievement of certain ends that would not be attainable in its absence.... In a farming community ... where one farmer got his hay baled by another and where farm tools are extensively borrowed and lent, the social capital allows each farmer to get his work done with less physical capital in the form of tools and equipment." Social capital, in short, enables Hume's farmers to surmount their dilemma of collective action.

Stocks of social capital, such as trust, norms, and networks, tend to be self-reinforcing and cumulative. Successful collaboration in one endeavor builds connections and trust—social assets that facilitate future collaboration in other, unrelated tasks. As with conventional capital, those who have social capital tend to accumulate more—them as has, gets. Social capital is what the social philosopher Albert O. Hirschman calls a "moral resource," that is, a resource whose supply increases rather than decreases through use and which (unlike physical capital) becomes depleted if *not* used.

Unlike conventional capital, social capital is a "public good," that is, it is not the private property of those who benefit from it. Like other public goods, from clean air to safe streets, social capital tends to be under provided by private agents. This means that social capital must often be a by-product of other social activities. Social capital typically consists in ties, norms, and trust transferable from one social setting to another. Members of Florentine choral societies participate because they like to sing, not because their participation strengthens the Tuscan social fabric. But it does.

SOCIAL CAPITAL AND ECONOMIC DEVELOPMENT

Social capital is coming to be seen as a vital ingredient in economic development around the world. Scores of studies of rural development have shown that a vigorous network of indigenous grassroots associations can be as essential to growth as physical investment, appropriate technology, or (that nostrum of neoclassical economists) "getting prices right." Political scientist Elinor Ostrom has explored why some cooperative efforts to manage common pool resources, like grazing grounds and water supplies, succeed, while others fail. Existing stocks of social capital are an important part of the story. Conversely, government interventions that neglect or undermine this social infrastructure can go seriously awry.

Studies of the rapidly growing economies of East Asia almost always emphasize the importance of dense social networks, so that these economies are sometimes said to represent a new brand of "network capitalism." These networks, often based on the extended family or on close-knit ethnic communities like the overseas Chinese, foster trust, lower transaction costs, and speed information and innovation. Social capital can be transmuted, so to speak, into financial capital: In novelist Amy Tan's *Joy Luck Club*, a group of mah-jong-playing friends evolves into a joint investment association. China's extraordinary economic growth over the last decade has depended less on formal institutions than on *guanxi* (personal connections) to underpin contracts and to channel savings and investment.

Social capital, we are discovering, is also important in the development of advanced Western economies. Economic sociologist Mark Granovetter has pointed out that economic transactions like contracting or job searches are more efficient when they are embedded in social networks. It is no accident that one of the pervasive stratagems of ambitious yuppies is "networking." Studies of highly efficient, highly flexible "industrial districts" (a term coined by Alfred Marshall, one of the founders of modern economics) emphasize networks of collaboration among workers and small entrepreneurs. Such concentrations of social capital, far from being paleo-industrial anachronisms, fuel ultra-modern industries from the high tech of Silicon Valley to the high fashion of Benetton. Even in mainstream economics the so-called "new growth theory" pays more attention to social structure (the "externalities of human capital") than do conventional neoclassical models. Robert Lucas, a founder of "rational expectations" economics, acknowledges that "human capital accumulation is a fundamentally *social* activity, involving *groups* of people in a way that has no counterpart in the accumulation of physical capital."

The social capital approach can help us formulate new strategies for development. For example, current proposals for strengthening market economies and democratic institutions in the formerly Communist lands of Eurasia center almost exclusively on deficiencies in financial and human capital (thus calling for loans and technical assistance). However, the deficiencies in social capital in these countries are at least as alarming. Where are the efforts to encourage "social capital formation"? Exporting PTAs or Kiwanis clubs may seem a bit far-fetched, but how about patiently reconstructing those shards of indigenous civic associations that have survived decades of totalitarian rule....

SOCIAL CAPITAL AND AMERICA'S ILLS

Fifty-one deaths and $1 billion in property damage in Los Angeles ... [in 1992] put urban decay back on the American agenda. Yet if the ills are clear, the prescription is not. Even those most sympathetic to the plight of America's ghettos are not persuaded that simply reviving the social programs dismantled in the last decade or so will solve the problems. The erosion of social capital is an essential and under-appreciated part of the diagnosis.

Although most poor Americans do no reside in the inner city, there is something qualitatively different about the social and economic isolation experienced by the chronically poor blacks and Latinos who do. Joblessness, inadequate education, and poor health clearly truncate the opportunities of ghetto residents. Yet so do profound deficiencies in social capital.

Part of the problem facing blacks and Latinos in the inner city is that they lack "connections" in the most literal sense. Job-seekers in the ghetto have little access, for example, to conventional job referral networks. Labor economists Anne Case and Lawrence Katz have shown that, regardless of race, inner-city youth living in neighborhoods blessed with high levels of civic engagement are more likely to finish school, have a job, and avoid drugs and crime, controlling for the individual characteristics of the youth. That is, of two identical youths, the one unfortunate enough to live in a neighborhood whose social capital has eroded is more likely to end up hooked, booked, or dead. Several researchers seem to have found similar neighborhood effects on the incidence of teen pregnancy, among both blacks and whites, again controlling for personal characteristics. Where you live and whom you know—the social capital you can draw on—helps to define who you are and thus to determine your fate.

Racial and class inequalities in access to social capital, if properly measured, may be as great as inequalities in financial and human capital, and no less portentous. Economist Glenn Loury has used the term "social capital" to capture the fundamental fact that racial segregation, coupled with socially inherited differences in community networks and norms, means that individually targeted "equal opportunity" policies may not eliminate racial inequality, even in the long run. Research suggests that the life chances of today's generation depend not only on their parents' social resources, but also on the social resources of their parents' ethnic group. Even workplace integration and upward mobility by successful members of minority groups cannot overcome these persistent effects of inequalities in social capital. William Julius Wilson has described in tragic detail how the exodus of middle-class and working-class families from the ghetto has eroded the social capital available to those left behind. The settlement houses that nurtured sewing clubs and civic activism a century ago, embodying community as much as charity, are now mostly derelict.

It would be a dreadful mistake, of course, to overlook the repositories of social capital within America's minority communities. The neighborhood restaurant eponymously portrayed in Mitchell Duneier's recent *Slim's Table*, for example, nurtures fellowship and intercourse that enable blacks (and whites) in Chicago's South Side to sustain a modicum of collective life. Historically, the black church has been the most bounteous treasure-house of social capital for African Americans. The church provided the organizational infrastructure for political mobilization in the civil rights movement. Recent work on American political participation by political scientist Sidney Verba and his colleagues shows that the church is a uniquely powerful resource for political engagement among blacks—an arena in which to learn about public affairs and hone political skills and make connections.

In tackling the ills of Americas cities, investments in physical capital, financial capital, human capital, and social capital are complementary, not competing alternatives. Investments in jobs and education, for example, will be more effective if they are coupled with reinvigoration of community associations.

Some churches provide job banks and serve as informal credit bureaus, for example, using their reputational capital to vouch for members who may be ex-convicts, former drug addicts, or high school dropouts. In such cases the church does not merely provide referral networks. More fundamentally, wary employers and financial institutions bank on the church's ability to identify parishioners whose formal credentials understate their reliability. At the same time, because these parishioners value their standing in the church, and because the church has put its own reputation on the line, they have an additional incentive to perform. Like conventional capital for conventional borrowers, social capital serves as a kind of collateral for men and women who are excluded from ordinary credit or labor markets. In effect, the participants pledge their social connections, leveraging social capital to improve the efficiency with which markets operate.

The importance of social capital for America's domestic agenda is not limited to minority communities. Take public education, for instance. The success of private schools is attributable, according to James Coleman's massive research, not so much to what happens in the classroom nor to the endowments of individual students, but rather to the greater engagement of parents and community members in private school activities. Educational reformers like child psychologist James Comer seek to improve schooling not merely by "treating" individual children but by deliberately involving parents and others in the educational process. Educational policymakers need to move beyond debates about curriculum and governance to consider the effects of social capital. Indeed, most commonly discussed proposals for "choice" are deeply flawed by their profoundly individualist conception of education. If states and localities are to experiment with voucher systems for education or child care, why not encourage vouchers to be spent in ways that strengthen community organization, not weaken it? Once we recognize the importance of social capital, we ought to be able to design programs that creatively combine individual choice with collective engagement.

Many people today are concerned about revitalizing American democracy. Although discussion of political reform in the United States focuses nowadays on such procedural issues as term limits and campaign financing, some of the ills that afflict the American polity reflect deeper, largely unnoticed social changes.

"Some people say that you usually can trust people. Others say that you must be wary in relations with people. Which is your view?" Responses to this question, posed repeatedly in national surveys for several decades, suggest that social trust in the United States has declined for more than a quarter century. By contrast, American politics benefited from plentiful stocks of social capital in earlier times. Recent historical work on the Progressive Era, for example, has uncovered evidence of the powerful role played by nominally nonpolitical associations (such as women's literary societies) precisely because they provided a dense social network. Is our current predicament the result of a long-term erosion of social capital, such as community engagement and social trust?

Economist Juliet Schorr's discovery of "the unexpected decline of leisure" in America suggests that our generation is less engaged with one another outside the marketplace and thus less prepared to cooperate for shared goals. Mobile, two-career (or one-parent) families often must use the market for child care and other services formerly provided through family and neighborhood networks. Even if market-based services, considered individually, are of high quality, this deeper social trend is eroding social capital. There are more empty seats at the PTA and in church pews these days. While celebrating the productive, liberating effects of fuller equality in the workplace, we must replace the social capital that this movement has depleted....

Classic liberal social policy is designed to enhance the opportunities of *individuals*, but if social capital is important, this emphasis is partially misplaced. Instead we must focus on community development, allowing space for religious organizations and choral societies and Little Leagues that may seem to have little to do with politics or economics. Government policies, whatever their intended effects, should be vetted for their indirect effects on social capital. If, as some suspect, social capital is fostered more by home ownership than by public or private tenancy, then we should design housing policy accordingly. Similarly, as Theda Skocpol has suggested, the direct benefits of national service programs might be dwarfed by the indirect benefits that could flow from the creation of social networks that cross class and racial lines. In any comprehensive strategy for improving the plight of America's communities, rebuilding social capital is as important as investing in human and physical capital.

Urbanism as a Way of Life

Louis Wirth (1897–1952), a 1930s University of Chicago sociologist, was a theorist and a founder of the International Sociological Society. Wirth contributed heavily to the study of social organization, mass society, minorities, the sociology of knowledge, and urbanism as a way of life. He was also among the first to introduce the concept of social planning. He was concerned about the manipulation of public opinion by politicians; he therefore stressed democracy as a process of intercommunication, discussion, debate, negotiation, compromise, and toleration.

In the following selection from "Urbanism as a Way of Life," *American Journal of Sociology* (July 1938), Wirth discusses his view of urbanism as it emerged in Chicago during the 1920s and 1930s. Wirth defines the city as a densely populated area of socially heterogeneous individuals. In a far-ranging discussion, he provides an understanding, directly and indirectly, of why social relations in the city are anonymous and thus limited to specific activities. His theory explains how and why urbanism is conducive to social mobility, leveling, and a breakdown of caste lines and why it creates heterogeneity and the demise of the homogeneous community.

Key Concept: heterogeneity

*F*or sociological purposes a city may be defined as a relatively *large, dense,* and permanent settlement of socially *heterogeneous* individuals. On the basis of the postulates which this minimal definition suggests, a theory of urbanism may be formulated in the light of existing knowledge concerning social groups.

A THEORY OF URBANISM

In the pages that follow we shall seek to set forth a limited number of identifying characteristics of the city. Given these characteristics we shall then indicate what consequences or further characteristics follow from them in the light of general sociological theory and empirical research. We hope in this manner to arrive at the essential propositions comprising a theory of urbanism. Some of these propositions can be supported by a considerable body of already available research materials; others may be accepted as hypotheses for which a certain amount of presumptive evidence exists, but for which more ample and exact verification would be required. At least such a procedure will, it is hoped, show what in the way of systematic knowledge of the city we now have and what are the crucial and fruitful hypotheses for future research....

Size of the Population Aggregate

Ever since Aristotle's *Politics*, it has been recognized that increasing the number of inhabitants in a settlement beyond a certain limit will affect the relationships between them and the character of the city. Large numbers involve, as has been pointed out, a greater range of individual variation. Furthermore, the greater the number of individuals participating in a process of interaction, the greater is the *potential* differentiation between them. The personal traits, the occupations, the cultural life, and the ideas of the members of an urban community may, therefore, be expected to range between more widely separated poles than those of rural inhabitants.

That such variations should give rise to the spatial segregation of individuals according to color, ethnic heritage, economic and social status, tastes and preferences, may readily be inferred. The bonds of kinship, of neighborliness, and the sentiments arising out of living together for generations under a common folk tradition are likely to be absent or, at best, relatively weak in an aggregate the members of which have such diverse origins and backgrounds. Under such circumstances competition and formal control mechanisms furnish the substitutes for the bonds of solidarity that are relied upon to hold a folk society together.

Increase in the number of inhabitants of a community beyond a few hundred is bound to limit the possibility of each member of the community knowing all the others personally. Max Weber, in recognizing the social significance of this fact, pointed out that from a sociological point of view large numbers of inhabitants and density of settlement mean that the personal mutual acquaintanceship between the inhabitants which ordinarily inheres in a neighborhood is lacking. The increase in numbers thus involves a changed character of the social relationships. As [Georg] Simmel points out:

> [If] the unceasing external contact of numbers of persons in the city should be met by the same number of inner reactions as in the small town, in which one knows almost every person he meets and to each of whom he has a positive relationship, one would be completely atomized internally and would fall into an unthinkable mental condition.

The multiplication of persons in a state of interaction under conditions which make their contact as full personalities impossible produces that segmentalization of human relationships which has sometimes been seized upon by students of the mental life of the cities as an explanation for the "schizoid" character of urban personality. This is not to say that the urban inhabitants have fewer acquaintances than rural inhabitants, for the reverse may actually be true;

it means rather that in relation to the number of people whom they see and with whom they rub elbows in the course of daily life, they know a smaller proportion, and of these they have less intensive knowledge.

Characteristically, urbanites meet one another in highly segmental roles. They are, to be sure, dependent upon more people for the satisfactions of their life-needs than are rural people and thus are associated with a greater number of organized groups, but they are less dependent upon particular persons, and their dependence upon others is confined to a highly fractionalized aspect of the other's round of activity. This is essentially what is meant by saying that the city is characterized by secondary rather than primary contacts. The contacts of the city may indeed be face to face, but they are nevertheless impersonal, superficial, transitory, and segmental. The reserve, the indifference, and the blasé outlook which urbanites manifest in their relationships may thus be regarded as devices for immunizing themselves against the personal claims and expectations of others.

The superficiality, the anonymity, and the transitory character of urban-social relations make intelligible, also, the sophistication and the rationality generally ascribed to city-dwellers. Our acquaintances tend to stand in a relationship of utility to us in the sense that the role which each one plays in our life is overwhelmingly regarded as a means for the achievement of our own ends. Whereas, therefore, the individual gains, on the one hand, a certain degree of emancipation or freedom from the personal and emotional controls of intimate groups, he loses, on the other hand, the spontaneous self-expression, the morale, and the sense of participation that comes with living in an integrated society. This constitutes essentially the state of *anomie* or the social void to which [Emile] Durkheim alludes in attempting to account for the various forms of social disorganization in technological society....

In a community composed of a larger number of individuals than can know one another intimately and can be assembled in one spot, it becomes necessary to communicate through indirect mediums and to articulate individual interests by a process of delegation. Typically in the city, interests are made effective through representation. The individual counts for little, but the voice of the representative is heard with a deference roughly proportional to the numbers for whom he speaks....

Density

As in the case of numbers, so in the case of concentration in limited space, certain consequences of relevance in sociological analysis of the city emerge. Of these only a few can be indicated.

As Darwin pointed out for flora and fauna and as Durkheim noted in the case of human societies, an increase in numbers when area is held constant (i.e., an increase in density) tends to produce differentiation and specialization, since only in this way can the area support increased numbers. Density thus reinforces the effect of numbers in diversifying men and their activities and in increasing the complexity of the social structure.

On the subjective side, as Simmel has suggested, the close physical contact of numerous individuals necessarily produces a shift in the mediums through which we orient ourselves to the urban milieu, especially to our fellow-men. Typically, our physical contacts are close but our social contacts are distant. The urban world puts a premium on visual recognition. We see the uniform which denotes the role of the functionaries and are oblivious to the personal eccentricities that are hidden behind the uniform. We tend to acquire and develop a sensitivity to a world of artefacts and become progressively farther removed from the world of nature.

We are exposed to glaring contrasts between splendor and squalor, between riches and poverty, intelligence and ignorance, order and chaos. The competition for space is great, so that each area generally tends to be put to the use which yields the greatest economic return. Place of work tends to become dissociated from place of residence, for the proximity of industrial and commercial establishments makes an area both economically and socially undesirable for residential purposes.

Density, land values, rentals, accessibility, healthfulness, prestige, aesthetic consideration, absence of nuisances such as noise, smoke, and dirt determine the desirability of various areas of the city as places of settlement for different sections of the population. Place and nature of work, income, racial and ethnic characteristics, social status, custom, habit, taste, preference, and prejudice are among the significant factors in accordance with which the urban population is selected and distributed into more or less distinct settlements. Diverse population elements inhabiting a compact settlement thus tend to become segregated from one another in the degree in which their requirements and modes of life are incompatible with one another and in the measure in which they are antagonistic to one another. Similarly, persons of homogeneous status and needs unwittingly drift into, consciously select, or are forced by circumstances into, the same area. The different parts of the city thus acquire specialized functions. The city consequently tends to resemble a mosaic of social worlds in which the transition from one to the other is abrupt. The juxtaposition of divergent personalities and modes of life tends to produce a relativistic perspective and a sense of toleration of differences which may be regarded as prerequisites for rationality and which lead toward the secularization of life.

The close living together and working together of individuals who have no sentimental and emotional ties foster a spirit of competition, aggrandizement, and mutual exploitation. To counteract irresponsibility and potential disorder, formal controls tend to be resorted to. Without rigid adherence to predictable routines a large compact society would scarcely be able to maintain itself. The clock and the traffic signal are symbolic of the basis of our social order in the urban world. Frequent close physical contact, coupled with great social distance, accentuates the reserve of unattached individuals toward one another and, unless compensated for by other opportunities for response, gives rise to loneliness. The necessary frequent movement of great numbers of individuals to a congested habitat gives occasion to friction and irritation. Nervous tensions which derive from such personal frustrations are accentuated by the rapid tempo and the complicated technology under which life in dense areas must be lived.

The social interaction among such a variety of personality types in the urban milieu tends to break down the rigidity of caste lines and to complicate the class structure, and thus induces a more ramified and differentiated framework of social stratification than is found in more integrated societies. The heightened mobility of the individual, which brings him within the range of stimulation by a great number of diverse individuals and subjects him to fluctuating status in the differentiated social groups that compose the social structure of the city, tends toward the acceptance of instability and insecurity in the world at large as a norm. This fact helps to account, too, for the sophistication and cosmopolitanism of the urbanite. No single group has the undivided allegiance of the individual. The groups with which he is affiliated do not lend themselves readily to a simple hierarchical arrangement. By virtue of his different interests arising out of different aspects of social life, the individual acquires membership in widely divergent groups, each of which functions only with reference to a single segment of his personality. Nor do these groups easily permit of a concentric arrangement so that the narrower ones fall within the circumference of the more inclusive ones, as is more likely to be the case in the rural community or in primitive societies. Rather the groups with which the person typically is affiliated are tangential to each other or intersect in highly variable fashion.

6.4 MAX WEBER

Bureaucracy

German sociologist Max Weber (1864–1920) has probably had more influence on Western sociology than any other individual. His studies ranged widely, but he will be remembered primarily for his theory of modern Western history and the industrial revolution. He saw the latter as involving economic factors, but he also felt that Protestant religious ideas played a decisive role in the development of capitalism. The importance of his analysis lies in its refutation of Karl Marx's economic determinism. Weber's interpretation of modern Western history was also groundbreaking. He saw it as dominated by the expansion of rationalism, which expressed itself in the growth of science and technology, the disenchantment of the world, the growing rule of law, and the growth of a relatively new form of organization that Weber classified as rational-legal organizations and called bureaucracies. His work on the latter initiated the sociology of formal organizations and is still relevant today.

Most organizations are family businesses and operate partly by rational (efficiency) norms and partly by family norms. Big modern organizations, however, are best understood as rational-legal organizations. These are based on explicit rules and formal definitions of authority and responsibilities for each position in the hierarchal structure of the organization. To analyze them, Weber constructed an ideal type of bureaucracy, which he presents in the following selection from his essay "Bureaucracy," published in H. H. Gerth and C. Wright Mills, eds. and trans., *From Max Weber: Essays in Sociology* (Oxford University Press, 1958). According to Weber, an ideal type of bureaucracy is a composite of all the essential characteristics of a category, though no actual case embodies them all. It can serve as a model against which real cases can be compared. Normally, deviations from the ideal type signal problems. The ideal type of bureaucracy, for example, is a smooth-running machine, but many pathologies can be found in most real bureaucracies. In fact, the finding and documentation of these pathologies has become a cottage industry in organizational studies.

Key Concept: bureaucracy

CHARACTERISTICS OF BUREAUCRACY

Modern officialdom functions in the following specific manner:

I. There is the principle of fixed and official jurisdictional areas, which are generally ordered by rules, that is, by laws or administrative regulations.

1. The regular activities required for the purposes of the bureaucratically governed structure are distributed in a fixed way as official duties.
2. The authority to give the commands required for the discharge of these duties is distributed in a stable way and is strictly delimited by rules concerning the coercive means, physical, sacerdotal, or otherwise, which may be placed at the disposal of officials.
3. Methodical provision is made for the regular and continuous fulfilment of these duties and for the execution of the corresponding rights; only persons who have the generally regulated qualifications to serve are employed.

In public and lawful government these three elements constitute 'bureaucratic authority.' In private economic domination, they constitute bureaucratic 'management.' Bureaucracy, thus understood, is fully developed in political and ecclesiastical communities only in the modern state, and, in the private economy, only in the most advanced institutions of capitalism. Permanent and public office authority, with fixed jurisdiction, is not the historical rule but rather the exception. This is so even in large political structures such as those of the ancient Orient, the Germanic and Mongolian empires of conquest, or of many feudal structures of state. In all these cases, the ruler executes the most important measures through personal trustees, table-companions, or court-servants. Their commissions and authority are not precisely delimited and are temporarily called into being for each case.

II. The principles of office hierarchy and of levels of graded authority mean a firmly ordered system of super- and subordination in which there is a supervision of the lower offices by the higher ones. Such a system offers the governed the possibility of appealing the decision of a lower office to its higher authority, in a definitely regulated manner. With the full development of the bureaucratic type, the office hierarchy is monocratically organized. The principle of hierarchical office authority is found in all bureaucratic structures: in state and ecclesiastical structures as well as in large party organizations and private enterprises. It does not matter for the character of bureaucracy whether its authority is called 'private' or 'public.' ...

III. The management of the modern office is based upon written documents ('the files'), which are preserved in their original or draught form. There is, therefore, a staff of subaltern officials and scribes of all sorts. The body of officials actively engaged in a 'public' office, along with the respective apparatus of material implements and the files, make up a 'bureau.' In private enterprise, 'the bureau' is often called 'the office.' ...

IV. Office management, at least all specialized office management—and such management is distinctly modern—usually presupposes thorough and expert training. This increasingly holds for the modern executive and employee of private enterprises, in the same manner as it holds for the state official.

V. When the office is fully developed, official activity demands the full working capacity of the official, irrespective of the fact that his obligatory time in the bureau may be firmly delimited. In the normal case, this is only the product of a long development, in the public as well as in the private office. Formerly, in all cases, the normal state of affairs was reversed: official business was discharged as a secondary activity.

VI. The management of the office follows general rules, which are more or less stable, more or less exhaustive, and which can be learned. Knowledge of these rules represents a special technical learning which the officials possess. It involves jurisprudence, or administrative or business management. . . .

THE POSITION OF THE OFFICIAL

All this results in the following for the internal and external position of the official:

I. Office holding is a 'vocation.' This is shown, first, in the requirement of a firmly prescribed course of training, which demands the entire capacity for work for a long period of time, and in the generally prescribed and special examinations which are prerequisites of employment. Furthermore, the position of the official is in the nature of a duty. This determines the internal structure of his relations, in the following manner: Legally and actually, office holding is not considered a source to be exploited for rents or emoluments, as was normally the case during the Middle Ages and frequently up to the threshold of recent times. Nor is office holding considered a usual exchange of services for equivalents, as is the case with free labor contracts. Entrance into an office, including one in the private economy, is considered an acceptance of a specific obligation of faithful management in return for a secure existence. It is decisive for the specific nature of modern loyalty to an office that, in the pure type, it does not establish a relationship to a *person*, like the vassal's or disciple's faith in feudal or in patrimonial relations of authority. Modern loyalty is devoted to impersonal and functional purposes. Behind the functional purposes, of course, 'ideas of culture-values' usually stand. These are *ersatz* for the earthly or supramundane personal master: ideas such as 'state,' 'church,' 'community,' 'party,' or 'enterprise' are thought of as being realized in a community; they provide an ideological halo for the master. . . .

II. The personal position of the official is patterned in the following way:

1. Whether he is in a private office or a public bureau, the modern official always strives and usually enjoys a distinct *social esteem* as compared with the governed. . . .

2. The pure type of bureaucratic official is *appointed* by a superior authority. An official elected by the governed is not a purely bureaucratic figure. Of course, the formal existence of an election does not by itself mean that no appointment hides behind the election—in the state, especially, appointment by party chiefs. . . .

3. Normally, the position of the official is held for life, at least in public bureaucracies; and this is increasingly the case for all similar structures....

4. The official receives the regular *pecuniary* compensation of a normally fixed *salary* and the old age security provided by a pension. The salary is not measured like a wage in terms of work done, but according to 'status,' that is, according to the kind of function (the 'rank') and, in addition, possibly, according to the length of service. The relatively great security of the official's income, as well as the rewards of social esteem, make the office a sought-after position, especially in countries which no longer provide opportunities for colonial profits. In such countries, this situation permits relatively low salaries for officials.

5. The official is set for a *'career'* within the hierarchical order of the public service. He moves from the lower, less important, and lower paid to the higher positions. The average official naturally desires a mechanical fixing of the conditions of promotion: if not of the offices, at least of the salary levels. He wants these conditions fixed in terms of 'seniority,' or possibly according to grades achieved in a developed system of expert examinations....

TECHNICAL ADVANTAGES OF BUREAUCRATIC ORGANIZATION

The decisive reason for the advance of bureaucratic organization has always been its purely technical superiority over any other form of organization. The fully developed bureaucratic mechanism compares with other organizations exactly as does the machine with the non-mechanical modes of production.

Precision, speed, unambiguity, knowledge of the files, continuity, discretion, unity, strict subordination, reduction of friction and of material and personal costs—these are raised to the optimum point in the strictly bureaucratic administration, and especially in its monocratic form. As compared with all collegiate, honorific, and avocational forms of administration, trained bureaucracy is superior on all these points. And as far as complicated tasks are concerned, paid bureaucratic work is not only more precise but, in the last analysis, it is often cheaper than even formally unremunerated honorific service....

Today, it is primarily the capitalist market economy which demands that the official business of the administration be discharged precisely, unambiguously, continuously, and with as much speed as possible. Normally, the very large, modern capitalist enterprises are themselves unequalled models of strict bureaucratic organization. Business management throughout rests on increasing precision, steadiness, and, above all, the speed of operations. This, in turn, is determined by the peculiar nature of the modern means of communication, including, among other things, the news service of the press. The extraordinary increase in the speed by which public announcements, as well as economic and political facts, are transmitted exerts a steady and sharp pressure in the direction of speeding up the tempo of administrative reaction towards various situations. The optimum of such reaction time is normally attained only by a strictly bureaucratic organization.[1]

Bureaucratization offers above all the optimum possibility for carrying through the principle of specializing administrative functions according to purely objective considerations. Individual performances are allocated to functionaries who have specialized training and who by constant practice learn more and more. The 'objective' discharge of business primarily means a discharge of business according to *calculable rules* and 'without regard for persons.'...

The second element mentioned, 'calculable rules,' also is of paramount importance for modern bureaucracy. The peculiarity of modern culture, and specifically of its technical and economic basis, demands this very 'calculability' of results. When fully developed, bureaucracy also stands, in a specific sense, under the principle of *sine ira ac studio* ["without hostility or fanaticism"]. Its specific nature, which is welcomed by capitalism, develops the more perfectly the more the bureaucracy is 'dehumanized,' the more completely it succeeds in eliminating from official business love, hatred, and all purely personal, irrational, and emotional elements which escape calculation. This is the specific nature of bureaucracy and it is appraised as its special virtue.

The more complicated and specialized modern culture becomes, the more its external supporting apparatus demands the personally detached and strictly 'objective' *expert*, in lieu of the master of older social structures, who was moved by personal sympathy and favor, by grace and gratitude. Bureaucracy offers the attitudes demanded by the external apparatus of modern culture in the most favorable combination. As a rule, only bureaucracy has established the foundation for the administration of a rational law conceptually systematized on the basis of such enactments as the latter Roman imperial period first created with a high degree of technical perfection. During the Middle Ages, this law was received along with the bureaucratization of legal administration, that is to say, with the displacement of the old trial procedure which was bound to tradition or to irrational presuppositions, by the rationally trained and specialized expert.

NOTES

1. Here we cannot discuss in detail how the bureaucratic apparatus may, and actually does, produce definite obstacles to the discharge of business in a manner suitable for the single case.

PART THREE

Stratification

On the Internet . . .

Sites appropriate to Part Three

This Web site of the magazine *American Scientist* allows students of sociology to access a variety of articles and to explore issues and concepts related to race and gender.

    http://www.amsci.org/amsci/amsci.html

This site provides a handy reference to the prevailing concepts of race and the causes of human variability since ancient times. It can serve as a valuable starting point for research and understanding into the concept of race.

    http://www.as.ua.edu/ant/bindon/ant101/
        syllabus/race/race1.htm

Open this page to find definitions and tables related to poverty and poverty areas. The site provides answers to frequently asked questions about poverty, facts about poverty, and discussion of the myths of poverty versus the realities. Welfare reform is also addressed.

    http://www.mindspring.com/~nexweb21/
        povindex.htm

The Urban Institute offers lengthy discussions of issues related to welfare and its reform. This page starts with the assertion, "No one likes the current welfare system."

    http://www.urban.org/welfare/overview.htm

CHAPTER 7 Social Inequality

7.1 KARL MARX AND FRIEDRICH ENGELS

On Class

In no society are all people equal. All societies are stratified. The major dimensions of stratification systems are wealth, power, and status, and usually they are strongly related to each other. The powerful are typically wealthy and highly esteemed and vice versa. Many early sociologists located the factors that account for social inequalities in social systems, not in the nature of human beings. One of the most insightful analyses of structured inequality was presented by the German philosopher Karl Marx (1818–1883). Marx was a revolutionary thinker and writer, and his works formed the basis of European socialism in the late nineteenth century. Together with his collaborator Friedrich Engels (1820–1895), who later served as the leading authority on Marx and his philosophies, he published the *Manifest der Kommunistischen Partei* (1848), or what is commonly known as *The Communist Manifesto.* For Marx and Engels, this work was as much a theory of history and social change and an economic analysis of social stratification as it was a call to arms.

In the following excerpt from *The Communist Manifesto,* Marx and Engels describe one type of power as the critical dimension for understanding all stratification systems: the ownership and control of the means of production. In their view, most other inequalities derive from this one. The owners of the land in agricultural societies and the owners of the factories and businesses in industrial societies control, exploit, and oppress the land-less and the wage workers. In fact, all human history, according to Marx and Engels, has been a struggle between the haves and the have-nots. Those who have power are determined to keep it (hence the class struggle), and those who

155

control the economy (in a capitalist society they are the bourgeoisie) control all the other institutions in society.

Sociologists continue to find Marx and Engels's perspective profoundly useful.

Key Concept: class and class warfare

BOURGEOIS AND PROLETARIANS[1]

The history of all hitherto existing society is the history of class struggles.

Freeman and slave, patrician and plebeian, lord and serf, guild-master and journeyman, in a word, oppressor and oppressed stood in constant opposition to one another, carried on an uninterrupted, now hidden, now open fight, a fight that each time ended, either in a revolutionary reconstitution of society at large, or in the common ruin of the contending classes.

In the earlier epochs of history, we find almost everywhere a complicated arrangement of society into various orders, a manifold gradation of social rank. In ancient Rome we have patricians, knights, plebeians, slaves; in the Middle Ages, feudal lords, vassals, guild-masters, journeymen, apprentices, serfs; in almost all of these classes, again, subordinate gradations.

The modern bourgeois society that has sprouted from the from the ruins of feudal society has not done away with class antagonisms. It has but established new classes, new conditions of oppression, new forms of struggle in place of the old ones.

Our epoch, the epoch of the bourgeoisie, possesses, however, this distinctive feature: It has simplified the class antagonisms. Society as a whole is more and more splitting up into two great hostile camps, into two great classes directly facing each other—bourgeoisie and proletariat.

From the serfs of the Middle Ages sprang the chartered burghers of the earliest towns. From these burgesses the first elements of the bourgeoisie were developed.

The discovery of America, the rounding of the Cape, opened up fresh ground for the rising bourgeoisie. The East-Indian and Chinese markets, the colonisation of America, trade with the colonies, the increase in the means of exchange and in commodities generally, gave to commerce, to navigation, to industry, an impulse never before known, and thereby, to the revolutionary element in the tottering feudal society, a rapid development.

The feudal system of industry, in which industrial production was monopolised by closed guilds, now no longer sufficed for the growing wants of the new markets. The manufacturing system took its place. The guild-masters were pushed aside by the manufacturing middle class; division of labour between the different corporate guilds vanished in the face of division of labor in each single workshop.

Meantime the markets kept ever growing, the demand ever rising. Even manufacture no longer sufficed. Thereupon, steam and machinery revolutionised industrial production. The place of manufacture was taken by the giant, modern industry, the place of the industrial middle class by industrial millionaires, the leaders of whole industrial armies, the modern bourgeois.

Modern industry has established the world market, for which the discovery of America paved the way. This market has given an immense development to commerce, to navigation, to communication by land. This development has, in its turn, reacted on the extension of industry; and in proportion as industry, commerce, navigation, railways extended, in the same proportion the bourgeoisie developed, increased its capital, and pushed into the background every class handed down from the Middle Ages.

We see, therefore, how the modern bourgeoisie is itself the product of a long course of development, of a series of revolutions in the modes of production and of exchange.

Each step in the development of the bourgeoisie was accompanied by a corresponding political advance of that class. An oppressed class under the sway of the feudal nobility, an armed and self-governing association in the mediaeval commune; here independent urban republic (as in Italy and Germany), there taxable "third estate" of the monarchy (as in France); afterwards, in the period of manufacture proper, serving either the semi-feudal or the absolute monarchy as a counterpoise against the nobility, and, in fact, corner-stone of the great monarchies in general—the bourgeoisie has at last, since the establishment of modern industry and of the world market, conquered for itself, in the modern representative state, exclusive political sway. The executive of the modern state is but a committee for managing the common affairs of the whole bourgeoisie.

The bourgeoisie, historically, has played a most revolutionary part.

The bourgeoisie, wherever it has got the upper hand, has put an end to all feudal, patriarchal, idyllic relations. It has pitilessly torn asunder the motley feudal ties that bound man to his "natural superiors," and has left no other nexus between man and man than naked self-interest, than callous "cash payment." It has drowned the most heavenly ecstasies of religious fervour, of chivalrous enthusiasm, of philistine sentimentalism, in the icy water of egotistical calculation. It has resolved personal worth into exchange value, and in place of the numberless indefeasible chartered freedoms, has set up that single, unconscionable freedom—Free Trade. In one word, for exploitation, veiled by religious and political illusions, it has substituted naked, shameless, direct brutal exploitation.

The bourgeoisie has stripped of its halo every occupation hitherto honoured and looked up to with reverent awe. It has converted the physician, the lawyer, the priest, the poet, the man of science, into its paid wage labourers.

The bourgeoisie has torn away from the family its sentimental veil, and has reduced the family relation to a mere money relation.

The bourgeoisie has disclosed how it came to pass that the brutal display of vigour in the Middle Ages, which reactionaries so much admire, found its fitting complement in the most slothful indolence. It has been the first to show what man's activity can bring about. It has accomplished wonders far surpassing Egyptian pyramids, Roman aqueducts, and Gothic cathedrals; it has conducted expeditions that put in the shade all former exoduses of nations and crusades.

The bourgeoisie cannot exist without constantly revolutionising the instruments of production, and thereby the relations of production, and with them the whole relations of society. Conservation of the old modes of production in unaltered form, was, on the contrary, the first condition of existence for all earlier industrial classes. Constant revolutionising of production, uninterrupted disturbance of all social conditions, everlasting uncertainty and agitation distinguish the bourgeois epoch from all earlier ones. All fixed, fast frozen relations, with their train of ancient and venerable prejudices and opinions, are swept away, all new-formed ones become antiquated before they can ossify. All that is solid melts into air, all that is holy is profaned, and man is at last compelled to face with sober senses his real conditions of life and his relations with his kind.

The need of a constantly expanding market for its products chases the bourgeoisie over the whole surface of the globe. It must nestle everywhere, settle everywhere, establish connections everywhere.

The bourgeoisie has through its exploitation of the world market given a cosmopolitan character to production and consumption in every country. To the great chagrin of reactionaries, it has drawn from under the feet of industry the national ground on which it stood. All old-established national industries have been destroyed or are daily being destroyed. They are dislodged by new industries, whose introduction becomes a life and death question for all civilised nations, by industries that no longer work up indigenous raw material, but raw material drawn from the remotest zones; industries whose products are consumed, not only at home, but in every quarter of the globe. In place of the old wants, satisfied by the production of the country, we find new wants, requiring for their satisfaction the products of distant lands and climes. In place of the old local and national seclusion and self-sufficiency, we have intercourse in every direction, universal inter-dependence of nations. And as in material, so also in intellectual production. The intellectual creations of individual nations become common property. National one-sidedness and narrow-mindedness become more and more impossible, and from the numerous national and local literatures there arises a world literature.

The bourgeoisie, by the rapid improvement of all instruments of production, by the immensely facilitated means of communication, draws all, even the most barbarian, nations into civilisation. The cheap prices of its commodities are the heavy artillery with which it batters down all Chinese walls, with which it forces the barbarians' intensely obstinate hatred of foreigners to capitulate. It compels all nations, on pain of extinction, to adopt the bourgeois mode of production; it compels them to introduce what it calls civilisation into their midst, *i.e.*, to become bourgeois themselves. In one word, it creates a world after its own image.

The bourgeois has subjected the country to the rule of the towns. It has created enormous cities, has greatly increased the urban population as compared with the rural, and has thus rescued a considerable part of the population from the idiocy of rural life. Just as it has made the country dependent on the towns, so it has made barbarian and semi-barbarian countries dependent on the civilised ones, nations of peasants on nations of bourgeois, the East on the West.

The bourgeoisie keeps more and more doing away with the scattered state of the population, of the means of production, and of property. It has agglomerated population, centralised means of production, and has concentrated property in a few hands. The necessary consequence of this was political centralisation. Independent, or but loosely connected provinces, with separate interests, laws, governments and systems of taxation, became lumped together into one nation, with one government, one code of laws, one national class interest, one frontier and one customs tariff.

The bourgeoisie, during its rule of scarce one hundred years, has created more massive and more colossal productive forces than have all preceding generations together. Subjection of nature's forces to man, machinery, application of chemistry to industry and agriculture, steam navigation, railways, electric telegraphs, clearing of whole continents for cultivation, canalisation of rivers, whole populations conjured out of the ground—what earlier century had even a presentiment that such productive forces slumbered in the lap of social labour?

We see then: the means of production and of exchange, on whose foundation the bourgeoisie built itself up, were generated in feudal society. At a certain stage in the development of these means of production and of exchange, the conditions under which feudal society produced and exchanged, the feudal organisation of agriculture and manufacturing industry, in one word, the feudal relations of property became no longer compatible with the already developed productive forces; they became so many fetters. They had to be burst asunder; they were burst asunder.

Into their place stepped free competition, accompanied by a social and political constitution adapted to it, and by the economic and political sway of the bourgeois class.

A similar movement is going on before our own eyes. Modern bourgeois society with its relations of production, of exchange and of property, a society that has conjured up such gigantic means of production and of exchange, is like the sorcerer who is no longer able to control the powers of the nether world whom he has called up by his spells. For many a decade past the history of industry and commerce is but the history of the revolt of modern productive forces against modern conditions of production, against the property relations that are the conditions for the existence of the bourgeoisie and of its rule. It is enough to mention the commercial crises that by their periodical return put the existence of the entire bourgeois society on its trial, each time more threateningly. In these crises a great part not only of the existing products, but also of the previously created productive forces, are periodically destroyed. In these crises there breaks out an epidemic that, in all earlier epochs, would have seemed an absurdity—the epidemic of over-production. Society suddenly finds itself put back into a state of momentary barbarism; it appears as if a famine, a universal war of devastation had cut off the supply of every means of subsistence; industry and commerce seem to be destroyed. And why? Because there is too much civilisation, too much means of subsistence, too much industry, too much commerce. The productive forces at the disposal of society no longer tend to further the development of the conditions of bourgeois property; on the contrary, they have become too powerful for these conditions, by which they are fettered, and so soon as they overcome these fetters, they bring disorder into the whole of bourgeois society, endanger the existence of bourgeois property. The conditions of bourgeois society are too narrow to comprise the wealth created by them. And how does the bourgeoisie get over these crises? On the one hand, by enforced destruction of a mass of productive forces; on the other, by the conquest of new markets, and by the more thorough exploitation of the old ones. That is to say, by paving the way for more extensive and more destructive crises, and by diminishing the means whereby crises are prevented.

The weapons with which the bourgeoisie felled feudalism to the ground are now turned against the bourgeoisie itself.

But not only has the bourgeoisie forged the weapons that bring death to itself; it has also called into existence the men who are to wield those weapons —the modern working class—the proletarians.

In proportion as the bourgeoisie, *i.e.,* capital, is developed, in the same proportion is the proletariat, the modern working class, developed—a class of labourers, who live only so long as they find work, and who find work only so long as their labour increases capital. These labourers, who must sell themselves piecemeal, are a commodity, like every other article of commerce, and are consequently exposed to all the vicissitudes of competition, to all the fluctuations of the market.

Owing to the extensive use of machinery and to division of labour, the work of the proletarians has lost all individual character, and, consequently, all charm for the workman. He becomes an appendage of the machine, and it is only the most simple, most monotonous, and most easily acquired knack, that is required of him. Hence, the cost of production of a workman is restricted, almost entirely, to the means of subsistence that he requires for his maintenance, and for the propagation of his race. But the price of a commodity, and therefore also of labour, is equal to its cost of production. In proportion, therefore, as the repulsiveness of the work increases, the wage decreases. Nay more, in proportion as the use of machinery and division of labour increases, in the same proportion the burden of toil also increases, whether by prolongation of the working hours, by increase of the work exacted in a given time, or by increased speed of the machinery, etc.

Modern industry has converted the little workshop of the patriarchal master into the great factory of the industrial capitalist. Masses of labourers, crowded into the factory, are organised like soldiers. As privates of the industrial army they are placed under the command of a perfect hierarchy of officers and sergeants. Not only are they slaves of the bourgeois class, and of the bourgeois state; they are daily and hourly enslaved by the machine, by the overlooker, and, above all, by the individual bourgeois manufacturer himself. The more openly this despotism proclaims gain to be its end and aim, the more petty, the more hateful and the more embittering it is.

The less the skill and exertion of strength implied in manual labour, in other words, the more modern industry becomes developed, the more is the labour of men superseded by that of women. Differences of age and sex have no longer any distinctive social validity for the working class. All are instruments of labour, more or less expensive to use, according to their age and sex.

No sooner is the exploitation of the labourer by the manufacturer, so far at an end, that he receives his wages in cash, than he is set upon by the other portions of the bourgeoisie, the landlord, the shopkeeper, the pawnbroker, etc.

The lower strata of the middle class—the small tradespeople, shopkeepers, and retired tradesmen generally, the handicraftsmen and peasants—all these sink gradually into the proletariat, partly because their diminutive capital does not suffice for the scale on which modern industry is carried on, and is swamped in the competition with the large capitalists, partly because their specialised skill is rendered worthless by new methods of production. Thus the proletariat is recruited from all classes of the population.

The proletariat goes through various stages of development. With its birth begins its struggle with the bourgeoisie. At first the contest is carried on by individual labourers, then by the work people of a factory, then by the operatives of one trade, in one locality, against the individual bourgeois who directly exploits them. They direct their attacks not against the bourgeois conditions of production, but against the instruments of production themselves; they destroy imported wares that compete with their labour, they smash to pieces machinery, they set factories ablaze, they seek to restore by force the vanished status of the workman of the Middle Ages.

At this stage the labourers still form an incoherent mass scattered over the whole country, and broken up by their mutual competition. If anywhere they unite to form more compact bodies, this is not yet the consequence of their own active union, but of the union of the bourgeoisie, which class, in order to attain its own political ends, is compelled to set the whole proletariat in motion, and is moreover yet, for a time, able to do so. At this stage, therefore, the proletarians do not fight their enemies, but the enemies of their enemies, the remnants of absolute monarchy, the landowners, the non-industrial bourgeois, the petty bourgeoisie. Thus the whole historical movement is concentrated in the hands of the bourgeoisie; every victory so obtained is a victory for the bourgeoisie.

But with the development of industry the proletariat not only increases in number; it becomes concentrated in greater masses, its strength grows, and it feels that strength more. The various interests and conditions of life within the ranks of the proletariat are more and more equalised, in proportion as machinery obliterates all distinctions of labour, and nearly everywhere reduces wages to the same low level. The growing competition among the bourgeois, and the resulting commercial crises, make the wages of the workers ever more fluctuating. The unceasing improvement of machinery, ever more rapidly developing, makes their livelihood more and more precarious; the collisions between individual workmen and individual bourgeois take more and more the character of collisions between two classes. Thereupon the workers begin to form combinations (trades unions) against the bourgeois; they club together in order to keep up the rate of wages; they found permanent associations in order to make provisions beforehand for these occasional revolts. Here and there the contest breaks out into riots.

Now and then the workers are victorious, but only for a time. The real fruit of their battles lies, not in the immediate result, but in the ever expanding union of the workers. This union is helped on by the improved means of communication that are created by modern industry, and that place the workers of different localities in contact with one another. It was just this contact that was needed to centralise the numerous local struggles, all of the same character, into one national struggle between classes. But every class struggle is a political struggle. And that union, to attain which the burghers of the Middle Ages, with their miserable highways, required centuries, the modern proletarians, thanks to railways, achieve in a few years.

This organisation of the proletarians into a class, and consequently into a political party, is continually being upset again by the competition between the workers themselves. But it ever rises up again, stronger, firmer, mightier. It compels legislative recognition of particular interests of the workers, by taking advantage of the divisions among the bourgeoisie itself. Thus the ten-hours' bill in England was carried.

Altogether, collisions between the classes of the old society further in many ways the course of development of the proletariat. The bourgeoisie finds itself involved in a constant battle. At first with the aristocracy; later on, with those portions of the bourgeoisie itself, whose interests have become antagonistic to the progress of industry; at all times with the bourgeoisie of foreign countries. In all these battles it sees itself compelled to appeal to the proletariat, to ask for its help, and thus, to drag it into the political arena. The bourgeoisie itself, therefore, supplies the proletariat with its own elements of political and general education, in other words, it furnishes the proletariat with weapons for fighting the bourgeoisie.

Further, as we have already seen, entire sections of the ruling classes are, by the advance of industry, precipitated into the proletariat, or are at least threatened in their conditions of existence. These also supply the proletariat with fresh elements of enlightenment and progress.

Finally, in times when the class struggle nears the decisive hour, the process of dissolution going on within the ruling class, in fact within the whole range of old society, assumes such a violent, glaring character, that a small section of the ruling class cuts itself adrift, and joins the revolutionary class, the class that holds the future in its hands. Just as, therefore, at an earlier period, a section of the nobility went over to the bourgeoisie, so now a portion of the bourgeoisie goes over to the proletariat, and in particular, a portion of the bourgeois ideologists, who have raised themselves to the level of comprehending theoretically the historical movement as a whole.

Of all the classes that stand face to face with the bourgeoisie today, the proletariat alone is a really revolutionary class. The other classes decay and finally disappear in the face of modern industry; the proletariat is its special and essential product. The lower middle class, the small manufacturer, the shopkeeper, the artisan, the peasant, all these fight against the bourgeoisie, to save from extinction their existence as fractions of the middle class. They are therefore not revolutionary, but conservative. Nay more, they are reactionary, for they try to roll back the wheel of history. If by chance they are revolutionary, they are so only in view of their impending transfer into the proletariat; they thus defend not their present, but their future interests; they desert their own standpoint to place themselves at that of the proletariat.

The "dangerous class," the social scum, that passively rotting mass thrown off by the lowest layers of old society, may, here and there, be swept into the movement by a proletarian revolution; its conditions of life, however, prepare it far more for the part of a bribed tool of reactionary intrigue.

In the conditions of the proletariat, those of old society at large are already virtually swamped. The proletarian is without property; his relation to his wife and children has no longer anything in common with the bourgeois family relations: modern industrial labour, modern subjection to capital, the same in England as in France, in America as in Germany, has stripped him of every trace of national character. Law, morality, religion, are to him so many bourgeois prejudices, behind which lurk in ambush just as many bourgeois interests.

All the preceding classes that got the upper hand, sought to fortify their already acquired status by subjecting society at large to their conditions of appropriation. The proletarians cannot become masters of the productive forces of society, except by abolishing their own previous mode of appropriation, and thereby also every other previous mode of appropriation. They have nothing of their own to secure and to fortify: their mission is to destroy all previous securities for, and insurances of, individual property.

All previous historical movements were movements of minorities, or in the interest of minorities. The proletarian movement is the self-conscious, independent movement of the immense majority, in the interest of the immense majority. The proletariat, the lowest stratum of our present society, cannot stir, cannot raise itself up, without the whole superincumbent strata of official society being sprung into the air.

Though not in substance, yet in form, the struggle of the proletariat with the bourgeoisie is at first a national struggle. The proletariat of each country must, of course, first of all settle matters with its own bourgeoisie.

In depicting the most general phases of the development of the proletariat, we traced the more or less veiled civil war, raging within existing society, up to the point where that war breaks out into open revolution, and where the violent overthrow of the bourgeoisie lays the foundation for the ways of the proletariat.

Hitherto, every form of society has been based, as we have already seen, on the antagonism of oppressing and oppressed classes. But in order to oppress a class, certain conditions must be assured to it under which it can, at least, continue its slavish existence. The serf, in the period of serfdom, raised himself to membership in the commune, just as the petty bourgeois, under the yoke of feudal absolutism, managed to develop into a bourgeois. The modern labourer, on the contrary, instead of rising with the progress of industry, sinks deeper and deeper below the conditions of existence of his own class. He becomes a pauper, and pauperism develops more rapidly than population and wealth. And here it becomes evident, that the bourgeoisie is unfit any longer to be the ruling class in society, and to impose its conditions of existence upon society as an overriding law. It is unfit to rule because it is incompetent to assure an existence to its slave within his slavery, because it cannot help letting him sink into such a state, that it has to feed him, instead of being fed by him. Society can no longer live under this bourgeoisie, in other words, its existence is no longer compatible with society.

The essential condition for the existence and for the sway of the bourgeois class, is the formation and augmentation of capital; the condition for capital is wage labour. Wage labour rests exclusively on competition between the labourers. The advance of industry, whose involuntary promoter is the bourgeoisie, replaces the isolation of the labourers, due to competition, by their revolutionary combination, due to association. The development of modern industry, therefore, cuts from under its feet the very foundation on which the bourgeoisie produces and appropriates products. What the bourgeoisie therefore produces, above all, are its own grave-diggers. Its fall and the victory of the proletariat are equally inevitable.

NOTES

1. By bourgeoisie is meant the class of modern capitalists, owners of the means of social production and employers of wage labour. By proletariat, the class of modern wage labourers who, having no means of production of their own, are reduced to selling their labour power in order to live. [*Note by F. Engels to the English edition of 1888.*]

7.2 KINGSLEY DAVIS AND WILBERT E. MOORE

Some Principles of Stratification

Kingsley Davis (b. 1908) is a professor emeritus of sociology at the Hoover Institute, Stanford University, and a member of the Behavioral Science Division of the National Research Council. His research mainly focused on comparing population structures, urbanization, and marriage and family among different countries, and especially on the causes and consequences of population change. Wilbert E. Moore (1914–1987) was a professor of sociology and law at the University of Denver. His interests included the measurement of social change. Both men were students of Talcott Parsons, a prominent U.S. sociologist of the 1950s.

Davis and Moore discuss their functional theory of stratification in the following selection from "Some Principles of Stratification," *American Sociological Review* (vol. 10, no. 2, 1945). They argue that income inequalities are good for the effective functioning of societies and that certain positions in a society are more important for the well-being and survival of society than others. In order to ensure that the more competent members of society seek the more important positions and that they are willing to undergo long and arduous training, it is necessary for those positions to provide sufficient rewards in the form of wealth, status, honor, and power. Accordingly, doctors earn more than garbage collectors.

This notion that social stratification is functional has been subject to considerable criticism. Some sociologists have argued that Davis and Moore have provided an ideology in support of social inequality and not an explanation for the functional necessity of social stratification. The failure of communist societies, however, has validated Davis and Moore's perspective. Other critics question the functional necessity of wealth, honor, and power for professional athletes, movie stars, and musical performers. Still others suggest that the expenditure of resources to train for the highly rewarded positions tends to preserve the privileges of those who already have the resources. Thus, not only does the system exclude the have-nots, but it also limits the pool of the available talent, restricts competition, and favors the well-off.

Key Concept: the functions of stratification

In a previous paper some concepts for handling the phenomena of social inequality were presented. In the present paper a further step in stratification theory is undertaken—an attempt to show the relationship between stratification and the rest of the social order. Starting from the proposition that no society is "classless," or unstratified, an effort is made to explain, in functional terms, the universal necessity which calls forth stratification in any social system. Next, an attempt is made to explain the roughly uniform distribution of prestige as between the major types of positions in every society. Since, however, there occur between one society and another great differences in the degree and kind of stratification, some attention is also given to the varieties of social inequality and the variable factors that give rise to them.

Clearly, the present task requires two different lines of analysis—one to understand the universal, the other to understand the variable features of stratification. Naturally each line of inquiry aids the other and is indispensable, and in the treatment that follows the two will be interwoven, although, because of space limitations, the emphasis will be on the universals.

Throughout, it will be necessary to keep in mind one thing—namely, that the discussion relates to the system of positions, not to the individuals occupying those positions. It is one thing to ask why different positions carry different degrees of prestige, and quite another to ask how certain individuals get into those positions. Although, as the argument will try to show, both questions are related, it is essential to keep them separate in our thinking. Most of the literature on stratification has tried to answer the second question (particularly with regard to the ease or difficulty of mobility between strata) without tackling the first. The first question, however, is logically prior and, in the case of any particular individual or group, factually prior.

THE FUNCTIONAL NECESSITY
OF STRATIFICATION

Curiously, however, the main functional necessity explaining the universal presence of stratification is precisely the requirement faced by any society of placing and motivating individuals in the social structure. As a functioning mechanism a society must somehow distribute its members in social positions and induce them to perform the duties of these positions. It must thus concern itself with motivation at two different levels: to instill in the proper individuals the desire to fill certain positions, and, once in these positions, the desire to perform the duties attached to them. Even though the social order may be relatively static in form, there is a continuous process of metabolism as new individuals are born into it, shift with age, and die off. Their absorption into the positional system must somehow be arranged and motivated. This is true whether the system is competitive or non-competitive. A competitive system gives greater importance to the motivation to achieve positions, whereas a non-competitive system gives perhaps greater importance to the motivation to perform the duties of the positions; but in any system both types of motivation are required.

If the duties associated with the various positions were all equally pleasant to the human organism, all equally important to societal survival, and all equally in need of the same ability or talent, it would make no difference who got into which positions, and the problem of social placement would be greatly reduced. But actually it does make a great deal of difference who gets into which positions, not only because some positions are inherently more agreeable than others, but also because some require special talents or training and some are functionally more important than others. Also, it is essential that the duties of the positions be performed with the diligence that their importance requires. Inevitably, then, a society must have, first, some kind of rewards that it can use as inducements, and, second, some way of distributing these rewards differentially according to positions. The rewards and their distribution become a part of the social order, and thus give rise to stratification.

One may ask what kind of rewards a society has at its disposal in distributing its personnel and securing essential services. It has, first of all, the things that contribute to sustenance and comfort. It has, second, the things that contribute to humor and diversion. And it has, finally, the things that contribute to self-respect and ego expansion. The last, because of the peculiarly social character of the self, is largely a function of the opinion of others, but it nonetheless ranks in importance with the first two. In any social system all three kinds of rewards must be dispensed differentially according to positions.

In a sense the rewards are "built into" the position. They consist in the "rights" associated with the position, plus what may be called its accompaniments or perquisites. Often the rights, and sometimes the accompaniments, are functionally related to the duties of the position. (Rights as viewed by the incumbent are usually duties as viewed by other members of the community.) However, there may be a host of subsidiary rights and perquisites that are not essential to the function of the position and have only an indirect and symbolic connection with its duties, but which still may be of considerable importance in inducing people to seek the positions and fulfil the essential duties.

If the rights and perquisites of different positions in a society must be unequal, then the society must be stratified, because that is precisely what stratification means. Social inequality is thus an unconsciously evolved device by which societies insure that the most important positions are conscientiously filled by the most qualified persons. Hence every society, no matter how simple or complex, must differentiate persons in terms of both prestige and esteem, and must therefore possess a certain amount of institutionalized inequality.

It does not follow that the amount or type of inequality need be the same in all societies. This is largely a function of factors that will be discussed presently.

THE TWO DETERMINANTS
OF POSITIONAL RANK

Granting the general function that inequality subserves, one can specify the two factors that determine the relative rank of different positions. In general those positions convey the best reward, and hence have the highest rank, which (a) have the greatest importance for the society and (b) require the greatest training or talent. The first factor concerns function and is a matter of relative significance; the second concerns means and is a matter of scarcity.

Differential functional importance. Actually a society does not need to reward positions in proportion to their functional importance. It merely needs to give sufficient reward to them to insure that they will be filled competently. In other words, it must see that less essential positions do not compete successfully with more essential ones. If a position is easily filled, it need not be heavily rewarded, even though important. On the other hand, if it is important but hard to fill, the reward must be high enough to get it filled anyway. Functional importance is therefore a necessary but not a sufficient cause of high rank being assigned to a position.

Differential scarcity of personnel. Practically all positions, no matter how acquired, require some form of skill or capacity for performance. This is implicit in the very notion of position, which implies that the incumbent must, by virtue of his incumbency, accomplish certain things.

There are, ultimately, only two ways in which a person's qualifications come about: through inherent capacity or through training. Obviously, in concrete activities both are always necessary, but from a practical standpoint the scarcity may lie primarily in one or the other, as well as in both. Some positions require innate talents of such high degree that the persons who fill them are bound to be rare. In many cases, however, talent is fairly abundant in the population but the training process is so long, costly, and elaborate that relatively few can qualify. Modern medicine, for example, is within the mental capacity of most individuals, but a medical education is so burdensome and expensive that virtually none would undertake it if the position of the M.D. did not carry a reward commensurate with the sacrifice.

If the talents required for a position are abundant and the training easy, the method of acquiring the position may have little to do with its duties. There may be, in fact, a virtually accidental relationship. But if the skills required are scarce by reason of the rarity of talent or the costliness of training, the position, if functionally important, must have an attractive power that will draw the necessary skills in competition with other positions. This means, in effect, that the position must be high in the social scale—must command great prestige, high salary, ample leisure, and the like.

How variations are to be understood. In so far as there is a difference between one system of stratification and another, it is attributable to whatever factors affect the two determinants of differential reward—namely, functional importance and scarcity of personnel. Positions important in one society may not be important in another, because the conditions faced by the societies, or their degree of internal development, may be different. The same conditions, in turn, may affect the question of scarcity; for in some societies the stage of development, or the external situation, may wholly obviate the necessity of certain kinds of skill or talent. Any particular system of stratification, then, can be understood as a product of the special conditions affecting the two aforementioned grounds of differential reward.

Kingsley Davis and Wilbert E. Moore

The Inequality Express

Barry Bluestone is a crusader for greater economic justice. The titles of two of his books exhibit some of his major concerns: *The Deindustrialization of America: Plant Closings, Community Abandonment, and the Dismantling of Basic Industry,* coauthored with Bennett Harrison (Basic Books, 1984), and *Low Wages and the Working Poor,* coauthored with William M. Murphy and Mary H. Stevenson (University of Michigan Institute of Labor & Industrial Relations, 1973).

While the last three decades have not been good to the average American worker, they have been good to top management and the rich. As a result, income inequality has increased. Bluestone is very concerned about this trend and tries to explain it in an effort to change it in the following selection from "The Inequality Express," which was published in Robert Kuttner's edited book *Ticking Time Bombs* (New Press, 1996). Bluestone identifies 10 possible causes of income inequality and concludes that they all contributed to it. His conclusion, which deeply distresses him, is that "every major economic trend in the U.S. contributes to growing inequality largely linked to merit. None of these trends shows the least sign of weakening."

In a section of the original article not reprinted here, Bluestone examines policy solutions to the inequality problem. He argues that the current search for solutions is limited to education and training, restricting most immigration to highly skilled immigrants, and traditional tax and transfer policies. He concludes that although these policies may help, they will not be enough. He instead proposes increasing the minimum wage, instituting labor law reform that would make it easier for unions to organize workers, and adopting progressive industrial and trade policies that allow selective forms of government interventions to temporarily protect American workers. Although these changes would be difficult to achieve while the Republicans control Congress, Bluestone cites analyses that suggest that they could work without precipitating the dire consequences that their opponents fear.

Bluestone is the Frank L. Boyden Professor of Political Economy at the University of Massachusetts in Boston, Massachusetts. His research interests include labor studies, domestic economic development, and income distribution. In addition to his books, he has published several articles in *The American Prospect.*

Key Concept: income inequality

*I*n his 1958 book, *The Rise of the Meritocracy, 1870–2033*, British sociologist Michael Young predicted that growing inequality in Britain's income distribution would spark a great populist rebellion in the year 2034. As British society moved closer to realizing the ideal of equal opportunity, Young wrote, it would also abandon any pretense of equal outcome: Each individual's socioeconomic status would depend less on lineage, family connections, and political influence, and more on intelligence, education, experience, and effort. Outright racial and gender discrimination and iniquitous privilege would be gone; inequality based on merit would take their place. The victims of this new inequality—those who were once protected by good union wages, civil service status, or seniority—would then take to the barricades.

We haven't seen any such revolution yet, but the rest of Young's prophecy today seems uncomfortably prescient. Virtually every number cruncher who has perused contemporary income data from the United States and the United Kingdom reports three clearly defined trends, each consistent with Young's forecast. First, the distribution of earnings in both countries increasingly reflects the distribution of formal education in the workforce. Second, the gap in earnings between the well educated and the not-so-well educated is steadily increasing. And finally, the real standard of living of a large proportion of the workforce—particularly those with less than a college degree—has steadily and sharply declined.

Universal acceptance of these trends has not, however, led to any agreement about their source. Some scholars emphasize increasing demand for skills in a high-technology economy. Others claim globalization of the economy has thrown workers in high-wage countries into competition with workers in low-wage ones. Still others indict deindustrialization, the decline of unions, rising immigration, and the proliferation of winner-take-all labor markets. This lack of consensus about causes has produced a lack of consensus about remedies.

Here we will attempt to solve the mystery of rising wage inequality, and in so doing consider what might be done to stymie it. The best primer for this exercise is Agatha Christie's *Murder on the Orient Express.*

MERIT OR MARKET?

When Young penned his satire, there appeared little reason to heed his warning. In the immediate postwar period, while Europe and the United States were enjoying the heady days of rapid growth, economic expansion almost always spawned greater equality. Class warfare was giving way to an implicit and generally peaceful social contract. The big trade-off between equality and growth so elegantly detailed by the American economist Arthur Okun seemed to hold more true in theory than in practice. In the U.S., real average weekly earnings would grow by 60 percent between 1947 and 1973. Median family income literally doubled. And over the same period, personal wages and family incomes became tangibly more equal, not less. Along with growth and greater equality, poverty declined across the nation. Those at the bottom of the distribution gained more—on a percentage basis—than those at the top. The higher wages of unionized workers did not come at the expense of other workers' living standards. If anything, the rising wages of higher-paid labor were extracted from the profits that traditionally went to the wealthy.

There is little dispute that by 1973 this trend had come to an end. Inequality actually rose, especially during the 1980s. Many initially blamed a slowdown in overall economic growth. But the expansion of the economy after the 1980–82 recession suggested a new dynamic at work: Faster growth no longer reduced inequality or did much to increase the earnings of those at the bottom of the skill ladder. Wage dispersion returned to levels not seen since before the 1960s. By the late 1980s, family income inequality was higher than at the end of World War II.

Wage dispersion, of course, is not the only source of economic inequality. Another source is demographic trends, such as the simultaneous rise in the number of dual income couples and single-parent families. The tremendous increase during the 1980s in non-wage sources of income for the well-to-do—interest, dividends, rent, and capital gains—plays an important role as well. But whatever role these other causes may play, changes in the distribution of wages and salaries are clearly a primary factor in rising inequality.

Racial and gender discrimination continue to be the basis of large earnings differences. However, as the influence of more virulent prejudices has declined in the labor market, differences in education and skill have had a greater impact on wages. One manifestation of this trend is the increasing wage ratio of college-educated workers to high school dropouts. In 1963, the mean annual earnings of those with four years of college or more stood at just over twice (2.11 times) the mean annual earnings of those who had not completed high school. By 1979, this ratio had increased to 2.39. This was but a harbinger of things to come. By 1987, the education-to-earnings ratio had skyrocketed to nearly three to one (2.91). The trend continues today.

In fact, the entire pattern of wage growth during the 1980s reflects a remarkable labor market "twist" tied to schooling. During this decade, the average real wage of male high school dropouts fell by over 18 percent, while male high school graduates suffered nearly a 13 percent real earnings loss. At the other end of the distribution, men who completed at least a master's degree emerged as the only real winners. Their earnings rose by more than 9 percent. Note that even men who had attended college without graduating saw a serious erosion in their earning power. And men who completed college discovered that their undergraduate degrees merely served to prevent a decline in inflation-adjusted wages....

THE ECONOMISTS' LINEUP

To explain the crisis, economists have offered up ten suspects:

SUSPECT ONE: TECHNOLOGY Robert Lawrence of Harvard's John F. Kennedy School of Government and Paul Krugman, now at Stanford University, are the leading advocates of this position. They believe that the new information technologies skew the earnings distribution by placing an extraordinary premium on skilled labor while reducing the demand, and hence the wage, for those of lesser skill. This, they contend, is about all you need to explain current earnings trends.

The problem is that no one has any direct measure of the skill content of technology. Proving this hypothesis would require proving not just skill-biased technological change but also a tremendous acceleration in new technology during the 1980s. After all, at least some level of technological change occurred in earlier decades without such an adverse impact on earnings equality. What's so different about technology in the 1980s and 1990s? According to David Howell (see "The Skills Myth," *Ticking Time Bombs* [1996]), and Lawrence Mishel and Jared Bernstein in an Economic Policy Institute working paper, there is little evidence that the pace of innovation—the speed at which new machines are brought to factories and new products are developed—was any faster than during the 1960s and 1970s. Most businesses are not introducing technology that requires vastly improved skill. Many are simply paying less for the same skills they have been using all along while others are hiring better educated workers at lower wage rates to do the work previously relegated to lesser-educated employees.

SUSPECT TWO: THE SERVICE-BASED ECONOMY   Other researchers, including George Borjas of the University of California at San Diego, have argued that a primary suspect is deindustrialization—the shift of jobs from goods-producing sectors to the service sector. In previous writings, I have estimated that between 1963 and 1987 the earnings ratio between college graduates and high school dropouts working in the goods-producing sector (mining, construction, and manufacturing) increased from 2.11 to 2.42—a jump of 15 percent. In the service sector, however, the education-to-earnings ratio mushroomed from 2.20 to 3.52—a 60 percent increase. All of the employment growth in the economy during the 1980s came in the services sector, where wages were polarizing between high school dropouts and college graduates four times faster than the goods-producing industries. Hence, this could explain at least part of the dramatic increase in earnings inequality.

SUSPECT THREE: DEREGULATION   Government deregulation of the airlines, trucking and telecommunications industries very likely has produced the same effect. In each of these industries, intense competition from new non-union, low-wage entrants, such as the short-lived People Express in the airline industry, forced existing firms to extract large wage concessions from their employees to keep from going bankrupt. How much this has contributed to overall earnings inequality remains an open question.

SUSPECT FOUR: DECLINING UNIONIZATION   Unions have historically negotiated wage packages that narrow earnings differentials. They have tended to improve wages the most for workers with modest educations. As Richard Freeman of Harvard and a number of other economists have noted, the higher rate of union membership is one of the reasons for the smaller dispersion of wages found in manufacturing. That unions have made only modest inroads into the service economy may explain in part why earnings inequality in this sector outstrips inequality in the goods-producing sector.

SUSPECT FIVE: DOWNSIZING   The restructuring of corporate enterprise toward lean production and the destruction of internal job ladders as firms rely more heavily on part-time, temporary, and leased employees is still another suspect in this mystery, according to Bennett Harrison of Carnegie Mellon. The new enterprise regime creates what labor economists call "segmented" labor force of insiders and outsiders whose job security and earnings potential can differ markedly.

SUSPECT SIX: WINNER-TAKE-ALL LABOR MARKETS   The heightened competitive market, which forces firms toward lean production, may also, according to Robert Frank and Philip Cook, be creating a whole new structure of free-agency, "winner-take-all" labor markets. As Frank has explained ("Talent and the Winner-Take-All Society," *The American Prospect*, Spring 1994, No. 17), in winner-take-all markets, "a handful of top performers walk away with the lion's share of total rewards." The difference between commercial success and failure in such markets may depend on just a few "star" performers—in movies the director and leading actor or actress; in the O. J. Simpson trial the conduct of just one or two trial attorneys. Given the high stakes involved in a multimillion dollar movie project or a murder trial involving a well-to-do client, investors are willing to pay a bundle to make sure they employ the "best in the business."

Today, the fields of law, journalism, consulting, investment banking, corporate management, design, fashion, and even academia are generating payoff structures that once were common only in the entertainment and professional sports industries. Just a handful of Alan Dershowitzes, Michael Milkens, and Michael Eisners can have a sizeable impact on the dispersion of wages in each of their occupations. There is considerable evidence that inequality is not only rising across education groups but within them, very likely reflecting such winner-take-all dynamics.

SUSPECT SEVEN: TRADE   Even more fundamental to the recent restructuring of the labor market—and a likely proximate cause of deindustrialization, deunionization, lean production, and perhaps even the free-agency syndrome—is the expansion of unfettered global trade. According to trade theory, increased trade alone is sufficient—*without* any accompanying multinational capital investment or low-wage worker immigration—to induce the wages of similarly skilled workers to equalize across trading countries. Economists call this dynamic "factor price equalization." As the global economy moves toward free trade, lower transportation costs, better communications, and the same "best practice" production techniques available to all countries, factor price equalization is likely to occur.

Unfortunately, in a world like ours where there is a plentiful supply of unskilled labor juxtaposed to a continued relative scarcity of well-educated workers, this "price equalization" *within* skill categories leads to a "wage polarization" *between* skill categories. The gap between the compensation of low-skilled workers and high-skilled workers everywhere will tend to grow.

According to the well-respected trade theorist Edward Leamer of the University of California at Los Angeles, freer trade will ultimately reduce the wages of less-skilled U.S. workers by about a thousand dollars a year, partly as a result of NAFTA [North American Free Trade Agreement]. If factor price equalization is a chief source of wage dispersion today, just consider the implications when China and India with their immense unskilled workforces enter fully into global markets.

SUSPECT EIGHT: CAPITAL MOBILITY   Freer trade generally provides for the unrestricted movement of investment capital across borders. This inevitably accelerates the process of growing wage inequality. Modern transportation and communications technologies, combined with fewer government restrictions on foreign capital investment, have led to increased multinational capital flows between countries. To the extent that companies move to take advantage of cheaper unskilled labor, transnational investment adds to the effective supply of low-skilled workers available to American firms, thus reinforcing factor price equalization.

SUSPECT NINE: IMMIGRATION   Increased immigration potentially has the same effect, if a disproportionate share of new immigrants enters with limited skills and schooling. This is true at least for legal immigrants. The typical legal immigrant in the U.S. today has nearly a year less schooling than native citizens. Undocumented immigrants surely have even less. As such, while many immigrants to the U.S. come here with excellent education and skills, there is little doubt that the large number of Central American, Caribbean, and Southeast Asians seeking refuge in this country has had the unfortunate side effect of at least temporarily boosting the supply of low-skill workers seeking jobs.

SUSPECT TEN: TRADE DEFICITS   The trade gap has contributed to the decline in those sectors of the economy that have in the past helped to restrain earnings inequality. Moreover, trade data indicate that the import surplus itself is disproportionately composed of products made by low-skilled and modestly skilled labor. This boosts the effective supply of workers at the bottom of the education-to-earnings distribution and thus depresses their relative wages.

WHODUNNIT?

Thus, in our rogue's gallery we have ten suspects: skill-based technological change, deindustrialization, industry deregulation, the decline of unions, lean production, winner-take-all labor markets, free trade, transnational capital mobility, immigration, and a persistent trade deficit. Quantitatively parsing out the relative impact of all of these forces on wage distribution is fraught with enormous difficulty. Still, Richard Freeman and Lawrence Katz have attempted to do something like this, at least for the wage gap between men with a college degree and those with a high school diploma.

TABLE 1

Sources of Inequality

Factors responsible for the increase in the male college/high school wage differential during the 1980s

Technological Change	7%–25%
Deindustrialization	25%–33%
Deunionization	20%
Trade and Immigration	15%–20%
Trade Deficit	15%

Source: Richard B. Freeman and Lawrence F. Katz, "Rising Wage Inequality: The United States vs. Other Advanced Countries," in Richard Freeman, ed., *Working Under Different Rules*. Russel Sage, 1994.

What do these results suggest? If the Freeman and Katz estimates are in the right ballpark, the answer to our mystery is the same denouement as Agatha Christie's in *Murder on the Orient Express*. They all did it. Every major economic trend in the U.S. contributes to growing inequality largely linked to merit. None of these trends shows the least sign of weakening.

Each trend reflects the growth of market forces and the decline of institutional constraints on competition. This was Young's essential message more than 30 years ago. Increased reliance on domestic market dynamics as the sole determinant of earnings produces inequality. Heightened competition within these markets, as a consequence of fuller integration into the global economy, exacerbates this wage dispersion. While it may be sinister, there is nothing conspiratorial about this phenomenon. It is embedded in the very nature of laissez-faire market dynamics. For this reason, meritocratic inequality is much harder to remedy than overt forms of discrimination based on race and sex.

7.4 DANIEL D. HUFF

Upside-Down Welfare

One sociological theory that all sociologists accept is that the upper groups in a society dominate the political system, make the rules of society, and have a major influence on its policies. Therefore, sociologists expect that government "welfare" will be more generous to the rich and the middle class than to the poor; after all, the poor do not have much influence on policies. Of course, welfare for the well off is not called "welfare," which has negative connotations for its recipients. It is called "tax breaks," including tax deductions for mortage interest payments, subsidized loans, free or subsidized education, subsidies to businesses, and many thousands of special arrangements to powerful interests. Some of these forms of welfare for the better off may have positive impacts on the nation as a whole, but most of them clearly help the few at the expense of the whole. They are a blemish on the reputation of America as a just and equitable society, and it is the job of sociology to expose these transfers from the less well off to the better off and to explain how the stratification system produces these results.

The selection that follows is from "Upside-Down Welfare," *Public Welfare* (Winter 1992). In it, Daniel D. Huff, a professor of social work at Boise State University in Idaho, examines the upside-down welfare system and even tries to quantify it. His quantification is incomplete, however, because much of the welfare for the better off is hidden and hard to trace. Furthermore, his classification scheme can be criticized by defenders of the current redistribution system. Nevertheless, most sociologists would support Huff's point that the welfare for the better off dwarfs the welfare for the poor.

Key Concept: gilded welfare, or welfare for the nonpoor

*A*t this writing George Bush's "kinder, gentler nation" is still rather callous. One in four of our nation's children is now born into poverty, up from one in five a decade ago. One in six has no health insurance. Following years of progress in preventing infant deaths, improvements in infant mortality have stopped; our rate is now worse than in nineteen other nations (a black baby born in Boston or Washington, D.C., is more likely to die before his or her first birthday than a baby born in Jamaica). Twenty million Americans remain hungry; a half million children malnourished. The average American's real wages have declined since 1980. For the poor and the near poor, the drop has been more severe. Meanwhile, the

share of household income of the richest fifth of the American population continues to rise. The gap between the two groups is now wider than at any time in the
last fifty years.

—Robert B. Reich
The Resurgent Liberal

The decade of the eighties was hard. For many of us who came of age
in the sixties and early seventies, watching low-income individuals and families lose most of the meager gains won during that now dim and distant past
has been frustrating. Not only have low-income people grown both in numbers
and proportion of population, but also those who now find themselves economically disadvantaged are predominantly women and children, with strong
representation from mentally ill and developmentally disabled people. Iron-
ically, those who should be the highest on any rational list of priorities for
government assistance are receiving the least.

Our conservative friends tell us that we are now spending more of our
national budget on welfare programs than at any time in our past. But how can
that be? How can poverty be growing—particularly among our most vulnerable populations—at the same time that we are spending hundreds of billions of
dollars for welfare?

The answer lies in our understanding of what social welfare is and who it
should help. In fact, we have developed a set of extremely elaborate programs
that are designed to shift income from one group of citizens to another, but
need is seldom a criterion for receiving benefits. Presently, we have three types
of welfare programs. First are the poverty programs, such as Food Stamps and
Aid to Families with Dependent Children (AFDC), which represent a relatively
small amount of money and are designed to serve only low-income people.

Second are those programs, such as Social Security and Medicare, whose
benefits serve mostly middle- and upper-income individuals. The third category of welfare is a newer set of programs designed to redistribute wealth to
American businesses. Unlike the traditional poverty programs, these "upside-
down welfare" programs are not customarily called "welfare." Many of their
benefits are funneled through obscure and "off-budget" devices that avoid the
scrutiny and debate that normally accompany implementation of more conventional welfare designs. Upside-down welfare represents an immense redistribution of our national wealth and explains why so little has been done for
low-income people over the past decade. While we have been redistributing
our nation's wealth through a variety of benefits, most of this money has not
gone to help poor people.

The upside-down welfare state is extensive and breaks naturally into two
different categories. First are those schemes primarily benefiting middle- and
upper-income persons. That system represents a "gilded" welfare state, which
provides the nonpoor with such benefits as low-cost government insurance for
their oceanside homes, tax breaks for their investments, subsidized medical
care, and supplemental retirement benefits. The second is reserved for corporations, rather than individuals, and provides a redistribution system that annually transfers billions of dollars from ordinary taxpayers to the richest and
largest corporations in America—a welfare program for Wall Street.

TABLE 1

Welfare Spending by Program

Welfare Programs for Individuals	Amount (in billions)
Means-Tested Poverty Programs	
Medicaid	$49
AFDC	17
SSI	13
Food Stamps	15
Other (loans, etc.)	24
Total	$117
Gilded Welfare Middle-Class Programs	
Social Security	247
Medicare	104
Other retirement programs	62
Miscellaneous benefits	50
Tax expenditures	300
Fringe benefits (health & retirement)	385
Total	$1,148
Grand Total	$1,265

Source: U.S. Budget, 1990; Statistical Abstracts of the United States, 1990

WALL STREET WELFARE AND BUSINESS SUBSIDIES

I live in a Northwestern city that is a hub for a large agricultural area. My rural neighbors are among the first to shout about too much government spending and are particularly angered when some big-city liberal advocates increased budgets for poverty programs. As a rule, my neighbors are anti-government in attitude and intolerant of what they call "government handouts." In spite of these attitudes, my farmer friends receive immense benefits from a wide variety of government programs.

In this area of the country, almost all the farming is done under irrigation. Water is provided to farmers by the government at a rate so low that the farmers' water bills represent only a fraction of the cost of water usage. For every dollar spent by the Bureau of Reclamation to provide water, the farmer pays the government 10 cents. During the course of the year, my farmer friends typically take advantage of subsidized loans to purchase various necessities and subsidized insurance to protect them from the perils of pests and weather. When harvest season arrives, the local agricultural community lines up for government loans on their crops—loans they have to repay only if the crop values are greater than the so-called target prices set by the U.S. Department of Agriculture (USDA).

Many of the farms in this area are devoted to growing the sugar beet, an ugly plant that only reluctantly surrenders its sugar after extensive and expensive processing. The sole reason there is any market at all for these beets rests on a government trade policy that does not allow imports of cheaper cane sugar. This indirect subsidy to the sugar beet growers and processors costs consumers $3 billion a year.

Government programs designed to increase the income of the nation's farms cost approximately $25 billion a year. USDA estimated that fewer than five million Americans lived on farms in 1990. We disburse $25 billion a year for five million people on farms, while spending only $15 billion a year to support 11 million women and children on AFDC. Paradoxically, most of these funds never even reach the poorer segments of rural America. Clifton Luttrell, agricultural economist for the CATO Institute, estimates that less than 20 percent of farm subsidies trickle down to the poorest farmers. He explains that if the real purpose of farm subsidies is to eliminate farm poverty, the government could send every low-income farmer in America a check of sufficient size to pull him or her out of poverty for a cost of $2 billion to $3 billion. Clearly, our current farm programs are not a very efficient means of helping the country's poorer farmers.

Unfortunately, the upside-down welfare that benefits farmers is only a small illustration of an extensive system. Local manufacturers wishing to sell their wares abroad to sometimes unstable and unreliable governments arrange for government loans at rates far below those available at commercial banks. The source of these loans, the Export-Import Bank (Ex-Im Bank), has been accused of falsifying its books in an attempt to make this subsidy appear smaller than it really is. An example of what one observer termed "creative bookkeeping" was listing loans to prerevolutionary China as fully collectible. In 1989, House Banking Committee Chair Henry Gonzales suggested that the Ex-Im Bank was so awash in red ink that even if it were liquidated, it would leave a shortfall of $4 billion to $6 billion—a loss that would be passed directly to American taxpayers.

Much larger subsidies are received by the defense industry, which since World War II has enjoyed the free use of more than $100 billion worth of plants and machinery owned by the U.S. Department of Defense and has accepted gifts of more than $10 billion worth of shops and equipment.

The savings and loan (S&L) debacle is a more current example of upside-down welfare. The General Accounting Office now estimates that the financial rescue of the S&L industry will cost the American taxpayer $500 billion. This gigantic public relief program for the S&L industry is necessary because of deregulation policies that enriched a small number of investors and developers in a handful of states. Taxpayers from all over the country will end up paying

FIGURE 1

Welfare Spending for Individuals

Daniel D. Huff

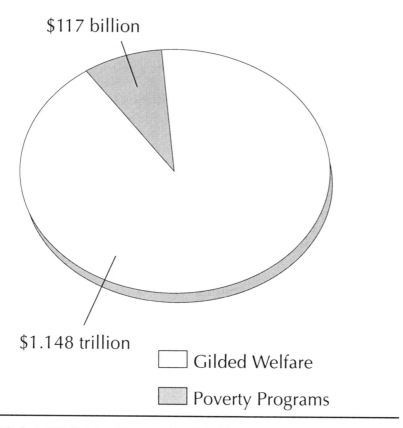

Total = $1.265 trillion

$117 billion

$1.148 trillion

☐ Gilded Welfare

▨ Poverty Programs

Source: U.S. Budget, 1990; Statistical Abstracts of the United States, 1990

the bill for what amounts to one of the largest transfer-of-wealth programs in American history.

Corporate welfare programs represent a huge income redistribution system, providing American business interests with more than $200 billion a year.

GILDED WELFARE: PUBLIC ASSISTANCE FOR THE MIDDLE AND UPPER CLASSES

I have a wealthy friend who is adamant in his denunciation of government handouts. Programs for low-income people earn his special disdain, for he believes such policies sap incentive and subsidize immoral behavior. He seems to harbor no such fears for his own set of personal subsidies, however, which are substantial. My comrade enjoys flying his own airplane at our local airport, which happily provides him services at fees representing only a fraction of their true costs. His beachfront vacation home is located in an area that is so frequently exposed to heavy weather that he cannot obtain private insurance and instead is forced to use subsidized government insurance. My friend spends many of his summer weekends camping in a neighboring national park where the fees he pays represent about one-third the actual costs of maintaining the park and its facilities. His considerable use of electricity, both at home and at his place of business, is subsidized through our regional power supplier at rates approximately one-half of those paid by consumers on the East Coast.

Needless to say, my friend is hardly alone. Most of us view our personal subsidies as important benefits and just compensation for the taxes we pay. Unfortunately, while the middle- and upper-income groups have become sophisticated in lobbying and advocating for their welfare benefits, low-income Americans have proven to be less capable at seizing their share of government benefits. This fact is evident if we examine two of the largest categories of the current federal budget, Social Security and tax expenditures.

Social Security represents annual allocations of more than $240 billion. Although one might imagine that the bulk of those dollars are divided among relatively low-income retirees, in fact in 1988 only 20 percent of Social Security benefits went to recipients with incomes less than 200 percent of the poverty level. Although Social Security is commonly seen as an insurance program, current Social Security benefits are heavily subsidized by current workers and are two to five times greater than those of comparable private retirement programs.

Social Security, therefore, is an inelegant solution to poverty, since 96 percent of the approximately 35 million low-income Americans are not elderly. The total spending for all the programs specifically designated for low-income people of all ages is only about $100 billion, while we spend $250 billion on retirees. According to Alice Munnell of the Brookings Institute, sending every American in poverty a check large enough to raise his or her income above the poverty level would cost only $130 billion to $160 billion.

In spite of Social Security's beneficence, it is not very effective as an antipoverty program. Even staunch advocates of the system, like policy analysts Merton and Joan Bernstein, admit that although more than two-thirds of Social Security recipients had incomes higher than 125 percent of the poverty level, 27 percent—almost one-third—of all beneficiaries collect so little in benefits that they are forced to live in poverty. The record is even more disheartening for minorities. In 1990, more than 40 percent of all black women currently receiving Social Security benefits were living below the poverty line.

The system of tax breaks for individuals highly favors the rich. Tax breaks —or, in current budgetary parlance, "tax expenditures"—represent uncollected revenues and are every bit as real as actual expenditures. Not collecting taxes has the same fiscal impact as a grant or subsidy, with the obvious advantage that tax expenditures are "off budget" and not subject to the same scrutiny as direct spending. Uncollected personal taxes made possible by the assorted tax breaks written into the 1986 tax reform bill came to a staggering $281 billion per year in 1990. Obviously, the bulk of savings generated by those tax breaks is distributed among the affluent. In 1990, *Wall Street Journal* reporters David Wessel and Jeffrey Birnbaum estimated that three-quarters of all itemized deductions are taken by individuals earning $50,000 or more per year. Half the benefits from the interest deductions on mortgages went to the wealthiest 10 percent of the population, and 80 percent of the benefits claimed through the deductibility of state and local taxes goes to individuals with annual incomes of more than $30,000.

The $90 billion a year in tax breaks represented by the exemption granted to employer-paid health and retirement plans represents a double inequity. Not only do lower-income workers benefit far less from the tax savings, but they enjoy coverage from these programs at proportionally lower rates than do upper-income workers. According to a study conducted by the U.S. Agency for Health Care Policy and Research, lower-income workers are twice as unlikely to have health insurance than their more affluent colleagues. Kevin Phillips in his book, *The Politics of Rich and Poor,* notes that only four in 10 American workers even have retirement plans.

Even the ostensibly benign private charity system has been accused of unfairly disbursing its largess. Most of the more than $100 billion collected every year by private nonprofits is spent on activities that only remotely affect lower-income Americans. According to Lester Solomon's Urban Institute study on private nonprofits, less than $22 billion annually is earmarked for social services, with the bulk of philanthropic spending directed to such enterprises as private hospitals, preparatory schools, universities, and a variety of cultural activities. Even money spent on social services is, upon closer inspection, suspect. The highly visible United Way programs have come under attack from such organizations as the United Black Fund for underwriting mostly middle class and white "charities," such as the Boy Scouts, the Young Men's Christian Association, and the Red Cross.

Altogether, Americans spend more than a trillion dollars every year on welfare; but less than 10 percent of that is specifically earmarked for low-income people. The rest, such as Social Security, private charity, tax breaks, fringe benefits, and assorted subsidies for American businesses, benefit primarily those who are relatively well-to-do. Although nothing is inherently wrong or immoral about any individual component of this upside-down welfare, spending so much on the nonpoor while cutting poverty programs seems shamefully hypocritical at best, and at worst inimical to the nation's economic and social stability.

> So there is the fundamental paradox of the welfare state: that it is not built for the desperate, but for those who are already capable of helping themselves. As long as the illusion persists that the poor are merrily freeloading on the public dole, so long will the other America continue unthreatened. The truth, it must be understood, is the exact opposite. The poor get less out of the welfare state than any group in America.
>
> — Michael Harrington
> *The Other America*

CHAPTER 8 Views of the Top and the Bottom

8.1 MICHAEL USEEM

The Inner Circle

Ever since C. Wright Mills published *The Power Elite* in 1959, sociologists have paid close attention to elites: who are they, how do they function, and do they make the government serve their interests ahead of the public's interests? Mills theorized that important political decisions affecting the entire United States are made by top corporate, military, and political officials who interact socially and share common values and belief systems. Although Mills and others could plainly see that power was very unevenly distributed in society, there was little evidence that the economic elite were sufficiently united in their interests and actions to "govern." Now changes in the structure of corporate America have created the basis on which the corporate world can act collectively for its general interests. Michael Useem has identified these changes and analyzed their consequences for the corporate domination of the political system. In Mills's day the top managers ran the corporations and faced minimal challenges from stockholders and the board of directors that represented them. Because these managers had many conflicting interests, it was hard for them to act collectively, so Mills never firmly established his thesis. Since then, however, an increasing proportion of stocks have been acquired by institutional investors, and their holdings are large enough to give them some power over top management. As Useem points out, managerial capitalism is being transformed into institutional capitalism, and the latter is far easier to organize for the pursuit of the general interests of corporate capitalism than the former. Useem questions how harmful (or beneficial) the increased political power of the corporate world is to the public interest, because the inner circle of institutional capitalism enables it to act in concert. He observes that institutional capitalism seeks the curtailment of regulations and government interference in business, limitations on social programs, shrinking of the public sector, and the reduced influence of unions over government, all of which constitute an important part of Congress's program today.

Useem is a professor of sociology at the University of Pennsylvania. He has written a number of books on social movements and elites, including *Executive Defense* (Harvard University Press, 1993) and *Investor Capitalism: How Money Managers Are Changing the Face of Corporate America* (Basic Books, 1996). The following selection is excerpted from *The Inner Circle: Large Corporations and the Rise of Business Political Activity in the U.S. and U.K.* (Oxford University Press, 1984).

Key Concept: the inner circle and elites

ORGANIZING BUSINESS

This [selection] offers a new thesis concerning the nature of contemporary political activity by large business firms. I will argue that a politicized leading edge of the leadership of a number of major corporations has come to play a major role in defining and promoting the shared needs of large corporations in two of the industrial democracies, the United States and the United Kingdom. Rooted in intercorporate networks through shared ownership and directorship of large companies in both countries, this politically active group of directors and top managers gives coherence and direction to the politics of business. Most business leaders are not part of what I shall term here the *inner circle*. Their concerns extend little beyond the immediate welfare of their own firms. But those few whose positions make them sensitive to the welfare of a wide range of firms have come to exercise a voice on behalf of the entire business community.

Central members of the inner circle are both top officers of large firms and directors of several other large corporations operating in diverse environments. Though defined by their corporate positions, the members of the inner circle constitute a distinct, semi-autonomous network, one that transcends company, regional, sectoral, and other politically divisive fault lines within the corporate community.

The inner circle is at the forefront of business outreach to government, nonprofit organizations, and the public. Whether it be support for political candidates, consultation with the highest levels of the national administration, public defense of the "free enterprise system," or the governance of foundations and universities, this politically dominant segment of the corporate community assumes a leading role, and corporations whose leadership involves itself in this pan-corporate network assume their own distinct political role as well. Large companies closely allied to the highest circle are more active than other firms in promoting legislation favorable to all big business and in assuming a more visible presence in public affairs, ranging from philanthropy to local community service.

The inner circle has assumed a particularly critical role during the past decade. Evidence we shall examine indicates that the 1970s and early 1980s

186

Chapter 8
Views of the Top
and the Bottom

were a period of unprecedented expansion of corporate political activities, whether through direct subvention of candidates, informal lobbying at the highest levels of government, or formal access to governmental decision-making processes through numerous business-dominated panels created to advise government agencies and ministries. This political mobilization of business can be traced to the decline of company profits in both the United States and the United Kingdom and to heightened government regulation in America and labor's challenge of management prerogatives in Britain. As large companies have increasingly sought to influence the political process, the inner circle has helped direct their activities toward political ends that will yield benefits for all large firms, not just those that are most active. This select group of directors and senior managers has thus added a coherence and effectiveness to the political voice of business, one never before so evident. The rise to power of governments attentive to the voice of business, if not always responsive to its specific proposals, is, in part, a consequence of the mobilization of corporate politics during the past decade and the inner circle's channeling of this new energy into a range of organizational vehicles.

Both the emergence of the inner circle and the degree to which it has come to define the political interests of the entire business community are unforeseen consequences of a far-reaching transformation of the ways in which large corporations and the business communities are organized. In the early years of the rise of the modern corporation, self-made entrepreneurs were at the organizational helm, ownership was shared with, but limited to, kin and descendents, and the owning families merged into a distinct, intermarrying upper class. It was the era of family capitalism, and upper-class concerns critically informed business political activity. In time, however, family capitalism was slowly but inexorably pushed aside by the emergence of a new pattern of corporate organization and control—managerial capitalism. Business political activity increasingly came to address corporate, rather upper-class, agendas, as the corporation itself became the central organizing force. If family capitalism was at its height at the end of the nineteenth century and managerial capitalism was ascendent during the first half of the twentieth, both are now yielding in this era to institutional capitalism, a development dating to the postwar period and rapidly gaining momentum in recent decades. In the era of institutional capitalism, it is not only family or individual corporate interests that serve to define how business political activity is organized and expressed but rather concerns much more classwide—the shared interests and needs of all large corporations taken together. Increasingly a consciousness of a generalized corporate outlook shapes the content of corporate political action.

The large business communities in Britain and America have thus evolved, for the most part without conscious design, the means for aggregating and promoting their common interests. While government agencies add further coherence to the policies sought, the inner circle now serves to fashion, albeit in still highly imperfect ways, the main elements of public policies suited to serve the broader requirements of the entire corporate community. This conclusion is not in accord with predominant thinking, nor with those theories about business-government relations more fully described below. Of these, most fall into one of two opposing schools. According to the first, corporate leadership is presumed to be either too-little organized to act politically at all, or, as the second goes, so fully organized that it acts as a single, politically unified bloc. This book rejects both schools of thought and argues for a new perception, a new theory of the nature of the politics of big business in contemporary British and American society.

A new conception of the business firm is also needed. Most corporate business decisions are viewed, correctly, as a product of the internal logic of the firm. Yet when decisions are made on the allocation of company monies to political candidates, the direction of its philanthropic activities, and other forms of political outreach, an external logic is important as well. This is the logic of classwide benefits, involving considerations that lead to company decisions beneficial to all large companies, even when there is no discernible, direct gain for the individual firm. The inner circle is the carrier of this extracorporate logic; the strategic presence of its members in the executive suites of major companies allows it to shape corporate actions to serve the entire corporate community.

The power of the transcorporate network even extends into the selection of company senior managers. In considering an executive for promotion to the uppermost positions in a firm, the manager's reputation within the firm remains of paramount importance, but it is not the only reputation that has come to count. The executive's standing within the broader corporate community—as cultivated through successful service on the boards of several other large companies, leadership in major business associations, and the assumption of civic and public responsibilities—is increasingly a factor. Acceptance by the inner circle has thus become almost a prerequisite for accession to the stewardship of many of the nation's largest corporations. Our traditional conception of the firm must accordingly be modified. No longer is the large company an entirely independent actor, striving for its own profitable success without regard for how its actions are affecting the profitability of others. While it retains its independence in many areas of decision-making, its autonomy is compromised. And this is especially true for company actions targeted at improving the political environment. Through the agency of the inner circle, large corporations are now subject to a new form of collective political discipline by their corporate brethren.

Finally, our thinking about democratic politics in Britain and America requires revision as well. The theory of democratic political practice rests on the traditional assumption that individual voters, special-interest groups, and political parties are the fundamental building blocks of the political order. Yet individual action is increasingly structured and mobilized through large-scale institutions nominally apolitical in purpose. Large corporations, through their ability to expand, contract, or simply redefine employment opportunities, productive capacity, and other of society's resources have become among the most important of these large-scale institutions. When these corporations are feuding and atomized, their political impact tends to be inconsistent, at times contradictory, and thus neutralized. When less divided and better organized for collective action, however, they can be very effective in finding and promoting their shared concerns.

Certainly a common awareness among those with wealth, those with economic power, those with titles or in positions of authority has always existed. They have long shared the presumption that by virtue of ownership or perfor-

188

*Chapter 8
Views of the Top
and the Bottom*

mance they had the right to run their own firm or institution, and certainly to veto or compromise reform and other legislative measures aimed at undermining their ability to rule and protect their own organization. Notwithstanding the continuing jealousies between old company money and new corporate wealth, financiers and industrialists, self-made entrepreneurs and professional management cadres, among those at the very top there is now a far stronger sense of an imperative to act together. Rather than defensively protecting only their own company's interests, those in the highest circles of corporate leadership now share a clearer understanding that what divides them is modest compared to what separates them from those who would presume to exercise power over economic decisions from bases other than those of private economic power.

So while a sense of class affinity based on company stewardship can hardly be said to be new, the strength of the bond has increased, and a select circle of those in corporate power are now far more willing to work toward goals that serve all large companies. Through the advancement of consensually determined positions on the issues of the day, this community of corporate leaders has been able to acquire a special role in the democratic process. While voter preferences and prejudices have not suddenly become impotent and special-interest lobbying remains decisive on many issues, a vastly powerful new institution, with organizational skills to match its economic power, has joined the political fray....

Principles of Social Organization

To facilitate our inquiry, it may be useful to describe several competing forms of internal social organization of the business community. In both countries, the organization is simultaneously structured by a number of distinct principles, of which three are of overriding importance. Each contains a fundamentally different implication for the ways in which business enters the political arena.

The *upper-class principle* asserts that the first and foremost defining element is a social network of established wealthy families, sharing a distinct culture, occupying a common social status, and unified through intermarriage and common experience in exclusive settings, ranging from boarding schools to private clubs....

The *corporate principle* of organization suggests by contrast that the primary defining element is the corporation itself. Location is determined not by patrician lineage, but by the individual's responsibilities in the firm and the firm's position in the economy. Coordinates for the latter include such standard dimensions as company size, market power, sector, organizational complexity, source of control, financial performance, and the like. Upper-class allegiances are largely incidental to this definition of location, for the manager is locked into corporate-determined priorities no matter what family loyalties may still be maintained....

The *classwide principle* resides on still different premises about the main elements defining the social organization of the corporate community. In this framework, location is primarily determined by position in a set of interrelated, quasi-autonomous networks encompassing virtually all large corporations. Acquaintanceship circles, interlocking directorates, webs of interfirm ownership, and major business associations are among the central strands of these networks. Entry into the transcorporate networks is contingent on successfully reaching the executive suite of some large company, and it is further facilitated by old school ties and kindred signs of a proper breeding. But corporate credentials and upper-class origins are here subordinated to a distinct logic of classwide organization.

The relative importance of these three principles in shaping the social organizations of the business community has a major bearing on a fundamental question of corporate politics in both countries: To what extent does the corporate community formulate and promote public policies that are in accord with the broader, longer-range concerns of all large corporations? Neither the upper-class principle nor the corporate principle would suggest that the interest aggregation could be effectively achieved, for neither principle organizes company interests in a suitable fashion. The upper class may inveigh against confiscatory inheritance policies, burdensome capital-gains taxes, and state-mandated invasions of its club sanctuaries, but a positive, detailed program for economic growth and profit expansion will not be a foremost priority....

Upper-class, corporate, and classwide principles of social organization distinctively shape the basic thrust of business political activity. Thus, their relative importance is of fundamental interest for comprehending contemporary corporate activity—from the orchestration of public opinion on behalf of "reindustrialization" to renewed assaults on organized labor and government regulation. The underlying theme of the present analysis is that the relative balance long ago shifted in the U.S. from upper-class to corporate principle, and that American business is currently undergoing still another transformation, this time from corporate to classwide principles of organization. By the middle of this century, family capitalism had largely given way to managerial capitalism, and in recent decades managerial capitalism itself has been giving way to institutional capitalism, bringing us into an era in which classwide principles are increasingly dominant....

INNER CIRCLE ORGANIZATION

Rarely, if ever, does big business act collectively to promote its political interests, classwide or otherwise, for as a bloc it lacks even the most rudimentary means for identifying and agreeing on its common needs, let alone a vehicle for pursuing them. The inner circle, by contrast, is opportunely situated to overcome these lacks.... [I]t possesses the intercorporate connections and organizational capacities to transcend the parochial interests of single companies and sectors, and to offer a more integrated vision of the broader, longer-term needs of business....

190

*Chapter 8
Views of the Top
and the Bottom*

Reform, regulation, and state intervention are less onerous to those central to the transcorporate network than to those on its margins. Interviewing 130 business leaders in the early 1970s, for instance, Allen Barton found that those most active in the major business associations, such as the Committee for Economic Development and the Council on Foreign Relations, and those most identified by other leaders as key figures in the inner world of national policy formulation, hold distinct political outlooks: Keynesian economic policies and reformist social policies are seen far more favorably. For example, those most active in the business associations and most identified as opinion leaders were more opposed than other business managers to the position, "In times of recession, government spending should be held down to avoid a deficit." They were more favorable toward such positions as "The federal government should support the creation of jobs in the public sector for those to whom the private sector does not provide employment," and a plan then being promoted by the White House to rationalize the welfare system. In my own interviews, similar elements of moderation were evident on the single, most-pressing issue then, the rise of government regulation. The one-company managers were adamant in their opposition to the actions and policies of the cross-industry regulatory agencies. Those traveling the inner circle were no less opposed, for they too were cognizant of the costs to their firms. Yet they were less certain that wholesale dismantling was the proper solution. Public opinion could be inflamed, they feared, and they were aware that environmental, consumer, women's, and labor groups had sufficient power to require a compromising attitude in any case, not the issuance of non-negotiable demands.

Historians of American business have often noted that large corporation leaders, or some fraction of them, have frequently adopted a more "progressive" attitude toward unions, labor legislation, and social reform. Sometimes termed "corporate liberalism," this attitude is rooted not in a commitment to reform, nor in an enlightened acceptance of labor and government opponents, but rather in the recognition that the entire business community and the future of the private economy will best prosper if it assumes a posture of compromise. It is this rejection of a rigid opposition to everything that organized labor and government programs represent, an embracing of that complex of attitudes perhaps best termed "corporate liberalism," that distinguishes the inner circle's views. . . .

Institutional Capitalism and Classwide Politics

The rise of institutional capitalism in the U.S. and U.K. contributed to the rise of more conservative political climates in the early 1980s. Though the new corporate political activity was not decisive, its significance should not be underestimated. A central objective of the business political mobilization on both sides of the Atlantic was to restore company profits to levels of an earlier decade. In pursuing "reindustrialization" and "recapitalizing capitalism," government spending was targeted as the chief impediment to such prosperity. In the American case, excessive government restraint on business decisions was also named as a critical target; in Britain, government failure to resist and control organized labor was identified by business as another top priority. With differing emphasis both business communities pointed toward government reductions in social spending, the dismantling of agencies that regulate business, and the scaling back of programs beneficial to labor.

The electoral success and political thrust of the Thatcher and Reagan governments were in no small part products of this business venture into politics. Both governments did sharply reduce controllable social spending, lift controls on business, and cut back unemployment benefits, welfare and other programs of special interest to labor. The squeeze on the private sector was thus translated into a shrinking public sector, with the exception of military spending. The decline of the welfare state, the slowing of social spending, and the end of activist government in the U.S. and U.K. were thus not simply, and indeed not largely, a product of spontaneous public disaffection with the socially interventionist state. Nor were they the result of an unarticulated, inchoate response to the chronic stagnation of the "British disease" and its American strain. Nor did they derive from an unorganized aggregation of business protest against the seemingly antibusiness posture of the national government.

Rather, the rise of the new conservative forces that were among the pillars of the Republican and Conservative governments was a product of the formation of both sides of the Atlantic of informal and formal organizational networks linking together most large corporations. These networks facilitated the political mobilization of business—by helping business to identify the public policies most needed for its aggregate welfare, and by helping it to express its consensual preferences in electoral campaigns, government lobbying, and other forms of political intervention.

REFERENCES

Barton, Allen H. 1982. "Determinants of attitudes in the American business elite." Paper presented at the World Congress of Sociology, Mexico City.

Poverty's Children: Growing Up in the South Bronx

The following selection is from Jonathan Kozol's "Poverty's Children: Growing Up in the South Bronx," *The Progressive* (October 1995). The poverty and deprivation that is described herein are truly awesome. How this reality can be part of a society in which many have overwhelming power and financial resources is somewhat of a mystery. It can be partly explained by an analysis of laissez-faire capitalism, which lets the rich get richer and the poor get poorer, but which does not account for the failure of the moral system to alter this picture. The Judeo-Christian heritage that America lays claim to obligates its followers to care for the poor, vulnerable, and needy. Sociologists expect the behavior of most people to fall far short of the ideal, but some realities like the ones described here are so bad as to shock even sociologists. This is why Kozol journeyed into the South Bronx: to cry out for these people and to disturb us. Kozol seems to be calling for people to return to their ideals through the stories he tells. He lets the people he meets speak for themselves so that we can see that they are just like us but in different circumstances. Sociology is sophisticated argument, intelligent use and interpretation of numbers, and stories that teach. The arguments and analyses without the stories cannot explain social life nor move us sufficiently to change what needs to be changed. Perhaps one reason why these conditions exist is that so few researchers include people like Cliffie and Mrs. Washington in the numbers with which they work.

Key Concept: everything breaks down in a place like this

T he Number Six train from Manhattan to the South Bronx makes nine stops in the eighteen-minute ride between East 59th Street and Brook Avenue. When you enter the train, you are in the seventh richest Congressional district in the nation. When you leave, you are in the poorest. The 600,000 people who live here and the 450,000 people who live in Washington Heights and Harlem, across the river, make up one of the largest racially segregated concentrations of poor people in our nation.

Brook Avenue, the tenth stop on the local, lies in the center of Mott Haven, whose 48,000 people are the poorest in the South Bronx. Walking into St. Ann's Church in Mott Haven on a hot summer afternoon, one is immediately in the presence of small children. They seem to be everywhere: in the garden, in the hallways, in the kitchen, in the chapel, on the stairs. The first time I see the pastor, Martha Overall, she is carrying a newborn baby in her arms and is surrounded by three lively and excited little girls. In one of the most diseased and dangerous communities in any city of the Western world, the beautiful, old, stone church on St. Ann's Avenue is a gentle sanctuary from the terrors of the streets outside.

A seven-year-old boy named Cliffie, whose mother has come to the church to talk with the Reverend Overall, agrees to take me for a walk around the neighborhood. Reaching up to take my hand the moment we leave the church, he starts a running commentary almost instantly, interrupting now and then to say hello to men and women on the street, dozens of whom are standing just outside the gateway to St. Ann's, waiting for a soup kitchen to open.

At a tiny park in a vacant lot less than a block away, he points to a number of stuffed animals that are attached to the branches of a tree.

"Bears," he says.

"Why are there bears in the tree?" I ask.

He doesn't answer me but smiles at the bears affectionately. "I saw a boy shot in the head right over there," he says a moment later. He looks up at me pleasantly. "Would you like a chocolate-chip cookie?"

"No, thank you," I say.

He has a package of cookies and removes one. He breaks it in half, returns half to the package, and munches on the other half as we are walking. We walk a long block to a rutted street called Cypress Avenue. He gestures down a hill toward what he calls "the bad place," and asks if I want to go see it.

I say, "OK."

"They're burning bodies down there," he announces ominously.

"What kind of bodies?" I ask.

"The bodies of people!" he says in a spooky voice, as if enjoying the opportunity to terrify a grownup.

The place Cliffie is referring to turns out to be a waste incinerator that went into operation recently over the objections of the parents in the neighborhood. The incinerator, I am later reassured by the Reverend Overall, does not burn entire "bodies." What it burns are so-called red-bag products, such as amputated limbs and fetal tissue, bedding, bandages, and syringes that are transported here from New York City hospitals.

Munching another cookie as we walk, Cliffie asks me, "Do you want to go on Jackson Avenue?" Although I don't know one street from another, I agree.

"Come on," he says, "I'll take you there. We have to go around this block." He pauses, however, and pulls an asthma inhaler from his pocket, holds it to his mouth, presses it twice, and then puts it away.

As confident and grown-up as he seems in some ways, he has the round face of a baby and is scarcely more than three-and-a-half feet tall. When he has bad dreams, he tells me, "I go in my mommy's bed and crawl under the covers."

194

*Chapter 8
Views of the Top
and the Bottom*

At other times, when he's upset, he says, "I sleep with a picture of my mother and I dream of her."

Unlike many children I meet these days, he has an absolutely literal religious faith. When I ask him how he pictures God, he says, "He has long hair and He can walk on the deep water." To make sure I understand how unusual this is, he says, "Nobody else can."

He seems to take the lessons of religion literally also. Speaking of a time his mother sent him to the store, "to get a pizza"—"three slices, one for my mom, one for my dad, and one for me"—he says he saw a homeless man who told him he was hungry. "But he was too cold to move his mouth! He couldn't talk."

"How did you know that he was hungry if he couldn't talk?"

"He pointed to my pizza."

"What did you do?"

"I gave him some!"

"Were your parents mad at you?"

He looks surprised by this. "Why would they be mad?" he asks. "God told us, 'Share!'"

When I ask him who his heroes are he first says "Michael Jackson," and then, "Oprah!"—like that, with an exclamation on the word. I try to get him to speak about "important" persons as the schools tend to define them: "Have you read about George Washington?"

"I don't even know the man," he says.

We follow Jackson Avenue past several boarded buildings and a "flat-fix" shop, stop briefly in front of a fenced-in lot where the police of New York City bring impounded cars, and then turn left and go two blocks to a highway with an elevated road above it, where a sign says BRUCKNER BOULEVARD. Crossing beneath the elevated road, we soon arrive at Locust Avenue.

The medical waste incinerator is a new-looking building, gun-metal blue on top of cinder blocks. From one of its metal sliding doors, a sourly unpleasant odor drifts into the street. Standing in front of the building, Cliffie grumbles slightly, but does not seem terribly concerned. "You sure that you don't want a cookie?"

Again I say, "No, thank you."

"I think I'll have another one," he says, and takes one for himself.

"You want to go the hard way or the easy way back to the church?"

"Let's go the easy way," I say.

Next to another vacant lot where someone has dumped a heap of auto tires and some rusted auto parts, he points to a hypodermic needle in the tangled grass and to the bright-colored caps of crack containers, then, for no reason that I can discern, starts puffing up his cheeks and blowing out the air, a curious behavior that seems whimsical and absent-minded and disconsolate at the same time.

"The day is coming when the world will be destroyed," he finally announces. "Everyone is going to be burned to crispy cookies." He reaches into the package for another cookie, only to discover they're all gone.

Cliffie's mother is a small, wiry woman wearing blue jeans and a baseball cap, a former cocaine addict who now helps addicted women and their kids.

Inside the church, when I return Cliffie to her, she looks at me with some amusement on her face and asks, "Did this child wear you out?"

"No," I say. "I enjoyed the walk." I mention, however, that he took me to the waste incinerator and I share with her his comment about "burning bodies." She responds by giving him a half-sarcastic look, hesitating, and then saying, "Hey! You never know! Maybe this child knows something we haven't heard."

She gives him another pleasantly suspicious look and leans back in her chair. "The point is they put a *lot* of things into our neighborhood that no one wants," she says. "The waste incinerator is just one more lovely way of showing their affection."

I ask, "Does it insult you?"

"It used to," she replies. "The truth is, you get used to the offense. There's trashy things all over. There's a garbage dump three blocks away. Then there's all the trucks that come through stinking up the air, heading for the Hunts Point Market. Drivers get their drugs there and their prostitutes."

She tells me that 3,000 homeless families have been relocated by the city in this neighborhood during the past few years and asks a question I hear from many other people here. "Why do you want to put so many people with small children in a place with so much sickness? This is the *last* place in New York that they should put poor children. Clumping so many people, all with the same symptoms and same problems, in one crowded place with nothing they can grow on? Our children start to mourn themselves before their time."

Cliffie, who is listening to this while leaning on his elbow like a pensive grownup, offers his tentative approval to his mother's words. "Yes," he says. "I think that's probably true."

He says it with so much thought, and grown-up reserve, that his mother can't help smiling, even though it's not a funny statement. She looks at him hard, grabs him suddenly around the neck, and kisses him.

Alice Washington lives on a street called Boston Road, close to East Tremont Avenue, but two miles north of St. Ann's Church. Visibly fragile as a consequence of having AIDS and highly susceptible to chest infections, she lives with her son, who is a high-school senior, in a first-floor apartment with three steel locks on the door. A nurse comes once a month to take her temperature and check her heart and her blood pressure.

The nurse, says Mrs. Washington one evening when we're sitting in her kitchen, has another sixteen patients in the building. "Some are children born with AIDS. Some are older people. One is a child, twelve years old, shot in a crossfire at the bus stop on the corner. The bullet ricocheted and got her in the back. She's lost her hair. Can't go to school. She's paralyzed. I see her mother all the time. They wheel her outside in the summer.

"This happened last year, on the Fourth of July. Summer had just begun. I feel so sorry for that child."

I ask how many people in the building now have AIDS.

196

*Chapter 8
Views of the Top
and the Bottom*

"In this building? Including the children, maybe twenty-seven people. That's just in this section. In the other building over there, there's maybe twenty more. Then there's lots of other people have it but don't know, afraid to know, and don't want to be tested. We're living in a bad time. What else can I say?"

She tells me that her food stamps and her welfare check have been cut off. It's a complicated story, but it seems that her food stamps and her welfare payment had been stolen from her in the street some months before. When she began the process of replacing them, there was a computer error that removed her from the rolls entirely.

She relates a story that I've heard many times from people in New York who have lost their welfare payments. "To get an emergency replacement for my check," she says, "I needed to bring three letters to the welfare office—one from my doctor, one from the hospital, and one from my social worker....

"I got the doctor's letter and the social worker's letter, but the hospital's letter didn't come. So I went back and forth from welfare to the hospital—it took a week and finally I got the letter. I brought in all the letters and I waited for another week and then I went to the computer. I put my card in, but it didn't work... then the man there said, 'Your card is dead. You've been cut off.'

"My doctor says, when it comes to the poor, they can't get nothin' right. Anyway, they got me runnin' uptown, downtown, to the hospital, to 34th Street, to the welfare, with the streets so hot and everyone at welfare so impatient. I've got no choice but I don't think I can go through it anymore. I feel like somebody beat me up."

Listening to her voice, which does sound like that of someone who is feeling beaten, I find myself thinking of the words of certain politicians who believe that we have got to get much tougher with unmarried, indigent, non-working women. How much tougher could we get with Mrs. Washington, I wonder, without settling for plain extermination?

"If poor people behaved rationally," says Lawrence Mead, a professor of political science at New York University, "they would seldom be poor for long in the first place." Many social scientists appear to hold this point of view today and argue that the largest portion of the suffering that poor people undergo has to be blamed upon their own behaviors.

But even from the most severe of academic viewpoints about "rationality" or "good" and "bad" behaviors, what has Mrs. Washington done wrong?

She was born in 1944 in New York City. She grew up in Harlem and the Bronx and went to segregated public schools, not something of her choosing, nor that of her mother and her father. She finished high school, studied bookkeeping at a secretarial college, and went to work when she was nineteen.

When she married, at the age of twenty-five, she had to choose her husband from that segregated "marriage pool," to which our social scientists sometimes quite icily refer, of frequently unemployable black men, some of whom have been involved in drugs or spent some time in prison. From her husband, after many years of what she thought to be monogamous matrimony, she contracted the AIDS virus.

She left her husband after he began to beat her. Cancer of her fallopian tubes was detected at this time, then cancer of her uterus. She had three operations. Too frail to keep on with the second of two jobs that she had held, in all, for nearly twenty years, she was forced to turn for mercy to the city of New York.

In 1983, at the age of thirty-nine, she landed with her children in a homeless shelter two blocks from Times Square, an old hotel in which the plumbing did not work and from which she and her son David and his sister had to carry buckets to a bar across the street in order to get water. After spending close to four years in three shelters in Manhattan, she was moved by the city to the neighborhood where she now lives in the South Bronx. It was at this time that she learned she carried the AIDS virus. Since the time I met Mrs. Washington, I have spent hundreds of hours talking with her in her kitchen. I have yet to figure out what she has done that was irrational.

The entire discussion of poor women and their children and their values seems to take place out of any realistic context that includes the physical surroundings of their lives.

The statement, for example, heard so often now as to assume the character of incantation, that low-income neighborhoods like the South Bronx have undergone a "breakdown of family structure" infuriates many poor women I have met, not because they think it is not true but because those who employ this phrase do so with no reference to the absolute collapse of almost every other form of life-affirming institution in the same communities.

"Nothing works here in my neighborhood," a mother named Elizabeth has told me. "Keeping a man is not the biggest problem. Keeping from being killed is bigger. Keeping your kids alive is bigger. If nothing else works, why should a marriage work? I'd rather have a peaceful little life just with my kids than live with somebody who knows that he's a failure. Men like that make everyone feel rotten."

Perhaps it is partly for this reason that so much of the debate about the breakdown of the family has a note of the unreal or incomplete to many of the poorest women I know, and to many of the priests and organizers who work with them. "Of course the family structure breaks down in a place like the South Bronx!" says a white minister who works in one of New York City's poorest neighborhoods. "Everything breaks down in a place like this. The pipes break down. The phone breaks down. The electricity and heat break down. The spirit breaks down. The body breaks down. The immune agents of the heart break down. Why wouldn't the family break down also?

"If we saw the children in these neighborhoods as part of the same human family to which we belong, we'd never put them in such places to begin with. But we do *not* think of them that way. That is one area of 'family breakdown' that the sociologists and the newspapers do not often speak of."

Mrs. Shirley Flowers, whose neighbors call her "Miss Shirley," sits for several hours every day at a table in the lobby of her building to keep out drug dealers.

198

*Chapter 8
Views of the Top
and the Bottom*

When I visit, we talk for a while of some of the children I have met at St. Ann's Church, almost all of whom have relatives in prison. Mrs. Flowers speaks of one of these kids, a fourteen-year-old boy who used to live here in this building but whose mother has since died of cancer.

"The family lived upstairs. The daughter's out at Rikers Island. Been there several times. Had two of her babies there. Now a brother of hers is out there, too. Another brother's dead."

"What happens to the kids," I ask, "when mothers are in prison?"

"Some of them, their relatives take them in. Others go in foster care. Other times," she says, "a neighbor takes the baby."

She speaks of toddlers in the streets who sometimes don't know where their mothers are. "If it's dinnertime, I'll bring them in and feed them. If they're dirty, I'll give them their bath." Many of the kids, she says, have little bugs all over them. "*Piojos* is the word the Puerto Rican children use. They get into their hair and skin. I say to them, 'Stay here with me. I'll keep you safe until your mamma's home.' The children know me, so they know that they don't need to be afraid."

For the past seven years, a gang of murderers and dealers has been based four doors away from Mrs. Flower's home on Beekman Avenue. They marketed crack in a distinctive vial with a red and orange cap, and disciplined dishonest dealers by such terrifying means as mutilations. In one mid-day mutilation, *Newsday* reported, gang enforcers punished a refractory gang member by taking him to St. Mary's Park, right at the end of Beekman Avenue, where "they hacked at him with machetes" and a serrated knife, "opening wounds so severe that some of his organs spilled out." A crowd including children from a nearby junior high school watched the killing.

In one massacre that took place on the street two years before, a man and woman were shot dead for buying crack from the wrong dealer, the dealer was shot and killed as well, and a fourth person who had no drug involvement but was walking in the alley at the wrong time was chased down the street into St. Mary's Park and shot there fourteen times.

I ask Mrs. Flowers, "Have you ever seen a shooting victim die before your eyes?"

"I've seen a *generation* die," she answers. "Some of them were killed with guns. Some lost their minds from drugs. Some from disease. Now we have AIDS, the great plague, the plague of AIDS, the plague that can't be cured. It's true. I've seen it. I've been there. I've been here in this building twenty-four years and I've seen it all."

Despite the horrors she has seen, she seems a fearless person and almost serene. I ask, "How do you keep yourself composed?"

"I pray. I talk to God. I tell him, 'Lord, it is your work. Put me to rest at night and wake me in the morning.' "

"Do your children have the same belief in God that you do?"

"Yes," she says, nodding at her daughter and her son-in-law. "They do. This family talks to God."

Before I leave, she shows me a handful of photocopied clippings from newspapers that have sent reporters here to talk with her. It occurs to me that I must be one in a long line of people who have come to ask her questions. "Do you ever get sick of all these people knocking at your door year after year to pick your brain?" I ask her.

"No," she says, "I don't get sick of it because a lot of them have been nice people. The trouble is, you answer their questions and you give them your opinions. They collect your story from you. Then you see it and you read it. You think, 'Good.' But nothing happens. It's just 'there' and then it drops. It's like they put you in a bucket, like a wishing well. Only it's a wishing well where wishes don't come true."

Anthony is waiting for me at St. Ann's, where he is playing with a furry dog who sleeps outside the front door of the church except on freezing winter nights, when the Reverend Overall brings him in to sleep inside her office. "Mother Martha does not have a heart of stone. She has a heart of gold," says this remarkable boy.

We walk down the street to Children's Park, and then, because there are too many addicts there and it is growing very cold, we walk another block and find a sandwich shop where we can sit inside and talk. When I first met Anthony, the Reverend Overall had told me that he was "unusual." Nothing, however, has prepared me for the fascination and intelligence this thirteen-year-old displays as he describes the things that interest him and those that sadden him. He speaks, moreover, in a frequently inverted syntax, which I take at first to be the consequences of his bilingualism, but soon discover also has some other, more literary explanations.

When I ask him, "Anthony, do you have a happy life?" he answers, "Mr. Jonathan, my life is like the life of Edgar Allan Poe."

I ask him how he knows of Edgar Allan Poe.

"Because I have read his books," he says. "Did you know he lived here in the Bronx?"

"No," I say. "I didn't."

"Yes. It's true. He lived here in a cottage with his wife."

I ask him what he's read of Poe, and he replies, "*The Masque of the Red Death*—and many other stories."

"Why is your life like his?"

"Because he had not a very happy life. He always began a job but for some reason never finished it, which is my problem, too." He adds, "His wife had tuberculosis, but he loved her anyway. After she died, he had a breakdown he could never get out of."

I ask about *The Masque of the Red Death,* which I have never read.

"It's about a plague that stalks the Earth," he says. "For many, many days has it been on the Earth. But a man decides to hold a party because he is not afraid. He thinks the plague will never come to him if he can make things very safe. So he closes all the windows, all the gates, and all the doors, even the little peepholes in the doors. 'Seal them!' he said. And they sealed them. This was because he didn't want the plague to get inside."

"What was this plague like?" I ask.

200

*Chapter 8
Views of the Top
and the Bottom*

"Little, sharp pins, like tuberculosis," he replies. "Or else like AIDS, because of the disease that gets into the blood, but maybe more like cancer. There was not AIDS in those days. I know that there was cancer."

I press him a bit and ask, "What is the meaning of this 'plague'?"

"A plague is an evil in one way," he says, "but not an evil in another way, because it could have a purpose." He then launches into a brief lecture on the history of plagues. "Now there was also a plague of Egypt where the firstborn died. The plague of Egypt is, of course, not over. It's over in Egypt but it could have gone to other places. Plagues are never really over. They can move from place to place.

"Sadness is one plague today. Desperate would be a plague. Drugs are a plague also but the one who gets it does not have to be the firstborn. It can be the second son. It could be the youngest."

"Anthony, what should we do to end this plague?"

"Mr. Jonathan," he answers, "only God can do that. I cannot be God."

I ask him when he thinks this plague will end "or else go someplace else."

"Mr. Jonathan," he says again, "I don't know when. I think it will only happen in the Kingdom of Heaven, but even the angels do not know when that will come. I only know that this is not His kingdom."

"How can you be sure of that?" I ask.

"This," he says with a gesture out the window that seems to take in many things beyond the dealers on the sidewalk and the tawdry-looking storefront medical office and the *"Farmacia"* sign across the street, "this out here is not God's kingdom. A kingdom is a place of glory. This is a place of pain."

Anthony meets me in the garden of St. Ann's and takes me for a walk to see the building where he lives, a few blocks to the west and north, and the building where his grandmother lives, which is close to the same neighborhood and which he says he likes to visit because "my grandma feeds me."

His grandmother, he tells me, is "the happiest person that I know."

I ask him why he thinks that she is happy.

"I don't know why," he says. "I think that feeding people makes her happy." Children from the neighborhood, he says, come to her house and she makes ices for them and bakes cookies. "I think that she likes children more than grownups."

His uncle, however, who lives with his grandmother, is, he says, "not happy. He has many troubles."

His eyes look worried when he says this.

"Anthony," I ask. "What troubles does your uncle have?"

"Mr. Jonathan, my uncle is a sick man. He has AIDS."

"What does he do during the day?" I ask. "Is he well enough to go outside?"

"Yes, he goes out. . . ." Then, in a grown-up voice, he adds, "How can I say this? He goes out but he stays in. He stays inside himself. He does not look at people. He looks down. The man looks at the ground. I don't know why. I think that he's afraid to look up at the world."

"Anthony, is your uncle a drug-user?"

"That," he answers, "is something that I do not want to know."

"Do you cry for your Uncle?"

"Yes, I cry. It's not a sin to cry."

"Do you know other children who cry?"

"Many cry."

"Do you know children who are happy?"

"Truly happy? No."

"Happy at all?"

"Not many.... Well, to tell the truth, not any who are happy for more than one day." Then he corrects himself. "No! Not for one day. For fifteen minutes." He thinks this over, as if to check that he is being accurate, then reports, "Not any. That's no lie."

I wonder at times if a sense of the dramatic might lead Anthony to overstate his answers to my questions, so I challenge him by telling him that I've met children in the schoolyard who seem cheerful.

"Cheerful? Yes. Happy is not the same as cheerful," he replies.

"I think there are certain children who are happy anywhere," I tell him. But he holds his ground.

"Whenever you see a child who enjoys life in this neighborhood, come and see me right away. I'll have to go and see a doctor."

He stops at that moment and waves his hand around him at the neighborhood. "Would you be happy if you had to live here?"

"No, Anthony. I wouldn't," I reply.

We walk as far as Alexander Avenue, then circle back. As we walk, we pass a painted memorial to a victim of gunfire that has been partly whited over in one of the periodic cleanups by the city. A name and date can still be read, however. Sometimes, the Reverend Overall has told me, the city needs to use sandblasters to remove these tributes to the dead.

"How old would you like to live to be?" I ask Anthony.

"That's easy," he replies. "One hundred and thirteen."

"That number's quite exact," I say. "How did you decide on that?"

"I'm thirteen. I'd like to live another 100 years."

"Why *exactly* 100 years?"

"I would like to live to see the human race grow up."

CHAPTER 9 Racial and Sexual Inequality

9.1 ANDREW HACKER

Two Nations: Black and White, Separate, Hostile, Unequal

In 1944 the Swedish sociologist and economist Gunnar Myrdal published a book on race in America titled *An American Dilemma: The Negro Problem and Modern Democracy.* The great dilemma for America then was the flagrant contradiction between American values of universal justice and equality and the oppression of blacks. Myrdal showed that America was a caste society, with justice and equal opportunity existing for whites only. Over a half-century later the situation of blacks is far better, but the contradiction remains.

In 1968 the National Advisory Commission on Civil Disorders concluded, "Our nation is moving toward two societies, one black, one white, separate and unequal." Change has been in the positive direction since this report, but two separate and unequal societies remain. Social scientist Andrew Hacker demonstrates this in the following selection from his book *Two Nations: Black and White, Separate, Hostile, Unequal* (Ballantine Books, 1995).

Several states have legislated against affirmative action, mainly because of the perception that affirmative action is unjust (i.e., that blacks get too much of an advantage through affirmative action). These legislative actions raise good questions about the distribution of advantages in America. In *Two Nations,* Hacker carefully sorts through reams of data to present an accurate picture of the true status of blacks in America, which is still quite disadvantaged. One of Hacker's noteworthy accomplishments is his artful presentation of the psychological deprivation of blacks and the complicated negative attitudes of whites toward blacks. These are usually overlooked when anti–affirmative action legislation is debated. Hacker also presents a thorough examination of the racial income gap. Basically, the gap for men closed significantly between 1940 and 1960, then slowed down and essentially did not change from 1970 to 1992. Consequently, a considerable gap remains.

Key Concept: the value of a white skin

DIVIDING AMERICAN SOCIETY

... Black Americans are Americans, yet they still subsist as aliens in the only land they know. Other groups may remain outside the mainstream—some religious sects, for example—but they do so voluntarily. In contrast, blacks must endure a segregation that is far from freely chosen. So America may be seen as two separate nations. Of course, there are places where the races mingle. Yet in most significant respects, the separation is pervasive and penetrating. As a social and human division, it surpasses all others—even gender—in intensity and subordination.

If white Americans regard the United States as their nation, they also see it beset with racial problems they feel are not of their making. Some contrast current conditions with earlier times, when blacks appeared more willing to accept a subordinate status. Most whites will protest that they bear neither responsibility nor blame for the conditions blacks face. Neither they nor their forebears ever owned slaves, nor can they see themselves as having held anyone back or down. Most white Americans believe that for at least the last generation, blacks have been given more than a fair chance and at least equal opportunity, if not outright advantages. Moreover, few white Americans feel obliged to ponder how membership in the major race gives them powers and privileges....

BEING BLACK IN AMERICA

Most white Americans will say that, all things considered, things aren't so bad for black people in the United States. Of course, they will grant that many problems remain. Still, whites feel there has been steady improvement, bringing blacks closer to parity, especially when compared with conditions in the past. Some have even been heard to muse that it's better to be black, since affirmative action policies make it a disadvantage to be white.

What white people seldom stop to ask is how they may benefit from belonging to their race. Nor is this surprising. People who can see do not regard their vision as a gift for which they should offer thanks. It may also be replied that having a white skin does not immunize a person from misfortune or failure. Yet even for those who fall to the bottom, being white has worth. What could that value be?

Let us try to find out by means of a parable. Suspend disbelief for a moment, and assume that what follows might actually happen.

The Visit

You will be visited tonight by an official you have never met. He begins by telling you that he is extremely embarrassed. The organization he represents has made a mistake, something that hardly ever happens.

According to their records, he goes on, you were to have been born black: to another set of parents, far from where you were raised.

However, the rules being what they are, this error must be rectified, and as soon as possible. So at midnight tonight, you will become black. And this will mean not simply a darker skin, but the bodily and facial features associated with African ancestry. However, inside, you will be the person you always were. Your knowledge and ideas will remain intact. But outwardly you will not be recognizable to anyone you now know.

Your visitor emphasizes that being born to the wrong parents was in no way your fault. Consequently, his organization is prepared to offer you some reasonable recompense. Would you, he asks, care to name a sum of money you might consider appropriate? He adds that his group is by no means poor. It can be quite generous when the circumstances warrant, as they seem to in your case. He finishes by saying that their records also show you are scheduled to live another fifty years—as a black man or woman in America.

How much financial recompense would you request?

When this parable has been put to white students, most seemed to feel that it would not be out of place to ask for $50 million, or $1 million for each coming black year. And this calculation conveys, as well as anything, the value that white people place on their own skins. Indeed, to be white is to possess a gift whose value can be appreciated only after it has been taken away. And why ask for so large a sum? Surely this needs no detailing. The money would be used, as best it could, to buy protection from the discriminations and dangers white people know they would face once they were perceived to be black.

Of course, no one who is white can understand what it is like to be black in America. Still, were they to spend time in a black body, here are some of the things they would learn.

In the eyes of white Americans, being black encapsulates your identity. No other racial or national origin is seen as having so pervasive a personality or character. Even if you write a book on Euclidean algorithms or Renaissance sculpture, you will still be described as a "black author." Although you are a native American with a longer lineage than most, you will never be accorded full membership in the nation or society. More than that, you early learn that this nation feels no need or desire for your physical presence. (Indeed, your people are no longer in demand as cheap labor.) You sense that most white citizens would heave a sigh of relief were you simply to disappear. While few openly propose that you return to Africa, they would be greatly pleased were you to make that decision for yourself....

[Y]ou sense that in mainstream occupations, your prospects are quite limited. In most areas of employment, even after playing by the rules, you find yourself hitting a not-so-invisible ceiling. You wonder if you are simply corporate wallpaper, a protective coloration they find it prudent to display. You begin to suspect that a "qualification" you will always lack is white pigmentation.

In theory, all Americans with financial means and a respectable demeanor can choose where they want to live. For over a generation, courts across the country have decreed that a person's race cannot be a reason for refusing to rent or sell a residence. However, the law seems to have had little impact on practice, since almost all residential areas are entirely black or white. Most whites prefer it that way. Some will say they would like a black family nearby, if only to be able to report that their area is integrated. But not many do. Most white Americans do not move in circles where racial integration wins social or moral credit.

This does not mean it is absolutely impossible for a black family to find a home in a white area. Some have, and others undoubtedly will. Even so, black Americans have no illusions about the hurdles they will face. If you look outside your designated areas, you can expect chilly receptions, evasive responses, and outright lies; a humiliating experience, rendered all the more enraging because it is so repeated and prolonged. After a while, it becomes too draining to continue the search. Still, if you have the income, you will find an area to your liking; but it will probably be all black. In various suburbs and at the outer edges of cities, one can see well-kept homes, outwardly like other such settings. But a closer view shows all the householders to be black.

This is the place to consider residential apartheid—and that is what it is—in its full perspective. Black segregation differs markedly from that imposed on any other group. Even newly arrived immigrants are more readily accepted in white neighborhoods.

Nor should it be assumed that most black householders prefer the racial ratios in areas where they currently reside. Successive surveys have shown that, on average, only about one in eight say they prefer a neighborhood that is all or mostly black, which is the condition most presently confront. The vast majority—usually about 85 percent—state they would like an equal mixture of black and white neighbors. Unfortunately, this degree of racial balance has virtually no chance of being realized. The reason, very simply, is that hardly any whites will live in a neighborhood or community where half the residents are black. So directly or indirectly, white Americans have the power to decide the racial composition of communities and neighborhoods. Most egregious have been instances where acts of arson or vandalism force black families to leave. But such methods are exceptional. There are other, less blatant, ways to prevent residential integration from passing a certain "tipping" point.

Here we have no shortage of studies. By and large, this research agrees that white residents will stay—and some new ones may move in—if black arrivals do not exceed 8 percent. But once the black proportion passes that point, whites begin to leave the neighborhood, and no new ones will move in. The vacated houses or apartments will be bought or rented by blacks, and the area will be on its way to becoming all black.

What makes integration difficult if not impossible is that so few whites will accept even a racial composition reflecting the overall national proportion of 12 or 13 percent....

If you are black, these white reactions brand you as a carrier of contaminations. No matter what your talents or attainments, you are seen as infecting a neighborhood simply because of your race. This is the ultimate insult of segregation. It opens wounds that never really heal and leaves scars to remind you how far you stand from full citizenship....

THE RACIAL INCOME GAP

Since their first arrival, and continuing after they started receiving wages, black Americans have figured disproportionately among the nation's poor. Of course, differences in incomes can have explanations apart from race. After all, a lot of white people are poor, and a number of blacks are very visibly rich. Even so, after other factors have been accounted for, race still seems to play a role in how people fare financially....

In 1992, the most recent figures available at this writing, personal income received by everyone living within the country added up to a grand total of $4.1 trillion. While black Americans made up 12.1 percent of the tabulated population, they ended up with only 7.3 percent of the monetary pie....

Between 1940 and 1960, the earnings of black men relative to whites improved by over a third....

However, during the past twenty-two years, as [Table 1] shows, the relative earnings of black men have tapered off. Between 1970 and 1992, their earnings relative to those of white workers improved by only $17; in fact, black men lost ground during this period's second decade. (And this was a period when affirmative action supposedly gave blacks preferences in hirings and promotions.) The decline in blue-collar employment hit black men especially hard. Each year found the economy offering fewer factory jobs, while more were being created in the white-collar sector.

... Since 1975, unemployment rates for blacks have remained at double-digit levels, and they have not fallen below twice the white rate since 1976. Even more depressing, the gap between the black and white figures grew during the 1980s, suggesting that the economy has little interest in enlisting black contributions....

What black Americans want is no more and no less than what white Americans want: a fair chance for steady employment at decent pay. But this opportunity has been one that the nation's economy continues to withhold. To be black in America is to know that you remain last in line for so basic a

TABLE 1

Earnings of Black Workers: 1940–1992 (per $1,000 for Whites)

Year	Men	Women
1940	$450	$379
1950	$613	$369
1960	$669	$696
1970	$704	$851
1980	$751	$917
1992	$721	$915

requisite as the means of supporting yourself and your family. More than that, you have much less choice among jobs than workers who are white. . . .

[T]he Bureau of Labor Statistics has created a category it calls "discouraged workers." These are individuals who say they would like to work but have ceased looking because they have become convinced that they will never find a job. So they have been dropped from the "labor force" category and are no longer even counted among the unemployed.

On a typical day, the bureau is able to identify almost a million of these "discouraged workers." The true total has to be considerably higher, since many in this plight cannot be found for interviews or refuse to give out information about themselves. Of the recorded "discouraged workers," close to 30 percent are black, a much higher proportion than on the official list of the unemployed who say they are actively looking for work. . . . [S]ome of these "nonworkers" support themselves on the streets by providing products and services in the underground economy. Others resort to theft, which means that sooner or later they will join yet another cohort of the nonemployed: the growing number of Americans who languish in this nation's prisons.

It is frequently proposed that the economy should create more semiskilled jobs at decent wages, which will be made available to black men. Just what kinds of positions they would be are seldom specified. As hardly needs mentioning, machines now perform many of the tasks once handled by human beings, while a lot of factory work once done within this country is being contracted overseas. Moreover, recent trends have expanded the sectors of the workforce open to women. Even if special jobs were devised, it is not clear how they could pay what today's men regard as a living wage. For at least a decade, newly created positions have been offering wages and salaries lower than those of the jobs they replaced. As a result, they are usually taken by women or teenagers or immigrants, who are willing to work at those rates because they have no other option. Put another way, many native-born men cannot see how they can work for such wages and still maintain a self-respect integral to their identity.

But the larger point is that this country cannot revert to a sweat-and-muscle economy of earlier eras. More than that, to contrive blue-collar jobs for black men would rouse not only charges of preferential treatment but accusations of racism as well, since it would imply that work requiring physical skills is all that black men can be expected to do.

EQUITY IN EMPLOYMENT

… Not so many years ago, entire spheres of employment were almost completely closed to blacks. As recently as 1980, the census could find only 254 black optometrists, 185 black actuaries, and 122 black auctioneers. In addition, blacks accounted for only 138 nuclear engineers, 89 theology professors, and 70 sheet metal apprentices. At present, it can be said that absolute barriers have been broken, and every occupation has some blacks among its practitioners. In many areas, however, the numbers remain exceedingly small…. Even now, blacks remain underrepresented in the professions of engineering, law, and medicine, as well as architecture and dentistry. Until lately, black students felt little incentive to train for these fields, since there were few if any prospects of obtaining a job. (Paul Robeson turned to acting because he had no serious offers after graduating from Columbia Law School.) While virtually all professions are saying they would like to have more blacks on their payrolls, it still remains to be seen whether they simply want a few faces for showcase purposes or if they mean jobs with real responsibilities.

… [P]ublic and nonprofit organizations have become havens for much of the black workforce. Over a third of all black lawyers work for government departments, as do almost 30 percent of black scientists. Blacks account for over 20 percent of the nation's armed services, twice their proportion in the civilian economy. They hold almost a fifth of all positions in the Postal Service and have similar ratios in many urban agencies. Unfortunately, this makes middle-class blacks vulnerable to public budget cuts.

On the whole, then, the business world has not done much to expand black employment….

Companies realize that too few black faces could lead to charges of bias, causing unpleasant publicity. At the same time, they worry lest they are seen as having "too many" black employees or as promoting blacks too liberally. In this vein, they may fear that "too black" an appearance will jeopardize their image for competence and credibility. Firms also become uneasy if one of their products—a brand of outdoor wear, for example, or a certain birth control device—becomes identified with a black clientele. Perhaps projecting some of their own anxieties, they sense that white customers will shy away from items they feel have become associated with black preferences and tastes.

All the while, businesses can be expected to protest that they are "color blind" in both policy and practice, seeking only the best talent they can find, regardless of race or creed or gender. If there appear to be few black people on their payrolls, they will insist it is because hardly any have applied or not enough live near their facilities or have the necessary qualifications. What is not openly addressed is how far possessing a skin of a certain color might figure as one of those "qualifications."

Business has always been inherently conservative, waiting until other sectors take steps toward social change. In part, this attitude stems from anxieties about how their customers will react. Will they buy, or buy as much, from salespeople who are black? And can blacks join in the socializing so often needed to clinch a deal? Will users of your product feel confident that a black technician can work competently with complex equipment? Hence the tendency to play it safe, which usually means hiring as white a workforce as possible....

In more secluded settings, white employees and supervisors may be heard to say that they find blacks hard to work with ("We had one, but he didn't work out.") They will cite cases of coldness or hostility or chips on the shoulder compounded by a readiness to imagine racial insults. Or they will allude to an unwillingness of black men to relax in workplace relationships. Rather than inquire why this reluctance persists or how it might be remedied, the tendency is to evade the issue by hiring and promoting as few blacks as possible. At that point, personal biases become transmuted into institutional racism.

Small wonder, then, that black Americans have always agreed among themselves that if they want to get ahead, they have to work harder and do better than white people. Given all the misgivings of white executives and supervisors, it would seem self-evident that blacks must put in a lot more effort simply to satisfy the standards their employers set. It is not as if they could simply walk in and start doing a job. All eyes are on them, as if a Great Experiment were under way.

It is not easy buckling down to a job when you have to expend so much of your energy contriving a "white" personality—or at least the appearance of one—so as to put your white workmates at ease. Nor is it easy to establish one's authority, since simply having a black face raises doubts in many white minds. Added to which is having to read nuances and allusions that whites recognize as a matter of course. All this demands much more from black workers than is ever asked of whites. If white people have any doubts on this score, they might imagine spending their entire careers with a foreign company, where they find that no matter how much they study its ways, it still refuses to grant that they can ever master the assignments at hand.

The Truly Disadvantaged: The Inner City, the Underclass, and Public Policy

The opportunities for African Americans have changed significantly since the civil rights movement of the 1960s. African Americans have more schooling, hold more political offices, have better jobs and a greater variety of jobs to choose from, and live in more diverse neighborhoods, compared to the time before the passage of the 1964 Civil Rights Act. This legislation outlawed discrimination in public accommodations and employment based on race, religion, national origin, or sex. These improvements, however, may have bypassed poor blacks in urban centers.

The story of black America since 1964 is two-sided. William Julius Wilson asserts that middle-class blacks have been closing the gap with their white counterparts while poor blacks are falling further behind in pockets of truly disadvantaged neighborhoods. Wilson suggests that many urban ghettos have changed from multiclass African American neighborhoods to concentrations of poor people. Middle-class African Americans and stable blue-collar families have moved out of the city and have been replaced by a young population with few skills. As the economy changed and industrial jobs disappeared, many of the young men had difficulty getting jobs. The high rates of joblessness turned some to crime or drugs. Young women in these areas were confronted with a shortage of marriageable men, and the number of out-of-wedlock births and woman-headed families greatly increased. These trends, Wilson says, have created an environment that is not conducive to children learning the habits and behaviors that can advance them in society. This in turn deepens the cycle of disadvantages in the ghetto.

Wilson (b. 1935), a member of the faculty at Harvard University for over 20 years, is currently the Malcolm Wiener Professor of Social Policy at Harvard. He is a former president of the American Sociological Association and a MacArthur Prize Fellow. His most recent book is *When Work Disappears: The World of the New Urban Poor* (Alfred A. Knopf, 1996). The following selection is from Wilson's book *The Truly Disadvantaged: The Inner City, the Underclass, and Public Policy* (University of Chicago Press, 1987).

William Julius Wilson

Key Concept: truly disadvantaged black America

THE TANGLE OF PATHOLOGY IN THE INNER CITY

When figures on black crime, teenage pregnancy, female-headed families, and welfare dependency are released to the public without sufficient explanation, racial stereotypes are reinforced....

These problems cannot be accounted for simply in terms of racial discrimination or in terms of a culture of poverty. Rather, they must be seen as having complex sociological antecedents that range from demographic changes to problems of economic organization. But before turning to these explanatory factors, I should like to outline the growing problems of social dislocation in the inner city, beginning first with violent crime.

Race and Violent Crime

Only one of nine persons in the United States is black; yet in 1984 nearly one of every two persons arrested for murder and nonnegligent manslaughter was black, and 41 percent of all murder victims were black. As Norval Morris and Michael Tonry indicate, "Homicide is the leading cause of death of black men and women aged 25 to 34." Furthermore, 61 percent of all persons arrested for robbery and 38 percent of those arrested for aggravated assault in 1984 were black. Moreover, the rate of black imprisonment in 1984 was 6.25 times greater than the rate of white imprisonment....

In examining the figures on homicide in Chicago it is important to recognize that the rates vary significantly according to the economic status of the community, with the highest rates of violent crime associated with the communities of the underclass. More than half of the 1983 murders and aggravated assaults in Chicago occurred in seven of the city's twenty-four police districts, the areas with a heavy concentration of low-income black and Latino residents.

The most violent area is the overwhelmingly black Wentworth Avenue police district on the South Side of Chicago. Indeed, in 1983, 81 murders (11 percent of city total) and 1,691 aggravated assaults (13 percent of city total) occurred in this four-square-mile district which contains only 3.4 percent of the city's total population.

The Wentworth figures on violent crime are high partly because the Robert Taylor Homes, the largest public-housing project in the city of Chicago, is located there. Robert Taylor Homes is a complex of twenty-eight sixteen-story buildings covering ninety-two acres. The official population in 1980 was almost 20,000.... The median family income was $5,470. Ninety-three percent of the families with children were headed by a single parent. Eighty-three percent of the (nonelderly headed) families with children received Aid to Families with Dependent Children (AFDC). Unemployment was estimated to be 47 percent in 1980. Although in 1980 only a little more than 0.5 percent of Chicago's more than 3 million people lived in the Robert Taylor Homes, "11 percent of the city's murders, 9 percent of its rapes, and 10 percent of its aggravated assaults were committed in the projects."...

Family Dissolution and Welfare Dependency

What is true of the structure of families and welfare dependency in the Robert Taylor Homes... is typical of all the CHA (Chicago Housing Authority) housing projects. In 1983, of the 25,000 families with children living in CHA projects, only 8 percent were married-couple families, and 80 percent of the family households received AFDC. But female-headed families and welfare dependency are not confined to public-housing projects. The projects simply magnify these problems, which permeate ghetto neighborhoods and to a lesser extent metropolitan areas generally....

Even if a female householder is employed full time, her earnings are usually substantially less than that of a male worker and are not likely to be supplemented with income from a second full-time employed member of the household. For women who head families and are not employed (including those who have never been employed, have dropped out of the labor force to become full-time mothers, or are employed only part time), the economic situation is often desperate. In 1983 the median income of female-headed families ($11,789) was only 43 percent of the median income of husband-wife families ($27,286); the median income of families headed by black women ($7,999) was only 37 percent of the median income of husband-wife black families ($21,840). In 1983, of the roughly 3.6 million families that reported incomes of less than $5000, 57 percent were headed by women....

The rise of female-headed families among blacks corresponds closely with the increase in the ratio of out-of-wedlock births. Only 15 percent of all black births in 1959 were out of wedlock. This figure jumped to roughly 24 percent in 1965 and 57 percent in 1982, almost five times greater than the white ratio....

These developments have significant implications for the problems of welfare dependency. In 1977 the proportion of families receiving AFDC that were black (43 percent) slightly exceeded the proportion that were white other than Spanish (42.5 percent), despite the great difference in total population. It is estimated that about 60 percent of the children who are born out of wedlock and are alive and not adopted receive welfare. A study by the Urban Institute pointed out that "more than half of all AFDC assistance in 1975 was paid to women who were or had been teenage mothers."...

TOWARD A COMPREHENSIVE EXPLANATION

There is no single explanation for the racial or ethnic variations in the rates of social dislocations I have described. But I should like to suggest several interrelated explanations that represent a comprehensive set of variables—including societal, demographic, and neighborhood variables....

The Effects of Historic and Contemporary Discrimination

Discrimination is the most frequently invoked explanation of social dislocations in the urban ghetto. However, proponents of the discrimination thesis often fail to make a distinction between the effects of historic discrimination, that is, discrimination before the middle of the twentieth century, and the effects of discrimination following that time. They therefore find it difficult to explain why the economic position of poor urban blacks actually deteriorated during the very period in which the most sweeping antidiscrimination legislation and programs were enacted and implemented. Their emphasis on discrimination becomes even more problematic in view of the economic progress of the black middle class during the same period.

There is no doubt that contemporary discrimination has contributed to or aggravated the social and economic problems of the ghetto underclass. But is discrimination greater today than in 1948, when ... black unemployment was less than half the 1980 rate, and the black-white unemployment ratio was almost one-fourth less than the 1980 ratio?...

It should ... be emphasized that, contrary to prevailing opinion, the black family showed signs of significant deterioration not before, but after, the middle of the twentieth century. Until the publication of Herbert Gutman's impressive historical study on the black family, scholars had assumed that the current problems of the black family could be traced back to slavery.... Gutman presented data that convincingly demonstrated that the black family was not particularly disorganized during slavery or during the early years of blacks' first migration to the urban North beginning after the turn of the century. The problems of the modern black family, he suggests, are a product of more recent social forces.

But are these problems mainly a consequence of present-day discrimination, or are they related to other factors that may have little or nothing to do with race? If contemporary discrimination is the main culprit, why did it produce the most severe problems of urban social dislocation during the 1970's, a decade that followed an unprecedented period of civil rights legislation and ushered in the affirmative action programs? The problem, as I see it, is unraveling the effects of present-day discrimination, on the one hand, and of historic discrimination, on the other.

My own view is that historic discrimination is far more important than contemporary discrimination in explaining the plight of the ghetto underclass....

One of the legacies of historic discrimination is the presence of a large black underclass in central cities. Blacks constituted approximately 23 percent of the population of central cities in 1983, but they were 43 percent of the poor in these cities. In accounting for the historical developments that contributed to this concentration of urban black poverty, I should like to draw briefly upon Stanley Lieberson's work. On the basis of a systematic analysis of early United States censuses and other sources of data, Lieberson concluded that in many spheres of life, including the labor market, blacks were discriminated against far more severely in the early twentieth century than were the new white immigrants from southern, central, and eastern Europe. The disadvantage of skin color, in the sense that the dominant white population preferred whites over nonwhites, is one that blacks shared with the Japanese, Chinese, and other nonwhite groups. However, skin color per se "was not an insurmountable obstacle." Because changes in immigration policy cut off Asian migration to America in the late nineteenth century, the Chinese and Japanese populations did not reach large numbers and, therefore, did not pose as great a threat as did blacks. Lieberson was aware that the "response of whites to Chinese and Japanese was of the same violent and savage character in areas where they were concentrated," but he emphasized that "the threat was quickly stopped through changes in immigration policy." Furthermore, the discontinuation of large-scale immigration from China and Japan enabled those already here to solidify networks of ethnic contacts and to occupy particular occupational niches in small, relatively stable communities.

If different population sizes accounted for much of the difference in the economic success of blacks and Asians, they also helped to determine the dissimilar rates of progress of urban blacks and the new European arrivals. The dynamic factor behind these differences, and perhaps the most important single contributor to the varying rates of urban racial and ethnic progress in the twentieth-century United States, is the flow of migrants. After the changes in immigration policy that halted Asian immigration to America came drastic restrictions on new European immigration. However, black migration to the urban North continued in substantial numbers for several decades. The sizable and continuous migration of blacks from the South to the North, coupled with the curtailment of immigration from eastern, central and southern Europe, created a situation in which other whites muffled their negative disposition toward the new Europeans and directed their antagonisms against blacks. According to Lieberson, "the presence of blacks made it harder to discriminate against the new Europeans because the alternative was viewed less favorably."

The flow of migrants also made it much more difficult for blacks to follow the path of both the new Europeans and the Asian-Americans in overcoming the negative effects of discrimination by finding special occupational niches. Only a small part of a group's total work force can be absorbed in such specialities when the group's population increases rapidly or is a sizable proportion of the total population. Furthermore, the continuing flow of migrants had a harmful effect on the urban blacks who had arrived earlier....

The flow of migrants also affects the average age of an ethnic group. For example, the black migration to urban centers—the continual replenishment of urban black populations by poor newcomers—predictably skewed the age profile of the urban black community and kept it relatively young. The higher the median age of a group, the greater its representation in higher income categories and professional positions. It is therefore not surprising that ethnic groups such as blacks and Hispanics, who on average are younger than whites, also tend to have high unemployment and crime rates. . . .

In the nation's central cities in 1977, the median age for whites was 30.3, for blacks 23.9, and for Hispanics 21.8. One cannot overemphasize the importance of the sudden growth of young minorities in the central cities. The number of central-city blacks aged fourteen to twenty-four rose by 78 percent from 1960 to 1970, compared with an increase of only 23 percent for whites of the same age. From 1970 to 1977 the increase in the number of young blacks slackened off somewhat, but it was still substantial. . . .

On the basis of these demographic changes alone one would expect blacks and Hispanics to contribute disproportionately to the increasing rates of social dislocation in the central city, such as crime. Indeed, 66 percent of all those arrested for violent and property crimes in American cities in 1980 were under twenty-five years of age.

Youth is not only a factor in crime; it is also associated with out-of-wedlock births, female-headed homes, and welfare dependency. Teenagers accounted for 38 percent of all out-of-wedlock births in 1982, and 78 percent of all illegitimate black births in that year were to teenage and young adult women. The median age of female householders has decreased substantially in recent years, and the explosion of teenage births has contributed significantly to the rise in the number of children on AFDC, from roughly 35 per 1,000 children under eighteen in 1960 to around 114 per 1,000 in 1982.

In short, much of what has gone awry in the inner city is due in part to the sheer increase in the number of young people, especially young minorities. However, as James Q. Wilson has pointed out in his analysis of the proliferation of social problems in the 1960's (a period of general economic prosperity), "changes in the age structure of the population cannot alone account for the social dislocations" of that decade. . . .

Wilson advances the hypothesis that an abrupt rise in the number of young persons has an "exponential effect on the rate of certain social problems." In other words, there may be a "critical mass" of young persons in a given community such that when that mass is reached or is increased suddenly and substantially, "a self-sustaining chain reaction is set off that creates an explosive increase in the amount of crime, addiction, and welfare dependency."

This hypothesis seems to be especially relevant to inner-city neighborhoods and even more so to those with large public-housing projects. Opposition from organized community groups to the construction of public housing in their neighborhoods has "led to massive, segregated housing projects, which become ghettos for minorities and the economically disadvantaged." As the earlier description of the Robert Taylor Homes . . . in Chicago suggests, when large poor families were placed in high-density housing projects in the ghetto, both family and neighborhood life suffered. High crime rates, family dissolution, and vandalism flourished in these projects. In St. Louis, the Pruit-Igoe project, which included about ten thousand adults and children, developed serious problems five years after it opened and "it became so unlivable that it was destroyed in 1976, 22 years after it was built."

In both the housing projects and other inner-city neighborhoods, residents have difficulty identifying their neighbors. They are, therefore, less likely to engage in reciprocal guardian behavior. Events in one part of the block or neighborhood tend to be of little concern to those residing in other parts. These conditions of social disorganization are as acute as they are because of the unprecedented increase in the number of teenage and young adult minorities in these neighborhoods, many of whom are jobless, not enrolled in school, and a source of delinquency, crime, and unrest. . . .

The Impact of Basic Economic Changes

The population explosion among minority youths occurred at a time when changes in the economy posed serious problems for unskilled individuals, both in and out of the labor force. Urban minorities have been particularly vulnerable to structural economic changes, such as the shift from goods-producing to service-producing industries, the increasing polarization of the labor market into low-wage and high-wage sectors, technological innovations, and the relocation of manufacturing industries out of the central cities. . . .

Whereas job losses in these cities have been greatest in industries with lower educational requirements, job growth has been concentrated in industries that require higher levels of education. . . .

What are the implications of this transformation of the urban economy for poor minorities? First of all, cities in the North that have experienced the greatest decline of jobs in the lower-education-requisite industries since 1970 have had, at the same time, significant increases in minority residents who are seldom employed in the high-growth industries. Indeed, despite increases in educational attainment since 1970, "black males (over age sixteen) in northern cities are still most concentrated in the education completed category where employment opportunities declined the fastest and are least represented in that category where northern central city employment has most expanded since 1970." This has created "a serious mismatch between the current education distribution of minority residents in large northern cities and the changing education requirements of their rapidly transforming industries bases. This mismatch is one major reason why both unemployment rates and labor-force dropout rates among central-city blacks are much higher than those of central-city residents, and why black unemployment rates have not responded well to economic recovery in many northern cities." . . .

Concentration Effects: The Significance of the
Social Transformation of the Inner City

William Julius
Wilson

... It is the growth of the high- and extreme-poverty areas that epitomizes the social transformation of the inner city, a transformation that represents a change in the class structure in many inner-city neighborhoods as the nonpoor black middle and working classes tend no longer to reside in these neighborhoods, thereby increasing the proportion of truly disadvantaged individuals and families. What are the effects of this growing concentration of poverty on individual and families in the inner city?

... I believe that the exodus of middle- and working-class families from many ghetto neighborhoods removes an important "social buffer" that could deflect the full impact of the kind of prolonged and increasing joblessness that plagued inner-city neighborhoods in the 1970s and early 1980s, joblessness created by uneven economic growth and periodic recessions. This argument is based on the assumption that even if the truly disadvantaged segments of an inner-city area experience a significant increase in long-term spells of joblessness, the basic institutions in that area (churches, schools, stores, recreational facilities, etc.) would remain viable if much of the base of their support comes from the more economically stable and secure families. Moreover, the very presence of these families during such periods provides mainstream role models that help keep alive the perception that education is meaningful, that steady employment is a viable alternative to welfare, and that family stability is the norm, not the exception.

Thus, a perceptive ghetto youngster in a neighborhood that includes a good number of working and professional families may observe increasing joblessness and idleness but he will also witness many individuals regularly going to and from work; he may sense an increase in school dropouts but he can also see a connection between education and meaningful employment. ...

Thus, in a neighborhood with a paucity of regularly employed families and with the overwhelming majority of families having spells of long-term joblessness, people experience a social isolation that excludes them from the job network system that permeates other neighborhoods and that is so important in learning about or being recommended for jobs that become available in various parts of the city. And as the prospects for employment diminish, other alternatives such as welfare and the underground economy are not only increasingly relied on, they come to be seen as a way of life. Moreover, unlike the situation in earlier years, girls who become pregnant out of wedlock invariably give birth out of wedlock because of a shrinking pool of marriageable, that is, employed, black males. ...

The communities of the underclass are plagued by massive joblessness, flagrant and open lawlessness, and low-achieving schools, and therefore tend to be avoided by outsiders. Consequently, the residents of these areas, whether women and children of welfare families or aggressive street criminals, have become increasingly socially isolated from mainstream patterns of behavior.

If I had to use one term to capture the differences in the experiences of low-income families who live in inner-city areas from the experiences of those who live in other areas in the central city today, that term would be *concentration effects.* The social transformation of the inner city has resulted in a disproportionate concentration of the most disadvantaged segments of the urban black population, creating a social milieu significantly different from the environment that existed in these communities several decades ago....

The ... degree of social isolation—defined in this context as the lack of contact or of sustained interaction with individuals and institutions that represent mainstream society—in these highly concentrated poverty areas has become far greater than we had previously assumed. What are the effects of this kind of social isolation?

Inner-city social isolation makes it much more difficult for those who are looking for jobs to be tied into the job network. Even in those situations where job vacancies become available in an industry near or within an inner-city neighborhood, workers who live outside the inner city may find out about these vacancies sooner than those who live near the industry because the latter are not tied into the job network....

Inner-city social isolation also generates behavior not conducive to good work histories. The patterns of behavior that are associated with a life of casual work (tardiness and absenteeism) are quite different from those that accompany a life of regular or steady work (e.g., the habit of waking up early in the morning to a ringing alarm clock). In neighborhoods in which nearly every family has at least one person who is steadily employed, the norms and behavior patterns that emanate from a life of regularized employment become part of the community gestalt. On the other hand, in neighborhoods in which most families do not have a steadily employed breadwinner, the norms and behavior patterns associated with steady work compete with those associated with casual or infrequent work. Accordingly, the less frequent the regular contact with those who have steady and full-time employment (that is, the greater the degree of social isolation), the more likely that initial job performance will be characterized by tardiness, absenteeism, and, thereby, low retention. In other words, a person's patterns and norms of behavior tend to be shaped by those with which he or she has had the most frequent or sustained contact and interaction. Moreover, since the jobs that are available to the inner-city poor are the very ones that alienate even persons with long and stable work histories, the combination of unattractive jobs and lack of community norms to reinforce work increases the likelihood that individuals will turn to either underground illegal activity or idleness or both.

The key theoretical concept, therefore, is not *culture of poverty* but *social isolation.* Culture of poverty implies that basic values and attitudes of the ghetto subculture have been internalized and thereby influence behavior. Accordingly, efforts to enhance the life chances of groups such as the ghetto underclass require, from this perspective, social policies (e.g., programs of training and education as embodied in manditory workfare) aimed at directly changing these subcultural traits. Social isolation, on the other hand, not only implies that contact between groups of different class and/or racial backgrounds is either lacking or has become increasingly intermittent but that the nature of this contact enhances the effects of living in a highly concentrated poverty area. These concentration effects include the constraints and opportunities in neighborhoods in which the population is overwhelmingly socially disadvantaged—constraints and opportunities that include the kinds of ecological niches that the residents of these neighborhoods occupy in terms of access to jobs and job networks, availability of marriageable partners, involvement in quality schools, and exposure to conventional role models.

... To emphasize the concept *social isolation* does not mean that cultural traits are irrelevant in understanding behavior in highly concentrated poverty areas; rather, it highlights the fact that culture is a response to social structural constraints and opportunities. From a public-policy perspective, this would mean shifting the focus from changing subcultural traits (as suggested by the "culture of poverty" thesis) to changing the structure of constraints and opportunities. The increasing social isolation of the inner city is a product of the class transformation of the inner city, including the growing concentration of poverty in inner-city neighborhoods. And the class transformation of the inner city cannot be understood without considering the effects of fundamental changes in the urban economy on the lower-income minorities, effects that include joblessness and that thereby increase the chances of long-term residence in highly concentrated poverty areas.

CONCLUSION TO THIS SECTION

In this section, I have tried to show that the factors associated with the recent increases in social dislocation among the ghetto underclass are complex and cannot be reduced to the easy explanation of racism or racial discrimination. Although present-day discrimination undoubtedly has contributed to the increasing social and economic woes of the ghetto underclass, I have argued that these problems have been due far more to a complex web of other factors that include shifts in the American economy—which have produced extraordinary rates of black joblessness that have exacerbated other social problems in the inner city—the historic flow of migrants, changes in the urban minority age structure, population changes in the central city, and the class transformation of the inner city....

The Role of Joblessness

... [T]he weight of the evidence on the relationship between the employment status of men, and family life and married life suggests that the increasing rate of joblessness among black men merits serious consideration as a major underlying factor in the rise of black single mothers and female-headed households. Moreover, when the factor of joblessness is combined with high black-male mortality and incarceration rates, the proportion of black men in stable economic situations is even lower than that conveyed in the current unemployment and labor-force figures.

... [T]he effect of male joblessness trends, in combination with the effects of male mortality and incarceration rates, [can be shown] by presenting the rates of employed civilian men to women of the same race and age-group. This ratio may be described as a "male marriageable pool index." The number of women is used as the denominator in order to convey the situation of young women in the "marriage market." ... [F]or men sixteen to twenty-four years of age, [there was]: a sharp decline in the nonwhite ratios beginning in the 1960s, which is even more startling when compared with the rising ratios for white men. ... [F]or men twenty-five to fifty-four years of age, [there was] a more gradual decline for black men relative to white men. Clearly, what our "male marriageable pool index" reveals is a long-term decline in the proportion of black men, and particularly young black men, who are in a position to support a family. ...

In the 1960s scholars readily attributed black family deterioration to the problems of male joblessness. However, in the last ten to fifteen years, in the face of the overwhelming focus on welfare as the major source of black family breakup, concerns about the importance of male joblessness have receded into the background. We argue ... that the available evidence justifies renewed scholarly and public policy attention to the connection between the disintegration of poor families and black male prospects for stable employment. ...

Although changing social and cultural trends have often been invoked to explain some of the dynamic changes in the structure of the family, they appear to have more relevance for shifts in family structure among whites. And contrary to popular opinion, there is little evidence to provide a strong case for welfare as the primary cause of family breakups, female-headed households, and out-of-wedlock births. Welfare does seem to have a modest effect on separation and divorce, especially for white women, but recent evidence suggests that its total effect on the size of the population of female householders is small. As shown in Ellwood and Bane's impressive study, if welfare does have a major influence on female-headed families, it is in the living arrangements of single mothers. ...

By contrast, the evidence for the influence of male joblessness is much more persuasive. Research has demonstrated, for example, a connection between the early marriage of young people and an encouraging economic situation. In this connection, we have tried to show that black women are more likely to delay marriage and less likely to remarry. We further noted that although black teenagers expect to become parents at about the same ages as whites, they expect to marry at later ages. And we argue that both the black delay in marriage and the lower rate of remarriage, each of which is associated with high percentages of out-of-wedlock births and female-headed households, can be directly tied to the labor-market status of black males. As we have documented, black women, especially young black women, are facing a shrinking pool of "marriageable" (i.e., economically stable) men.

9.3 JUDITH LORBER

Paradoxes of Gender

In Beijing on September 15, 1995, the United Nations Fourth World Conference on Women ended with total agreement on at least one major point —that women all over the world are not treated fairly. Not all the delegates agreed with the 150-page document drafted during the conference to provide guidelines for establishing and protecting women's rights around the world, but they all agreed that women everywhere need economic empowerment. The women's movement that has fought against the disadvantaged position of women in the United States is now spearheading a worldwide social revolution.

In the following selection from *Paradoxes of Gender* (Yale University Press, 1994), Judith Lorber identifies some of the gender inequalities that afflict women today. Although most of her data and specific analyses are based on women's situation in the United States, much of her discussion is general and applies to women worldwide. For example, the former Soviet Union was a leader with regard to the percentage of employed women and the percentage of women in the professions. But the degree of job segregation by gender did not differ from that of Western societies. Furthermore, 75 percent of physicians in the former Soviet Union are women, but physicians are now among the lowest paid and least prestigious professionals in that region. Lorber would argue that the low wages and prestige are a result of the profession's becoming a "woman's job."

Lorber asserts that, in addition to job segregation, women are greatly disadvantaged by inequities in pay, promotion opportunities, and household work. She suggests that the rapid decline in the percentage of women workers on ascending rungs of the promotion ladder indicates that women are more severely discriminated against with each higher rung. What explains these inequalities in the workplace? Lorber presents a cogent and straightforward Marxian explanation.

Lorber is a professor of sociology at the Graduate School and University Center of the City University of New York. She is the author of *Women Physicians: Careers, Status and Power* (Routledge, Chapman & Hall, 1985) and *Gender and the Social Construction of Illness* (Sage Publications, 1997), and she is coeditor, with Susan A. Farrell, of *The Social Construction of Gender* (Sage Publications, 1990).

Key Concept: gender inequality in the workplace

SEPARATE AND NOT EQUAL: THE
GENDERED DIVISION OF PAID WORK

Although modern industrialized workplaces have different segregation patterns, one type of sorting is endemic: *Almost every workplace in modern industrial societies is either gender-segregated or all one gender.* One group of researchers studying the organization of work in over four hundred firms in California from 1959 to 1979 found that "men and women shared job assignments in organizations so rarely that we could usually be certain that an apparent exception reflected coding or key-punch error.... We were amazed at the pervasiveness of women's concentration in organizational ghettos" (Baron and Bielby 1985, 235). The organizations ranged in size, extent of bureaucracy, and mixture of occupations, yet in virtually all of them, women worked with women and men worked with men (Bielby and Baron 1984, 1986); 59 percent were *totally* segregated by gender (Baron and Bielby 1985).

There are women and men workers in most occupations, but the extent of clustering is such that 60 to 70 percent of men (or women) workers in the United States would have to change occupations to desegregate them, a situation that has persisted throughout the twentieth century. During the 1970s, a decade in which women were thought to have made inroads into many occupations previously dominated by men in the United States, only 33 of 537 occupations saw an increase of women workers of at least 9 percent, or twice the percentage increase of women into the paid labor force during that decade (Reskin and Roos 1990, 16–21). In the 1980s, in 22 of these occupations, women's representation increased twice as rapidly as their increase in the labor force as a whole, which was only 2.4 percent....

Specific *jobs* are even more gender-segregated. An analysis of 645 occupational categories in 290 work organizations in California found that over three-fourths of the women (or men) would have to be reclassified to degender the occupational categories, and that 96 percent of the 10,525 different job titles were gender-segregated (Bielby and Baron 1986). Only 8 percent of the 50,838 workers shared job titles with a member of the opposite gender: "Our findings indicate that small differences in job requirements get amplified into large differences in gender composition.... With few exceptions, a job was either inappropriate for women or appropriate only for women, regardless of the amount of overlap in the attributes of prospective male and female employees" (Bielby and Baron, 1985, 782)....

Promotion ladders are also gender-segregated. Women and men who are not of the dominant racial ethnic group tend not to rise to the top in their work organization, unless practically all the workers are women or men of the same racial ethnic group. White men tend to dominate positions of authority whether or not they are numerically predominant. Even in occupations where the majority of the workers are women, positions of authority tend to be held by men —elementary school teachers are predominantly women in the United States, but principals and superintendents are predominantly men. That is, token men in a woman's occupation tend to be promoted faster than the women workers; the workplace has to be virtually all women for women to be promoted to supervisory positions(Baron and Bielby 1985, 224; C. L. Williams 1992). If bosses of dominant-group men were women or members of subordinate groups, the gendered and racial assumptions of current organizational hierarchies would be challenged (Acker 1989a, 207–23; 1990)....

The gendered division of paid labor dovetails with the gendered division of domestic labor. Low pay and uninteresting jobs encourage single women to marry and married women to devote energy and attention to child rearing and domestic work. Better job opportunities for men encourage them to devote their energy and attention to paid work. Employers (mostly men) benefit from women's cheap labor and men's need to earn more to support a family; men who live with women benefit from women's unpaid labor at home....

Despite twenty years of legislation mandating nondiscrimination in the United State, the better a job is ranked by workers, the more likely it still is to be held by a well-educated white man of high-status background and extensive work experience (Jencks, Perman, and Rainwater 1988). As the members of subordinate racial ethnic groups garner more social resources, they move into the better sectors of the economic system, but the women do not benefit as much as the men from the group's upward mobility. The men, as putative heads of households, monopolize the better opportunities for education, jobs, and starting businesses (Almquist 1987). Women of different racial ethnic groups, however, compete with each other, and as with men, being white is often an advantage (Glenn and Tolbert 1987; Glazer 1993). In teaching, for example, 82.5 percent of Black women teachers were employed in the public sector in fifteen large U.S. cities in 1983, compared to 66.7 percent of white women teachers (E. Higginbotham 1987, table 4.3)....

The Wage Gap

Equal pay for equal work is a generally accepted princple that not only guarantees that women doing men's work receive a man's salary but also ensures that an employer cannot undercut men's wages by hiring women at a cheaper rate (Kessler-Harris 1990, 81–112). The shifting boundaries of occupational gender segregation maintain the principle and undermine it at the same time. Women and men do not do "equal" work—they do different work, or the same work in different industries, or the same work in a different part of a work organization under a different job title (Goldin 1990, 58–82; Strang and Baron 1990). As William Bielby and James Baron say: "men's jobs are rewarded according to their standing within the hierarchy of men's work, and women's jobs are rewarded according to their standing within the hierarchy of women's work. The legitimacy of this system is easy to sustain in a segregated workplace" (1987, 226).

The result is the familiar gendered wage gap. In the United States, the ratio of white women's to white men's wages for full-time, year-round work rose from .46 to .56 from 1890 to 1930, but from 1950 to 1980 hovered around .60 and rose to about .65 by 1989 (Blum 1991, 29; Goldin 1990, 59). The ratio is somewhat better when Black and Hispanic women and men workers are compared, but only because men of color earn less than white men. Most of the early increase in white women's wages was due to their greater work experience and education, but most of the later increase was due to the decline in white men's earnings. The dollar value of "human capital" factors, such as education and experience, is consistently less for all women and for men of subordinate racial ethnic groups than for dominant-group men workers, and this unexplained difference is attributed to the "wage discrimination" that occurs in industrialized countries.

Wage discrimination occurs in two major ways: Wage scales of jobs, occupations, sectors, and segments where dominant-group men are in the majority are consistently higher, and in *any* job, women and subordinate-group men tend to be paid less as workers. Gender differentials are more prevalent than racial gaps. Men who do "women's work" earn less than men who work in occupations where most of the workers are men, but they tend to earn more than the women in these occupations because they are promoted faster. Women who do "men's work" earn more than women who do "women's work" because the occupation or profession as a whole is likely to be better paid; however, since women in "men's work" are not likely to be promoted as fast or as high as their men colleagues, if at all, they rarely outearn men.

In addition to the wage gap produced by the proportion of women to men workers and by the gendered inequalities in advancement, occupations that encompass authority or supervision pay more than similar jobs that do not need managerial skills, and jobs that require workers to deal with clients in an interpersonal or nuturant way pay less than similar non-people-oriented jobs (England 1992). Since authority is more likely to characterize higher-level jobs, where men predominate, and nurturance the lower-level jobs where the majority of the workers are women, all the types of wage discrimination coincide.

Pay Equity or Comparable Worth

One way of achieving pay equity in the face of persistent gender segregation is to compare to actual work content of women's and men's jobs and to pay the same salaries for those that are equally complex or skilled or have similar responsibilities. The strategy of comparable worth is to break a job down into components that add up to points. Such components can be education or training needed to get the job, skills needed to do the job, the extent of responsibility for others' work and for finances, dangerousness, dirtiness, and so on. Evaluation schemes usually assign "worth points" for knowledge and skills, mental demands, accountability, and working conditions.

Comparable worth or pay equity lawsuits claim that women and men workers in jobs with the same number of points should be paid the same in order to redress gendered wage discrimination. For example, in Minnesota, the highest grade of clerk-typists, all women, earned $1,274 a month, while senior highway maintenance workers, almost all men, earned, $1,521 a month. In the pay equity evaluation, the clerk-typist job was given 169 points; the highway maintenance job 154 points (Evans and Nelson 1989, table 1.1, 9). In San Jose, California, before the implementation of a pay equity plan, a nurse earned $9,120 a year less than a fire truck mechanic; a legal secretary made $7,288 a year less than an equipment mechanic; the mayor's secretary made 47 percent less than a senior air conditioning mechanic (Blum 1991, 82–83)....

Judith Lorber

GUARDING THE GATES:
THE MICROPOLITICS OF GENDER

Twenty-five years ago, Muriel F. Siebert bought a seat on the New York Stock Exchange, the first woman to be permitted to do so. In 1992, receiving an award for her accomplishments, she said bluntly that despite the numbers of women coming into high finance, the professions, and government, the arenas of power are still overwhelmingly dominated by men (Henriques 1992). The numbers bear her out.... [I]n the past decade, in the United States, where women composed between 42.4 and 45.4 percent of the work force, and numbered between 42.1 and 53.5 million, a total of five women were heads of the largest corporations (Marsh 1991). When *Fortune* culled the lists of the highest paid officers and directors of 799 U.S. industrial and service companies, out of 4,012 it found 19 women, or less than one-half of 1 percent (Fierman 1990).

The belief that upward mobility and leadership positions would automatically follow if women increased their numbers in the workplace greatly underestimated the social processes that get some people onto the fast track and systematically derail others. These processes are used by those at the top to ensure that those coming up will be as similar as possible to themselves so that their values and ideas about how things should be done will be perpetuated. The markers of homogeneity are gender, race, religion, ethnicity, education, and social background. The few heterogeneous "tokens" who make it past the gate-keepers first must prove their similarity to the elite in outlook and behavior. The numbers at the bottom in any field have little relation to the numbers at the top, where power politics is played and social policies are shaped.

The gender segregation so evident in the modern work world is exacerbated at the top echelons of business, the professions, and politics by gendered concepts of authority and leadership potential. Women are seen as legitimate leaders only in areas considered of direct concern to women, usually health, education, and welfare. Women's accomplishments in men's fields tend to be invisible or denigrated by the men in the field, and so women rarely achieve the stature to be considered leaders in science or space, for example. The U.S. National Aeronautics and Space Administration put twenty-five women pilots through rigorous physical and psychological testing from 1959 to 1961. Thirteen demonstrated "exceptional suitability" for space flight, but neither they nor seventeen women with advanced science degrees were chosen to be astronauts or space scientists, even though the Russians had sent Valentina Tereshkova into space in 1963 (McCullough 1973). As Gloria Steinem said, recalling these invisible women almost twenty years later, women's demonstrating they have the "right stuff" turns into the "wrong stuff" without the approval of the men in charge (1992).

When a leader is chosen among colleagues, women are often overlooked by the men of the group, and there are usually too few women to support one another. Even where women are the majority of workers, men tend to be favored for positions of authority because women and men will accept men leaders as representing their general interests but will see women as representing only women's interests (Izraeli 1984). As a result, men in occupations where most of the workers are women, such as nursing and social work, tend to be overrepresented in high-level administrative positions, and women in occupations where most of the workers are men rarely reach the top ranks (C. L. Williams 1989, 95–98; Zunz 1991)....

The Glass Ceiling

The pervasive phenomenon of women going just so far and no further in their occupations and professions has come to be known as the *glass ceiling*. This concept assumes that women have the motivation, ambition, and capacity for positions of power and prestige, but invisible barriers keep them from reaching the top. They can see their goal, but they bump their heads on a ceiling that is both hidden and impenetrable. The U.S. Department of Labor defines the glass ceiling as "those artificial barriers based on attitudinal or organizational bias that prevent qualified individuals from advancing upward in their organization into management level positions" (L. Martin 1991, 1).

A recent study of the pipelines to power in large-scale corporations conducted by the U.S. Department of Labor found that the glass ceiling was lower than previously thought—in middle management. Members of disadvantaged groups were even less likely than white women to be promoted to top positions, and the upper rungs were "nearly impenetrable" for women of color (L. Martin 1991). A random sample of ninety-four reviews of personnel in corporate headquarters found that of 147,179 employees, 37.2 percent were women and 15.5 percent were minorities Of these employees, 31,184 were in all levels of management, from clerical supervisor to chief executive officer; 16.9 percent were women and 6 percent were minorities. Of 4,491 managers at the level of assistant vice president and higher, 6.6 percent were women and 2.6 percent were minorities. Thus, in this survey, the higher the corporate position, the smaller the proportion of women; if the numbers of women in the top ranks had been proportional with the number of women in the lower ranks, over a third of the vice presidents, presidents, and executive officers would have been women....

The ways that most people move up in their careers are through *networking* (finding out about job opportunities through word-of-mouth and being recommended by someone already there), *mentoring* (being coached through the informal norms of the workplace), and *sponsorship* (being helped to advance by a senior colleague). In civil service bureaucracies, where promotion depends on passing a test or getting on additional credential, those who receive encouragement and advice from senior members of the organization tend to take the qualifying tests or obtain the requisite training (Poll 1978). In the sciences, research productivity depends to a significant degree on where you work, whom you work with, and what resources are available to you. All these processes of advancement depend on the support of colleagues and superiors, which means that in a workplace where men outnumber women and whites outnumber any other racial ethnic group, white women and women and men of disadvantaged racial ethnic groups have to be helped by white if they are to be helped at all.

An in-depth study of nine Fortune 500 companies with a broad range of products and services located in different parts of the country found that despite differences in organizational structure, corporate culture, and personnel policies, the same practices results in a glass ceiling for women, especially women of color (L. Martin 1991, 4–5). These practices were recruitment policies for upper-management levels that depended on word-of-mouth networking and employee referrals. When "head hunters" were used, they were not instructed to look for women and men of social groups underrepresented at managerial levels. The few white women and women and men of color who were already hired were not given the opportunity to build up their credentials or enhance their careers by assignment to corporate committees, task forces, and special projects. These are traditional avenues of advancement, since they bring junior members into contact with senior members of the organization and give them visibility and the chance to show what they can do....

Bands of Brothers

Parallel to the formal organization of a large, modern workplace, which is structured as a task-related, bureaucratic hierarchy, is the informal organization, which is based on trust, loyalty, and reciprocal favors (Lorber [1979] 1989a). Because the unspoken rules are often a significant to the way business is conducted as the written rules, colleagues want to work with people who know what goes without saying: "In order that men [*sic*] may communicate freely and confidentially, they must be able to take a good deal of each other's sentiments for granted. They must feel easy about their silences as well as about their utterances. These factors conspire to make colleagues, with a large body of unspoken understandings, uncomfortable in the presence of what they consider odd kinds of fellows" (Hughes 1971, 146)....

In twentieth-century businesses, professions, and politics, trust and loyalty are built not through kin ties (which is considered nepotism) but through *homosociality*—the bonding of men of the same race, religion, and social-class background (Lipman-Blumen 1976). These men have the economic, political, professional, and social resources to do each other favors. Women with the same social characteristics may be included in men's circles when they have equivalent wealth, power, and social position (C. F. Epstein 1981, 265–302; Lorber 1984, 57–63). Most men and women, however, relate to each other socially only in familial or sexual roles (G. Moore 1990)....

Inner Circles, Friendly Colleagues, and Tokens

The discriminatory aspects of the sorting and tracking that occur in every occupation and profession with long career ladders are obscured because colleagues who are not considered for the top jobs are not fired. They simply fail to make it into the inner circle. Colleagues are organized, informally, into three concentric circles—*inner circles, friendly colleagues,* and *isolated loners.* Power is concentrated and policy is made in inner circles, which are usually homogeneous on gender, race, religion, ethnicity, social class, and education or training. Friendly colleagues usually have some, but not all, of the social characteristics members of the inner circle have. Although they are not totally excluded from the informal colleague network, they are rarely groomed to be part of the inner circle. Women with excellent credentials and work performance in occupations and professions dominated by men tend to end up friendly colleagues if they are of the same race and social class as the men of the inner circle and do similar kinds of work; otherwise, they become loners. Women professionals have formed their own separate colleague groups or professional networks, but many ambitious women do not want to be professionally segregated. They often try to fit in with the men or work on their own and hope that their worth will eventually be recognized by the gatekeepers of their profession or occupation.

Although inner circles tend to be homogeneous on gender, religion, race, ethnicity, education, and class background, a few people with different social characteristics may be accepted if they have a respected sponsor and demonstrate that in all other ways, they are just like the others. They are the true "tokens" (J. L. Laws 1975). They are actively discouraged from bringing more of their kind into the inner circle or from competing for the very top positions in the organization. Tokens usually are eager to fit in and not embarrass their sponsor, so they do not challenge these restrictions or the views, values, or work practices of the inner circle. Indeed, they may outdo the others in upholding the prevailing perspectives and exclusionary practices. That is why token women tend to "one of the boys." ...

GENDER AND EQUALITY

The defeated Equal Rights Amendment to the United States Constitution read simply, "Equality of rights under the law shall not be denied or abridged by the United States or any state on account of sex." Equal rights for women is a goal that resonates with individualism and freedom of choice. Yet that goal failed because, legally, in order to be treated alike, people have to *be* alike, and the prevailing belief in Western societies is that women and men are intrinsically different. Biological rationales for gender inequality not only are still part of the taken-for-granted assumptions of everyday reality in Western countries; they are built into public policy and law....

Exploiting Women

As a group, men own most of the private property, monopolize the better jobs, and make the laws. The outcome of this inequality is men's double exploitation of women in the job market and in the home. Even is they have no other privileges, men reap the advantages of women's domestic labor. Procreative differences are not the cause of women's exploitation but its justification. Women are subordinated in all industrial societies not because they are child bearers or child minders but because owners, managers, and governments depend on them as low-paid, accessible, responsible workers. They are the primary child carers not because of their procreative capabilities but because they are economically disadvantaged and have little choice but to do the unwaged work of social reproduction. Each form of exploitation of women's labor reinforces the other. Women's economic value as waged and unwaged workers is the *main* reason for their subordination in modern societies; they are the "last colony" (Mies, Bennholdt-Thomsen, and von Werlhof 1988).

An often-cited United Nations report (1980) claims that women do two-thirds of the world's work, receive 10 percent of the income, and own 1 percent of the property. Underlying that statement is the world economic system that exploits working-class women and, in particular, women of color by paying them barely subsistence-level wages so that they must expand their nonwaged work in order to maintain their families. Working-class women's labor as unpaid housewives and poorly paid domestic servants, child carers, sex workers, subsistence farmers, sellers and traders of petty commodities, and pieceworkers in the home and in sweatshop factories, combined with middle-class women's work as low-paid office workers, service workers, teachers, nurses, librarians, and social workers, adds up to the two-thirds of the world's work at one-tenth of the world's income....

Working-class women are exploited the most in the job market and in the home. They are systematically deprived of well-paying jobs and so provide cheap labor in the world's factories and offices. Because they do not have a secure place in the labor market, they continue to be exploitable as low-paid domestic workers, dependent on better-paid workers to supplement their inadequate income. In their own homes, their unpaid domestic labor swells capital accumulation because the workers in the household do not have to buy the goods and services they provide for free, and so employers can keep wages down. Working-class women need their husbands' economic support, so they continue to shoulder the burden of the double day....

The fault lines in this gendered social order are single parenthood for women and unemployment for men; both circumstances upset the complementary role expectations that tie women to individual men in order to have a family of their own and give individual men the resources for their dominant status. Bringing up children on the poor salary of a woman's job or on assistance from a government that questions their moral status can radicalize women, just as long-term unemployment has led men to question the legitimacy of an economy that deprives them of work. Rebellious men, once they have jobs, are likely to want a secure and even traditional family life; rebellious women have the potential to challenge the whole gendered social structure that makes it so difficult for them to live both comfortably and independently.

Can You Have Gender and Equality, Too?

I have argued... that gender is a social creation, a product of human inventiveness adopted for its usefulness in allocating reciprocal rights and responsibilities, work tasks, and the physical and social reproduction of new members of any society. The gendered division of work in early societies did not separate subsistence labor and child care—women did both—and many of these societies were egalitarian or possibly even woman-dominated, given women's important contribution to the food supply and their evident role in the procreation of valued children. Accidentally or deliberately, but in any case probably quite gradually, gender got inextricably built into stratification and inequality, producing a subordinate group, "women," whose labor, sexuality, and childbearing could be exploited.

The unequal distribution of power, property, and prestige between women and men is now part of the structure of modern societies. Gender statuses today are inherently unequal, and the whole point of gendering is to produce structured gender inequality. Subordination of women is an intrinsic part of the modern social order not because men are naturally superior or dominant ... or because women bear children. . . . The subordination of women persists because it produces a group that can be exploited as workers, sexual partners, childbearers, and emotional nurturers in the marketplace and in the household. Policies that could establish true gender equality are not seriously implemented because they would erode the exploitation of women's labor, sexuality, and emotions. Societies and communities that have tried to establish egalitarianism rarely give as much attention to gender inequality as they do to economic inequity, the main concern of men. . . .

A truly radical goal for feminism would be not just gender equality but "a society in which maleness and femaleness are socially irrelevant, in which men and women, as we know them, will no longer exist" (Jaggar 1983, 330), a society without gender. A more pragmatic goal (but ultimately equally radical) would be a society without economic inequities, racial distinctions, or sexual exploitation, since they are all implicated in the social production of gender inequality.

9.4 TONI NELSON

Violence Against Women

Although no one has measured suffering rates for groups, many would agree that women do most of the suffering in the world. Sociologists would attribute the cause of this to "structure" and "culture," which, in the case of women's unequal suffering, means patriarchy. Men occupy the more powerful positions and make the rules that govern societies, which naturally benefit men. They also dominate the processes that make and change the culture of societies to create, justify, and protect their advantages. As a result, any unfairness is rationalized as "the way things ought to be."

In the twentieth century men's cozy situation has been attacked and altered by women. This fight and its effects are very unevenly distributed throughout the world. In no place has true equality between the genders been achieved. However, in the United States and Sweden the effects of women's efforts are becoming noticeable.

The most egregious examples of gender inequality can be found in the less developed countries. These include horrendous violence against women, as Toni Nelson, a staff researcher at the Worldwatch Institute, describes in the following selection from "Violence Against Women," *World Watch* (July/August 1996). Only two decades ago violence toward women worldwide received scant attention. Now women around the world have made it an issue for international organizations, national politics, and research agendas. New research is beginning to document women's pain throughout the world. Women and civil rights activists are becoming increasingly organized to fight abuses against women, and many governments are passing laws. There is progress and there is hope.

Key Concept: gender-based violence

A GIRL IS MUTILATED IN EGYPT

It is not a ritual that many people would expect—much less want—to witness. Yet in the fall of 1994, the television network CNN brought the practice of female genital mutilation (FGM) into living rooms around the world, by broadcasting the amputation of a young Egyptian girl's clitoris. Coinciding with the United Nations International Conference on Population and Development in Cairo, the broadcast was one of several recent events that have galvanized efforts to combat the various forms of violence that threaten women and girls

231

throughout the world. The experience suffered by 10-year-old Nagla Hamza focused international attention on the plight of the more than 100 million women and girls in Africa victimized by FGM. In doing so, it helped spur conference delegates into formulating an official "Programme of Action" that condemned FGM and outlined measures to eliminate the practice.

Euphemistically referred to as female circumcision, FGM encompasses a variety of practices ranging from excision, the partial or total removal of the clitoris and labia minora, to infibulation, in which all the external genitals are cut away and the area is restitched, leaving only a small opening for the passage of urine and menstrual blood. Nagla's mutilation, performed by a local barber without anesthesia or sanitary precautions, was typical. Although the physical and psychological consequences of FGM are severe and often life-threatening, the practice persists due to beliefs that emerged from ancient tribal customs but which have now come to be associated with certain major religions. In Israel, for instance, FGM is practiced by Jewish migrants from the Ethiopian Falasha community; elsewhere in Africa, it is found among Christian and Islamic populations. But FGM has no inherent association with any of these religions. Although some Islamic scholars consider it an important part of that religion, FGM actually predates Islam, and neither the Qur'an, the primary source for Islamic law, nor the Hadith, collections of the Prophet Mohammed's lessons, explicitly require the practice.

Justifications for FGM vary among the societies where it occurs (FGM is practiced in 28 African nations, as well as in scattered tribal communities in the Arabian Peninsula and various parts of South Asia). But most explanations relate in some way to male interest in controlling women's emotions and sexual behavior. One of the most common explanations is the need to lessen desire so women will preserve their virginity until marriage. The late Gad-Alhaq Ali Gad-Alhaq, Sheik of Cairo's al-Azhar Islamic University at the time of the CNN broadcast, explained it this way: the purpose of FGM is "to moderate sexual desire while saving womanly pleasures in order that women may enjoy their husbands." For Mimi Ramsey, an anti-FGM activist in the United States who was mutilated in her native Ethiopia at age six, FGM is meant to reinforce the power men have over women: "the reason for my mutilation is for a man to be able to control me, to make me a good wife." Today, migrants are bringing FGM out of its traditional societies and into Europe, North America, and Australia. Approximately 2 million girls are at risk each year....

VIOLENCE IS A UNIVERSAL THREAT

... Throughout the world, women's inferior social status makes them vulnerable to abuse and denies them the financial and legal means necessary to improve their situations. Over the past decade, women's groups around the world have succeeded in showing how prevalent this problem is and how much violence it is causing—a major accomplishment, given the fact that the issue was not even mentioned during the first UN Women's Conference in 1975 or in the

1979 UN Convention on All Forms of Discrimination Against Women. But as the situation in Egypt demonstrates, effective policy responses remain elusive.

Violence stalks women throughout their lives, "from cradle to grave"—in the judgment of *Human Development Report 1995*, the UN's annual assessment of social and economic progress around the world. Gender-specific violence is almost a cultural constant, both emerging from and reinforcing the social relationships that give men power over women. This is most obvious in the implicit acceptance, across cultures, of domestic violence—of a man's prerogative to beat his wife. Large-scale surveys in 10 countries, including Colombia, Canada, and the United States, estimate that as many as one-third of women have been physically assaulted by an intimate male partner. More limited studies report that rates of physical abuse among some groups in Latin America, Asia, and Africa may reach 60 percent or more.

Belying the oft-cried cliché about "family values," studies have shown that the biggest threat to women is domestic violence. In 1992, the *Journal of the American Medical Association* published a study that found that women in the United States are more likely to be assaulted, injured, raped, or murdered by a current or former male partner than by all other types of attackers combined. In Canada, a 1987 study showed that 62 percent of the women murdered in that year were killed by an intimate male partner. And in India, the husband or in-laws of a newly married woman may think it justified to murder her if they consider her dowry inadequate, so that a more lucrative match can be made. One popular method is to pour kerosene on the woman and set her on fire— hence the term "bride burning." One in four deaths among women aged 16 to 24 in the urban areas of Maharashtra state (including Bombay) is attributed to "accidental burns." About 5,000 "dowry deaths" occur in India every year, according to government estimates, and some observers think the number is actually much higher. Subhadra Chaturvedi, one of India's leading attorneys, puts the death toll at a minimum of 12,000 a year.

The preference for sons, common in many cultures, can lead to violence against female infants—and even against female fetuses. In India, for example, a 1990 study of amniocentesis in a large Bombay hospital found that 95.5 percent of fetuses identified as female were aborted, compared with only a small percentage of male fetuses. (Amniocentesis involves the removal of a sample of amniotic fluid from the womb; this can be used to determine the baby's sex and the presence of certain inherited diseases.) Female infanticide is still practiced in rural areas of India; a 1992 study by Cornell University demographer Sabu George found that 58 percent of female infant deaths (19 of 33) within a 12-village region of Tamil Nadu state were due to infanticide. The problem is especially pronounced in China, where the imposition of the one-child-per-family rule has led to a precipitous decline in the number of girls: studies in 1987 and 1994 found a half-million fewer female infants in each of those years than would be expected, given the typical biological ratio of male to female births.

Women are also the primary victims of sexual crimes, which include sexual abuse, rape, and forced prostitution. Girls are the overwhelming target of child sexual assaults; in the United States, 78 percent of substantiated child sexual abuse cases involve girls. According to a 1994 World Bank study, *Violence Against Women: The Hidden Health Burden*, national surveys suggest that up to one-third of women in Norway, the United States, Canada, New Zealand, Barbados, and the Netherlands are sexually abused during childhood. Often very young children are the victims: a national study in the United States and studies in several Latin American cities indicate that 13 to 32 percent of abused girls are age 10 and under.

Rape haunts women throughout their lives, exposing them to unwanted pregnancy, disease, social stigma, and psychological trauma. In the United States, which has some of the best data on the problem, a 1993 review of rape studies suggests that between 14 and 20 percent of women will be victims of completed rapes during their lifetimes. In some cultures, a woman who has been raped is perceived as having violated the family honor, and she may be forced to marry her attacker or even killed. One study of female homicide in Alexandria, Egypt, for example, found that 47 percent of women murdered were killed by a family member following a rape.

In war, rape is often used as both a physical and psychological weapon. An investigation of recent conflicts in the former Yugoslavia, Peru, Kashmir, and Somalia by the international human rights group, Human Rights Watch, found that "rape of women civilians has been deployed as a tactical weapon to terrorize civilian communities or to achieve 'ethnic cleansing'." Studies suggest that tens of thousands of Muslim and Serbian women in Bosnia have been raped during the conflict there.

A growing number of women and girls, particularly in developing countries, are being forced into prostitution. Typically, girls from poor, remote villages are purchased outright from their families or lured away with promises of jobs or false marriage proposals. They are then taken to brothels, often in other countries, and forced to work there until they pay off their "debts"—a task that becomes almost impossible as the brothel owner charges them for clothes, food, medicine, and often even their own purchase price. According to Human Rights Watch, an estimated 20,000 to 30,000 Burmese girls and women currently work in brothels in Thailand; their ranks are now expanding by as many as 10,000 new recruits each year. Some 20,000 to 50,000 Nepalese girls are working in Indian brothels. As the fear of AIDS intensifies, customers are demanding ever younger prostitutes, and the age at which girls are being forced into prostitution is dropping; the average age of the Nepalese recruits, for example, declined from 14–16 years in the 1980s, to 10–14 years by 1994....

WOMEN BREAK THE SILENCE

"These women are holding back a silent scream so strong it could shake the earth." That is how Dr. Nahid Toubia, Executive Director of the U.S.-based anti-FGM organization RAINBO, described FGM victims when she testified at the 1993 Global Tribunal on Violations of Women's Human Rights. Yet her statement would apply just as well to the millions of women all over the world who have been victims of other forms of violence. Until recently, the problem of gender-based violence has remained largely invisible. Because the stigma attached to many forms of violence makes them difficult to discuss openly, and because violence typically occurs inside the home, accurate information on the magnitude of the problem has been extremely scarce. Governments, by claiming jurisdiction only over human rights abuses perpetrated in the public sphere by agents of the state, have reinforced this invisibility. Even human rights work has traditionally confined itself to the public sphere and largely ignored many of the abuses to which women are most vulnerable.

But today, the victims of violence are beginning to find their voices. Women's groups have won a place for "private sphere" violence on human rights agendas, and they are achieving important changes in both national laws and international conventions. The first major reform came in June 1993, at the UN Second World Conference on Human Rights in Vienna. In a drive leading up to the conference, activists collected almost half a million signatures from 124 countries on a petition insisting that the conference address gender violence. The result: for the first time, violence against women was recognized as an abuse of women's human rights, and nine paragraphs on "The equal status and human rights of women" were incorporated into the Vienna Declaration and Programme of Action.

More recently, 18 members of the Organization of American States have ratified the Inter-American Convention on the Prevention, Punishment and Eradication of Violence Against Women. Many activists consider this convention, which went into effect on March 5, 1995, the strongest existing piece of international legislation in the field. And the Pan American Health Organization (PAHO) has become the first development agency to make a significant financial commitment to the issue. PAHO has received $4 million from Sweden, Norway, and the Netherlands, with the possibility of an additional $2.5 million from the Inter-American Development Bank, to conduct research on violence and establish support services for women in Latin America.

National governments are also drawing up legislation to combat various forms of gender violence. A growing number of countries, including South Africa, Israel, Argentina, the Bahamas, Australia, and the United States have all passed special domestic violence laws. Typically, these clarify the definition of domestic violence and strengthen protections available to the victims. In September 1994, India passed its "Pre-natal Diagnostic Techniques (Regulation and Prevention of Misuse) Act," which outlaws the use of prenatal testing for sex-selection. India is also developing a program to eradicate female infanticide. FGM is being banned in a growing number of countries, too. At least nine European countries now prohibit the practice, as does Australia. In the United States, a bill criminalizing FGM was passed by the Senate in May, but had yet to become law. More significant, perhaps, is the African legislation: FGM is now illegal in both Ghana and Kenya.

It is true, of course, that laws don't necessarily translate into real-life changes. But it is possible that the movement to stop FGM will yield the first solid success in the struggle to make human rights a reality for women. Over the past decade, the Inter-African Committee on Traditional Practices Affecting the Health of Women and Children, an NGO dedicated to abolishing FGM, has set up committees in 25 African countries. And in March 1995, Ghana used its anti-FGM statute to arrest the parents and circumciser of an eight-year-old girl who was rushed to the hospital with excessive bleeding. In Burkina Faso, some circumcising midwives have been convicted under more general legislation. These are modest steps, perhaps, but legal precedent can be a powerful tool for reform.

In the United States, an important precedent is currently being set by a 19-year-old woman from the nation of Togo, in west Africa. Fleeing an arranged marriage and the ritual FGM that would accompany it, Fauziya Kasinga arrived in the United States seeking asylum in December 1994. She has spent much of the time since then in prison, and her request for asylum, denied by a lower court, is at the time of writing under appeal. People are eligible for asylum in the United States if they are judged to have a reasonable fear of persecution due to their race, religion, nationality, political opinions, or membership in a social group. However, U.S. asylum law makes no explicit provision for gender-based violence. In 1993, Canada became the world's first country to make the threat of FGM grounds for granting refugee status.

Whichever way the decision on Kasinga's case goes, it will be adopted as a binding general precedent in U.S. immigration cases (barring the passage of federal legislation that reverses it). But even while her fate remains in doubt, Kasinga has already won an important moral victory. Her insistence on her right *not* to be mutilated—and on the moral obligation of others to shield her from violence if they can—has made the threat she faces a matter of conscience, of politics, and of policy. Given the accumulating evidence of how deeply gender-based violence infects our societies, in both the developing and the industrialized countries, we have little choice but to recognize it as the fundamental moral and economic challenge that it is.

PART FOUR

Social Institutions

On the Internet . . .

Sites appropriate to Part Four

The Marketplace of Political Ideas is a valuable collection of
links to campaign, conservative/liberal perspective, and
political party sites. These include general political sites,
Democratic sites, Republican sites, and third-party sites.

```
http://info.lib.uh.edu/politics/
   markind.htm
```

The National Center for Policy Analysis site offers links to
discussions of an array of topics that are of major interest in
the study of American politics and government from a
sociological perspective, including regulatory policy,
affirmative action, and income.

```
http://www.public-policy.org/~ncpa/pd/
   pdindex.html
```

The Futurist is a monthly magazine of forecasts, trends, and
ideas about the future. It is published by the World Future
Society and is read by 30,000 members worldwide.

```
http://www.wfs.org/futurist.htm
```

The December 1996 issue of the Dutch journal Sociale
Wetenschappen ("Social Sciences") is devoted to a discussion of
George Ritzer's McDonaldization of society thesis. This
special issue contains an opening article by Ritzer followed by
four critical articles. Ritzer closes the discussion with a reply
to his critics.

```
http://www.mi.fgg.eur.nl/fsw/mcd/
```

CHAPTER 10 The Political System

10.1 G. WILLIAM DOMHOFF

Who Rules America?

The key question concerning the political system for the sociologist is, What is the structure of power? Since the founding of history's first democratic national government in the United States, there have been countless claims that it is dominated by the elite and nondemocratic. C. Wright Mills launched his attack on the myth of democratic rule in the United States in his 1957 book *The Power Elite.* According to Mills, the few people who occupy the command post positions of the large, powerful organizations in the economy, government, and military control the country through their control of these organizations. His theory was criticized for not demonstrating how these elites were organized into a unified ruling group. The members of this group, it was argued, had conflicting interests and did not meet together. Without some explicit means of coordination, these people, though powerful, would not be a ruling group.

Since Mills, the major proponent of the elite rule view has been political sociologist G. William Domhoff. In *Who Rules America* (1967) he argued that America has an upper class of wealth and power that is identifiable largely by membership in the social registers of the country. Its members occupy the majority of the ruling positions in the government, the corporations, the media, and the policy-forming institutions. Where it does not occupy the key positions it rules by various forms of influence. For example, its members do not occupy the majority of the seats in Congress, but they do control Congress through contributions and lobbying.

Over time Domhoff softened his equation of the ruling elite with the upper class as defined largely by the social registers. He now defines the elite group more in terms of corporate capitalism. His latest work, from which the following selection has been taken, is *Who Rules America? Power and Politics in the Year 2000,* 3rd ed. (Mayfield, 1998). In it, Domhoff states his theory thusly: "The owners and top-level managers in large income-producing properties are far and away the dominant power figures in the United States. Their corporations, banks, and agribusinesses come together as a *corporate community* that dominates the federal government in Washington."

Key Concept: power elite

POWER AND CLASS IN THE UNITED STATES

Power and *class* are terms that make Americans a little uneasy, and concepts like *power elite* and *dominant class* immediately put people on guard. The idea that a relatively fixed group of privileged people might shape the economy and government for their own benefit goes against the American grain. Nevertheless,... the owners and top-level managers in large income-producing properties are far and away the dominant power figures in the United States. Their corporations, banks, and agribusinesses come together as a *corporate community* that dominates the federal government in Washington. Their real estate, construction, and land development companies form *growth coalitions* that dominate most local governments. Granted, there is competition within both the corporate community and the local growth coalitions for profits and investment opportunities, and there are sometimes tensions between national corporations and local growth coalitions, but both are cohesive on policy issues affecting their general welfare, and in the face of demands by organized workers, liberals, environmentalists, and neighborhoods.

As a result of their ability to organize and defend their interests, the owners and managers of large income-producing properties have a very great share of all income and wealth in the United States, greater than in any other industrial democracy. Making up at best 1 percent of the total population, by the early 1990s they earned 15.7 percent of the nation's yearly income and owned 37.2 percent of all privately held wealth, including 49.6 percent of all corporate stocks and 62.4 percent of all bonds. Due to their wealth and the lifestyle it makes possible, these owners and managers draw closer as a common social group. They belong to the same exclusive social clubs, frequent the same summer and winter resorts, and send their children to a relative handful of private schools. Members of the corporate community thereby become a *corporate rich* who create a nationwide *social upper class* through their social interaction.... Members of the growth coalitions, on the other hand, are *place entrepreneurs,* people who sell locations and buildings. They come together as local upper classes in their respective cities and sometimes mingle with the corporate rich in educational or resort settings.

The corporate rich and the growth entrepreneurs supplement their small numbers by developing and directing a wide variety of nonprofit organizations, the most important of which are a set of tax-free charitable foundations, think tanks, and policy-discussion groups. These specialized nonprofit groups constitute a *policy-formation network* at the national level. Chambers of commerce and policy groups affiliated with them form similar policy-formation networks at the local level, aided by a few national-level city development organizations that are available for local consulting.

Those corporate owners who have the interest and ability to take part in general governance join with top-level executives in the corporate community and the policy-formation network to form the *power elite*, which is the leadership group for the corporate rich as a whole. The concept of a power elite makes clear that not all members of the upper class are involved in governance; some of them simply enjoy the lifestyle that their great wealth affords them. At the same time, the focus on a leadership group allows for the fact that not all those in the power elite are members of the upper class; many of them are high-level employees in profit and nonprofit organizations controlled by the corporate rich....

The power elite is not united on all issues because it includes both moderate conservatives and ultraconservatives. Although both factions favor minimal reliance on government on all domestic issues, the moderate conservatives sometimes agree to legislation advocated by liberal elements of the society, especially in times of social upheaval like the Great Depression of the 1930s and the Civil Rights Movement of the early 1960s. Except on defense spending, ultraconservatives are characterized by a complete distaste for any kind of government programs under any circumstances—even to the point of opposing government support for corporations on some issues. Moderate conservatives often favor foreign aid, working through the United Nations, and making attempts to win over foreign enemies through patient diplomacy, treaties, and trade agreements. Historically, ultraconservatives have opposed most forms of foreign involvement, although they have become more tolerant of foreign trade agreements over the past thirty or forty years. At the same time, their hostility to the United Nations continues unabated.

Members of the power elite enter into the electoral arena as the leaders within a *corporate-conservative coalition*, where they are aided by a wide variety of patriotic, antitax, and other single-issue organizations. These conservative advocacy organizations are funded in varying degrees by the corporate rich, direct-mail appeals, and middle-class conservatives. This coalition has played a large role in both political parties at the presidential level and usually succeeds in electing a conservative majority to both houses of Congress. Historically, the conservative majority in Congress was made up of most Northern Republicans and most Southern Democrats, but that arrangement has been changing gradually since the 1960s as the conservative Democrats of the South are replaced by even more conservative Southern Republicans. The corporate-conservative coalition also has access to the federal government in Washington through lobbying and the appointment of its members to top positions in the executive branch....

Despite their preponderant power within the federal government and the many useful policies it carries out for them, members of the power elite are constantly critical of government as an alleged enemy of freedom and economic growth. Although their wariness toward government is expressed in terms of a dislike for taxes and government regulations, I believe their underlying concern is that government could change the power relations in the private sphere by aiding average Americans through a number of different avenues: (1) creating government jobs for the unemployed; (2) making health, unemployment, and welfare benefits more generous; (3) helping employees gain greater workplace rights and protections; and (4) helping workers organize unions. All of these initiatives are opposed by members of the power elite because they would increase wages and taxes, but the deepest opposition is toward any government support for unions because unions are a potential organizational base for advocating the whole range of issues opposed by the corporate rich....

Where Does Democracy Fit In?

... [T]o claim that the corporate rich have enough power to be considered a dominant class does not imply that lower social classes are totally powerless. *Domination* means the power to set the terms under which other groups and classes must operate, not total control. Highly trained professionals with an interest in environmental and consumer issues have been able to couple their technical information and their understanding of the legislative and judicial processes with well-timed publicity, lobbying, and lawsuits to win governmental restrictions on some corporate practices. Wage and salary employees, when they are organized into unions and have the right to strike, have been able to gain pay increases, shorter hours, better working conditions, and social benefits such as health insurance. Even the most powerless of people—the very poor and those discriminated against—sometimes develop the capacity to influence the power structure through sit-ins, demonstrations, social movements, and other forms of social disruption, and there is evidence that such activities do bring about some redress of grievances, at least for a short time.

More generally, the various challengers to the power elite sometimes work together on policy issues as a *liberal-labor coalition* that is based in unions, local environmental organizations, some minority group communities, university and arts communities, liberal churches, and small newspapers and magazines. Despite a decline in membership over the past twenty years, unions are the largest and best-financed part of the coalition, and the largest organized social force in the country (aside from churches). They also cut across racial and ethnic lines more than any other institutionalized sector of American society....

The policy conflicts between the corporate-conservative and liberal-labor coalitions are best described as *class conflicts* because they primarily concern the distribution of profits and wages, the rate and progressivity of taxation, the usefulness of labor unions, and the degree to which business should be regulated by government. The liberal-labor coalition wants corporations to pay higher wages to employees and higher taxes to government. It wants government to regulate a wide range of business practices, including many that are related to the environment, and help employees to organize unions. The corporate-conservative coalition resists all these policy objectives to a greater or lesser degree, claiming they endanger the freedom of individuals and the efficient workings of the economic marketplace. The conflicts these disagreements generate can manifest themselves in many different ways: workplace protests, industrywide boycotts, massive demonstrations in cities, pressure on Congress, and the outcome of elections.

Neither the corporate-conservative nor the liberal-labor coalition includes a very large percentage of the American population, although each has the regular support of about 25–30 percent of the voters. Both coalitions are made up primarily of financial donors, policy experts, political consultants, and party activists. . . .

Pluralism. The main alternative theory [I] address . . . claims that power is more widely dispersed among groups and classes than a class-dominance theory allows. This general perspective is usually called *pluralism*, meaning there is no one dominant power group. It is the theory most favored by social scientists. In its strongest version, pluralism holds that power is held by the general public through the pressure that public opinion and voting put on elected officials. According to this version, citizens form voluntary groups and pressure groups that shape public opinion, lobby elected officials, and back sympathetic political candidates in the electoral process. . . .

The second version of pluralism sees power as rooted in a wide range of well-organized "interest groups" that are often based in economic interests (e.g., industrialists, bankers, labor unions), but also in other interests as well (e.g., environmental, consumer, and civil rights groups). These interest groups join together in different coalitions depending on the specific issues. Proponents of this version of pluralism sometimes concede that public opinion and voting have only a minimal or indirect influence, but they see business groups as too fragmented and antagonistic to form a cohesive dominant class. They also claim that some business interest groups occasionally join coalitions with liberal or labor groups on specific issues, and that business-dominated coalitions sometimes lose. Furthermore, some proponents of this version of pluralism believe that the Democratic Party is responsive to the wishes of liberal and labor interest groups.

In contrast, I argue that the business interest groups are part of a tightly knit corporate community that is able to develop classwide cohesion on the issues of greatest concern to it: opposition to unions, high taxes, and government regulation. When a business group loses on a specific issue, it is often because other business groups have been opposed; in other words, there are arguments within the corporate community, and these arguments are usually settled within the governmental arena. I also claim that liberal and labor groups are rarely part of coalitions with business groups and that for most of its history the Democratic Party has been dominated by corporate and agribusiness interests in the Southern states, in partnership with the growth coalitions in large urban areas outside the South. Finally, I show that business interests rarely lose on labor and regulatory issues except in times of extreme social disruption like the 1930s and 1960s, when differences of opinion between Northern and Southern corporate leaders made victories for the liberal-labor coalition possible. . . .

HOW THE POWER ELITE
DOMINATES GOVERNMENT

This [section] shows how the power elite builds on the ideas developed in the policy-formation process and its success in the electoral arena to dominate the federal government. Lobbyists from corporations, law firms, and trade associations play a key role in shaping government on narrow issues of concern to specific corporations or business sectors, but their importance should not be overestimated because a majority of those elected to Congress are predisposed to agree with them. The corporate community and the policy-formation network supply top-level governmental appointees and new policy directions on major issues.

Once again, as seen in the battles for public opinion and electoral success, the power elite faces opposition from a minority of elected officials and their supporters in labor unions and liberal advocacy groups. These opponents are sometimes successful in blocking ultra-conservative initiatives, but most of the victories for the liberal-labor coalition are the result of support from moderate conservatives. . . .

Appointees to Government

The first way to test a class-dominance view of the federal government is to study the social and occupational backgrounds of the people who are appointed to manage the major departments of the executive branch, such as state, treasury, defense, and justice. If pluralists are correct, these appointees should come from a wide range of interest groups. If the state autonomy theorists are correct, they should be disproportionately former elected officials or longtime government employees. If the class-dominance view is correct, they should come disproportionately from the upper class, the corporate community, and the policy-formation network.

There have been numerous studies over the years of major governmental appointees under both Republican and Democratic administrations, usually focusing on the top appointees in the departments that are represented in the president's cabinet. These studies are unanimous in their conclusion that most top appointees in both Republican and Democratic administrations are corporate executives and corporate lawyers—and hence members of the power elite. . . .

Conclusion

This [section] has demonstrated the power elite's wide-ranging access to government through the interest-group and policy-formation processes, as well as through its ability to influence appointments to major government positions. When coupled with the several different kinds of power discussed in earlier [sections] this access and involvement add up to power elite domination of the federal government.

By *domination,* as stated in the first [section], social scientists mean the ability of a class or group to set the terms under which other classes or groups within a social system must operate. By this definition, domination does not mean control on each and every issue, and it does not rest solely on involvement in government. Influence over government is only the final and most visible aspect of power elite domination, which has its roots in the class structure, the corporate control of the investment function, and the operation of the policy-formation network. If government officials did not have to wait for corporate leaders to decide where and when they will invest, and if government officials were not further limited by the general public's acceptance of policy recommendations from the policy-formation network, then power elite involvement in elections and government would count for a lot less than they do under present conditions.

Domination by the power elite does not negate the reality of continuing conflict over government policies, but few conflicts, it has been shown, involve challenges to the rules that create privileges for the upper class and domination by the power elite. Most of the numerous battles within the interest-group process, for example, are only over specific spoils and favors; they often involve disagreements among competing business interests.

Similarly, conflicts within the policy-making process of government often involve differences between the moderate conservative and ultraconservative segments of the dominant class. At other times they involve issues in which the needs of the corporate community as a whole come into conflict with the needs of specific industries, which is what happens to some extent on tariff policies and also on some environmental legislation. In neither case does the nature of the conflict call into question the domination of government by the power elite.

...Contrary to what pluralists claim, there is not a single case study on any issue of any significance that shows a liberal-labor victory over a united corporate-conservative coalition, which is strong evidence for a class-domination theory on the "Who wins?" power indicator. The classic case studies frequently cited by pluralists have been shown to be gravely deficient as evidence for their views. Most of these studies reveal either conflicts among rival groups within the power elite or situations in which the moderate conservatives have decided for their own reasons to side with the liberal-labor coalition....

More generally, it now can be concluded that all four indicators of power introduced in [the first section] point to the corporate rich and their power elite as the dominant organizational structure in American society. First, the wealth and income distributions are skewed in their favor more than in any other industrialized democracy. They are clearly the most powerful group in American society in terms of "Who benefits?" Second, the appointees to government come overwhelmingly from the corporate community and its associated policy-formation network. Thus, the power elite is clearly the most powerful in terms of "Who sits?"

Third, the power elite wins far more often than it loses on policy issues resolved in the federal government. Thus, it is the most powerful in terms of "Who wins?" Finally, as shown in reputational studies in the 1950s and 1970s,... corporate leaders are the most powerful group in terms of "Who shines?" By the usual rules of evidence in a social science investigation using multiple indicators, the owners and managers of large income-producing properties are the dominant class in the United States.

Still, as noted at the end of the first [section], power structures are not immutable. Societies change and power structures evolve or crumble from time to unpredictable time, especially in the face of challenge. When it is added that the liberal-labor coalition persists in the face of its numerous defeats, and that free speech and free elections are not at risk, there remains the possibility that class domination could be replaced by a greater sharing of power in the future.

10.2 MARVIN J. CETRON AND OWEN DAVIES

The Future Face of Terrorism

Until the bombing of the World Trade Center in New York City in 1993 and a federal building in Oklahoma City in 1995, America had been free of mass terrorist acts, which have afflicted many other nations. Now the potential for terrorism in the United States is a major concern. The defense and law enforcement establishments have initiated considerable research on terrorism but are reluctant to disseminate the findings.

Recent events have greatly increased the opportunities for terrorism. The collapse of the Soviet Union has given birth to new states with primitive infrastructures and unreliable security systems but also with an array of sophisticated weapons and numerous scientists, technicians, and military experts. Some fear that these experts might sell their expertise and knowledge to religious and ethnically motivated terrorists or rogue nation-states for the right price.

Marvin J. Cetron and Owen Davies, leading terrorist researchers for the U.S. Department of Defense, provide their major conclusions on the future of terrorism in the following selection, which is from "The Future Face of Terrorism," *The Futurist* (November/December 1994). They suggest that the future will be the age of superterrorism: No longer will terrorists use a narrow range of limited impact weapons that kill only hundreds; they will use *nuclear, chemical, and biological weapons* that can kill millions of people. Furthermore, some terrorists will seek the complete annihilation of their enemies, not just to reach political goals.

Governments, note Cetron and Davies, respond to terrorism by increasing the security in governmental buildings and limiting or closing off access to all governmental structures. Indeed, following the bombing of the federal building in Oklahoma City, for the first time in the history of the United States several streets with direct access to the White House were permanently closed to motorists. But generally, the authors contend, governments are not responding enough to terrorism.

Cetron is the founder and president of Forecasting International and is one of the world's leading futurists. He is the author of *Technological Forecasting* (Technology Forecasting Institute, 1969). Davies is the former senior editor of *Omni* magazine and coauthor, with Cetron, of *American*

Renaissance: Our Life at the Turn of the Twenty-first Century (St. Martin's
Press, 1989).

Key Concept: superterrorism

In the past, terrorists have been ruthless opportunists, using bloody, but
relatively narrow, range of weapons to further clear, political ends. The next 15
years may well be the age of superterrorism, when they gain access to weapons
of mass destruction and show a new willingness to use them. Tomorrow's most
dangerous terrorists will be motivated not by political ideology, but by fierce
ethnic and religious hatreds. Their goal will not be political control, but the utter
destruction of their chosen enemies. Nuclear, biological, and chemical weapons
are ideal for their purpose.

They will increasingly be joined by another variety of terrorist—criminals
with the goal of maximizing profit, minimizing risk, and protecting their enterprises by intimidating or co-opting government officials. We have already seen
their brand of terrorism in Colombia and Italy, but "criminal terrorism" has not
yet been fully accepted as a legitimate target for the antiterrorist community.
We use counterterrorist forces against "narcoterrorists," for example, but still
believe we are diverting specialized resources to aid the "war on drugs." Before
the 1990s are over, we will be forced to recognize that it is the method, not the
motive, that makes a terrorist.

Alongside all of these developments, the traditional brand of terrorism—
seeking political power through the violent intimidation of noncombatants—
will continue to grow at the global rate of about 15% per year. Instability bred
by the proliferation of the more-violent religious and ethnic terrorist groups,
coupled with an almost exponential growth in "mini-states" in the former Soviet Union and eastern Europe, could produce a two- to three-fold increase in
international terrorist incidents by the turn of the century.

Technology in particular has made terrorism more attractive to dissident
groups and rogue states. In the high-tech global village that the world is fast
becoming, modern telecommunications provides near real-time coverage of terrorist attacks, whether in Beirut, Buenos Aires, Khartoum, or New York. As
terrorism expert Brian Jenkins has noted, terrorism is theater and terrorists can
now play to a global audience. As we move into the twenty-first century, new
and even more powerful communications links will give terrorism still greater
power and appeal.

SUPERTERRORISM

The most ominous trend in terrorism is also a matter of technology. With the
end of the Cold War, weapons of mass destruction have slipped from their traditional controls. If nuclear, biological, or chemical weapons are not yet available
to terrorist organizations and the states that support them, they soon will be.

Marvin J. Cetron and Owen Davies

The proliferation of mass-destruction technologies and of groups that actively seek to inflict mass casualties has forever changed the face of terrorism. This confluence of means and will is a benchmark development that has qualitatively changed the nature of the terrorist challenge. According to members of both the Futurist and Terrorist Advisory Boards, assembled by Forecasting International, an improvised nuclear, biological, or chemical attack on the United States is increasingly probable—perhaps within the next five years.

Though North Korea's weapons program represents a pressing concern, the former Soviet Union and its one-time satellite states present the greater risk. In North Korea, such weapons remain under the firm control of a strong central government, whose willingness to distribute them is a troubling possibility, but is not yet clear. In many former communist states, control over many of these weapons has been so badly weakened that it may not matter what their central government intends.

Throughout the former East Bloc, scientists, technicians, and military personnel have families to feed, but suddenly lack jobs to pay their way. Many have firsthand knowledge of biological, chemical, and nuclear weapons. Therefore, many states and terrorist groups are hungry for their expertise and able to pay handsomely for it.

The weapons themselves may also be an immediate danger. While strategic nuclear weapons remain too well guarded to be stolen or sold, tactical weapons lie scattered across what is left of the Soviet Union. Controls over these weapons are reportedly lax, and there is little hope that they will remain where Soviet troops left them. A single artillery round could provide enough material for a crude but effective nuclear device, particularly if it were designed for contamination rather than for use as a conventional nuclear weapon.

Chemical and biological weapons are even easier to acquire. Neurotoxins are closely related to many pesticides. Anyone capable of making common agricultural chemicals can make these poisons. As early as 1972, American authorities broke an ultra-right-wing terrorist organization and discovered a weapons cache that included 80 pounds of botulin toxin, a deadly food poison. Today, genetic engineering is sophisticated enough to produce even more virulent, custom-tailored pathogens. With such technology within the reach of many would-be terrorists, this is one form of proliferation that no one can even hope to prevent.

Easy access to biological, chemical, and nuclear technologies will bring many new players to the game of mass destruction. They may not even be limited to states and traditional terrorist groups. Organized crime, fanatical single-issue groups, and even individuals will all be able to acquire weapons once limited to regional and world powers.

Using chemical or nuclear-type weapons effectively would be easy, too. For example, if the World Trade Center bombers had packed their van with cobalt-60 or iodine-131 (both commonly available in medical industrial laboratories), they might well have rendered New York's financial district uninhabitable for generations. Pulmonary anthrax kills 99% of the victims it infects, and only a few grams would be needed to kill virtually everyone in a major government office complex. If released in a subway tunnel, the convection currents created by the passing trains would carry the spores throughout the system, to be inhaled by thousands of commuters. Clinging to people's clothing, the anthrax spores would also be spread through offices, public buildings, and suburban homes. Thousands would die. It would be days before we even knew we had been attacked, and it would be virtually impossible to assign blame.

Those weapons will be used, and not only because once possessed they represent an overwhelming temptation, but because—in the United States particularly—the public pays attention only to the spectacular. A year after the World Trade Center bombing, the blast was little more than a dim memory, to be revived only briefly when the perpetrators were brought to trial. Future terrorists will find that they need ever more spectacular horrors to overcome people's capacity to absorb and forget what previously would have seemed intolerable.

In the past, other concerns would have restrained terrorists from using weapons of mass destruction. Politically motivated terrorists require popular support to function. That support is seldom as committed or ruthless as the violent core of a terrorist movement, and the true extremists must temper their actions so as to avoid alienating the sympathies of those they hope to recruit, as well as those who provide money and logistical support. But for many of those now embarking on terrorist careers, those restraints do not apply.

ETHNORELIGIOUS TERRORISM

Since the end of the Cold War, many forces have combined to unleash terrorist causes that either are new or had been buried under the crushing weight of the Soviet security apparatus. Where most old-line terrorist organizations served political causes, in the early twenty-first century they will be joined by a growing number of terrorist groups that are motivated by religious fervor or ethnic hatred. This is a dangerous development. With many traditional terrorist groups, we could assume that their targets and tactics would be constrained by the need to retain political sympathies. We appear to be entering an era in which few, if any, restraints will remain.

Religious and ethnically motivated terrorists are more willing than most to pursue their aims by whatever means necessary. Unlike politically motivated terrorists, religious fanatics do not shrink from mass murder, because they are struggling against what they perceive as "the forces of darkness" or are striving to preserve such quasi-mystical concepts as "the purity of the race." Mass casualties are not to be shunned, because they demonstrate the cataclysmic nature of divine retribution. If innocents suffer, God will sort them out. The late Hussein Mussawi, leader of the Shiite Muslim group Hezbollah, once commented, "We are not fighting so that the enemy recognizes us and offers us something. We are fighting to wipe out the enemy." Radical Islam not only attacks moderate Arab regimes, but has spread beyond the Middle East. It now has significant followings in Muslim communities in Africa, Asia, Europe, and the Americas.

Ethnically motivated terrorists are driven by forces almost as powerful—a visceral, tribal fealty with a mystical and almost religious overlay. These terrorists are defending their family and community, the memory of their ancestors, their cultural heritage, and the identity of their people, many of whom have suffered and died simply because they were Armenians, Bosnians, Basques, Irish, Quiche, Ibo, or Kurds. They believe that their enemies seek the subjugation or annihilation of their people. It is the ethnoterrorist's sacred duty to prevent this evil, not only for the sake of the living and future generations, but out of reverence for the dead.

Given such powerful motives, ethno-religious extremists are the terrorists most likely to kill indiscriminately and to embrace weapons of mass destruction. Thus, Hezbollah, the Basque ETA, and the Tamil Tigers rank among the world's most professional and deadly terrorist groups.

Many ethnic groups, liberated by the collapse of communism, are now free to act on their ancient hatreds. Their animosities threaten to engulf the patchwork of states and independent republics that have emerged from the ruins of the Soviet empire. Only now are we beginning to learn their names, histories, and agendas.

Because such groups were of little interest to the traditional intelligence collector, Western security services know little about their ethnic allies or their depth of support, either on their home turf or in other countries.

ECONOMIC TERRORISM

Terrorist operations that target a nation's economy can be extremely effective. Radical Egyptian Islamists attacking foreign tourists have all but destroyed Egypt's lucrative tourist trade, dealing a serious blow to the nation's economy. The discovery of two cyanide-tainted grapes almost destroyed the export market for Chilean produce. Even Mother Nature can be enlisted in the terrorist cause. One potential weapon could be the Mediterranean fruit fly, a voracious agricultural pest that feeds on some 250 varieties of fruits, plants, and nuts. A malevolent Johnny Appleseed could single-handedly devastate the economies of whole regions. California produce, for example, earns the state $18.1 billion annually.

Recent reports of a sophisticated counterfeiting operation in Lebanon's Bekka Valley underscores how counterfeiting may be used as a more unconventional weapon. Using state-of-the-art equipment, American $100 bills are being churned out by terrorists. They are of such high quality that even experienced bank officials were fooled. If terrorists were to flood a country with high-quality counterfeit currency, economic confidence and faith in the government could take a nosedive, particularly if such an operation were combined with other forms of economic warfare and more-conventional forms of terrorism.

Other operations could target a nation's infrastructure. Our increasing dependence on the information superhighway could provide terrorists a new spectrum of targets. Several nations are believed to be developing computer viruses to disrupt military command and control systems, as well as other vital computer-dependent components of a nation's infrastructure. A massive disruption of East Coast telephone service in 1992, coupled with the airlines' dependence on it, forced flights scheduled to land in New York and other eastern cities to divert and major airports to close down. The failure was attributed to the system's dependence on telephone networks, which were handling an unusually high volume of holiday traffic. We must expect that rogue states and terrorist groups are exploring techniques to induce such failures by attacking the critical nodes of interdependent communications systems.

International banking systems would also be particularly lucrative targets for both terrorists and criminal elements. Doubtless, such groups are exploring ways to penetrate and alter account information, as well as to manipulate electronic fund transfers. Stock exchanges would similarly be at risk.

DEFENDING AGAINST TERRORISM

Governments generally respond to increased terrorism by beefing up the security of government installations, key components of the nation's infrastructure, and other lucrative targets. This pressures the terrorists to seek softer targets that effectively coerce the government to meet their demands. Operations that generate large civilian casualties fit these parameters and are anywhere large numbers of people gather. Choice targets include sports arenas, shopping malls, houses of worship, and movie theaters. Targets such as the World Trade Center not only provide the requisite casualties but, because of their symbolic nature, provide more bang for the buck. In order to maximize their odds for success, terrorist groups will likely consider mounting multiple, simultaneous operations with the aim of overtaxing a government's ability to respond, as well as demonstrating their professionalism and reach.

Despite all this, terrorism will remain a back-burner issue for Western leaders as long as the violence strikes in distant lands and has little impact on their fortunes or those of their constituents. Until a country's citizens believe that terrorism poses a significant threat, traditional economic and political concerns will remain paramount. The industrialized nations will be too busy jockeying for access to markets and resources to be concerned with the less immediate problems.

In a world dominated by economic and political interests, most of the industrialized West will deal with terrorism one incident at a time, playing it by ear. Many developed states will seek accommodation with terrorists and their sponsors, as long as they can find a "fig leaf" to minimize potential embarrassment. France and Germany have done business this way for many years. Both to secure immunity and for commercial advantage, Paris and Bonn have tacit agreements with some of the world's most-lethal terrorist groups and their state supporters. France has reportedly formalized some of these arrangements in writing.

Terrorists in the early years of the twenty-first century will reflect the causes that excite passion and move people to violence. During this period of tumult and transition, terrorism and other forms of low-intensity conflict will increase until a new stasis or "world order" is established. Religious and ethnically motivated terrorists, who exhibit few constraints now, will have within their grasp the potential to create the Armageddon they seek.

It is this confluence of will and means that has forever changed the face of terrorism. As a consequence, we will face future dangers that would have seemed wildly improbable only a few years ago, and we must prepare to defend ourselves against them.

*Marvin J.
Cetron and
Owen Davies*

CHAPTER **11** The Corporate World

11.1   ROSABETH MOSS KANTER,
BARRY A. STEIN, AND TODD D. JICK

The Challenge of Organizational Change: How Companies Experience It and Leaders Guide It

One of the major problems in the progress of sociology is the degree to which the world changes even as sociologists try to carefully develop empirically supported generalizations about how it works. In the 1960s the field of organizational sociology was developing rapidly based on a systematic study of dozens and even hundreds of cases. Organizations had identifiable members, relatively clear boundaries, and relatively regular patterns of association between environment, structure, and performance. Since that time the world has changed considerably, especially the world of business

254

organizations. Many of the old generalizations are no longer accurate. Organizational members are harder to identify clearly because there are now more temporary employees, part-time workers, and contracted work. Even the causal patterns are changing. Classic articles on organizations do not capture the present reality. Rosabeth Moss Kanter, Barry A. Stein, and Todd D. Jick attempt to do so in their book *The Challenge of Organizational Change: How Companies Experience It and Leaders Guide It* (Free Press, 1994), from which the following selection has been excerpted. The organizing principle of the new world of organizations is *flexibility,* not bureaucracy. The authors contend that centralization and hierarchy are generally dysfunctional and that decentralization and networks are functional. The new organizational forms and environments require new types of managers and new management patterns, and the authors discuss effective management practices and behaviors.

Kanter is a professor at the Harvard Business School and a recent editor of the *Harvard Business Review*. Her books include *The Change Masters* (Simon & Schuster, 1983), *When Giants Learn to Dance: Mastering the Challenge of Strategy, Management and Careers in the 1990s* (Simon & Schuster, 1989), and *Frontiers of Management* (Harvard University Press, 1997). Stein is a management consultant and a consulting firm executive. Jick is a professor at the Harvard Business School.

Key Concept: flexible organizations responding to change

The approach of the year 2000, with its millennial label and transformational implications, suggests the possibility of an equally profound change in our economic life and the institutions—primarily business firms—that populate it. In fact, even though the number has a highly spurious precision, its symbolism is appropriate. The world is undergoing many major transitions, some of which involve the meaning of business and the character and shape of the organizations that carry it out.

Most striking is the strong convergence of streams of thought and experience alike coming from academic theorists and practicing managers, from avowed free-market partisans and committed social democrats, from regulators and those regulated, from countries as diverse as Singapore and South Africa, the U.S.A. and the former U.S.S.R., Vietnam and Venezuela. This trend —or more accurately, this tidal wave—is becoming a universal model for organizations, especially large ones.

This model describes more flexible organizations, adaptable to change, with relatively few levels of formal hierarchy and loose boundaries among functions and units, sensitive and responsive to the environment; concerned with stakeholders of all sorts—employees, communities, customers, suppliers, and shareholders. These organizations empower people to take action and be entrepreneurial, reward them for contributions and help them gain in skill and "employability." Overall, these are global organizations characterized by internal and external relationships, including joint ventures, alliances, consortia, and partnerships....

THE IMPORTANCE OF MOTION:
AN ACTION VIEW OF ORGANIZATIONS

Our view, then, . . . stresses continuous flow. Organizations, as we see them, are bundles of activity with common elements that allow activities and people to be grouped and treated as an entity. As activities shift, as new or different units or people are included in activity clusters, what is identified as "the organization" also shifts.

Organizations are always in motion. There is some central thrust or directional tendency—"keeping the herd roughly moving West," as Tom Peters once put it—that results from a combination of the trajectory of past events, pushes arising from the environment, and pulls arising from the strategies embraced by the organization's dominant coalition, all within the context of the organization's character. Of course, the activity clusters (task units, division, projects, interest groups, alliances, etc.) themselves are also in motion, and their movements at any time may or may not be in step with each other or with the overall direction.

This framework creates situations similar to the "agency" problem in economics (Pratt and Zeckhauser, 1985)—the problem that occurs when "principals" who own an asset must delegate responsibility for it to "agents" whose stake, interests, and understanding are different. But this framework goes far beyond agency theory in identifying a *coordination* problem and an *implementation* problem as well as a *delegation* problem. These are necessary additions, because organizations consist of *multiple* stakeholders conducting multiple but overlapping activities, and because even coordinated actions do not automatically produce intended results.

This view of organizations is well suited to the demands of the 1990s. Global economic competition coupled with continuous technological change is hastening the evolution of an organizational model that defines the boundaries of organizations as fluid and permeable. It recognizes that influence over organizational acts comes from many sources and directions, and through many pathways, rather than "down" a "chain of command." It understands the limits of authoritative intentions in the face of an organization's tendency to continue on preexisting paths. Organizational names, legal ownership, and charts with formal reporting relationships thus do not entirely or usefully define the ways action occurs—or the way change occurs. Intentional "strategic" acts said to represent *the* organization are only one form of action. There are multiple strategists, and organizational purpose is itself problematic and debatable.

Thus, organizational action in the new model needs to be viewed in terms of *clusters of activity sets* whose membership, composition, ownership, and goals are constantly changing, and in which *projects* rather than *positions* are central. In such an image of an organization, the bonds between actors are more meaningful and ongoing than those of single market transactions but less rigid and immutable than those of positions in authority structures. Action possibilities are neither as fully open as in a market transaction nor as fully constrained and circumscribed as in the classic theory of bureaucracy.

Furthermore, there is great variety in the relationships of individuals to these organizational activity sets. While some people's roles are defined primarily by positions in a hierarchy of authority (e.g., "employees" carrying out predefined tasks through specified procedures), others are defined by the ability to mobilize resources and develop commitment to new tasks (e.g., "corporate entrepreneurs" on the payroll as employees but also receiving additional social, psychic, and/or economic inducements for initiative). Others are defined by market exchanges without the organizational membership bond (e.g., subcontractors and contingent workers). And still others are defined by their dual positions in several hierarchies (e.g., as a contributor to company X in a joint venture or alliance while still "employed" by company Y).

More critically, many of these activity sets are themselves only minimally "institutionalized." They do not exist or persist irrespective of the people occupying them. While the named entity under whose auspices activities occur (e.g., Ford Motor Company) may have an existence independent of persons, the limited-purpose associations (project teams) within it may come and go with the initiative and enthusiasm of particular people. For social scientists, this more fluid view of organizations suggests that perhaps network theory or social movement theory is more relevant to the emerging economic world than is bureaucratic theory. At the same time, this also suggests the possibility of formalizing some of these nonhierarchical mechanisms, in their form if not in their details of composition, as "parallel organizations" (Stein and Kanter, 1980).

Viewing an organization as a coalition of interests and a network of activities within a momentum-bearing structure has two implications that are essential for the perspective used [here]. First, change of one sort or another is always occurring, though it may not always be guided by organizational leaders nor be consistent with the purposes of the principal stakeholders. Second, managers concerned with *controlling* events or *guiding* change must be aware of both the nature of the networks within and around the organization (so they are able to form or work through coalitions of interests in order to induce multiple activities and interests to coalesce) and the sources and effects of the organization's momentum.

In this sense, "stability" in an organization is an idealization rather than a reality, an epiphenomenon or a quasi-equilibrium. "Stability" is just motion that is so smooth and involves so little conflict or challenge that it appears on the surface that nothing is moving. Or, to use more technical language, "stability" is better thought of as *unified motion stemming from a coalescence of interests and activities in an environment of adequate relative consistency and certainty.*

Apparent "stability" occurs when resources are abundant and easily obtained; competitors are few and competition is geographically confined by protected markets; technologies are standard and understood; individual and group ambition is constrained (people accept what they have); disasters or system failures are few or are accepted fatalistically; commitments are clear and acceptable to stakeholders; and interests are adequately aligned. General Motors in the United States in the 1950s and 1960s enjoyed this kind of "stability"; so did the telecommunications monopolies in most major countries through the 1970s.

Depart from any of these conditions, as in the globalizing economy of the 1980s, and suddenly the motion is apparent, with change taking center stage. Depart from all of them at once, as seems to be the case in the 1990s, and *responding to change, harnessing change, and creating change become the major management challenges.*

Consider the situation facing most organizations and their leaders today: Resources are scarcer and are obtained with more difficulty. New technologies arise frequently. Individual and group ambition is given free rein, in ever more countries. Crises are common but assumed to be solvable if only managers are good enough. Commitments—of customers, employees, or other stakeholders—are fragile or short-lived because of numerous choices and alternatives. And interests shift and diverge frequently.

How can so much motion be conceptualized and understood, so that leaders can manage it? . . .

LOOKING BACKWARD OR LOOKING FORWARD? MULTIPLE POSSIBILITIES AND THE OPPORTUNITIES FOR MANAGERS

. . . Managers spend considerable sums on analyses designed to project, predict, and forecast, and model all known variables and complex relationships in the quest for underlying inevitabilities of markets or other trends. But the increased motion of today's activated environment makes analyses of this kind more and more suspect except in narrow, constrained domains.

But managers act anyway, even in the absence of perfect knowledge. Without knowing what *must* be, as we look backward from history, they consider what *can* or *might* be. Managers see *multiple possibilities* rather than a single inevitable ending. . . .

Multiple possibility theory is in fact particularly well suited to a view of organizations as activity clusters in constant motion, guided by managers trying to steer. Of course, from a historian's perspective, viewed from far away and over a long period of time, coherence and identity may be more apparent than constant motion. But from the point of view of the actors confronting the situation, the choices are far less clear, the options less structured, the results inevitably more mixed, and the rationales highly arguable.

A reasonable, though slightly cynical, view of the world says: "If life gives you lemons, learn to like lemonade." Similarly, if organizational life involves continuous flow, then go with that flow. Understanding all the forces and variables involved in organizational change can help managers place their bets in a world of complex motion and multiple possibilities. Ultimately, despite the limits upon what people can control, it is still up to people to act and in acting they do more than predict the future, they invent it. . . .

Implementing change. The phrase sounds reasonable enough, and yet "managing" change is probably one of the most troubling and challenging tasks facing organizations today. Implementing a major and lasting change requires managers to develop skills akin to a juggler's. Instead of balls, however, managers must juggle tasks, striking a delicate balance between individual and collective actions, paying attention to the content as well as the process of change, and pursuing both short-term and long-term goals.

Considering the complexity of the task, it is no wonder that many managers feel overwhelmed—unable to keep all the balls of change in the air at the same time. The vice president is too busy to add "change" related tasks to her already crowded schedule of "normal" activities; the production manager nods his head during the meeting on managing change, but forgets the message as soon as he's back on the factory floor; or the company launches a change effort with great fanfare and enthusiasm, but then loses momentum one year into the program and calls it quits. Consider the results of a 1990 *Wall Street Journal* survey of 164 chief executive officers. Although the CEOs recognized that personal communication helps create more employee commitment to change, 86 percent said other demands prevented them from devoting more time to communicating.

Another study examined the large gap between declared participatory management styles and what is actually practiced. A survey of 485 upper-level managers from 59 firms found unequivocal support for the concept of participatory management and a willingness and desire to support such a change. Nevertheless, managers generally did not install such systems, blaming an absence of opportunities to discuss the implementation process and a lack of leadership (Collins, Ross, and Ross, 1989).

To help address such problems, change experts have devised tactics over the years to help managers do a better job on everything from crafting a vision to rewarding employees for productive behavior. Most managers at medium- to large-size U.S. companies have been exposed to these tenets. Yet the track record overall is disappointing. ... [T]here continues to be a great deal of disquiet in the workplace over the effectiveness of change efforts. Despite volumes of literature on planned change, legions of consultants, and the best efforts of corporate leaders, organizational change still appears to be a chaotic process. It is frequently mismanaged, beset by unexpected developments, and often largely unfulfilled. ...

Fine-tuning is no longer enough.

Company survival today depends on courage and imagination—the courage to challenge prevailing business models, and the imagination to invent new services, new products, and new markets. Competitive success in the 1990s will belong to companies that escape the tyranny of their served markets to create new ones, a process that requires sweeping challenges to obsolete assumptions. Increasingly, neither business leaders nor rank-and-file employees question *whether* to change but *how*. ...

The best way to select initial actions with any likelihood of success is first to understand two things.

TABLE 1

Leader Actions: Comparing Bold Strokes and Long Marches

	Bold Strokes	*Long Marches*
Time frame	Fast	Slow
Locus of action	Decisions at top	Initiatives throughout
Leader control	High	Low
	can command results	can initiate but not command
Initial results	Clear acts, impact	Unclear acts, impact
Later results	Erratic	Dependable
Culture impact	Habits unchanged	Habits can change

1. *The sources of organizational success.* Whatever the specific changes sought, they are intended to promote success in some definable sense. That means knowing how organizations succeed, and what things help them do it more reliably, because those are the things that should be introduced or reinforced.
2. *The success factors in organizational change.* As we have tried to show ... many problems and failures associated with organizational change initiatives arise from naïve, inaccurate, or misleading prescriptions. These need to be replaced with more robust and accurate working models. ...

Successful Change: Bold Strokes and Long Marches

Leaders engage in two types of actions that help promote and sustain organizational success, which can be called "bold strokes" and "long marches."

Bold strokes are big strategic decisions or major economic initiatives, such as buying another company, closing some plants, or allocating critical resources to the development of a new product or technology. Long marches are more operational initiatives, such as combining several divisions, transforming quality or customer relationships, or enhancing organizational effectiveness.

These two action streams are very different in practice. Bold strokes can be mandated largely by the executive actions of one or a few people. Organizations are often forever changed when a CEO decides to buy this, sell that, discontinue product lines, or enter the European market. On the other hand, long marches, as the name suggests, require the personal support of many people and *cannot* be mandated in practice. Chief executives can attempt to order costs cut, cycle time reduced, management competence enhanced, or products developed faster, but these are only paper decisions. Improving quality, the integration of acquired units, or customer relationships are classic long marches. They simply cannot be done by fiat.

Consider the case of [Henry] Ford. Under Donald Petersen's leadership Ford executed a conspicuously successful turnabout in the early 1980s. The reasons articulated by Petersen himself, and by many who use Ford as an example, tend to focus on the operational change programs, including Petersen's personal leadership, quality ("Quality is Job 1"), participative management, reduced cycle time (at Ford mainly focused on parallel engineering), and continuous improvement.

These would not by themselves have produced visible results without several bold interventions. Very early in his tenure as CEO, Petersen shut several assembly plants and other facilities, cutting the payroll in the process, to the point where the company could be profitable on much smaller production runs.

He also fundamentally redirected the styling of Ford cars in a dramatic shift from tradition. Ford thus became the first American automaker to produce "European looking" vehicles as embodied in the Ford Taurus and the Mercury Sable. These cars won wide acclaim, from critics and consumers alike. And new relationships with suppliers were undertaken.

It was following these moves that Ford embarked on the more widely noted internal initiatives associated with quality and organizational adjustments. Although these had very beneficial effects, the company, according to insiders, is still highly bureaucratic, and many of these initiatives have been either sharply reduced or stopped altogether. Even at their peak, such things as participative management and QWL (quality of work life) methods were never really routinized across the whole company. Perhaps Ford's early success was driven more by Petersen's strategy than by his operational actions.

Petersen's change strategy thus began with some bold strokes, followed by a long march. Typically, however, long marches, precisely because they involve many or most of an organization's members and require unusual commitment sustained over a long time, are much more difficult. And Ford's ability to sustain it evidently dropped over time. Since then, Ford has visibly lost some of its momentum, a change that culminated in a very large loss in 1991....

But this is not to conclude that only bold strokes will work. Xerox,... rather dramatically turned itself around after a steep drop in market share in a market it created and once owned. Its strategy was much more of a long march than a bold stroke. The Xerox turnaround demonstrates how much visible commitment and top management attention is required to complete a long march successfully. General Motors, on the other hand,... appeared unwilling to make the necessary bold strokes, but was evidently equally unwilling to invest adequately in a long march. Indeed, the argument between Ross Perot and Roger Smith is illuminating; Perot urged bold strokes, which Smith rejected in favor of what he called a long march—but what turned out to be inadequate movement. Often it takes bold strokes to galvanize an organization into starting a march....

In theory, every organization needs both kinds of action. But in practice, because of characteristics of the firm, its industry, its leaders, and its relationship to the environment, some narrower orientation will be visible. Some companies, for example, will be more likely to launch bold strokes, while others will be engaged in a series of long marches. Organizations develop dispositions toward dealing with problems in a certain way. This is not merely a matter of management style; rather, it is driven by some realities of the organization, its economic and competitive environment, and its resource portfolio.

In general, it is clear that virtually all organizations succeed some of the time; the reasons are as variable as the situations. Therefore, it is *much* more interesting, as well as much more important, to look at firms that are successful over *extended* periods, particularly when those periods exhibit some turbulence and include a variety of contingencies. What counts is not the occasional or "one-off" success, but the capacity to succeed regularly and reliably. And here, in the task of routinizing success, the key ingredient is what might be called good organizational habits.

"Habits" are created and then supported by the organization's character, the mechanisms, standards, and procedures that assume and enable that particular style. In excellent organizations, habits will "work" for a relatively long time. Inevitably, however, there comes a time when a very different approach is required. At that point, the organization is likely to falter. This becomes a critical juncture; some firms make the transition and go on to continuing success, many do not.

This is one of the reasons organizational diagnosis and understanding are critical. Organizations succeed in part because they are competent to recognize and to understand exactly what factors and features encourage their people's patterned behavior, in both appropriate and inappropriate ways. From this point of view, both problems and successes represent important opportunities to reevaluate the organization's habits and the sort of behavior it systematically encourages in its people. To understand these things is to recognize how and where management can effectively intervene.

Every large and complex organization has many thousands of people who have each day the opportunity, or are literally required, to take action on something. We think of these as "choice points." For an organization to succeed, in any long-run sense, these millions of choices must be more or less appropriate and constructive, day in and day out. But this is an immensely difficult problem, because it requires the ultimate in decentralization—literally to the individual level—along with centralization in the sense that those individual choices must be coordinated and coherent.

As we have pointed out, the importance of coordinating and guiding those millions of individual choices varies to some degree with the organization's situation. Some strategic actions of the organization's leaders—long marches—require more continuing support from people within the organization than do others—such as bold strokes. Still, in setting a strategic focus on improving performance or competitive position, leaders are also, whether aware of it or not, inevitably launching a program of deliberate organizational change. The critical task of change implementors, our second change role, is to ensure congruent effort along both those objectives, the strategic management and the change management.

11.2 MARK DOWIE

Pinto Madness

It may be difficult to imagine that some of the leaders of American industries —persons who contribute to and perform good deeds for the community— would contemplate taking actions that would result in the deaths of innocent men, women, and children. Nevertheless, in the following excerpt, Mark Dowie describes how the leaders of the Ford Motor Company deliberately produced a new car that they knew was potentially lethal. In their judgment, the $11 per car required to install a safety device that would make it safer was too costly.

In the early 1970s Ford put the Pinto on the market to compete with foreign companies for the compact car market. When struck from the rear at relatively low speed, however, the car consistently exploded into a ball of fire. Minor changes would have corrected the flaw and saved lives, but it took nearly seven years of litigation to institute the safety standard that would force Ford to install a device that would prevent this type of accident. Finally, in 1978, all Pintos produced between 1971 and 1976 were recalled.

In "Pinto Madness," *Mother Jones* (September/October 1977), for which he won the National Magazine Award from Columbia University School of Journalism, Dowie describes with some incredulity the lengths to which Ford went to protect its investment. His forte as an investigative journalist lies in exposing business and government practices that are legal "but nonetheless reprehensible." Dowie (b. 1939) has also won numerous other journalism awards for his investigative reporting. The story of the Ford Pinto is a good sociological case study on corporate decision-making.

Key Concept: cost-benefit analysis

One evening in the mid-1960s, Arjay Miller was driving home from his office in Dearborn, Michigan, in the four-door Lincoln Continental that went with his job as president of the Ford Motor Company. On a crowded highway, another car struck his from the rear. The Continental spun around and burst into flames. Because he was wearing a shoulder-strap seat belt, Miller was unharmed by the crash, and because his doors didn't jam he escaped the flaming wreck. But the accident made a vivid impression on him. Several months later, on July 15, 1965, he recounted it to a U.S. Senate subcommittee that was hearing testimony on auto safety legislation. "I still have burning in my mind the image of that gas tank on fire," Miller said. He went on to express an almost passionate interest in controlling fuel-fed fires in cars that crash or roll over. He spoke with excitement about the fabric gas tank Ford was testing at that very moment. "If it proves out," he promised the senators, "it will be a feature you will see in our standard cars."

Almost seven years after Miller's testimony, a woman, whom for legal reasons we will call Sandra Gillespie, pulled onto a Minneapolis highway in her new Ford Pinto. Riding with her was a young boy, whom we'll call Robbie Carlton. As she entered a merge lane, Sandra Gillespie's car stalled. Another car rear-ended hers at an impact speed of 28 miles per hour. The Pinto's gas tank ruptured. Vapors from it mixed quickly with the air in the passenger compartment. A spark ignited the mixture and the car exploded in a ball of fire. Sandra died in agony a few hours later in an emergency hospital. Her passenger, 13-year-old Robbie Carlton, is still alive; he has just come home from another futile operation aimed at grafting a new ear and nose from skin on the few unscarred portions of his badly burned body. (This accident is real; the details are from police reports.)

Why did Sandra Gillespie's Ford Pinto catch fire so easily, seven years after Ford's Arjay Miller made his apparently sincere pronouncements—the same seven years that brought more safety improvements to cars than any other period in automotive history? An extensive investigation by *Mother Jones* over the past six months has found these answers:

Fighting strong competition from Volkswagen for the lucrative small-car market, the Ford Motor Company rushed the Pinto into production in much less than the usual time.

Ford engineers discovered in pre-production crash tests that rear-end collisions would rupture the Pinto's fuel system extremely easily.

Because assembly-line machinery was already tooled when engineers found this defect, top Ford officials decided to manufacture the car anyway—exploding gas tank and all—*even though Ford owned the patent on a much safer gas tank.*

For more than eight years afterwards, Ford successfully lobbied, with extraordinary vigor and some blatant lies, against a key government safety standard that would have forced the company to change the Pinto's fire-prone gas tank.

By conservative estimates Pinto crashes have caused 500 burn deaths to people who would not have been seriously injured if the car had not burst into flames. . . .

Ford knows the Pinto is a firetrap, yet it has paid out millions to settle damage suits out of court, and it is prepared to spend millions more lobbying against safety standards. With a half million cars rolling off the assembly lines each year, Pinto is the biggest-selling subcompact in America, and the company's operating profit on the car is fantastic. Finally, in 1977, new Pinto models have incorporated a few minor alterations necessary to meet that federal standard Ford managed to hold off for eight years. Why did the company delay so long in making these minimal inexpensive improvements?

Ford waited eight years because its internal "cost-benefit analysis," *which places a dollar value on human life,* said it wasn't profitable to make the changes sooner.

Before we get to the question of how much Ford thinks your life is worth, let's trace the history of the death trap itself. Although this particular story is about the Pinto, the way in which Ford made its decision is typical of the U.S. auto industry generally. There are plenty of similar stories about other cars made by other companies. But this case is the worst of them all. . . .

Mother Jones has studied hundreds of reports and documents on rear-end collisions involving Pintos. These reports conclusively reveal that if you ran into that Pinto you were following at over 30 miles per hour, the rear end of the car would buckle like an accordion, right up to the back seat. The tube leading to the gas-tank cap would be ripped away from the tank itself, and gas would immediately begin sloshing onto the road around the car. The buckled gas tank would be jammed up against the differential housing which contains four sharp protruding bolts likely to gash holes in the tank and spill still more gas. The welded seam between the main body frame and the wheel well would split, allowing gas to enter the interior of the car.

Now all you need is a spark from a cigarette, ignition, or scraping metal, and both cars would be engulfed in flames. If you gave the Pinto a really good whack—say, at 40 mph—chances are excellent that its doors would jam and you would have to stand by and watch its trapped passengers burn to death.

This scenario is no news to Ford. Internal company documents in our possession show that Ford has crash-tested the Pinto at a top-secret site more than 40 times and that *every* test made at over 25 mph without special structural alteration of the car has resulted in a ruptured fuel tank. Despite this, Ford officials denied having crash-tested the Pinto.

Eleven of these tests, averaging a 31-mph impact speed, came before Pintos started rolling out of the factories. Only three cars passed the test with unbroken fuel tanks. In one of them an inexpensive light-weight metal baffle was placed so those bolts would not perforate the tank. (Don't forget about that baffle which costs about a dollar and weighs about a pound. It plays an important role in our story later on.) In another successful test, a piece of steel was placed between the tank and the bumper. In the third test car the gas tank was lined with a rubber bladder. But none of these protective alterations was used in the mass-produced Pinto.

In preproduction planning, engineers seriously considered using in the Pinto the same kind of gas tank Ford uses in the Capri. The Capri tank rides over the rear axle and differential housing. It has been so successful in over 50 crash tests that Ford used it in its Experimental Safety Vehicle, which withstood rear-end impacts of 60 mph. So why wasn't the Capri tank used in the Pinto? Or, why wasn't that baffle placed between the tank and the axle—something that would have saved the life of Sandra Gillespie and hundreds like her. Why was a car known to be a serious fire hazard deliberately released to production in August of 1970?

Whether Ford should manufacture subcompacts at all was the subject of a bitter two-year debate at the company's Dearborn headquarters. The principals in the corporate struggle were the then-president Semon "Bunky" Knudsen, whom Henry Ford II had hired away from General Motors, and Lee Iacocca, a spunky young turk who had risen fast within the company on the enormous success of the Mustang. Iacocca argued forcefully that Volkswagen and the

Japanese were going to capture the entire American subcompact market unless Ford put out its own alternative to the VW Beetle. Bunky Knudsen said, in effect: let them have the small-car market; Ford makes good money on medium and large models. But he lost the battle and later resigned. Iacocca became president and almost immediately began a rush program to produce the Pinto.

Like the Mustang, the Pinto became known in the company as "Lee's car." Lee Iacocca wanted that little car in the showrooms of America with the 1971 models. So he ordered his engineering vice president, Bob Alexander, to oversee what was probably the shortest production planning period in modern automotive history. The normal time span from conception to production of a new car model is about 43 months. The Pinto schedule was set at just under 25.

Design, styling, product planning, advance engineering and quality assurance all have flexible time frames, and engineers can pretty much carry these on simultaneously. Tooling, on the other hand, has a fixed time frame of about 18 months. Normally, an auto company doesn't begin tooling until the other processes are almost over. *But Iacocca's speed-up meant Pinto tooling went on at the same time as product development.* So when crash tests revealed a serious defect in the gas tank, it was too late. The tooling was well under way.

When it was discovered the gas tank was unsafe, did anyone go to Iacocca and tell him? "Hell no," replied an engineer who worked on the Pinto, a high company official for many years, who, unlike several others at Ford, maintains a necessarily clandestine concern for safety. "That person would have been fired. Safety wasn't a popular subject around Ford in those days. With Lee it was taboo. . . ."

As Lee Iacocca was fond of saying, "Safety doesn't sell."

Heightening the anti-safety pressure on Pinto engineers was an important goal set by Iacocca known as "the limits of 2,000." The Pinto was not to weigh an ounce over 2,000 pounds and not to cost a cent over $2,000. "Iacocca enforced these limits with an iron hand," recalls the engineer quoted earlier. So, even when a crash test showed that that one-pound, one-dollar piece of metal stopped the puncture of the gas tank, it was thrown out as an extra cost and extra weight.

People shopping for subcompacts are watching every dollar. "You have to keep in mind," the engineer explained, "that the price elasticity on these subcompacts is extremely tight. You can price yourself right out of the market by adding $25 to the production cost of the model. And nobody understands that better than Iacocca."

Blame for Sandra Gillespie's death, Robbie Carlton's unrecognizable face and all the other injuries and deaths in Pintos since 1970 does not rest on the shoulders of Lee Iacocca alone. For, while he and his associates fought their battle against a safer Pinto in Dearborn, a larger war against safer cars raged in Washington. One skirmish in that war involved Ford's successful eight-year lobbying effort against Federal Motor Vehicle Safety Standard 301, the rear-end provisions of which would have forced Ford to redesign the Pinto.

But first some background:

During the early '60s, auto safety legislation became the *bête-noire* of American big business. The auto industry was the last great unregulated business, and if *it* couldn't reverse the tide of government regulation, the reasoning went, no one could....

[But] by 1965, most pundits and lobbyists saw the handwriting on the wall and prepared to accept government "meddling" in the last bastion of free enterprise. Not Henry [Ford II]. With bulldog tenacity, he held out for defeat of the legislation to the very end, loyal to his grandfather's invention and to the company that makes it. But the Safety Act passed the House and Senate unanimously, and was signed into law by Lyndon Johnson in 1966.

While lobbying for and against legislation is pretty much a process of high-level back-slapping, press-conferencing and speech-making, fighting a regulatory agency is a much subtler matter. Henry headed home to lick his wounds in Grosse Pointe, Michigan, and a planeload of the Ford Motor Company's best brains flew to Washington to start the "education" of the new federal auto safety bureaucrats.

Their job was to implant the official industry ideology in the minds of the new officials regulating auto safety. Briefly summarized, that ideology states that auto accidents are caused not by *cars*, but by people and highway conditions....

In light of an annual death rate approaching 50,000, they are forced to admit that driving is hazardous. But the car is, in the words of Arjay Miller, "the safest link in the safety chain."

Before the Ford experts left Washington to return to drafting tables in Dearborn they did one other thing. They managed to informally reach an agreement with the major public servants who would be making auto safety decisions. This agreement was that "cost-benefit" would be an acceptable mode of analysis by Detroit and its new regulators....

Cost-benefit analysis was used only occasionally in government until President Kennedy appointed Ford Motor Company President Robert McNamara to be Secretary of Defense. McNamara, originally an accountant, preached cost benefit with all the force of a Biblical zealot. Stated in its simplest terms, cost-benefit analysis says that if the cost is greater than the benefit, the project is not worth it—no matter what the benefit. Examine the cost of every action, decision, contract, part, or change, the doctrine says, then carefully evaluate the benefits (in dollars) to be certain that they exceed the cost before you begin a program or pass a regulation.

As a management tool in a business in which profits count over all else, cost-benefit analysis makes a certain amount of sense. Serious problems arise, however, when public officials who ought to have more than corporate profits at heart apply cost-benefit analysis to every conceivable decision. The inevitable result is that they must place a dollar value on human life.

Ever wonder what your life is worth in dollars? Perhaps $10 million? Ford has a better idea: $200,000.

Remember, Ford had gotten the federal regulators to agree to talk auto safety in terms of cost-benefit. But in order to be able to argue that various safety costs were greater than their benefits, Ford needed to have a dollar value figure for the "benefit." Rather than coming up with a price tag itself, the auto industry pressured the National Highway Traffic Safety Administration to do so. And in a 1972 report the agency determined that a human life lost on the highway was

TABLE 1

*What's Your Life Worth? Societal Cost
Components for Fatalities, 1972 NHTSA Study*

Component	1971 Costs
Future productivity losses	
Direct	$132,000
Indirect	41,300
Medical costs	
Hospital	700
Other	425
Property damage	1,500
Insurance administration	4,700
Legal and court	3,000
Employer losses	1,000
Victim's pain and suffering	10,000
Funeral	900
Assets (lost consumption)	5,000
Miscellaneous accident cost	200
Total per fatality: $200,725	

Here is a chart from a federal study showing how the National Highway Traffic Safety Administration has calculated the value of a human life. The estimate was arrived at under pressure from the auto industry. The Ford Motor Company has used it in cost-benefit analyses arguing why certain safety measures are not "worth" the savings in human lives. The calculation above is a breakdown of the estimated cost to society every time someone is killed in a car accident. We were not able to find anyone, either in the government or at Ford, who could explain how the $10,000 figure for "pain and suffering" had been arrived at.

worth $200,725 [Table 1]. Inflationary forces have recently pushed the figure up to $278,000.

Furnished with this useful tool, Ford immediately went to work using it to prove why various safety improvements were too expensive to make.

Nowhere did the company argue harder that it should make no changes than in the area of rupture-prone fuel tanks. Not long after the government arrived at the $200,725-per-life figure, it surfaced, rounded off to a cleaner $200,000, in an internal Ford memorandum. This cost-benefit analysis argued that Ford should not make an $11-per-car improvement that would prevent 180 fiery deaths a year.

This cold calculus [Table 2] is buried in a seven-page company memorandum entitled "Fatalities Associated with Crash-Induced Fuel Leakage and Fires."

The memo goes on to argue that there is no financial benefit in complying with proposed safety standards that would admittedly result in fewer auto fires, fewer burn deaths and fewer burn injuries. Naturally, memoranda that speak so casually of "burn deaths" and "burn injuries" are not released to the public.

TABLE 2

*Benefits and Costs Relating to Fuel Leakage Associated
With the Static Rollover Test Portion of FMVSS 208*

Benefits
Savings: 80 burn deaths, 180 serious burn injuries, 2,100 burned vehicles.
Unit cost: $200,000 per death, $67,000 per injury, $700 per vehicle.
Total benefit: 180 × ($200,000) + 180 × ($67,000) + 2,100 × ($700) = $49.5 million.

Costs
Sales: 11 million cars, 1.5 million light trucks.
Unit cost: $11 per car, $11 per truck.
Total cost: 11,000,000 × ($11) + 1,500,000 × ($11) = $137 million.

They are very effective, however, with Department of Transportation officials indoctrinated in McNamarian cost-benefit analysis.

All Ford had to do was convince men like John Volpe, Claude Brinegar and William Coleman (successive Secretaries of Transportation during the Nixon-Ford years) that certain safety standards would add so much to the price of cars that fewer people would buy them. This could damage the auto industry, which was still believed to be the bulwark of the American economy. "Compliance to these standards," Henry Ford II prophesied at more than one press conference, "will shut down the industry."

The Nixon Transportation Secretaries were the kind of regulatory officials big business dreams of. They understood and loved capitalism and thought like businessmen. Yet, best of all, they came into office uninformed on technical automotive matters. And you could talk "burn injuries" and "burn deaths" with these guys, and they didn't seem to envision children crying at funerals and people hiding in their homes with melted faces. Their minds appeared to have leapt right to the bottom line—more safety meant higher prices, higher prices meant lower sales and lower sales meant lower profits.

So when J. C. Echold, Director of Automotive Safety (chief anti-safety lobbyist) for Ford wrote to the Department of Transportation—which he still does frequently, at great length—he felt secure attaching a memorandum that in effect says it is acceptable to kill 180 people and burn another 180 every year, *even though we have the technology that could save their lives for $11 a car.*

Furthermore, Echold attached this memo, confident, evidently, that the Secretary would question neither his low death/injury statistics nor his high cost estimates. But it turns out, on closer examination, that both these findings were misleading.

First, note that Ford's table shows an equal number of burn deaths and burn injuries. This is false. All independent experts estimate that for each person who dies by an auto fire, many more are left with charred hands, faces and limbs. Andrew McGuire of the Northern California Burn Center estimates the ratio of burn injuries to deaths at ten to one instead of the one to one Ford shows here. Even though Ford values a burn at only a piddling $67,000 instead of the $200,000 price of life, the true ratio obviously throws the company's calculations way off.

The other side of the equation, the alleged $11 cost of a fire-prevention device, is also a misleading estimation. One document that was *not* sent to Washington by Ford was a "Confidential" cost analysis *Mother Jones* has managed to obtain, showing that crash fires could be largely prevented for considerably *less* than $11 a car. The cheapest method involves placing a heavy rubber bladder inside the gas tank to keep the fuel from spilling if the tank ruptures. Goodyear had developed the bladder and had demonstrated it to the automotive industry. We have in our possession crash-test reports showing that the Goodyear bladder worked well. On December 2, 1970 (*two years before* Echold sent his cost-benefit memo to Washington), Ford Motor Company ran a rear-end crash test on a car with the rubber bladder in the gas tank. The tank ruptured, but no fuel leaked. On January 15, 1971, Ford again tested the bladder and again it worked. The total purchase and installation cost of the bladder would have been $5.08 per car. That $5.08 could have saved the lives of Sandra Gillespie and several hundred others.

When a federal regulatory agency like the National Highway Traffic Safety Administration (NHTSA) decides to issue a new standard, the law usually requires it to invite all interested parties to respond before the standard is enforced—a reasonable enough custom on the surface. However, the auto industry has taken advantage of this process and has used it to delay lifesaving emission and safety standards for years. In the case of the standard that would have corrected that fragile Pinto fuel tank, the delay was for an incredible eight years.

The particular regulation involved here was Federal Motor Vehicle Safety Standard 301. Ford picked portions of Standard 301 for strong opposition back in 1968 when the Pinto was still in the blueprint stage. The intent of 301, and the 300 series that followed it, was to protect drivers and passengers *after* a crash occurs. Without question the worst postcrash hazard is fire. So Standard 301 originally proposed that all cars should be able to withstand a fixed barrier impact of 20 mph (that is, running into a wall at that speed) without losing fuel.

When the standard was proposed, Ford engineers pulled their crash-test results out of their files. The front ends of most cars were no problem—with minor alterations they could stand the impact without losing fuel. "We were already working on the front end," Ford engineer Dick Kimble admitted. "We knew we could meet the test on the front end." But with the Pinto particularly, a 20-mph rear-end standard meant redesigning the entire rear end of the car. With the Pinto scheduled for production in August of 1970, and with $200 million worth of tools in place, adoption of this standard would have created a minor financial disaster. So Standard 301 was targeted for delay, and, with some assistance from its industry associates, Ford succeeded beyond its wildest expectations: the standard was not adopted until the 1977 model year. Here is how it happened:

There are several main techniques in the art of combating a government safety standard: a) make your arguments in succession, so the feds can be working on disproving only one at a time; b) claim that the real problem is not X but Y (we already saw one instance of this in "the problem is not cars but people"); c) no matter how ridiculous each argument is, accompany it with thousands of pages of highly technical assertions it will take the government months or, preferably, years to test. Ford's large and active Washington office brought these techniques to new heights and became the envy of the lobbyists' trade.

The Ford people started arguing against Standard 301 way back in 1968 with a strong attack of technique b). Fire, they said, was not the real problem. Sure, cars catch fire and people burn occasionally. But statistically auto fires are such a minor problem that NHTSA should really concern itself with other matters.

Strange as it may seem, the Department of Transportation (NHTSA's parent agency) didn't know whether or not this was true. So it contracted with several independent research groups to study auto fires. The studies took months, often years, which was just what Ford wanted. The completed studies, however, showed auto fires to be more of a problem than Transportation officials ever dreamed of. A Washington research firm found that 400,000 cars were burning up every year, burning more than 3,000 people to death. Furthermore, auto fires were increasing five times as fast as building fires. Another study showed that 35 per cent of all fire deaths in the U.S. occurred in automobiles. Forty per cent of all fire department calls in the 1960s were to vehicle fires—a public cost of $350 million a year, a figure that, incidentally, never shows up in cost-benefit analyses.

Another study was done by the Highway Traffic Research Institute in Ann Arbor, Michigan, a safety think-tank funded primarily by the auto industry (the giveaway there is the words "highway traffic" rather than "automobile" in the group's name). It concluded that 40 per cent of the lives lost in fuel-fed fires could be saved if the manufacturers complied with proposed Standard 301. Finally, a third report was prepared for NHTSA. This report indicated that the Ford Motor Company makes 24 per cent of the cars on the American road, yet these cars account for 42 per cent of the collision-ruptured fuel tanks.

Ford lobbyists then used technique a)—bringing up a new argument. Their line then became: yes, perhaps burn accidents do happen, but rear-end collisions are relatively rare (note the echo of technique b) here as well). Thus Standard 301 was not needed. This set the NHTSA off on a new round of analyzing accident reports. The government's findings finally were that rear-end collisions were seven and a half times more likely to result in fuel spills than were front-end collisions. So much for that argument.

By now it was 1972; NHTSA had been researching and analyzing for four years to answer Ford's objections. During that time, nearly 9,000 people burned to death in flaming wrecks. Tens of thousands more were badly burned and scarred for life. And the four-year delay meant that well over 10 million new unsafe vehicles went on the road, vehicles that will be crashing, leaking fuel and incinerating people well into the 1980s.

Ford now had to enter its third round of battling the new regulations. On the "the problem is not X but Y" principle, the company had to look around for something new to get itself off the hook. One might have thought that, faced with all the latest statistics on the horrifying number of deaths in flaming accidents, Ford would find the task difficult. But the company's rhetoric was brilliant. The problem was not burns, but... impact! Most of the people killed in these fiery accidents, claimed Ford, would have died whether the car burned or not. They were killed by the kinetic force of the impact, not the fire.

And so once again, the ball bounced into the government's court and the absurdly pro-industry NHTSA began another slow-motion response. Once again it began a time-consuming round of test crashes and embarked on a study of accidents. The latter, however, revealed that a large and growing number of corpses taken from burned cars involved in rear-end crashes contained no cuts, bruises or broken bones. They clearly would have survived the accident unharmed if the cars had not caught fire. This pattern was confirmed in careful rear-end crash tests performed by the Insurance Institute for Highway Safety. A University of Miami study found an inordinate number of Pintos burning on rear-end impact and concluded that this demonstrated "a clear and present hazard to all Pinto owners."

Pressure on NHTSA from Ralph Nader and consumer groups began mounting. The industry-agency collusion was so obvious that Senator Joseph Montoya (D-N.M.) introduced legislation about Standard 301. NHTSA waffled some more and again announced its intentions to promulgate a rear-end collision standard.

Waiting, as it normally does, until the last day allowed for response, Ford filed with NHTSA a gargantuan batch of letters, studies and charts now arguing that the federal testing criteria were unfair. Ford also argued that design changes required to meet the standard would take 43 months, which seemed like a rather long time in light of the fact that the entire Pinto was designed in about two years. Specifically new complaints about the standard involved the weight of the test vehicle, whether or not the brakes should be engaged at the moment of impact and the claim that the standard should only apply to cars, not trucks or buses. Perhaps the most amusing argument was that the engine should not be idling during crash tests, the rationale being that an idling engine meant that the gas tank had to contain gasoline and that the hot lights needed to film the crash might ignite the gasoline and cause a fire.

Some of these complaints were accepted, others rejected. But they all required examination and testing by a weak kneed NHTSA, meaning more of those 18-month studies the industry loves so much. So the complaints served their real purpose—delay; all told, an eight-year delay, while Ford manufactured more than three million profitable, dangerously incendiary Pintos....

In 1977, however, an incredibly sluggish government has at last instituted Standard 301. Now Pintos will have to have rupture-proof gas tanks. Or will they?

To everyone's surprise, the 1977 Pinto recently passed a rear-end crash test in Phoenix, Arizona, for NHTSA. The agency was so convinced the Pinto would fail that it was the first car tested. Amazingly, it did not burst into flame.

"We have had so many Ford failures in the past," explained agency engineer Tom Grubbs, "I felt sure the Pinto would fail."

How did it pass?

Remember that one-dollar, one-pound metal baffle that was on one of the three modified Pintos that passed the pre-production crash tests nearly ten years ago? Well, it is a standard feature on the 1977 Pinto. In the Phoenix test it protected the gas tank from being perforated by those four bolts on the differential housing.

We asked Grubbs if he noticed any other substantial alterations in the rear-end structure of the car. "No," he replied, "the [baffle] seems to be the only noticeable change over the 1976 model."

But was it? What Tom Grubbs and the Department of Transportation didn't know when they tested the car was that it was manufactured in St. Thomas, Ontario. Ontario? The significance of that becomes clear when you learn that Canada has for years had extremely strict rear-end collision standards.

Tom Irwin is the business manager of Charlie Rossi Ford, the Scottsdale, Arizona, dealership that sold the Pinto to Tom Grubbs. He refused to explain why he was selling Fords made in Canada when there is a huge assembly plant much closer by in California. "I know why you're asking that question, and I'm not going to answer it," he blurted out. "You'll have to ask the company." . . .

The Department of Transportation is considering buying an American Pinto and running the test again. For now, it will only say that the situation is under investigation.

Whether the new American Pinto fails or passes the test, Standard 301 will never force the company to test or recall the more than two million pre-1977 Pintos still on the highway. Seventy or more people will burn to death in those cars every year for many years to come. If the past is any indication, Ford will continue to accept the deaths. . . .

The original draft of the Motor Vehicle Safety Act provided for criminal sanction against a manufacturer who willfully placed an unsafe car on the market. Early in the proceedings the auto industry lobbied the provision out of the bill. Since then, there have been those damage settlements, of course, but the only government punishment meted out to auto companies for non-compliance to standards has been a minuscule fine, usually $5,000 to $10,000. One wonders how long the Ford Motor Company would continue to market lethal cars were Henry Ford II and Lee Iacocca serving 20-year terms in Leavenworth for consumer homicide.

This article was published in September of 1977, and in February 1978 a jury awarded a sixteen-year-old boy, badly burned in a rear-end Pinto accident, $128 million in damages (the accident occurred in 1973 in Santa Ana, Calif.). That was the largest single personal injury judgment in history.

On May 8, 1978, the Department of Transportation announced that tests conducted in response to this article showed conclusively that the Pinto was defective in all respects described in the article and called for a recall of all 1971 to 1976 Pintos—the most expensive recall in automotive history.

The McDonaldization
of Society

Bureaucracies are basically designed for efficiency. A half-century ago, however, much of the economy was not subjected to the same relentless drive for efficiency, because other values were often taken into account. Food service is an example. Quality and atmosphere were other important goals. However, the franchising of McDonald's restaurants revolutionized the fast-food industry in that every aspect of the business was relentlessly reduced to efficiency criteria. Their competition had to follow suit or fail.

The success of McDonald's led to the diffusion of the principles of McDonald's to many other areas of the economy, including "education, work, health care, travel, leisure, dieting, politics, the family, and virtually every other aspect of society," according to George Ritzer. Ritzer details this process, which he calls *McDonaldization,* in the following selection from his book *The McDonaldization of Society: An Investigation into the Changing Character of Contemporary Social Life,* rev. ed. (Pine Forge Press, 1996). He is not convinced that the inexorable extension of McDonaldization is altogether good, because it tramples down some other worthwhile values. Nevertheless, he seeks to understand why it sweeps other organizational forms aside as it advances. Ritzer's conclusion is that "McDonald's has succeeded because it offers consumers, workers, and managers efficiency, calculability, predictability, and control."

Ritzer is a professor of sociology at the University of Maryland, where he has been named Distinguished Scholar-Teacher. His publications include *Frontiers of Sociological Theory* (Colombia University Press, 1991) and *Classic Theory in Sociology* (McGraw-Hill, 1996).

Key Concept: McDonaldization

AN INTRODUCTION TO McDONALDIZATION

Ray Kroc, the genius behind the franchising of McDonald's restaurants, was a man with big ideas and grand ambitions. But even Kroc could not have anticipated the astounding impact of his creation. McDonald's is one of the most influential developments in twentieth-century America. Its reverberations extend far beyond the confines of the United States and the fast-food business. It has influenced a wide range of undertakings, indeed the way of life, of a significant portion of the world. And that impact is likely to expand at an accelerating rate.

... McDonald's serves here as the major example, the "paradigm," of a wide-ranging process I call *McDonaldization*, that is,

> the process by which the principles of the fast-food restaurant are coming to dominate more and more sectors of American society as well as of the rest of the world.

... McDonaldization affects not only the restaurant business, but also education, work, health care, travel, leisure, dieting, politics, the family, and virtually every other aspect of society. McDonaldization has shown every sign of being an inexorable process by sweeping through seemingly impervious institutions and parts of the world.

McDonald's success is apparent: in 1993 its total sales reached $23.6 billion with profits of almost $1.1 billion. The average U.S. outlet has total sales of approximately $1.6 million in a year. Many entrepreneurs envy such sales and profits and seek to emulate McDonald's success. McDonald's, which first began franchising in 1955, opened its 12,000th outlet on March 11, 1991. By the end of 1993, McDonald's had almost 14,000 restaurants worldwide....

The Dimensions of McDonaldization

Why has the McDonald's model proven so irresistible? Four alluring dimensions lie at the heart of the success of this model and, more generally, of McDonaldization. In short, McDonald's has succeeded because it offers consumers, workers, and managers efficiency, calculability, predictability, and control.

First, McDonald's offers *efficiency,* or the optimum method for getting from one point to another. For consumers, this means that McDonald's offers the best available way to get from being hungry to being full. (Similarly, Woody Allen's orgasmatron offered an efficient method for getting people from quiescence to sexual gratification.) Other institutions, fashioned on the McDonald's model, offer similar efficiency in losing weight, lubricating cars, getting new glasses or contacts, or completing income-tax forms. In a society where both parents are likely to work, or where there may be only a single parent, efficiently satisfying the hunger and many other needs of people is very attractive. In a society where people rush, usually by car, from one spot to another, the efficiency of a fast-food meal, perhaps even without leaving their cars by wending their way along the drive-through lane, often proves impossible to resist. The fast-food model offers people, or at least appears to offer them, an efficient method for satisfying many needs.

Like their customers, workers in McDonaldized systems function efficiently. They are trained to work this way by managers, who watch over them closely to make sure they do. Organizational rules and regulations also help ensure highly efficient work.

Second, McDonald's offers *calculability*, or an emphasis on the quantitative aspects of products sold (portion size, cost) and service offered (the time it takes to get the product). Quantity has become equivalent to quality; a lot of something, or the quick delivery of it, means it must be good. As two observers of contemporary American culture put it, "As a culture, we tend to believe deeply that in general 'bigger is better.'" Thus, people order the *Quarter Pounder*, the *Big* Mac, the *large* fries. More recently, there is the lure of the "double this" (for instance, Burger King's "Double Whopper With Cheese") and the "triple that." People can quantify these things and feel that they are getting a lot of food for what appears to be a nominal sum of money. This calculation does not take into account an important point: the extraordinary profitability of fast-food outlets and other chains, which indicates that the owners, not the consumers, get the best deal.

People also tend to calculate how much time it will take to drive to McDonald's, be served the food, eat it, and return home; then, they compare that interval to the time required to prepare food at home. They often conclude, rightly or wrongly, that a trip to the fast-food restaurant will take less time than eating at home. This sort of calculation particularly supports home-delivery franchises such as Domino's, as well as other chains that emphasize time saving. A notable example of time saving in another sort of chain is Lens Crafters, which promises people, "Glasses fast, glasses in one hour."

Some McDonaldized institutions combine the emphases on time and money. Domino's promises pizza delivery in half an hour, or the pizza is free. Pizza Hut will serve a personal pan pizza in five minutes, or it, too, will be free.

Workers at McDonaldized systems also tend to emphasize the quantitative rather than the qualitative aspects of their works. Since the quality of the work is allowed to vary little, workers focus on such things as how quickly tasks can be accomplished. In a situation analogous to that of the customer, workers are expected to do a lot of work, very quickly, for low pay.

Third, McDonald's offers *predictability*, the assurance that their products and services will be the same over time and in all locales. The Egg McMuffin in New York will be, for all intents and purposes, identical to those in Chicago and Los Angeles. Also, those eaten next week or next year will be identical to those eaten today. There is great comfort in knowing that McDonald's offers no surprises. People know that the next Egg McMuffin they eat will taste about the same as the others they have eaten; it will not be awful, but it will not be exceptionally delicious, either. The success of the McDonald's model suggests that many people have come to prefer a world in which there are few surprises.

The workers in McDonaldized systems also behave in predictable ways. They follow corporate rules as well as the dictates of their managers. In many cases, not only what they do, but also what they say, is highly predictable. McDonaldized organizations often have scripts that employees are supposed to memorize and follow whenever the occasion arises. This scripted behavior helps create highly predictable interactions between workers and customers. While customers do not follow scripts, they tend to develop simple recipes for dealing with the employees of McDonaldized systems. As Robin Leidner argues,

> McDonald's pioneered the routinization of interactive service work and remains an exemplar of extreme standardization. Innovation is not discouraged... at least among managers and franchisees. Ironically, though, 'the object is to look for new, innovative ways to create an experience that is exactly the same no matter what McDonald's you walk into, no matter where it is in the world.'

Fourth, *control*, especially through the *substitution of nonhuman for human technology*, is exerted over the people who enter the world of McDonald's. A *human technology* (a screwdriver, for example) is controlled by people; a *nonhuman technology* (the assembly line, for instance) controls people. The people who eat in fast-food restaurants are controlled, albeit (usually) subtly. Lines, limited menus, few options, and uncomfortable seats all lead diners to do what management wishes them to do—eat quickly and leave. Further, the drive-through (in some cases walk-through) window leads diners to leave before they eat. In the Domino's model, customers never come in the first place.

The people who work in McDonaldized organizations are also controlled to a high degree, usually more blatantly and directly than customers. They are trained to do a limited number of things in precisely the way they are told to do them. The technologies used and the way the organization is set up reinforce this control. Managers and inspectors make sure that workers toe the line.

McDonald's also controls employees by threatening to use, and ultimately using, nonhuman technology to replace human workers. No matter how well they are programmed and controlled, workers can foul up the system's operation. A slow worker can make the preparation and delivery of a Big Mac inefficient. A worker who refuses to follow the rules might leave the pickles or special sauce off a hamburger, thereby making for unpredictability. And a distracted worker can put too few fries in the box, making an order of large fries seem skimpy. For these and other reasons, McDonald's has felt compelled to steadily replace human beings with nonhuman technologies, such as the soft-drink dispenser that shuts itself off when the glass is full, the french-fry machine that rings and lifts itself out of the oil when the fries are crisp, the preprogrammed cash register that eliminates the need for the cashier to calculate prices and amounts, and, perhaps at some future time, the robot capable of making hamburgers. This technology increases the corporation's control over workers. Thus, McDonald's can assure customers that their employees and service will be consistent....

EFFICIENCY

McDonaldization implies a search for maximum efficiency in increasingly numerous and diverse social settings. Efficient means choosing the optimum means to a given end. Let me clarify this definition. First, the truly optimum means to an end is rarely found. Rather, optimum in this definition implies the attempt to find and use the *best possible* means. According to the economist, Herbert Simon, people and organizations rarely maximize. However, the drive for efficiency implies the search for a far better means to an end than would be employed under ordinary circumstances. Second, the generality of the terms *means and ends* makes it clear that efficiency can be applied to innumerable means and ends. In other words, there can be a search for optimum means within settings that involve a large number of disparate ends. This means that the drive for efficiency can and does occur within a wide variety of social settings.

In a McDonaldized society, people rarely search for the best means to an end on their own. Rather, they rely on the optimum means that have been previously discovered and institutionalized in a variety of social settings. Thus, the best means may be part of a technology, written into an organization's rules and regulations, or taught to employees during the process of occupational socialization. It would be inefficient if people always had to discover for themselves the optimum means to ends.

Efficiency is clearly advantageous to consumers, who can obtain what they need more quickly with less effort. Similarly, workers can perform their tasks more rapidly and easily. Manager and owners gain because work gets done and because customers are served more efficiently. But, as is always the case, irrationalities such as surprising inefficiencies and the dehumanization of customers and workers crop up....

The Fast-Food Industry: We Do It All for Them...

Streamlining the Process. Above all else, Ray Kroc was impressed by the efficiency of the McDonald brothers' operation, as well as the enormous profit potential of such a system applied at a large number of sites. Here is how Kroc described his initial reactions to the McDonald's system:

> I was fascinated by the simplicity and effectiveness of the system.... each step in producing the limited menu was stripped down to its essence and accomplished with a minimum of effort. They sold hamburgers and cheeseburgers only. The burgers were... all fried the same way.

... Kroc and his associates experimented with each component of the hamburger to increase the efficiency of producing and serving it. For example, they started with only partially sliced buns that arrived in cardboard boxes. The griddle workers had to spend time opening the boxes, separating the buns, slicing them in half, and discarding the leftover paper and cardboard. Eventually, they found that buns sliced completely in half could be used more efficiently. In addition, buns were made efficient by having them separated and shipped in reusable boxes. The meat patty received similar attention. For example, the paper between the patties had to have just the right amount of wax so that the patties would readily slide off the paper and onto the grill. Kroc made it clear that he aimed at greater efficiency:

> The purpose of all these refinements, and we never lost sight of it, was to make our griddle man's job easier to do quickly and well. And the other considerations of cost cutting, inventory control, and so forth were important to be sure, but they were secondary to the critical detail of what happened there at the smoking griddle. This was the vital passage of our *assembly-line,* and the product had to flow through it smoothly or the whole plant would falter. [Italics added.]

Today, fast food restaurants prepare their menu items on a kind of assembly line involving a number of people in specialized operations (for example, the burger "dresser"). The ultimate application of the assembly line to the fast-food process is Burger King's conveyor belt: A raw, frozen hamburger placed on one end moves slowly via the conveyor under a flame and emerges in ninety-four seconds on the other end fully cooked. Similar techniques are employed at Dunkin' Donuts, Kentucky Fried Chicken (if you want spicy Cajun fried chicken you must wheel on down the road to Popeye's), Taco Bell, and Pizza Hut. A newer and even more specialized fast-food outlet, Cinnabon, has perfected the techniques to mass produce and serve cinnamon buns.

Getting diners into and out of the fast-food restaurant has also been streamlined. As three observers put it, McDonald's has done "everything to speed the way from secretion to excretion." Parking lots adjacent to the restaurant offer readily available parking spots. It's a short walk to the counter, and although there is sometimes a line, food is usually quickly ordered, obtained, and paid for. The highly limited menu makes the diner's choice easy, in contrast to the many choices available in other restaurants. With the food obtained, it is but a few steps to a table and the beginning of the "dining experience." Because there is little inducement to linger, the diners generally gather the leftover paper, styrofoam, and plastic, discard them in a nearby trash receptacle, and get back in their cars to drive to the next (often McDonaldized) activity.

Not too many years ago, those in charge of fast-food restaurants discovered that the drive-through window made this whole process far more efficient. McDonald's opened its first drive-through in 1975 in Oklahoma City; within four years, almost half its restaurants had one. Instead of the "laborious" and "inefficient" process of parking the car, walking to the counter, waiting in line, ordering, paying, carrying the food to the table, eating, and disposing of the remnants, the drive-through window offered diners the option of driving to the window (perhaps waiting in a line of cars), ordering, paying, and driving off with the meal. You could eat while driving if you wanted to be even more efficient. The drive-through window is also efficient for the fast-food restaurant. As more and more people use the drive-through window, fewer parking spaces, tables, and employees are needed. Further, consumers take their debris with them as they drive away, thereby eliminating the need for additional trash receptacles and employees to empty those receptacles periodically....

Simplifying the Product.   Another efficient aspect of the fast-food restaurant is the nature of the food served. Complex foods based on sophisticated recipes are, needless to say, not the norm at fast-food restaurants. The staples of the industry are foods that require relatively few ingredients and are simple to prepare, serve, and eat.

In fact, fast-food restaurants generally serve finger food, food that can be eaten without utensils. Hamburgers, french fries, fried chicken, slices of pizza, tacos—the staples of the fast-food business—are all finger foods. Many innovations over the years have greatly increased the number and types of finger foods available. The Egg McMuffin is an entire breakfast—egg, Canadian bacon, English muffin—combined into a handy sandwich. It is far more efficient to devour such a sandwich than to sit down with knife and fork and eat a plate full of eggs, bacon, and toast. The creation of the Chicken McNugget, perhaps the ultimate finger food, reflects the fact that chicken is pretty inefficient as far as McDonald's is concerned. Bones, gristle, and skin of the chicken—barriers to efficient consumption—have all been eliminated in the Chicken Mc-Nugget. Customers can pop the bite-size morsels of fried chicken right into their mouths even as they drive. Were they able to, the mass purveyors of chicken, for example, Perdue, would breed a more efficiently consumed chicken free of bones, gristle, and skin. McDonald's also offers an apple pie that, because it is completely encased in dough, can be munched like a sandwich.

The limited number of available choices and options also contributes to efficiency in the fast-food restaurant. McDonald's does not serve egg rolls (at least not yet), and Taco Bell does not offer fried chicken. In spite of what they tell people, fast-food restaurants are far from not only full-serve restaurants but also the old cafeterias that offered a vast array of foods.

Pity the consumer who has a special request in the fast-food restaurant. The fast-food advertisement, "We do it your way," implies that these chains happily accommodate special requests. However, because much of their efficiency stems from the fact that they virtually always do it one way—*their* way, the last thing that fast-food restaurants want to do is do it your way. The typical hamburger is usually so thin that it can only be cooked one way—well done. Bigger burgers (the McDonald's Quarter-Pounder, for example) can be prepared rare, but the fast-food restaurant prefers, for the sake of efficiency (and perhaps for health reasons), that they all be cooked one way. Customers with the temerity to ask for a rare burger or well-browned fries are likely to cool their heels for a long time waiting for such "exotica." Few customers are willing to do this because it defeats one of the main advantages of going to a fast-food restaurant—efficiency. The limited number of menu items also allows for highly efficient ordering of supplies and food delivery. In sum, what Henry Ford once said about cars has been extended to hamburgers, "Any customer can have a car painted any color that he wants so long as it is black."

Putting Customers to Work.   Two scholars have recently described how fast-food customers do unpaid labor:

> A few years ago, the fast food chain McDonald's came up with the slogan "We do it all for you." In reality, at McDonald's, we do it all for them. We stand in line, take the food to the table, dispose of the waste, and stack our trays. As labor costs rise and technology develops, the consumer often does more and more of the work.

The salad bar is a classic example of putting the consumer to work. The customer "buys" an empty plate and then ambles over to the salad bar to load up on the array of vegetables and other foods available that day. Quickly seeing the merit in this, many supermarkets have now installed their own salad bars with a more elaborate array of alternative foods available to the consumer. The salad lover can now work as a salad chef at lunch hour in the fast-food restaurant and then do it all over again in the evening at the supermarket. All this is very efficient from the perspective of the fast-food restaurant and the supermarket, since they need only a small number of employees to keep the various compartments well stocked.

In a number of fast-food restaurants, including Roy Rogers (owned by Hardee's), consumers are expected to take a naked burger to the "fixin' bar" to add such things as lettuce, tomatoes, and onions. In such cases, they end up logging a few minutes a week as sandwich makers. In a more recent innovation at Burger King and other franchises, people must fill their own cups with ice and soft drinks, thereby spending a few moments as "soda jerks." In some ultramodern fast-food restaurants such as Taco Bell, people must punch in their own orders on computer screens. In these and other ways, the fast-food restaurant has grown more efficient by putting customers to work....

Conclusion

No social institution lasts forever. While McDonaldization remains a powerful force in today's world, it, too, will pass from the scene. McDonaldized systems will remain powerful until the nature of society has changed so dramatically that they can no longer adapt to it. Even after it is gone, McDonald's will be remembered for the dramatic impact it had, both positive and negative, on the United States and much of the rest of the world.... When McDonald's has... receded in importance or even passed from the scene, it will be remembered as yet another precursor to what is likely to be a still more rational world.

CHAPTER 12

The Family

12.1 STEPHANIE COONTZ

The Way We Really Are

Most people know a good deal about the family because almost all of us have grown up in one. By experience we know how important good family life is. But do we accurately know how American families are changing? Experts say that the American family is disintegrating. Tied to this assertion are numerous reports about divorce, spouse abuse, child abuse, latchkey kids, runaways, neglected children, and so on. Blame for these problems is laid on the women's movement, working mothers, welfare, economic hardship, and the extension of the government into the family.

In fact, much of what we hear about these problems is wrong or only partially right, according to family historian Stephanie Coontz in the following selection from *The Way We Really Are: Coming to Terms With America's Changing Families* (Basic Books, 1997). The main source of error, says Coontz, is the common belief in an ideal "traditional" family of the past to which today's families are unfavorably compared. She maintains that the family of the past was not ideal and that few would want to turn the clock back. Coontz also maintains that the family of the present is not as weak as it is usually portrayed. For example, there are more high-quality and long-lasting marriages today than ever before, although there are also many short-lived, low-quality marriages. Coontz argues that the weak marriages get the attention and the good ones are overlooked. Coontz's careful analysis leads her to conclude that the answer to family problems is not to be found in the past. Rather, it is to be found in the future, with reforms at the workplace, and in a more compatible definition of husband and wife roles.

Coontz teaches history and family studies at the Evergreen State College in Olympia, Washington. A former Woodrow Wilson fellow, she has also taught at Kobe University in Japan and the University of Hawaii at Hilo. She is coeditor of *American Families: A Multicultural Reader* (Routledge, 1998).

Key Concept: short life of the male breadwinner family

INTRODUCTION

Five years ago I wrote a book called *The Way We Never Were: American Families and the Nostalgia Trap*. As a family historian bothered by widespread misconceptions in the popular press about "traditional" families, I hoped to get people to look more realistically at the strengths, weaknesses, and surprising variability of family life in the past....

In my last book, I demonstrated the tremendous variety of family types that have worked—and not worked—in American history. When families succeeded, it was often for reasons quite different than stereotypes about the past suggest—because they were flexible in their living arrangements, for example, or could call on people and institutions beyond the family for assistance or support. And when families failed, the results were often devastating. There never was a golden age of family life, a time when all families were capable of meeting the needs of their members and protecting them from poverty, violence, or sexual exploitation.

The "traditional" sexual double standard, for example, may have led more middle-class girls to delay sex at the end of the nineteenth century than today, but it also created higher proportions of young female prostitutes. Respect for elders may have received more lip service in the past, but elders were until very recently the segment of the population most likely to be destitute.

...[C]are must be taken in interpreting headlines about the explosion of unwed motherhood. Unwed motherhood has increased dramatically since 1970, but it's easy to overstate *how* dramatically, because much illegitimacy was covered up in the past and reporting methods have recently become much more sophisticated....

It's also important to distinguish between the ratio of unmarried to married births and the rate of births to unmarried women. Between 1960 and 1990, the nonmarital birth ratio increased by more than 500 percent, from 5.3 percent of all births to 28 percent. But birth rates to unmarried women only increased by a factor of 1.73, not quite twofold. What explains the larger figure is that births to unmarried women rose while births to married women fell, increasing the *relative* proportion of unmarried births much more than their *absolute* numbers. In some cases, a fall in marital fertility may be so large that unwed births become a larger proportion of all births even when rates of unwed childbearing are flat or falling. The probability that an unmarried African-American woman would have a child actually fell from 9.8 to 9.0 percent between 1960 and 1990, for example; but because married-couple childbearing decreased among African Americans even more sharply, the proportion of black children born to unwed mothers rose.

...[T]ake the question of whether marriage is a dying institution. In 1867 there were 9.6 marriages per 1,000 people. A hundred years later, in 1967, there were 9.7. The rate reached a low of 7.9 in 1932 and an all-time high of 16.4 in 1946, a peak quickly followed by a brief but huge surge in divorce. Marriage rates fell again from the early 1950s to 1958, rose slowly until the end of the 1960s, and then began to decline again. But the proportion of women who remain single all their lives is *lower* today than at the turn of the century, and fewer women now feel they have to forgo marriage entirely in order to do anything else in their lives. Periodic predictions to the contrary, it is unlikely that we will someday record the demise of the last married couple in America.

Nevertheless, marriage is certainly a *transformed* institution, and it plays a smaller role than ever before in organizing social and personal life. One reason is that marriage comes much later, for most people, than in the past. Men's average age at first marriage today is not unprecedented, though it has now regained the previous record high of 1890. But the average age of marriage for contemporary women is two years higher than its historical peak in 1890 and almost four years higher than in the 1950s. This figure approaches the highest age ever recorded for Western Europe, a region where marriage has always taken place later than almost anywhere else in the world. And although fewer women stay single all their lives than in 1900, a higher proportion of women than ever before experience a period of independent living and employment before marriage. Women's expectations of both marriage and work are unlikely to ever be the same as in the past.

The second reason for marriage's more limited role in people's lives is that it is no longer expected to last "until death do us part." Divorce rates in America rose steadily until World War II, fell briefly during the 1950s, and took off again during the late 1960s. The divorce rate crested near the end of the 1970s, leveled off in the 1980s, and very slightly receded from 1988 to 1993. This last trend was heralded by many commentators as a "real turnaround," a sign that Americans "are turning conservative, pro-family." But while demographers now say that only 40 percent, rather than 50 percent, of marriages will end in divorce, these remain among the highest divorce rates ever recorded. Furthermore, the cumulative effects of past divorces continue to mount. In 1960 there were 35 divorced men and women for every 1,000 married ones. By 1990 there were 140 divorced individuals for every 1,000 married ones.

People often misunderstand what statisticians mean when they estimate that one in every two or three marriages will end in divorce. The calculations refer to the chances of a marriage ending in divorce within 40 years. While rising divorce rates have increased the number of marriages at risk for dissolution, the gradual extension of life spans ensures that a marriage today has the potential to last three times longer than one of 200 years ago. Thus while the number of people who divorce is certainly unprecedented, so is the number of couples who celebrate their fortieth wedding anniversaries. In fact, the chances of doing so have never been better.

On the other hand, the average marriage that ends in divorce lasts only 6.3 years. We may be seeing more marriages that last longer and are more fulfilling than at any time in our history. But we are also seeing more marriages that are *less* committed and of shorter duration than in the past. Sociologist Valerie Oppenheimer suggests we are experiencing growing polarization between increasing numbers of very "high-quality," long-lasting marriages *and* increasing numbers of short-lived, medium- to "low-quality" ones where the partners are not committed enough to stay and work things through. Understanding this polarization helps explain some of the ambivalence Americans have about modern families. Very few people in a modern high-quality marriage would trade it for an older model where limited communication and a high degree of sexual dissatisfaction were taken for granted. And few adults in a very low-quality marriage, or their children, want to be trapped there for life. But the commitments and consequences of "medium-quality" marriages are more ambiguous, especially for kids, and this worries many Americans....

WHY WORKING MOTHERS ARE HERE TO STAY

The 1950s was clearly out of balance in one direction, with almost half the adult population restricted in their access to economic and political roles beyond the family. But the last few decades have been out of balance in the opposite direction. Many of us now feel that our expanding roles beyond the family have restricted our access to family life.

At first glance, it appears that the new imbalance results from women, especially mothers, entering the workforce. Certainly, that trend has produced a dramatic change in relation to the decade that most people use as their measure of "traditional" family life. In 1950, only a quarter of all wives were in the paid labor force, and just 16 percent of all children had mothers who worked outside the home. By 1991, more than 58 percent of all married women, and nearly two-thirds of all married women with children, were in the labor force. Of the total number of children in the country, 59 percent, including a majority of preschoolers, had mothers who worked outside the home.

But to analyze today's family imbalance as a conflict between work and mothering is to misread family history and to misdirect future family policy. Historically, productive work by mothers as well as fathers (and by young people) has not only been compatible with family life but has also strengthened family relationships. What's really out of balance is the relationship between market activities and nonmarket ones (including community as well as family ties). Our jobs don't make room for family obligations. The purchase of goods and services often substitutes for family or neighborhood activities. Phone calls, beepers, faxes and e-mail constantly intrude into family time. To correct this imbalance, we need to reorganize work to make it more compatible with family life. We need to reorganize family life to make sure that all members share in the work needed to sustain it. We need to redirect technology so that it serves rather than dominates our social and interpersonal relationships.

Instead, however, the family consensus brokers encourage us to cobble together personal marital arrangements that combine what they consider to be the best family features from both the 1950s and the 1990s. They reason that if we could convince women to take time off from work while their children are young, bolster male wages enough that more families could afford to make this choice, increase the incentives for marriage, and combat the excesses of individualism that lead to divorce or unwed motherhood, then surely we could solve the conflicts that parents now experience in balancing work and family. While recommending that men should help out more at home and expressing abstract support for equal pay and promotion opportunities for women on the job, the family values think tanks nevertheless propose that parents revive "relatively traditional marital gender roles" for the period "when children are young," cutting back on mothers' paid work.

In the absence of wider social change in work policies and family support systems, this is the individual solution that many men and women try to work out. And it may be a reasonable stopgap measure for parents who can afford it. But when such personal accommodations are put forward as an overarching political program for family life, they cease to sound quite so reasonable....

Women, the argument goes, are happy to care for children, but men's biological drives point them in a different direction. Men have to be coaxed and guided into responsible fatherhood, and societies have historically achieved this by granting husbands special status as moral educators, family authority figures, and breadwinners. When society stops viewing breadwinning "as a father's special task," we lose our most powerful way "to motivate fathers to provide for their children."

The family values crusaders believe that all men and women, at least during their parenting years, should organize their families with the man as primary provider and protector and the wife as primary nurturer. Before and after child rearing, a woman is welcome to work; but unless she has no other option, she should engage in "sequencing"—alternating work and child raising rather than trying to combine them. Popenoe proposes the wife take "at least a year" off work, then work part-time until her children are in their early to mid-teens. Even when both husband and wife are employed, the woman should remain primarily responsible for nurturing, with the man as "junior partner" at home. Husbands should help out more than in the past, but anything that smacks of "androgyny" is to be avoided like the plague. Society, he argues, must "disavow the popular notion of radical feminists that 'daddies can make good mommies.'"

Hostility to women's economic independence is a consistent subtext in "new consensus" writing. "Policies that encourage mothers to work instead of marry" are a large part of America's social problem, says Wade Horn of the National Fatherhood Initiative. Without providing any evidence, Dan Quayle claims studies show "that children whose parents work are *less likely* to have Mommy's undivided attention than children whose mothers stay home." Isn't it odd how quickly a discussion of working *parents* becomes an indictment of *Mommy*? According to this agenda, a male breadwinner–female homemaker division of labor is not an individual family choice but the correct model for every family. Women are told that there are compensations for giving up their aspirations to economic equality: "Even though the man is the head of the family, the woman is the neck, and she turns the head any way she wants." But if women are not willing to "give back" family leadership, groups such as the Promise Keepers advise men to "take it back.... Be sensitive. Treat the lady gently and lovingly. But lead!"

While we can debate the *merits* of these proposals for America's families, I am more interested in examining their *practicality*. How likely is it that a majority of mothers will once more withdraw from paid employment during the early years of child rearing? What can historical and sociological analysis teach us about how realistic it is to propose that we revive the breadwinner identity as the basis for men's commitment to marriage and child raising?

*Stephanie
Coontz*

One of the most common misconceptions about modern marriage is the notion that coprovider families are a new invention in human history. In fact, today's dual-earner family represents a return to older norms, after a very short interlude that people mistakenly identify as "traditional."

Throughout most of humanity's history women as well as men were family breadwinners. Contrary to cartoons of cavemen dragging home food to a wife waiting at the campfire, in the distant past of early gathering and hunting societies women contributed as much or more to family subsistence as men. Mothers left the hearth to forage for food, hunt small animals, trade with other groups, or tend crops.

On this continent, neither Native American, African-American, nor white women were originally seen as economic dependents. Among European colonists, men dominated women, but their authority was based on legal, political, and religious coercion, not on men's greater economic importance. The most common words for wives in seventeenth- and eighteenth-century colonial America were "yoke-mates" or "meet-helps," labels that indicated women's economic partnership with men. Until the early nineteenth century, men and women worked together on farms or in small household businesses, alongside other family members. Responsibility for family life and responsibility for breadwinning were not two different, specialized jobs.

But in the early 1800s, as capitalist production for the market replaced home-based production for local exchange and a wage-labor system supplanted widespread self-employment and farming, more and more work was conducted in centralized workplaces removed from the farm or home. A new division of labor then grew up within many families. Men (and older children) began to specialize in work outside the home, withdrawing from their traditional child-raising responsibilities. Household work and child care were delegated to wives, who gave up their older roles in production and barter. While slaves and free blacks continued to have high labor force participation by women, wives in most other ethnic and racial groups were increasingly likely to quit paid work outside the home after marriage.

But it's important to remember that this new division of work between husbands and wives came out of a *temporary* stage in the history of wage labor and industrialization. It corresponded to a transitional period when households could no longer get by primarily on things they made, grew, or bartered, but could not yet rely on purchased consumer goods. For example, families no longer produced their own homespun cotton, but ready-made clothing was not yet available at prices most families could afford. Women still had to sew clothes from cloth that men purchased with their pay. Most families still had to grow part of their food and bake their own bread. Food preparation and laundering required hours of work each day. Water often had to be hauled and heated.

Somebody had to go out to earn money in order to buy the things the family needed; but somebody else had to stay home and turn the things they bought into things they could actually use. Given the preexisting legal, political, and religious tradition of patriarchal dominance, husbands (and youths of both sexes) were assigned to work outside the home. Wives assumed exclusive responsibility for domestic matters that they had formerly shared with husbands or delegated to older children and apprentices. Many women supplemented their household labor with income-generating work that could be done at or around home—taking in boarders, doing extra sewing or laundering, keeping a few animals, or selling garden products. But this often arduous work was increasingly seen as secondary to wives' primary role of keeping house, raising the children, and getting dinner on the table.

The resulting identification of masculinity with economic activities and femininity with nurturing care, now often seen as the "natural" way of organizing the nuclear family, was in fact a historical product of this nineteenth-century transition from an agricultural household economy to an industrial wage economy. So even as an ideal, the male breadwinner family was a comparatively late arrival onto the historical scene. As a reality—a family form in which most people actually lived—it came about even later....

The Revival of Women's Role as Family Coprovider

... For approximately 50 years, from the 1920s through the 1960s, the growth in married women's work outside the home was smaller than the decline in child labor, so that the male breadwinner family became increasingly dominant. But even at its high point in the 1950s, less than 60 percent of American children spent their youth in an Ozzie and Harriet-type family where dad went to work and mom stayed home. And by the 1970s the fifty-year reign of this family form was definitely over....

After 1973, real wages for young men began falling, creating a larger proportion of families where the mother worked just to keep the family afloat. Housing inflation meant that families with young children were especially likely to need the wife to work, in order to afford the new home that their growing family motivated them to buy. By 1989, almost 80 percent of all home buyers came from two-income households. Another incentive was the rising cost of higher education, which increased nearly three times faster than household income between 1980 and 1994.

Today most families can no longer think of the earnings that wives and mothers bring home as a bonus that can be put aside when family needs call. Nor, increasingly, do the jobs women hold allow them the luxury of choosing to cut back or quit when family priorities change, any more than their husbands' jobs would. By 1993, married women working full-time contributed 41 percent of their families' incomes. Indeed, in 23 percent of two-earner couples, the wives earned *more* than their husbands.

The sequencing of mothering and paid employment that characterized many women's activities over the past 100 years is becoming a thing of the past. Through most of this century, even though labor participation rates for women rose steadily, they dropped significantly when women were in their twenties and thirties. By 1990, however, labor-force participation rates no longer dipped for women in their child-raising years. Today, fewer and fewer women leave their jobs while their children are very young.

Proponents of the modified male breadwinner family believe that if we could drastically reduce the number of single-mother households, raise wages for men, and convince families to get by on a little less, we might be able to get wives to quit work during their child-raising years. Polls consistently show that many women would like to cut back on work hours, though not quit entirely (and it's interesting that an almost equal number of men would also like to cut back their hours). But a return to the norm of male breadwinner families is simply not feasible for most Americans.

Why Wives and Mothers Will Continue to Work Outside the Home

It's not just a dollars-and-cents issue. Most women would not give up the satisfactions of their jobs even if they could afford to quit. They consistently tell interviewers they like the social respect, self-esteem, and friendship networks they gain from the job, despite the stress they may face finding acceptable child care and negotiating household chores with their husbands. In a 1995 survey by Louis Harris & Associates, for example, less than a third of working women said they would prefer to stay home even if money were no object.

Another reason women do not want to quit work is that they are not willing to surrender the increased leverage it gives them in the family. The simple truth is that women who do not earn income have much less decision-making power in marital relations than women who do. And no amount of goodwill on the part of husbands seems to lessen this imbalance. In one in-depth study of American families, researchers found that the primary determinant of power in all couples was who brings in the money. The only exception was among lesbians. Lesbian couples might be persuaded to have one partner stay home with the kids and the other earn the money, but I doubt that the Institute for American Values would consider this a positive step in the direction of "marital role complementarity."

Aside from women's own motivations to remain at work, the issue of whether a family can afford to have the wife stay home is quite debatable. One of the most longstanding American traditions, much older than the ideal of the male breadwinner, is the search for socioeconomic mobility. That's why many families came to America in the first place. It's what people were seeking when they crossed the plains in covered wagons, why farmers switched from diversified family crops to specialized market production, what parents have expected education to provide for their children.

From the mid-nineteenth to the mid-twentieth century, there were three main routes to family economic advancement. One was child labor, allowing parents to accumulate enough to buy a house and possibly send a later generation to school. Another was the move from farm to city, to take advantage of higher wage rates in urban areas. The third was investment in increased training and education for male members of the family.

But child labor was abolished in the early twentieth century, and even before 1950 most men had already obtained nonfarm jobs. By the mid-1960s there were diminishing returns to the gains families could expect from further education or training for men. As these older strategies ceased to guarantee continued mobility, women's employment became so central to family economic advancement that it could less and less often be postponed or interrupted for full-time child raising.

In other words, even for families where the uninterrupted work of wives isn't essential for minimum family subsistence, it is now the main route to even a modest amount of upward mobility. Those who tell women who "don't need to work" that they should go back to full-time child rearing are contradicting many of the other ideals most Americans hold dear. We're talking about abandoning the American dream here. The only way to get a significant number of families to make this choice would be to foster a thoroughly untraditional —some might even say un-American—acceptance of a stationary standard of living, a no-growth family economy. Some families may harbor such subversive ideals; yet the chances are slim that this will become a mass movement any time soon.

12.2 KATHLEEN GERSON

Coping With Commitment: Dilemmas and Conflicts of Family Life

During the long process of becoming a modern institution, the family lost many of its functions: economic—to the factory and office; educational—to institutions of education; and a share of social control—to law enforcement institutions. A significant part of the socialization process was quietly assumed by the school and peer groups. Since the 1960s radical changes have occurred. The women's movement, for example, challenged the ideal family of the 1950s in which the wife, mother, and homemaker (even when employed) did not question the role of the husband as the primary breadwinner or demand that he help much at home. The subsequent changes were not greeted by all as liberating. Women who accepted the traditional role as helpmates to their husbands and as mothers nurturing the future generation were opposed to the new message that these roles were not enough and that women should seek income, independence, and fulfillment in the workplace. Others, especially the young, responded to the message of women's liberation and changed the American family.

Members of the current generation, discussed in the following selection by Kathleen Gerson, are not the complete opposite of their parents. Social change, notes Gerson, remains inconsistent. It is dramatic for some and unchanging for others. Her research suggests that whether women are *work oriented* or *family oriented* depends mainly on the experiences that they have rather than their original values. She found that women who were exposed to change in marriage and work institutions were more likely to be work oriented, but those who were not exposed to change tended to be family oriented.

291

Current problems of the family, argues Gerson, are a consequence of the "inconsistent and contradictory nature of change" and dilemmas and conflicts created in balancing the demands of work and parenthood. It is the resolution of these dilemmas and conflicts that constitutes the central challenge to men and women.

Gerson is an associate professor of sociology at New York University. She has published many books on gender, the family, and social change, including *Hard Choices: How Women Decide About Work, Career, and Motherhood* (University of California Press, 1985) and *No Man's Land: Men's Changing Commitments to Family and Work* (Basic Books, 1993). She has a new book in progress tentatively titled *The Uncertain Revolution.* The following selection is from Gerson's essay "Coping With Commitment: Dilemmas and Conflicts of Family Life," in Alan Wolfe, ed., *America at Century's End* (University of California Press, 1991).

Key Concept: work orientation and family orientation

Since 1950, when the breadwinner-homemaker household accounted for almost two-thirds of all American households, widespread changes have occurred in the structure of American family life. Rising rates of divorce, separation, and cohabitation outside of marriage have created a growing percentage of single-parent and single-adult households. The explosion in the percentage of employed women, and especially employed mothers, has produced a rising tide of dual-earner couples whose patterns of child rearing differ substantially from the 1950s' norm of the stay-at-home mother....

Incomplete and unequal social change has created new personal dilemmas over how to balance parental and employment commitments and new social conflicts between those who have developed "traditional" and "nontraditional" resolutions to the intransigent conflicts between family and workplace demands. These dilemmas and conflicts pose the central challenges to which new generations of women, men, and children must respond.

PERSONAL DILEMMAS AND FAMILY DIVERSITY: THE CONSEQUENCES OF UNEQUAL SOCIAL CHANGE

Social change in family structure remains inconsistent in two consequential ways. First, some social arrangements have changed significantly, but others have not. Even though an increasing percentage of families depend on the earnings of wives and mothers, women continue to face discrimination at the workplace and still retain responsibility for the lion's share of household labor. Similarly, despite the growth of dual-earner and single-parent households, the structural conflicts between family and work continue to make it difficult for either women or men to combine child rearing with sustained employment commitment. The combination of dramatic change in some social arrangements (for example, women's influx into the labor force) and relatively little change in others (for example, employers' continuing expectation that job responsibilities should take precedence over family needs) has created new forms of gender inequality and new dilemmas for both women and men who confront the dual demands of employment and parenthood.

Second, social change is inconsistent because social groups differ greatly in how and to what degree they have been exposed to change. Not only are the alternatives that women and men face structured differently, but within each gender group, the alternatives vary significantly. A growing group of women, for example, have gained access to highly rewarded professional and managerial careers, but most women remain segregated in relatively ill-rewarded, female-dominated occupations. Similarly, the stagnation of real wages has eroded many men's ability to support wives and children on their paycheck alone, but most men still enjoy significant economic advantages. This variation in opportunities and constraints has, in turn, promoted contrasting orientations toward family change among differently situated groups of women and men. . . .

CHOOSING BETWEEN EMPLOYMENT AND MOTHERHOOD

Although most women, including most mothers, now participate in the paid labor force, this apparent similarity masks important differences in women's responses to the conflicts between employment and motherhood. Not only do some mothers continue to stay home to rear children, but many employed women work part time or intermittently and continue to emphasize family over employment commitments. These "domestically oriented" women stand in contrast to a growing group of "nondomestic" women, who have developed employment ties that rival, and for some surpass, family commitments. Women develop "domestic" or "nondomestic" orientations in response to specific sets of occupational and interpersonal experiences. These contrasting orientations to family life are not only rooted in different social circumstances; they also represent opposing responses to the conflicts between motherhood and employment.

All women face an altered social context, but they differ in how and to what extent they have been exposed to structural change. This uneven exposure to new opportunities and constraints has produced contrasting orientations toward employment and motherhood. In my research on how women make family and work decisions, I found that regardless of class position or early childhood experiences and expectations, those women who were exposed to change in marital and work institutions were more likely to develop nondomestic orientations as adults, whereas those who were sheltered from these changes tended to develop a domestic orientation in adulthood. About two-thirds of the respondents who held domestic orientations as children ultimately became work-committed. Similarly, over 60 percent of those who were ambivalent about childbearing or who held career aspirations as children became committed to domesticity in adulthood.

Unanticipated encounters with changing structures of marriage and employment led some women to veer away from domesticity and others to veer toward it. Those who experienced instability in their relationships with men, who encountered often unanticipated chances for advancement at the workplace, who were disillusioned with the experience of motherhood, and who met severe economic squeezes in their households tended to develop strong work commitments. These women found full-time mothering and homemaking relatively isolating, devalued, and unfulfilling compared to the rewards of paid jobs. Exposure to unanticipated opportunities outside the home combined with unexpected disappointment in domestic pursuits to encourage a nondomestic orientation even among those who had initially planned for a life of domesticity.

In contrast, women who encountered blocked mobility at work and became disillusioned by dead-end jobs decided that motherhood provided a more satisfying alternative to stifling work conditions. They were, furthermore, able to establish stable marital partnerships in which they could depend on economic support from husbands with secure careers. When the experience of blocked mobility at the workplace was combined with unexpected marital commitment to a securely employed spouse, even women who once held career aspirations were encouraged to loosen their employment ties and turn toward domestic pursuits. Over 60 percent of those who initially planned to have a work career ultimately opted for domesticity in response to constraints at the workplace and opportunities for domestic involvement. Amid the currents of social change, exposure to a traditional package of opportunities and constraints led these women to conclude that their best hope for a satisfying life depended on subordinating their employment goals to motherhood and family pursuits.

In sum, exposure to expanded opportunities outside the home (for example, upward employment mobility) and unanticipated insecurities within it (for example, marital instability or economic squeezes in the household) tends to promote a nondomestic orientation, even among women who once planned for full-time motherhood. Exposure to a more traditional package of opportunities and constraints (such as constricted employment options and stable marriage) tends, in contrast, to promote a domestic orientation even among those who felt ambivalent toward motherhood and domesticity as children....

Strategies of Domestically Oriented Women

Despite the forces leading other women out of the home, domestically oriented women confront ample reasons to avoid such a fate. Blocked occupational opportunities leave these women poorly positioned to enjoy the benefits of work outside the home. They have concluded that domestic pursuits offer significant advantages over workplace commitment. A homemaker and mother of two declared:

> I never plan to go back [to work]. I'm too spoiled now. I'm my own boss. I have independence; I have control; I have as much freedom as anyone is going to have in our society. No [paid] job can offer me those things.

Since their "freedom" depends on someone else's paycheck, domestically oriented women are willing to accept responsibility for the care of home and children in exchange for male economic support....

Whether or not they work, domestically oriented women put their family commitments first. When employed, they carefully define their work attachments as a discretionary choice that can be curtailed if necessary and that always comes second to their children's needs....

The rise of work-commitment among other women has not only provided an alternative to domesticity, it has also eroded the ideological hegemony that homemakers once enjoyed. Domestically oriented women feel unfairly devalued by others, as [this] ex-clerical worker explained:

> People put no value on a housewife. If you have a job, you're interesting. If you don't, you're really not very interesting, and sometimes I think people turn you off.

... The erosion of the structural and ideological supports for domesticity has left domestically oriented women feeling embattled. They are now forced to defend a personal choice and family arrangement that was once considered sacrosanct. For these reasons, domestically oriented women cannot afford to take a neutral stance toward social change, and many have developed ideologies of opposition to other people's choices. Domestically oriented women tend to view employed mothers as either selfish and dangerous to children or overburdened and miserable....

Finally, domestically oriented women support men's right and duty to be primary breadwinners. They frown on men who shirk their duties to support women and children....

Although their strategies have unfolded against the tide of social change, domestically oriented women illustrate the forces that not only limit the change but provide a powerful opposition to it. Their personal circumstances give them ample reason to view change as a dangerous threat to their own and their children's well-being, even when it leads in the direction of greater gender equality.

Strategies of Work-Committed Women

Work-committed women lack the option of domesticity, or the desire to opt for it, but they nevertheless face significant obstacles. Persistent wage inequality and occupational sex segregation continue to deny most employed women an equal opportunity to succeed at the workplace. In addition, limited change in the organization of work, especially in male-dominated occupations, combines with the "stalled revolution" in the sexual division of domestic work to make it difficult for employed women to integrate career-commitment with motherhood. Work-committed women have responded in several ways to this predicament. A small but significant proportion have decided to forgo child-bearing altogether, but the majority of work-committed women are attempting to balance child rearing with strong labor force attachment.

Childless women have concluded that childbearing is an unacceptably dangerous choice in a world where marriage is fragile and motherhood threatens to undermine employment prospects. A strong skepticism regarding the viability of marriage led a divorced executive to reject childbearing:

> [Having children] probably would set back my career... irretrievably. The real thing that fits in here is my doubts about men and marriage, because if I had real faith that the marriage would go on, and that this would be a family unit and be providing for these children, being set back in my career wouldn't be that big a deal....

Childless women also have considerable skepticism about men's willingness to assume the sacrifices and burdens of parenthood. Since gender equality in parenting seems out of reach, so does motherhood....

Most work-committed women, however, do eventually have children....

Work-committed mothers must create strategies to meet the competing demands of child rearing and employment. However, their strategic choices are severely limited by intransigence in the workplace. This aspiring banker lamented:

> [My bosses] figure that I'm to have my career, and what I do at home is my own business, but it better not interrupt the job....

Since most employers continue to penalize workers, regardless of gender, for parental involvement that interferes with the job, employed mothers have had to look elsewhere for relief from the competing demands of employment and child rearing. Three strategies, in particular, offer hope of easing their plight. First, employed mothers limit their demands by limiting family size. Although the two-child family remains the preferred alternative, the one-child family is gaining acceptance....

Employed mothers must also reevaluate and alter the beliefs about child rearing they inherited from earlier generations, who frowned on working mothers....

Finally, work-committed mothers have engaged in a protracted struggle to bring men into the process of parenting. Their male partners' support of their independence gives them leverage to demand sharing, even if it doesn't guarantee that such sharing will be equal....

Inconsistent and unequal social change has promoted differing strategic reactions among women that leave them socially divided and politically opposed. The contours of change, however, also depend on men's reactions to the emerging conflicts and dilemmas of family life.

CHOOSING BETWEEN PRIVILEGE AND SHARING: MEN'S RESPONSES TO GENDER AND FAMILY CHANGE

While the transformation in women's lives has garnered the most attention, significant changes have also occurred in men's family patterns. The primary breadwinner who emphasizes economic support and constricted participation in child rearing persists, but this model—like its female counterpart, the homemaker—no longer predominates. Alongside this pattern, several alternatives have gained adherents. An increasing proportion of men have moved away from family commitments—among them single and childless men who have chosen to forgo parenthood and divorced fathers who maintain weak ties to their offspring. Another group of men, however, has become more involved in the nurturing activities of family life. Although these "involved fathers" rarely assume equal responsibility for child rearing, they are nevertheless significantly more involved with their children than are primary breadwinners, past or present. Change in men's lives, while limited and contradictory, is nonetheless part of overall family change.

As with women's choices, men's family patterns reflect uneven exposure to structural change in family and work arrangements. In my research on men's changing patterns of parental involvement, I found that men who established employment stability in highly rewarded but demanding jobs, and who experience unexpected marital stability with a domestically oriented spouse, were pushed and pulled toward primary breadwinning even when they had originally hoped to avoid such a fate. In contrast, men who experienced employment instability and dissatisfaction with the "rat race" of high-pressure, bureaucratically controlled jobs tended to turn away from primary breadwinning. When these experiences were coupled with instability in heterosexual relationships and dissatisfying experiences with children, many rejected parental involvement altogether—opting instead for personal independence and freedom from children. When declining work commitments were coupled with unexpected pleasure in committed, egalitarian heterosexual relationships and unexpected fulfillment through involvement with children, men tended to become oriented toward involved fatherhood. Thus, while about 36 percent of the respondents developed a primary breadwinning orientation, the remaining men did not. . . .

ALTERNATIVES TO PRIMARY BREADWINNING AMONG MEN

Men who eschew primary breadwinning have concluded that the privileges afforded "good providers" are not worth the price that privilege entails. They view breadwinning responsibilities as burdensome and constricting, but their rejection of breadwinning poses its own dilemmas. The loosening bonds of marriage allow these men greater latitude to avoid parental responsibilities, both economic and social. On the other hand, the increasing number of work-committed women encourages and, indeed, pressures some nontraditional men to become more involved in the noneconomic aspects of family life than was typical of men a generation ago. These two patterns—forgoing parental commitments and becoming involved in caretaking—represent increasingly popular, if quite different, responses to the search for an alternative to traditional masculinity amid a contradictory and ambiguous set of options.

Forgoing Parental Commitments

Like permanently childless women, some men have opted to forgo parental responsibilities. This group includes childless men who do not wish or plan to become fathers and divorced fathers who have significantly curtailed their economic and social ties to their offspring in the wake of marital disruption. These men have come to value autonomy over commitment and to view children as a threat to their freedom of choice....

Some divorced fathers also develop a relatively weak emotional and social attachment to their children. Whether their reaction is a defense against the pain of loss or an extension of their lack of involvement in child rearing prior to divorce, divorced fathers who become distant from their children tend to discount the importance of parenthood....

Caretaking Fathers

A more equal sharing of both earning income and rearing children provides another alternative to primary breadwinning. While complete equality remains rare even among dual-earner couples, male participation in caretaking is nevertheless on the rise. Men who are married to work-committed women and divorced fathers who have retained either joint or sole custody of their children are particularly likely to participate in child rearing. In contrast to childless men, these men have placed family at the center of their lives. In contrast to primary breadwinners, they value spending time with their families as much as contributing money to them....

Some involved fathers view the time spent in child care not as simply helping out, but as an incomparably pleasurable activity and an essential component of good parenting. This thirty-seven-year-old construction worker chose to work the night shift so that he could spend his days with his newborn daughter while his wife pursued a dancing career:

> I take care of [my daughter] during the morning and the day. [My wife] takes care [of her] in the evenings. I work from three to eleven P.M. and wake up with the morning ahead of me, and that's important with a little one. Even if I'm pretty tired when I get up, all I have to do is look at that little face, and I feel good....

In sum, while women grapple with the choice between motherhood and committed employment, men are generally denied such a choice. Even when a man wishes to be an involved father, rarely is he able to trade full-time employment for parental involvement. The primary breadwinning surveyor noted, with some envy, that although women remain disadvantaged, many still retain the option not to work—an option few men enjoy:

> Women can have the best of both worlds, whereas men can only have one choice. A woman has a choice of which way she wants to go. If she wants to be a successful lawyer, she has that choice. If she wants to stay home, she also has that choice most of the time....

Structural and ideological barriers to men's participation in child rearing inhibit the prospects of genuine equality in parental and employment options. Limits on men's options constrain even the most feminist men's ability and willingness to embrace genuine symmetry in gender relations. The truncated range of choices available to men restricts the options open to women as well.

BEYOND THE DEBATE ON THE FAMILY

Social change in family arrangements has expanded the range of options adult women and men encounter, but the inconsistent nature of change has also created new personal dilemmas, more complex forms of gender inequality, and a growing social and ideological cleavage between more traditional family forms and the emerging alternatives. Since people have different exposure to changes in the structure of marriage, the economy, and the workplace, they have developed contrasting responses. Some have developed new patterns of family life that emphasize either greater freedom from family commitments (for example, childless women and men and uninvolved divorced fathers) or more equal sharing of breadwinning responsibilities (for example, work-committed women and involved fathers). Others have endeavored to re-create a more traditional model of gender exchange in spite of the social forces promoting change (for example, women who are domestically oriented and men who are primary breadwinners). The growth of alternative patterns of family life amid the persistence of more traditional forms has not produced a new consensus to replace the old, but rather an increasing competition among a diverse range of family types.

Marriage and the Construction of Reality

In the past, when marriage and the family were embedded in the community, neighbors, friends, and relatives supported and assisted the family. Community norms guarded against divorce, affairs, and other threats to the family. As a result, the stability of marriages and families appeared less problematic than it does today.

In contemporary society, the strain on most marriages is great, and the marital relationship is fragile. Consequently, the establishment of an identity as a couple is very important. In the following excerpt from "Marriage and the Construction of Reality," *Diogenes* (Summer 1964), Peter L. Berger and Hansfried Kellner provide a unique view of marriage. They discuss the process through which two individuals modify, redefine, and transform their pasts and construct a new mutual reality for themselves. They thereby demonstrate how the social-consruction-of-reality perspective can generate profound insights into the social world around us. Berger and Kellner explain how spouses create a new identity for themselves as a couple and validate each other's constructions of reality.

Berger (b. 1929), a sociologist with wide-ranging interests, supports what he calls "methodological atheism," which argues that explanations of society and social life should be based on scientific study. He is director of the Institute for the Study of Economic Culture at Boston University and the author of *The Heretical Imperative: Contemporary Possibilities of Religious Affirmation* (Doubleday, 1979), which was nominated for the 1980 American Book Award. Kellner (b. 1937?) is a professor of sociology at the University of Darmstadt in West Germany.

Key Concept: constructing a mutual reality in marriage

*E*ver since Durkheim it has been a commonplace of family sociology that marriage serves as a protection against anomie [normlessness] for the individual. Interesting and pragmatically useful though this insight is, it is but the negative side of a phenomenon of much broader significance. If one speaks of *anomic* states, then one ought properly to investigate also the *nomic* processes that, by their absence, lead to the aforementioned states. If, consequently, one finds a negative correlation between marriage and anomie, then one should be led to inquire into the character of marriage as a *nomos*-building instrumentality, that is, of marriage as a social arrangement that creates for the individual the sort of order in which he can experience his life as making sense. It is our intention here to discuss marriage in these terms. While this could be done in a macrosociological perspective, dealing with marriage as a major social institution related to other broad structures of society, our focus will be microsociological, dealing primarily with the social processes affecting the individuals in any specific marriage, although, of course, the larger framework of these processes will have to be understood. In what sense this discussion can be described as microsociology of knowledge will hopefully become clearer in the course of it.

Marriage is obviously only *one* social relationship in which this process of *nomos*-building takes place. It is, therefore, necessary to first look in more general terms at the character of this process. In doing so, we are influenced by three theoretical perspectives—the Weberian perspective on society as a network of meanings, the Meadian perspective on identity as a social phenomenon, and the phenomenological analysis of the social structuring of reality especially as given in the work of Schutz and Merleau-Ponty....

The process that interests us here is the one that constructs, maintains and modifies a consistent reality that can be meaningfully experienced by individuals. In its essential forms this process is determined by the society in which it occurs. Every society has its specific way of defining and perceiving reality—its world, its universe, its overarching organization of symbols. This is already given in the language that forms the symbolic base of the society. Erected over this base, and by means of it, is a system of ready-made *typifications* [stereotypical explanations of events in the world], through which the innumerable experiences of reality come to be ordered. These typifications and their order are held in common by the members of society, thus acquiring not only the character of objectivity, but being taken for granted as *the* world *tout court*, the only world that normal men can conceive of. The seemingly objective and taken-for-granted character of the social definitions of reality can be seen most clearly in the case of language itself, but it is important to keep in mind that the latter forms the base and instrumentality of a much larger world-erecting process.

The socially constructed world must be continually mediated to and actualized by the individual, so that it can become and remain indeed *his* world as well. The individual is given by his society certain decisive cornerstones for his everyday experience and conduct. Most importantly, the individual is supplied with specific sets of typifications and criteria of relevance, predefined for him by the society and made available to him for the order of his everyday life. This order or (in line with our opening considerations) nomic apparatus is biographically cumulative. It begins to be formed in the individual from the earliest stages of socialization on, then keeps on being enlarged and modified by himself throughout his biography. While there are individual biographical differences making for differences in the constitution of this apparatus in specific individuals, there exists in the society an overall consensus on the range of differences deemed to be tolerable. Without such consensus, indeed, society would be impossible as a going concern, since it would then lack the ordering principles by which alone experience can be shared and conduct can be mutually intelligible. This order, by which the individual comes to perceive and define his world, is thus not chosen by him, except perhaps for very small modifications. Rather, it is discovered by him as an external datum, a ready-made world that simply is *there* for him to go ahead and live in, though he modifies it continually in the process of living in it. Nevertheless, this world is in need of *validation*, perhaps precisely because of an ever-present glimmer of suspicion as to its social manufacture and relativity. This validation, while it must be undertaken by the individual himself, requires ongoing interaction with others who co-inhabit this same socially constructed world. In a broad sense, *all* the other co-inhabitants of this world serve a validating function. Every morning the newspaper boy validates the widest coordinates of my world and the mailman bears tangible validation of my own location within these coordinates. However, some validations are more significant than others. Every individual requires the ongoing validation of his world, including crucially the validation of his identity and place in this world, by those few who are his truly significant others. Just as the individual's deprivation of relationship with his significant others will plunge him into anomie, so their continued presence will sustain for him that *nomos* by which he can feel at home in the world at least most of the time. Again in a broad sense, all the actions of the significant others and even their simple presence serve this sustaining function. In everyday life, however, the principal method employed is speech. In this sense, it is proper to view the individual's relationship with his significant others as an ongoing conversation. As the latter occurs, it validates over and over again the fundamental definitions of reality once entered into, not, of course, so much by explicit articulation, but precisely by taking the definitions silently for granted and conversing about all conceivable matters on this taken-for-granted basis. Through the same conversation the individual is also made capable of adjusting to changing and new social contexts in his biography. In a very fundamental sense it can be said that one converses one's way through life.

If one concedes these points, one can now state a general sociological proposition: the plausibility and stability of the world, as socially defined, is dependent upon the strength and continuity of significant relationships in which conversation about this world can be continually carried on. Or, to put it a little differently: *the reality of the world is sustained through conversation with significant others.* This reality-bestowing force of social relationships depends on the degree of their nearness, that is, on the degree to which social relationships occur in face-to-face situations and to which they are credited with primary significance by the individual. In any empirical situation, there now emerge obvious sociological questions out of these considerations, namely, questions about the patterns of the world-building relationships, the social forms taken by the conversation with significant others. Sociologically, one must ask how these relationships are *objectively* structured and distributed, and one will also want to understand how they are *subjectively* perceived and experienced.

With these preliminary assumptions stated we can now arrive at our main thesis here. Namely, we would contend that marriage occupies a privileged status among the significant validating relationships for adults in our society. Put slightly differently: marriage is a crucial nomic instrumentality in our society.

We would further argue that the essential social functionality of this institution cannot be fully understood if this fact is not perceived.

We can now proceed with an ideal-typical analysis of marriage, that is, seek to abstract the essential features involved. Marriage in our society is a *dramatic* act in which two strangers come together and redefine themselves. The drama of the act is internally anticipated and socially legitimated long before it takes place in the individual's biography, and amplified by means of a pervasive ideology, the dominant themes of which (romantic love, sexual fulfillment, self-discovery and self-realization through love and sexuality, the nuclear family as the social site for these processes) can be found distributed through all strata of the society. The actualization of these ideologically predefined expectations in the life of the individual occurs to the accompaniment of one of the few traditional rites of passage that are still meaningful to almost all members of the society. It should be added that, in using the term "strangers," we do not mean, of course, that the candidates for the marriage come from widely discrepant social backgrounds—indeed, the data indicate that the contrary is the case. The strangeness rather lies in the fact that, unlike marriage candidates in many previous societies, those in ours typically come from different face-to-face contexts...

It goes without saying that this character of marriage has its root in much broader structural configurations of our society. The most important of these, for our purposes, is the crystalization of a so-called private sphere of existence, more and more segregated from the immediate controls of the public institutions (especially the economic and political ones), and yet defined and utilized as the main social area for the individual's self-realization.... [I]t is above all and, as a rule, only in the private sphere that the inividual can take a slice of reality and fashion it into his world. If one is aware of the decisive significance of this capacity and even necessity of men to externalize themselves in reality and to produce for themselves a world in which they can feel at home, then one will hardly be surprised at the great importance which the private sphere has come to have in modern society.

The private sphere includes a variety of social relationships. Among these, however, the relationships of the family occupy a central position and, in fact, serve as a focus for most of the other relationships (such as those with friends, neighbors, fellow-members of religious and other voluntary associations).... [T]he central relationship in this whole area is the marital one. It is on the basis of marriage that, for most adults in our society, existence in the private sphere is built up. It will be clear that this is not at all a universal or even a cross culturally wide function of marriage. Rather... marriage in our society [has] taken on a very peculiar character and functionality. It has been pointed out that marriage in contemporary society has lost some of its older functions and taken on new ones instead. This is certainly correct, but we would prefer to state the matter a little differently. Marriage and family used to be firmly embedded in a matrix of wider community relationships, serving as extensions and particularizations of the latter's social controls. There were few separating barriers between the world of the individual family and the wider community, a fact even to be seen in the physical conditions under which the family lived before the industrial revolution. The same social life pulsated through the house, the street and the community. In our terms, the family and within it the marital relationship were part and parcel of a considerably larger area of conversation. In our contemporary society, by contrast, each family constitutes its own segregated subworld, with its own controls and its own closed conversation.

This fact requires a much greater effort on the part of the marriage partners. Unlike an earlier situation in which the establishment of the new marriage simply added to the differentiation and complexity of an already existing social world, the marriage partners now are embarked on the often difficult task of constructing for themselves the little world in which they will live. To be sure, the larger society provides them with certain standard instructions as to how they should go about this task, but this does not change the fact that considerable effort of their own is required for its realization. The monogamous character of marriage enforces both the dramatic and the precarious nature of this undertaking. Success or failure hinges on the present idiosyncrasies and the fairly unpredictable future development of these idiosyncrasies of *only two individuals* (who, moreover, do not have a shared past)—as Simmel has shown, the most unstable of all possible social relationships. Not surprisingly, the decision to embark on this undertaking has a critical, even cataclysmic connotation in the popular imagination, which is underlined as well as psychologically assuaged by the ceremonialism that surrounds the event.

Every social relationship requires *objectivation,* that is, requires *a process by which subjectively experienced meanings become objective to the individual and*, in interaction with others, *become common property* and thereby massively objective. The degree of objectivation will depend on the number and the intensity of the social relationships that are its carriers. A relationship that consists of only two individuals called upon to sustain, by their own efforts, an ongoing social world will have to make up in intensity for the numerical poverty of the arrangement. This, in turn, accentuates the drama and the precariousness. The later addition of children will add to the, as it were, density of objectivation taking place within the nuclear family, thus rendering the latter a good deal less precarious. It remains true that the establishment and maintenance of such a social world make extremely high demands on the principal participants.

The attempt can now be made to outline the ideal-typical process that takes place as marriage functions as an instrumentality for the social construction of reality. The chief protagonists of the drama are two individuals, each with a biographically accumulated and available stock of experience. As members of a highly mobile society, these individuals have already internalized a degree of readiness to redefine themselves and to modify their stock of experience, thus bringing with them considerable psychological capacity for entering new relationships with others. Also, coming from broadly similar sectors of the larger society (in terms of region, class, ethnic and religious affiliations), the two individuals will have organized their stock of experience in similar fashion. In other words, *the two individuals have internalized the same overall world, including the general definitions and expectations of the marriage relationship itself.* Their society has provided them with a taken-for-granted image of marriage and has socialized them into an anticipation of stepping into the taken-for-granted roles of marriage. All the same, *these relatively empty projections now have to be actual-*

ized, lived through and filled with experiential content by the protagonists. This will require a dramatic change in their definitions of reality and of themselves.

Peter L. Berger and Hansfried Kellner

As of the marriage, most of each partner's actions must now be projected in conjunction with those of the other. Each partner's definitions of reality must be continually correlated with the definitions of the other. The other is present in nearly all horizons of everyday conduct. Furthermore, the identity of each now takes on a new character, having to be constantly matched with that of the other, indeed being typically perceived by the people at large as being symbiotically conjoined with the identity of the other. In each partner's psychological economy of significant others, the marriage partner becomes the other *par excellence*, the nearest and most decisive co-inhabitant of the world. Indeed, all other significant relationships have to be almost automatically reperceived and regrouped in accordance with this drastic shift.

In other words, from the beginning of the marriage each partner has new modes in his meaningful experience of the world in general, of other people and of himself. By definition, then, marriage constitutes a nomic rupture. In terms of each partner's biography, the event of marriage initiates a new nomic process. Now, the full implications of this fact are rarely apprehended by the protagonists with any degree of clarity. There rather is to be found the notion that one's world, one's other-relationships and, above all, oneself have remained what they were before—only, of course, that world, others and self will now be shared with the marriage partner. It should be clear by now that this notion is a grave misapprehension. Just because of this fact, marriage now propels the individual into an unintended and unarticulated development, in the course of which the nomic transformation takes place. What typically *is* apprehended are certain objective and concrete problems arising out of the marriage—such as tensions with in-laws, or with former friends, or religious differences between the partners, as well as immediate tensions between them. These are apprehended as external, situational and practical difficulties. What is *not* apprehended is the subjective side of these difficulties, namely, the transformation of *nomos* and identity that has occurred and that continues to go on, so that all problems and relationships are experienced in a quite new way, that is, experienced within a new and ever-changing reality.

Take a simple and frequent illustration—the male partner's relationships with male friends before and after the marriage. It is a common observation that such relationships, especially if the extramarital partners are single, rarely survive the marriage, or, if they do, are drastically redefined after it. This is typically the result of neither a deliberate decision by the husband nor deliberate sabotage by the wife. What rather happens, very simply, is a slow process in which the husband's image of his friend is transformed as he keeps talking about this friend with his wife. Even if no actual talking goes on, the mere presence of the wife forces him to see his friend differently. This need not mean that he adopts a negative image held by the wife. Regardless of what image she holds or is believed by him to hold, it will be different from that held by the husband. This difference will enter into the joint image that now must needs be fabricated in the course of the ongoing conversation between the marriage partners—and, in due course, must act powerfully on the image previously held by the husband. Again, typically, this process is rarely apprehended with any degree of lucidity. The old friend is more likely to fade out of the picture by slow degrees, as new kinds of friends take his place. The process, if commented upon at all within the marital conversation, can always be explained by socially available formulas about "people changing," "friends disappearing" or oneself "having become more mature." This process of conversational liquidation is especially powerful because it is one-sided—the husband typically talks with his wife about his friend, but *not* with his friend about his wife. Thus the friend is deprived of the defense of, as it were, counterdefining the relationship. *This dominance of the marital conversation over all others is one of its most important characteristics.* It may be mitigated by a certain amount of protective segregation of some non-marital relationships (say "Tuesday night out with the boys," or "Saturday lunch with mother"), but even then there are powerful emotional barriers against the sort of conversation (conversation *about* the marital relationship, that is) that would serve by way of counterdefinition.

Marriage thus posits a new reality. The individual's relationship with this new reality, however, is a dialectical one—he acts upon it, in collusion with the marriage partner, and it acts back upon both him and the partner, welding together their reality. Since, as we have argued before, the objectivation that constitutes this reality is precarious, the groups with which the couple associates are called upon to assist in co-defining the new reality. The couple is pushed towards groups that strengthen their new definition of themselves and the world, avoids those that weaken this definition. This in turn releases the commonly known pressures of group association, again acting upon the marriage partners to change their definitions of the world and of themselves. Thus the new reality is not posited once and for all, but goes on being redefined not only in the marital interaction itself but also in the various maritally based group relationships into which the couple enters. . . .

The reconstruction of the world in marriage occurs principally in the course of conversation, as we have suggested. *The implicit problem of this conversation is how to match two individual definitions of reality.* By the very logic of the relationship, a common overall definition must be arrived at—otherwise the conversation will become impossible and, *ipso facto*, the relationship will be endangered. Now, this conversation may be understood as the working away of an ordering and typifying apparatus—if one prefers, an objectivating apparatus. Each partner ongoingly contributes his conceptions of reality, which are then "talked through," usually not once but many times, and in the process become objectivated by the conversational apparatus. The longer this conversation goes on, the more massively real do the objectivations become to the partners. In the marital conversation a world is not only built, but it is also kept in a state of repair and ongoingly refurnished. The subjective reality of this world for the two partners is sustained by the same conversation. The nomic instrumentality of marriage is concretized over and over again, from bed to breakfast table, as the partners carry on the endless conversation that feeds on nearly all they individually or jointly experience. Indeed, it may happen eventually that no experience is fully real unless and until it has been thus "talked through."

This process has a very important result—namely, *a hardening or stabilization of the common objectivated reality.* It should be easy to see now how this comes about. The objectivations ongoingly performed and internalized by the marriage partners become ever more massively real, as they are confirmed and reconfirmed in the marital conversation. The world that is made up of these objectivations at the same time gains in stability. For example, the images of other people, which before or in the earlier stages of the marital conversation may have been rather ambiguous and shifting in the minds of the two partners, now become hardened into definite and stable characterizations.... The same process of stabilization may be observed with regard to self-definitions as well. In this way, the wife in our example will not only be pressured to assign stable characterizations to others but also to herself. Previously uninterested politically, she now identifies herself as liberal. Previously alternating between dimly articulated religious positions, she now declares herself an agnostic. Previously confused and uncertain about her sexual emotions, she now understands herself as an unabashed hedonist in this area. And so on and so forth, with the same reality—and identity—stabilizing process at work on the husband. Both world and self thus take on a firmer, more reliable character for both partners.

Furthermore, it is not only the ongoing experience of the two partners that is constantly shared and passed through the conversational apparatus. The same *sharing extends into the past.* The two distinct biographies, as subjectively apprehended by two individuals who have lived through them, are overruled and reinterpreted in the course of their conversations. Sooner or later, they will "tell all"—or, more correctly, they will tell it in such a way that it fits into the self-definitions objectivated in the marital relationship. The couple thus construct not only present reality but reconstruct past reality as well, fabricating a common memory that integrates the recollections of the two individual pasts. The comic fulfillment of this process may be seen in those cases when one partner "remembers" more clearly what happened in the other's past than the other does—and corrects him accordingly. Similarly, there occurs a *sharing of future horizons,* which leads not only to stabilization, but inevitably to a narrowing of the future projections of each partner. Before marriage the individual typically plays with quite discrepant daydreams in which his future self is projected.[17] Having now considerably stabilized his self-image, the married individual will have to project the future in accordance with this maritally defined identity. This narrowing of future horizons begins with the obvious external limitation that marriage entails, as, for example, with regard to vocational and career plans. However, it extends also to the more general possibilities of the individual's biography. To return to a previous illustration, the wife, having "found herself" as a liberal, an agnostic and a "sexually healthy" person, *ipso facto* liquidates the possibilities of becoming an anarchist, a Catholic or a Lesbian. At least until further notice she has decided upon who she is—and, by the same token, upon who she will be. The stabilization brought about by marriage thus affects that total reality in which the partners exist. In the most far-reaching sense of the word, the married individual "settles down"—and *must* do so, if the marriage is to be viable, in accordance with its contemporary institutional definition.

It cannot be sufficiently strongly emphasized that this process is typically unapprehended, almost automatic in character. The protagonists of the marriage drama do *not* set out deliberately to create their world. Each continues to live in a world that is taken for granted—and keeps its taken-for-granted character even as it is metamorphosed. The new world that the married partners, Prometheuslike, have called into being is perceived by them as the normal world in which they have lived before. Reconstructed present and reinterpreted past are perceived as a continuum, extending forward into a commonly projected future. *The dramatic change that has occurred remains in bulk, unapprehended and unarticulated.* And where it forces itself upon the individuals' attention, it is retrojected into the past, explained as having always been there, though perhaps in a hidden way. Typically, the reality that has been "invented" within the marital conversation is subjectively perceived as a "discovery." Thus the partners "discover" themselves and the world, "who they really are," "what they really believe," "how they really feel, and always have felt, about so-and-so." This retrojection of the world being produced all the time by themselves serves to enhance the stability of this world and at the same time to assuage the "existential anxiety" that, probably inevitably, accompanies the perception that nothing but one's own narrow shoulders supports the universe in which one has chosen to live. . . .

The use of the term "stabilization" should not detract from the insight into the difficulty and precariousness of this world-building enterprise. Often enough, the new universe collapses *in statu nascendi.* Many more times it continues over a period, swaying perilously back and forth as the two partners try to hold it up, finally to be abandoned as an impossible undertaking. If one conceives of the marital conversation as the principal drama and the two partners as the principal protagonists of the drama, then one can look upon the other individuals involved as the supporting chorus for the central dramatic action. Children, friends, relatives and casual acquaintances all have their part in reinforcing the tenuous structure of the new reality. It goes without saying that the *children form the most important part of this supporting chorus.* Their very existence is predicated on the maritally established world. The marital partners themselves are in charge of their socialization *into* this world, which to them has a pre-existent and self-evident character. They are taught from the beginning to speak precisely those lines that lend themselves to a supporting chorus, from their first invocations of "Daddy" and "Mummy" on to their adoption of the parents' ordering and typifying apparatus that now defines *their* world as well. The marital conversation is now in the process of becoming a family symposium, with the necessary consequence that its objectivations rapidly gain in density, plausibility and durability.

In sum: the process that we have been inquiring into is, ideal-typically, one in which reality is crystallized, narrowed and stabilized. Ambivalences are converted into certainties. Typifications of self and of others become settled. Most generally, possibilities become facticities. What is more, this process of transformation remains, most of the time, unapprehended by those who are both its authors and its objects.

CHAPTER 13 Other Institutions: Religion and Health Care

13.1 ROBERT WUTHNOW

How Small Groups Are Transforming Our Lives

Alcoholics Anonymous (AA) is considered by many to be the greatest so-cial invention of the twentieth century. This 12-step program has helped many millions of alcoholics live without alcohol and has greatly enriched their lives. Its basic principles of shared leadership, wide participation, ac-ceptance of others, a program for self-improvement, and weekly or frequent meetings have diffused widely, first to voluntary associations of other addicts and then to religious and other self-improvement groups.

In the following selection from "How Small Groups Are Transforming Our Lives," *Christianity Today* (February 7, 1994), sociologist Robert Wuth-now describes how small groups such as AA are changing communities and churches and giving their members caring and support. He says that these groups are spreading like wildfire and have "been effecting a quiet revolu-tion in American society." Although people are enjoying and getting much help from these groups, Wuthnow is ambivalent toward them. He feels that although the individual benefits are substantial, these groups nevertheless fail to create true community. For example, the group makes no demands on its members (come if you want to, speak if you feel like it, never criticize,

310

*Chapter 13
Other
Institutions:
Religion and
Health Care*

and leave if you are dissatisfied). Also, in the religious realm, Wuthnow says, "The deity of small groups is a God of love, comfort, order, and security. Gone is the God of judgment, wrath, justice, mystery, and punishment. Gone are concerns about the forces of evil." Wuthnow's concern is that religion should confront as well as comfort. The sinner should be understood and loved for such are all of us, but evil actions should be condemned and, when harmful to others, they should be punished. Wuthnow notes the group norm against breaking the harmony of the group, which serves to rule out holding anyone to high standards. He maintains that the sacred is humanized by many of these groups and is thereby made less sacred, mysterious, awesome, and challenging.

Wuthnow teaches sociology at Princeton University and directs the Center for the Study of American Religion. He is the author of *Poor Richard's Principle: Recovering the American Dream Through the Moral Dimension of Work, Business, and Money* (Princeton University Press, 1996).

Key Concept: the sense of community in small groups

*I*n the driveway across the street, a vintage silver Porsche sits on blocks as its owner tinkers with the engine. Next door, a man with thinning gray hair applies paint to the trim around his living-room window. But at 23 Springdale, something quite different is happening. About two-dozen people are kneeling in prayer, heads bowed, elbows resting on folding chairs in front of them. After praying, they will sing, then pray again, then discuss the Bible. They are young and old, men and women, Black and White. A teenage girl remarks after the meeting that she comes every week because the people are so warm and friendly. "They're not geeks; they just make me feel at home."

A few miles away at the largest Gothic structure in town, several people slip hastily through the darkness and enter a small door toward the rear of the building. Inside is a large circle of folding chairs. On the wall, a felt banner reads, "Alleluia Alleluia" (the two As are in red). Before long all the chairs are filled, and an attractive woman in her late thirties calls the group to order. "Hi, my name is Joan, and I'm an alcoholic."

"Hi, Joan," the group responds.

After a few announcements, Betty, a young woman just out of college, tells her story. Alcohol nearly killed her. Then, close to death in a halfway house, she found God. "I thought God hated me. But now I know there is a higher power I can talk to and know."

These two cases are so ordinary that it is easy to miss their significance. They are examples of a phenomenon that has spread like wildfire in recent years.

Most of us are vaguely aware of small groups that meet in our neighborhoods or at local churches and synagogues. We can scan a local newspaper and find support groups available for anything from underweight children to oversexed spouses. We may have a coworker who attends Alcoholics Anonymous or family members who have participated in youth groups or prayer groups. Perhaps we attend one ourselves.

At present, four out of every ten Americans belong to a small group that meets regularly and provides caring and support for its members. These are not simply informal gatherings of neighbors and friends, but organized groups: Sunday-school classes, Bible-study groups, Alcoholics Anonymous and other 12-step groups, singles groups, book discussion clubs, sports and hobby groups, and political or civic groups. Those who have joined these groups testify that their lives have been deeply enriched by the experience. They have found friends, received warm emotional support, overcome life-threatening addictions, and grown in their spirituality. They have learned how to forgive others and become more accepting of themselves.

Many people say their identity has been changed as a result of extended involvement in a small group. In fact, the majority have been attending their groups over a prolonged period of time, often for as long as five years, and nearly all attend faithfully, usually at least once a week.

Groups such as these seldom make the headlines or become the focus of public controversy. Few people are involved in small groups because they are trying to launch a political campaign or attract the attention of public officials. They are not staging protest marches or picketing in the nation's capital. They are, for the most part, off in the wings when others are clamoring about abortion rights or attempting to challenge the Supreme Court. Small groups are the private, largely invisible ways in which many individuals choose to spend a portion of their free time. Hence, in an era when the mass media increasingly define what is important, it is easy to dismiss the small-group phenomenon.

To overlook this trend, however, would be a serious mistake, for the small-group movement has been effecting a quiet revolution in American society. Its success has astounded even many of its leaders. Few of them were trying to unleash a revolution at all. Rather, they were responding to some need in their own lives or in the lives of people they knew. They started groups, let people talk about their problems or interests, and perhaps supplied them with reading material. The results were barely perceptible. The most noticeable were the addictions that people recovered from and the occasional suicide that was prevented.

The far more common happenings were the ordinary words of encouragement, the prayers that people spoke, their remarks about good days and bad days, and the cups of lukewarm coffee they consumed. What happened took place so incrementally that it could seldom be seen at all. It was, like most profound reorientations in life, so gradual that those involved saw it less as a revolution than as a journey. The change was concerned with daily life, with emotions, and with understanding of one's identity. It was personal rather than public, moral rather than political.

Nonetheless, this powerful movement is beginning to alter American society, both by changing our understandings of community and by redefining our spirituality. Its effects cannot be calculated simply at the individual level. What is important is not just that a teenager finds friends at a prayer meeting or that a young woman finds God in Alcoholics Anonymous. These stories have to be magnified a hundred thousand times to see how pervasive they have become in

312

*Chapter 13
Other
Institutions:
Religion and
Health Care*

our society. They must also be examined closely to see that what is happening now has never occurred at any previous time in history. Small groups are not only attracting participants on an unprecedented scale; they are also affecting the ways in which we relate to each other and how we view God.

A CUSTOM-MADE COMMUNITY

Providing people with a stronger sense of community has been a key aim of the small-group movement from its inception. There is a widespread assumption that community is sputtering to an undignified halt, leaving many people stranded and alone. Families are breaking down. Neighbors have become churlish or indifferent. The solution thus is to start intentional groups of like-minded individuals who can regain a sense of community.

And small groups are doing a better job than many critics would like to think. The communities they create are seldom frail. People feel cared for. They help one another. They share their intimate problems. They identify with their groups and participate regularly over extended periods of time.

Yet the kind of community small groups create is quite different from the communities in which people have lived in the past. These communities are more fluid and more concerned with the emotional states of the individual. Some small groups merely provide occasions for individuals to focus on themselves in the presence of others. What's more, the social contract binding members together asserts only the weakest of obligations. Come if you have time. Talk if you feel like it. Respect everyone's opinion. Never criticize. Leave quietly if you become dissatisfied. Families would never survive by following these operating norms. Close-knit communities in the past did not, either.

But times have changed, and small groups, as we know them, are a phenomenon of the late-twentieth century. There are good reasons for the way they are structured. They reflect the fluidity of our lives by allowing us to bond simply but to break our attachments with equivalent ease. If we fail to understand these reasons, we can easily view small groups as something other than what they are. We can imagine that they substitute for families, neighborhoods, and broader community attachments that demand lifelong commitments, when, in fact, they do not.

THE DOMESTICATED DEITY

Not only are small groups fostering a new sense of community, these groups are also affecting how we conceive of the sacred.

A majority of all small-group members say they joined because they wanted to deepen their faith and that their sense of the sacred has been profoundly influenced by their participation. But small groups are not simply drawing people back to the God of their fathers and mothers. They are dramatically changing the way God is understood. God is now less of an external authority and more of an internal presence. The sacred becomes more personal but, in the process, also becomes more manageable, more serviceable in meeting individual needs, and more a feature of the group process itself.

Interestingly, churches are among the primary proponents of the small-group phenomenon and its "user-friendly" deity. Nearly two-thirds of all small groups have some connection to churches or synagogues. Many have been initiated by clergy. Many devote their meetings to studying the Bible or to discussing other religious texts. Most include prayer. Embarking on a spiritual journey is a common theme among members. Some would argue that this trend is indicative simply of a thirst in the human heart for a relationship with God. But why now? Why has the small-group movement become the vehicle for expressing spiritual thirst? Why not churches? Or religious television? Or individual devotional readings and meditation?

The standard, though inaccurate, answer is that the churches have become weak—people want to know God but find no guidance when they attend religious services. The small-group movement is thus a way of revitalizing American religion, stemming the tide of secularity, and drawing the faithful back to God before the churches slide into oblivion.

But the standard answer is wrong on two counts. The small-group movement is flourishing in American society, not because the churches are weak, but because they are strong. People do not join groups simply because their hearts tell them to. They join because groups are available, because they have direct exposure to these groups, and because someone encourages them to attend. Groups are available because churches and synagogues sponsor them. Members of the clergy initiate them as part of an explicit plan for the future of their church or synagogue. They enlist leaders, create mechanisms for recruiting members, purchase study guides, and provide meeting space. In this sense, the small-group movement is an extension of the role that organized religion has always played in American society.

The standard view is also wrong in suggesting that small groups are stemming the tide of secularity. To be sure, they encourage people to pray and to think about spiritual truths. Nevertheless, they do little to increase the biblical knowledge of their members. Most of them do not assert the value of denominational traditions or pay much attention to the distinctive theological arguments that have identified variants of Christianity or Judaism in the past. Indeed, many of the groups encourage faith to be subjective and pragmatic. A person may feel that his or her faith has been deepened, but in what way is largely in the eye of the beholder. Biblical truths may be more meaningful, but the reason is that they calm anxiety and help one make it through the day.

The deity of small groups is a God of love, comfort, order, and security. Gone is the God of judgment, wrath, justice, mystery, and punishment. Gone are concerns about the forces of evil. Missing from most groups, even, is a distinct interest in heaven and hell, except for the small heavens and hells that people experience in their everyday lives.

Indeed, it does not overstate the case to suggest that the small-group movement is currently playing a major role in *adapting* American religion to the main currents of secular culture that have surfaced at the end of the twentieth century. Secularity is misunderstood if it is assumed to be a force that prevents

314

*Chapter 13
Other
Institutions:
Religion and
Health Care*

people from being spiritual at all. It is more aptly conceived as an orientation that encourages a safe, domesticated version of the sacred. From a secular perspective, a divine being is one who is there for our own gratification, like a house pet, rather than one who demands obedience from us, is too powerful or mysterious for us to understand, or who challenges us to a life of service. When spirituality has been tamed, it can accommodate the demands of a secular society. People can go about their daily business without having to alter their lives very much because they are interested in spirituality. Secular spirituality can even be put to good use, making people more effective in their careers, better lovers, and more responsible citizens. This is the kind of spirituality being nurtured in many small groups today.

The small-group movement is thus the latest in a series of cultural realignments. At the start of the eighteenth century, American religion underwent its first period of realignment. The state churches that colonists imported from Europe were disestablished. Denominational pluralism, later protected by a constitutional separation between church and state, was the result. During the nineteenth century, a second major realignment took place. The hegemony of a few Protestant denominations was undermined. Faith became more democratic and more thoroughly American. New denominations proliferated, congregational autonomy and diversity were strengthened, and Catholics and Jews gained a place alongside Protestants. Now, at the end of the twentieth century, denominational structures are waning considerably. Increasing numbers of people have switched from tradition to tradition to tradition. Clergy are under increased pressures to compete with other congregations for members. And the basis of competition has altered significantly—from doctrinal or liturgical distinctions to programmatic appeals.

Small groups provide greater variety and allow greater freedom in selecting the religion of one's choice than ever before. They make faith more fluid, championing change itself and creating modular communities that can be established and disbanded with relative ease.

Hence, small groups are effecting changes that have both salutary and worrisome consequences. They supply community and revitalize the sacred. But, for some of their members at least, these communities can be manipulated for personal ends, and the sacred can be reduced to a magical formula for alleviating anxiety.

THE SEARCH FOR THE SACRED

Overall, the small-group movement cannot be understood except in relation to the deep yearning for the sacred that characterizes much of the American public. Indeed, a great deal of the momentum for the movement as a whole comes from the fact that people are interested in spirituality, on the one hand, and from the availability of vast resources from religious organizations, on the other. As a result, small groups are dramatically redefining how Americans think about God.

We can imagine at the outset why this redefinition might be occurring if we remember that there is often a close connection between how people understand their relationships with each other and how they approach God. Religious traditions in which an intimate, emotion-laden relationship with God is valued are quite likely to emphasize the importance of intimacy in human relationships as well. At present, therefore, it would not be surprising to find that small groups oriented toward the intentional cultivation of caring relationships might also be interested in helping individuals cultivate such relationships with the divine as well.

It is, however, the intentionality of these relationships that is worth considering, not whether they emphasize caring. Most small groups that have anything to do with spirituality do not simply let the sacred emerge as a byproduct of their time together. Instead, they prescribe activities for growing closer to the sacred.

In many cultures, it would be unthinkable to engage in activities with the explicit purpose of discovering the sacred. Divine providence, grace, and the inscrutability of God would be emphasized instead. God would seek out the individual, like Yahweh capturing Moses' attention through the burning bush. But it would be less likely for the individual to set out to find God—and certainly unthinkable that deep spirituality could be found by following a set of prespecified guidelines or steps. Such quests are, of course, quite common in American culture, and they have been throughout our nation's history. Nevertheless, the small-group movement elevates the degree to which such activities are planned, calculated, and coordinated.

FROM CREEDS TO NORMS

Another way small groups are redefining the sacred is by replacing explicit creeds and doctrines with *implicit* norms devised by the group. Throughout the centuries, religious bodies have devoted much of their energy to hammering out doctrinal statements. They have sent representatives to church councils to debate the wording of creeds, and they have formed organizational structures around varying concepts of ecclesiastical authority. Making things explicit incurred huge costs, to be sure, including much sectarian strife and even religious wars, but believers assumed that it was important to know specifically what was right and what was wrong. The small-group movement is changing all of that.

Group members still have a sense of the importance of knowing what is right or wrong, but their groups seldom study religious history or formal theological statements. Rather, they discuss small portions of religious texts with an eye toward discovering how these texts apply to their personal lives. Personal testimonies carry enormous weight in such discussions, but these stories are also subject to group norms. These norms include implicit assumptions about whether one can be instructed directly by God, whether it is important to read the Bible to receive wisdom, what the role of intuition is, and how prayer should be understood.

316

*Chapter 13
Other
Institutions:
Religion and
Health Care*

In a very real sense, the group can become a manifestation of the sacred. Its members feel power within the group. They feel closer to God when they are gathered than when they are apart. They are sure the deity approves of the way they meet. They may be less sure that people can find God apart from the group. The group, then, encourages people to think about spirituality, but in the process it channels their thinking so that only some ideas about the sacred are acceptable. Spirituality becomes a matter of sincere seeking and of helping each other, all the while respecting whatever idiosyncratic notions of the sacred one's peers may develop.

STANDING AT THE CROSSROADS

When I say that the small-group movement is effecting a quiet revolution in American society, I mean that it is adding fuel to the fires of cultural change that have already been lit. The small-group movement may be providing community for people who feel the loss of personal ties, and it may be nurturing spirituality in an otherwise secular context. But it is not succeeding simply by filling these gaps. It is succeeding less because it is bucking the system than because it is going with the flow.

None of these observations should be construed to suggest that the small-group movement is in any way failing its members. Social institutions seldom do much more than help populations adjust to a changing environment. They solve day-to-day problems and work with envisioned realities, but they do not change reality as fundamentally as visionary leaders would like to think. The individual who finds God is no less blessed; the person who recovers from an addiction is no less important. But from a broader perspective, the same forces that have created these needs are at work in shaping the groups that help respond to them.

So, where does the small-group movement go from here? Despite the various criticisms already raised, its social effects have been largely beneficial. In responding to social and personal needs, this movement has been able to grow enormously. Consequently, it is now poised to exercise even greater influence on American society in the next decade than it has in the past two decades. The resources are there: models have been developed, leaders have been trained, national networks have been established, and millions of satisfied participants are ready to enlist their friends and neighbors. What it will do with these resources is yet to be seen.

Indeed, the movement stands at an important crossroads in its history, a turning point requiring it to choose which of two directions it will go. It can continue on its present course, or it can attempt to move to a higher level of interpersonal and spiritual quality.

Given the movement's success over the past two decades, it can easily maintain the status quo, drawing millions of participants by making them feel good about themselves and by encouraging them to develop a domesticated, pragmatic form of spirituality. Or it can focus less on numerical success and more on the quality of its offerings. By doing so, the movement may find itself challenging its members at deeper levels—to make more serious commitments to others who are in need, to serve the wider community, and to stand in worshipful, obedient awe of the sacred itself.

On Being Sane in Insane Places

In the labeling theory of deviance, the designation of a person as a deviant by officials has extensive consequences, including changes in the behavior of others toward that person. The result may well be to make that person become what he or she has been labeled. This theory has been applied to mental illness: It posits that when people are labeled as mentally ill they will be treated as such. Subsequently, they will see themselves as mentally ill, thus confirming the label. In the following selection from "On Being Sane in Insane Places," *Science* (January 19, 1973), D. L. Rosenhan tests another aspect of the labeling theory and raises an important issue: How does one tell the difference between a mentally healthy person and a mentally ill person?

In Rosenhan's experiment, healthy people presented themselves to 12 mental hospitals claiming they had symptoms that are associated with schizophrenia. Upon admission to the hospitals, they ceased to show these symptoms and behaved as they normally would. Nevertheless, Rosenhan found that throughout their stays, they were treated as mentally ill, in accordance with the initial diagnosis of schizophrenia. They were all eventually discharged with the label of "schizophrenia in remission." Thus, a long period without schizophrenia symptoms did not earn them the label of "sane."

Rosenhan expands on the details of this study and suggests that the label "mentally ill," once placed upon a person, will remain with that person regardless of his or her behavior, because the label influences the way other people interpret his or her sane behavior. Rosenhan's study also calls attention to the fact that the diagnosis of mental illness is difficult when there are no clear manifestations of psychosis and that such diagnoses have unacceptably large margins of error.

Rosenhan (b. 1929) is a professor of law and psychology at Stanford University. He is a social psychologist whose work is concerned with clinical and personality matters.

Key Concept: labeling theory

D. L. Rosenhan

*I*f sanity and insanity exist, how shall we know them?

The question is neither capricious nor itself insane. However much we may be personally convinced that we can tell the normal from the abnormal, the evidence is simply not compelling. It is commonplace, for example, to read about murder trials wherein eminent psychiatrists for the defense are contradicted by equally eminent psychiatrists for the prosecution on the matter of the defendant's sanity. More generally, there are a great deal of conflicting data on the reliability, utility, and meaning of such terms as "sanity," "insanity," "mental illness," and "schizophrenia." Finally, as early as 1934, [Ruth] Benedict suggested that normality and abnormality are not universal. What is viewed as normal in one culture may be seen as quite aberrant in another. Thus, notions of normality and abnormality may not be quite as accurate as people believe they are....

At its heart, the question of whether the sane can be distinguished from the insane (and whether degrees of insanity can be distinguished from each other) is a simple matter: do the salient characteristics that lead to diagnoses reside in the patients themselves or in the environments and contexts in which observers find them? From Bleuler, through Kretchmer, through the formulators of the recently revised *Diagnostic and Statistical Manual* of the American Psychiatric Association, the belief has been strong that patients present symptoms, that those symptoms can be categorized, and, implicitly, that the sane are distinguishable from the insane. More recently, however, this belief has been questioned. Based in part on theoretical and anthropological considerations, but also on philosophical, legal and therapeutic ones, the view has grown that psychological categorization of mental illness is useless at best and downright harmful, misleading, and pejorative at worst. Psychiatric diagnoses, in this view, are in the minds of the observers and are not valid summaries of characteristics displayed by the observed.

Gains can be made in deciding which of these is more nearly accurate by getting normal people (that is, people who do not have, and have never suffered, symptoms or serious psychiatric disorders) admitted to psychiatric hospitals and then determining whether they were discovered to be sane and, if so, how....

This article describes such an experiment. Eight sane people gained secret admission to 12 different hospitals. Their diagnostic experiences constitute the data of the first part of this article; the remainder is devoted to a description of their experiences in psychiatric institutions....

PSEUDOPATIENTS AND THEIR SETTINGS

The eight pseudopatients were a varied group. One was a psychology graduate student in his 20's. The remaining seven were older and "established." Among them were three psychologists, a pediatrician, a psychiatrist, a painter, and a housewife. Three pseudopatients were women, five were men. All of them employed pseudonyms, lest their alleged diagnoses embarrass them later. Those

320

*Chapter 13
Other
Institutions:
Religion and
Health Care*

who were in mental health professions alleged another occupation in order to avoid the special attentions that might be accorded by staff, as a matter of courtesy or caution, to ailing colleagues. With the exception of myself (I was the first pseudopatient and my presence was known to the hospital administrator and chief psychologist and, so far as I can tell, to them alone), the presence of pseudopatients and the nature of the research program was not known to the hospital staff....

After calling the hospital for an appointment, the pseudopatient arrived at the admissions office complaining that he had been hearing voices. Asked what the voices said, he replied that they were often unclear, but as far as he could tell they said "empty," "hollow," and "thud." The voices were unfamiliar and were of the same sex as the pseudopatient. The choice of these symptoms was occasioned by their apparent similarity to existential symptoms. Such symptoms are alleged to arise from painful concerns about the perceived meaninglessness of one's life. It is as if the hallucinating person were saying, "My life is empty and hollow." The choice of these symptoms was also determined by the *absence* of a single report of existential psychoses in the literature.

Beyond alleging the symptoms and falsifying name, vocation, and employment, no further alterations of person, history, or circumstances were made. The significant events of the pseudopatient's life history were presented as they had actually occurred. Relationships with parents and siblings, with spouse and children, with people at work and in school, consistent with the aforementioned exceptions, were described as they were or had been. Frustrations and upsets were described along with joys and satisfactions. These facts are important to remember. If anything, they strongly biased the subsequent results in favor of detecting sanity, since none of their histories or current behaviors were seriously pathological in any way.

Immediately upon admission to the psychiatric ward, the pseudopatient ceased simulating *any* symptoms of abnormality. In some cases, there was a brief period of mild nervousness and anxiety, since none of the pseudopatients really believed that they would be admitted so easily. Indeed, their shared fear was that they would be immediately exposed as frauds and greatly embarrassed. Moreover, many of them had never visited a psychiatric ward; even those who had nevertheless had some genuine fears about what might happen to them. Their nervousness, then, was quite appropriate to the novelty of the hospital setting, and it abated rapidly.

Apart from that short-lived nervousness, the pseudopatient behaved on the ward as he "normally" behaved. The pseudopatient spoke to patients and staff as he might ordinarily. Because there is uncommonly little to do on a psychiatric ward, he attempted to engage others in conversation. When asked by staff how he was feeling, he indicated that he was fine, that he no longer experienced symptoms. He responded to instructions from attendants to calls for medication (which was not swallowed), and to dining-hall instructions. Beyond such activities as were available to him on the admissions ward, he spent his time writing down his observations about the ward, its patients, and the staff. Initially these notes were written "secretly," but as it soon became clear that no one much cared, they were subsequently written on standard tablets of paper in such public places as the dayroom. No secret was made of these activities....

Despite their public "show" of sanity, the pseudopatients were never detected. Admitted, except in one case, with a diagnosis of schizophrenia, each was discharged with a diagnosis of schizophrenia "in remission." The label "in remission" should in no way be dismissed as a formality, for at no time during any hospitalization had any question been raised about any pseudopatient's simulation. Nor are there any indications in the hospital records that the pseudopatient's status was suspect. Rather, the evidence is strong that, once labeled schizophrenic, the pseudopatient was stuck with that label. If the pseudopatient was to be discharged, he must naturally be "in remission"; but he was not sane, nor, in the institution's view, had he ever been sane. . . .

Finally, it cannot be said that the failure to recognize the pseudopatients' sanity was due to the fact that they were not behaving sanely. While there was clearly some tension present in all of them, their daily visitors could detect no serious behavioral consequences—nor, indeed, could other patients. It was quite common for the patients to "detect" the pseudopatients' sanity. During the first three hospitalizations, when accurate counts were kept, 35 of a total of 118 patients on the admissions ward voiced their suspicions, some vigorously. "You're not crazy. You're a journalist, or a professor [referring to the continual note-taking]. You're checking up on the hospital." While most of the patients were reassured by the pseudopatient's insistence that he had been sick before he came in but was fine now, some continued to believe that the pseudopatient was sane throughout his hospitalization. The fact that the patients often recognized normality when staff did not raises important questions.

Failure to detect sanity during the course of hospitalization may be due to the fact that physicians operate with a strong bias toward what statisticians call the type 2 error. This is to say that physicians are more inclined to call a healthy person sick (a false positive, type 2) than a sick person healthy (a false negative, type 1). The reasons for this are not hard to find: it is clearly more dangerous to misdiagnose illness than health. Better to err on the side of caution, to suspect illness even among the healthy.

But what holds for medicine does not hold equally well for psychiatry. Medical illnesses, while unfortunate, are not commonly pejorative. Psychiatric diagnoses, on the contrary, carry with them personal, legal, and social stigmas. It was therefore important to see whether the tendency toward diagnosing the sane insane could be reversed. The following experiment was arranged at a research and teaching hospital whose staff had heard these findings but doubted that such an error could occur in their hospital. The staff was informed that at some time during the following 3 months, one or more pseudopatients would attempt to be admitted into the psychiatric hospital. Each staff member was asked to rate each patient who presented himself at admission or on the ward according to the likelihood that the patient was a pseudopatient. A 10-point scaled was used, with a 1 and 2 reflecting high confidence that the patient was a pseudopatient.

Judgments were obtained on 193 patients who were admitted for psychiatric treatment. All staff who had had sustained contact with or primary responsibility for the patient—attendants, nurses, psychiatrists, physicians, and

322

*Chapter 13
Other
Institutions:
Religion and
Health Care*

psychologists—were asked to make judgments. Forty-one patients were alleged, with high confidence, to be pseudopatients by at least one member of the staff. Twenty-three were considered suspect by at least one psychiatrist. Nineteen were suspected by one psychiatrist *and* one other staff member. Actually, no genuine pseudopatient (at least from my group) presented himself during this period....

THE STICKINESS OF PSYCHODIAGNOSTIC LABELS

Beyond the tendency to call the healthy sick—a tendency that accounts better for diagnostic behavior or admission than it does for such behavior after a lengthy period of exposure—the data speak to the massive role of labeling in psychiatric assessment. Having once been labeled schizophrenic, there is nothing the pseudopatient can do to overcome the tag. The tag profoundly colors others' perceptions of him and his behavior.

From one viewpoint, these data are hardly surprising, for it has long been known that elements are given meaning by the context in which they occur. Gestalt psychology made this point vigorously, and Asch demonstrated that there are "central" personality traits (such as "warm" versus "cold") which are so powerful that they markedly color the meaning of other information in forming an impression of a given personality. "Insane," "schizophrenic," "manic-depressive," and "crazy" are probably among the most powerful of such central traits. Once a person is designated abnormal, all of his other behaviors and characteristics are colored by that label. Indeed, that label is so powerful that many of the pseudopatients' normal behaviors were overlooked entirely or profoundly misinterpreted. Some examples may clarify this issue.

Earlier I indicated that there were no changes in the pseudopatient's personal history and current status beyond those of name, employment, and, where necessary, vocation. Otherwise, a veridical description of personal history and circumstances was offered. Those circumstances were not psychotic. How were they made consonant with the diagnosis of psychosis? Or were those diagnoses modified in such a way as to bring them into accord with the circumstances of the pseudopatient's life, as described by him?

As far as I can determine, diagnoses were in no way affected by the relative health of the circumstances of a pseudopatient's life. Rather, the reverse occurred: the perception of his circumstances was shaped entirely by the diagnosis. A clear example of such translation is found in the case of a pseudopatient who had had a close relationship with his mother but was rather remote from his father during his early childhood. During adolescence and beyond, however, his father became a close friend, while his relationship with his mother cooled. His present relationship with his wife was characteristically close and warm. Apart from occasional angry exchanges, friction was minimal. The children had rarely been spanked. Surely there is nothing especially pathological about such a history. Indeed, many readers may see a similar pattern in their own experiences, with no markedly deleterious consequences. Observe, however, how such a history was translated in the psychopathological context, this from the case summary prepared after the patient was discharged.

> This white 39-year-old male... manifests a long history of considerable ambivalence in close relationships, which begins in early childhood. A warm relationship with his mother cools during his adolescence. A distant relationship to his father is described as becoming very intense. Affective stability is absent. His attempts to control emotionality with his wife and children are punctuated by angry outbursts and, in the case of the children, spankings. And while he says that he has several good friends, one senses considerable ambivalence embedded in those relationships also....

The facts of the case were unintentionally distorted by the staff to achieve consistency with a popular theory of the dynamics of a schizophrenic reaction. Nothing of an ambivalent nature had been described in relations with parents, spouse, or friends. To the extent that ambivalence could be inferred, it was probably not greater than is found in all human relationships. It is true the pseudopatient's relationships with his parents changed over time, but in the ordinary context that would hardly be remarkable—indeed, it might very well be expected. Clearly, the meaning ascribed to his verbalizations (that is, ambivalence, affective instability) was determined by the diagnosis: schizophrenia. An entirely different meaning would have been ascribed if it were known that the man was "normal."...

One tacit characteristic of psychiatric diagnosis is that it locates the sources of aberration within the individual and only rarely within the complex of stimuli that surrounds him. Consequently, behaviors that are stimulated by the environment are commonly misattributed to the patient's disorder. For example, one kindly nurse found a pseudopatient pacing the long hospital corridors. "Nervous, Mr. X?" she asked. "No, bored," he said.

The notes kept by pseudopatients are full of patient behaviors that were misinterpreted by well-intentioned staff. Often enough, a patient would go "berserk" because he had, wittingly or unwittingly, been mistreated by, say, an attendant. A nurse coming upon the scene would rarely inquire even cursorily into the environmental stimuli of the patient's behavior. Rather, she assumed that his upset derived from his pathology, not from his present interactions with other staff members. Occasionally, the staff might assume that the patient's family (especially when they had recently visited) or other patients had stimulated the outburst. But never were the staff found to assume that one of themselves or the structure of the hospital had anything to do with a patient's behavior. One psychiatrist pointed to a group of patients who were sitting outside the cafeteria entrance half an hour before lunchtime. To a group of young residents he indicated that such behavior was characteristic of the oral-acquisitive nature of the syndrome. It seemed not to occur to him that there were very few things to anticipate in a psychiatric hospital besides eating.

A psychiatric label has a life and an influence of its own. Once the impression has been formed that the patient is schizophrenic, the expectation is that he will continue to be schizophrenic. When a sufficient amount of time has

324

*Chapter 13
Other
Institutions:
Religion and
Health Care*

passed, during which the patient has done nothing bizarre, he is considered to be in remission and available for discharge. But the label endures beyond discharge, with the unconfirmed expectation that he will behave as a schizophrenic again. Such labels, conferred by mental health professionals, are as influential on the patient as they are on his relatives and friends, and it should not surprise anyone that the diagnosis acts on all of them as a self-fulfilling prophecy. Eventually, the patient himself accepts the diagnosis, with all of its surplus meanings and expectations, and behaves accordingly.

The inferences to be made from these matters are quite simple. Much as Zigler and Phillips have demonstrated that there is enormous overlap in the symptoms presented by patients who have been variously diagnosed,[1] so there is enormous overlap in the behaviors of the sane and the insane. The sane are not "sane" all of the time. We lose our tempers "for no good reason." We are occasionally depressed or anxious, again for no good reason. And we find it difficult to get along with one or another person—again for no reason that we can specify. Similarly, the insane are not always insane. Indeed, it was the impression of the pseudopatients while living with them that they were sane for long periods of time—that the bizarre behaviors upon which their diagnoses were allegedly predicated constituted only a small fraction of their total behavior. If is makes no sense to label ourselves permanently depressed on the basis of an occasional depression, then it takes better evidence than is presently available to label all patients insane or schizophrenic on the basis of bizarre behaviors or cognitions.

NOTES

1. E. Zigler and L. Phillips, *J. Abnorm. Soc. Psychol.* **63,** 69 (1961).

PART FIVE

Social Change and the Future

On the Internet . . .

Sites appropriate to Part Five

The Economic Report of the President includes current and anticipated trends in the United States and annual numerical goals concerning such topics as employment, production, real income, and federal budget outlays. The database notes employment objectives for significant groups of the labor force, annual numeric goals, and a plan for carrying out program objectives.

```
http://www.library.nwu.edu/gpo/help/
    econr.html
```

This page, sponsored by the Tilburg Center of the John F. Kennedy School, is intended to serve as a resource, archive, and forum for people who are interested in globalization studies, a cross-disciplinary area that involves economics, political science, international law, ethics, and sociology.

```
http://www.globalize.org/index.html
```

The home page of the United Nations Environment Program (UNEP) contains links to environmental topics of critical concern to sociologists. The site will direct you to useful databases and global resource information.

```
http://www.unep.ch/
```

The William Davidson Institute at the University of Michigan Business School is dedicated to the understanding and promotion of economic transition. Consult this site for discussion of topics related to the changing global economy and the effects of globalization in general.

```
http://www.wdi.bus.umich.edu/
```

CHAPTER 14 Population, Environment, and the Future

14.1 ROBERT D. KAPLAN

The Coming Anarchy

The end of colonialism has not brought peace and prosperity to the nation-states in Africa. Rather, many of them are experiencing great demographic, environmental, economic, social, and political stress. In the following selection from "The Coming Anarchy," *The Atlantic Monthly* (February 1994), journalist Robert D. Kaplan uses the northwest African country of Sierra Leone to exemplify the problems of many other struggling Third World countries. Overpopulation and the overexploitation of resources are leading to environmental deterioration, which impoverishes people living off the land and destabilizes political and other institutions. The rain forest is being rapidly destroyed, the soils are eroding, the incidence of floods are increasing, hunger is widespread, and few people have access to a clean water supply or a sewage system. Crime and corruption are ever present. The government is ineffective and cannot maintain law and order outside the major cities and not even in many urban areas after dark. Anarchy afflicts many struggling African societies, which may exemplify the future of Asian and Latin American societies if their populations continue to put strains on dwindling environmental resources. Kaplan warns that the environment is the "national-security issue of the early twenty-first century" and requires immediate corrective actions.

Kaplan's analysis is rooted in what he has seen and heard, and his anarchy scenarios seem plausible, given current social science theories and findings.

Key Concept: demographic and environmental stress

*T*he Minister's eyes were like egg yolks, an aftereffect of some of the many illnesses, malaria especially, endemic in his country. There was also an irrefutable sadness in his eyes. He spoke in a slow and creaking voice, the voice of hope about to expire. Flame trees, coconut palms, and a ballpoint-blue Atlantic composed the background. None of it seemed beautiful, though. "In forty-five years I have never seen things so bad. We did not manage ourselves well after the British departed. But what we have now is something worse—the revenge of the poor, of the social failures, of the people least able to bring up children in a modern society." Then he referred to the recent coup in the West African country Sierra Leone. "The boys who took power in Sierra Leone come from houses like this." The Minister jabbed his finger at a corrugated metal shack teeming with children. "In three months these boys confiscated all the official Mercedes, Volvos, and BMWs and willfully wrecked them on the road." The Minister mentioned one of the coup's leaders, Solomon Anthony Joseph Musa, who shot the people who had paid for his schooling, "in order to erase the humiliation and mitigate the power his middle-class sponsors held over him."

Tyranny is nothing new in Sierra Leone or in the rest of West Africa. But it is now part and parcel of an increasing lawlessness that is far more significant that any coup, rebel incursion, or episodic experiment in democracy. Crime was what my friend—a top-ranking African official whose life would be threatened were I to identify him more precisely—really wanted to talk about. Crime is what makes West Africa a natural point of departure for my report on what the political character of our planet is likely to be in the twenty-first century.

The cities of West Africa at night are some of the unsafest places in the world. Streets are unlit; the police often lack gasoline for their vehicles: armed burglars, carjackers, and muggers proliferate. "The government in Sierra Leone has no writ after dark," says a foreign resident, shrugging. When I was in the capital, Freetown, last September, eight men armed with AK-47s broke into the house of an American man. They tied him up and stole everything of value. Forget Miami: direct flights between the United States and the Murtala Muhammed Airport, in neighboring Nigeria's largest city, Lagos, have been suspended by order of the U.S. Secretary of Transportation because of ineffective security at the terminal and its environs. A State Department report cited the airport for "extortion by law-enforcement and immigration officials." This is one of the few times that U.S. government has embargoed a foreign airport for reasons that are linked purely to crime. In Abidjan, effectively the capital of the Côte d'Ivoire, or Ivory Coast, restaurants have stick- and gun-wielding guards who walk you the fifteen feet or so between your car and the entrance, giving you an eerie taste of what American cities might be like in the future. . . .

"In the poor quarters of Arab North Africa," he continued, "there is much less crime, because Islam provides a social anchor: of education and indoctrination. Here in West Africa we have a lot of superficial Islam and superficial Christianity. Western religion is undermined by animist beliefs not suitable to a moral society, because they are based on irrational spirit power. Here spirits are used to wreak vengeance by one person against another, or one group against another."

A PREMONITION OF THE FUTURE

West Africa is becoming *the* symbol of worldwide demographic, environmental, and societal stress, in which criminal anarchy emerges as the real "strategic" danger. Disease, overpopulation, unprovoked crime, scarcity of resources, refugee migrations, the increasing erosion of nation-states and international borders, and the empowerment of private armies, security firms, and international drug cartels are now most tellingly demonstrated through a West African prism. West Africa provides an appropriate introduction to the issues, often extremely unpleasant to discuss, that will soon confront our civilization. To remap the political earth the way it will be a few decades hence—as I intend to do in this article—I find I must begin with West Africa.

There is no other place on the planet where political maps are so deceptive —where, in fact, they tell such lies—as in West Africa. Start with Sierra Leone. According to the map, it is a nation-state of defined borders, with a government in control of its territory. In truth the Sierra Leonian government, run by a twenty-seven-year-old army captain, Valentine Strasser, controls Freetown by day and by day also controls part of the rural interior. In the government's territory the national army is an unruly rabble threatening drivers and passengers at most checkpoints. In the other part of the country units of two separate armies from the war in Liberia have taken up residence, as has an army of Sierra Leonian rebels. The government force fighting the rebels is full of renegade commanders who have aligned themselves with disaffected village chiefs. A pre-modern formlessness governs the battlefield, evoking the wars in medieval Europe prior to the 1648 Peace of Westphalia, which ushered in the era of organized nation-states.

As a consequence, roughly 400,000 Sierra Leonians are internally displaced, 280,000 more have fled to neighboring Guinea, and another 100,000 have fled to Liberia, even as 400,000 Liberians have fled to Sierra Leone. The third largest city in Sierra Leone, Gondama, is a displaced-persons camp. With an additional 600,000 Liberians in Guinea and 250,000 in the Ivory Coast, the borders dividing these four countries have become largely meaningless. Even in quiet zones none of the governments except the Ivory Coast's maintains the schools, bridges, roads, and police forces in a manner necessary for functional sovereignty. The Koranko ethnic group in northeastern Sierra Leone does all its trading in Guinea. Sierra Leonian diamonds are more likely to be sold in Liberia than in Freetown. In the eastern provinces of Sierra Leone you can buy Liberian beer but not the local brand.

In Sierra Leone, as in Guinea, as in the Ivory Coast, as in Ghana, most of the primary rain forest and the secondary bush is being destroyed at an alarming rate. I saw convoys of trucks bearing majestic hardwood trunks to coastal ports. When Sierra Leone achieved its independence, in 1961, as much as 60 percent of the country was primary rain forest. Now six percent is. In the Ivory Coast the proportion has fallen from 38 percent to eight percent. The deforestation has led to soil erosion, which has led to more flooding and more mosquitoes. Virtually everyone in the West African interior has some form of malaria.

Sierra Leone is a microcosm of what is occurring, albeit in a more tempered and gradual manner, throughout West Africa and much of the underdeveloped world: the withering away of central governments, the rise of tribal and regional domains, the unchecked spread of disease, and the growing pervasiveness of war. West Africa is reverting to the Africa of the Victorian atlas. It consists now of a series of coastal trading posts, such as Freetown and Conakry, and an interior that, owing to violence, volatility, and disease, is again becoming, as Graham Greene once observed, "blank" and "unexplored." However, whereas Greene's vision implies a certain romance, as in the somnolent and charmingly seedy Freetown of his celebrated novel *The Heart of the Matter*, it is Thomas Malthus, the philosopher of demographic doomsday, who is now the prophet of West Africa's future. And West Africa's future, eventually, will also be that of most of the rest of the world....

Because the demographic reality of West Africa is a countryside draining into dense slums by the coast, ultimately the region's rulers will come to reflect the values of these shantytowns. There are signs of this already in Sierra Leone —and in Togo, where the dictator Etienne Eyadema, in power since 1967, was nearly toppled in 1991, not by democrats but by thousands of youths whom the London-based magazine *West Africa* described as "Soweto-like stone-throwing adolescents." Their behavior may herald a regime more brutal than Eyadema's repressive one.

... France *will* withdraw from former colonies like Benin, Togo, Niger, and the Ivory Coast, where it has been propping up local currencies. It will do so not only because its attention will be diverted to new challenges in Europe and Russia but also because younger French officials lack the older generation's emotional ties to the ex-colonies. However, even as Nigeria attempts to expand, it, too, is likely to split into several pieces. The State Department's Bureau of Intelligence and Research recently made the following points in an analysis of Nigeria:

> Prospects for a transition to civilian rule and democratization are slim.... The repressive apparatus of the state security service... will be difficult for any future civilian government to control.... The country is becoming increasingly ungovernable.... Ethnic and regional splits are deepening, a situation made worse by an increase in the number of states from 19 to 30 and a doubling in the number of local governing authorities; religious cleavages are more serious; Muslim fundamentalism and evangelical Christian militancy are on the rise; and northern

Muslim anxiety over southern [Christian] control of the economy is intense... the will to keep Nigeria together is now very weak.

Given that oil-rich Nigeria is a bellwether for the region—its population of roughly 90 million equals the populations of all the other West African states combined—it is apparent that Africa faces cataclysms that could make the Ethiopian and Somalian famines pale in comparison. This is especially so because Nigeria's population, including that of its largest city, Lagos, whose crime, pollution, and overcrowding make it the cliché par excellence of Third World urban dysfunction, is set to double during the next twenty-five years, while the country continues to deplete its natural resources....

And the cities keep growing. I got a general sense of the future while driving from the airport to downtown Conakry, the capital of Guinea. The forty-five-minute journey in heavy traffic was through one never-ending shantytown: a nightmarish Dickensian spectacle to which Dickens himself would never have given credence. The corrugated metal shacks and scabrous walls were coated with black slime. Stores were built out of rusted shipping containers, junked cars, and jumbles of wire mesh. The streets were one long puddle of floating garbage. Mosquitoes and flies were everywhere. Children, many of whom had protruding bellies, seemed as numerous as ants. When the tide went out, dead rats and the skeletons of cars were exposed on the mucky beach. In twenty-eight years Guinea's population will double if growth goes on at current rates. Hardwood logging continues at a madcap speed, and people flee the Guinean countryside for Conakry. It seemed to me that here, as elsewhere in Africa and the Third World, man is challenging nature far beyond its limits, and nature is now beginning to take its revenge.

Africa may be as relevant to the future character of world politics as the Balkans were a hundred years ago, prior to the two Balkan wars and the First World War. Then the threat was a collapse of empires and the birth of nations based solely on tribe. Now the threat is more elemental: *nature unchecked*. Africa's immediate future could be very bad. The coming upheaval, in which foreign embassies are shut down, states collapse, and contact with the outside world takes place through dangerous, disease-ridden coastal trading posts, will loom large in the century we are entering. (Nine of twenty-one U.S. foreign-aid missions to be closed over the next three years are in Africa—a prologue to a consolidation of U. S. embassies themselves.) Precisely because much of Africa is set to go over the edge at a time when the Cold War has ended, when environmental and demographic stress in other parts of the globe is becoming critical, and when the post-First World War system of nation-states—not just in the Balkans but perhaps also in the Middle East—is about to be toppled, Africa suggests what war, borders, and ethnic politics will be like a few decades hence.

To understand the events of the next fifty years, then, one must understand environmental scarcity, cultural and racial clash, geographic destiny, and

the transformation of war. The order in which I have named these is not accidental. Each concept except the first relies partly on the one or ones before it,
meaning that the last two—new approaches to mapmaking and to warfare—
are the most important. They are also the least understood. I will now look at
each idea, drawing upon the work of specialists and also my own travel experiences in various parts of the globe besides Africa, in order to fill in the blanks
of a new political atlas.

THE ENVIRONMENT AS A HOSTILE POWER

For a while the media will continue to ascribe riots and other violent upheavals
abroad mainly to ethnic and religious conflict. But as these conflicts multiply,
it will become apparent that something else is afoot, making more and more
places like Nigeria, India, and Brazil ungovernable.

Mention "the environment" or "diminishing natural resources" in foreign-
policy circles and you meet a brick wall of skepticism or boredom. To conservatives especially, the very terms seem flaky. Public-policy foundations have
contributed to the lack of interest, by funding narrowly focused environmental
studies replete with technical jargon which foreign-affairs experts just let pile
up on their desks.

It is time to understand "the environment" for what it is: *the* national-
security issue of the early twenty-first century. The political and strategic impact
of surging populations, spreading disease, deforestation and soil erosion, water
depletion, air pollution, and, possibly, rising sea levels in critical, overcrowded
regions like the Nile Delta and Bangladesh—developments that will prompt
mass migrations and, in turn, incite group conflicts—will be the core foreign-
policy challenge from which most others will ultimately emanate, arousing
the public and uniting assorted interests left over from the Cold War. In the
twenty-first century water will be in dangerously short supply in such diverse
locales as Saudi Arabia, Central Asia, and the southwestern United States. A
war could erupt between Egypt and Ethiopia over Nile River water. Even in
Europe tensions have arisen between Hungary and Slovakia over the damming
of the Danube, a classic case of how environmental disputes fuse with ethnic
and historical ones. The political scientist and erstwhile Clinton adviser Michael
Mandelbaum has said, "We have a foreign policy today in the shape of a doughnut—lots of peripheral interests but nothing at the center." The environment,
I will argue, is part of a terrifying array of problems that will define a new
threat to our security, filling the hole in Mandelbaum's doughnut and allowing
a post–Cold War foreign policy to emerge inexorably by need rather than by
design.

Our Cold War foreign policy truly began with George F. Kennan's famous article, signed "X," published in *Foreign Affairs* in July of 1947, in which Kennan
argued for a "firm and vigilant containment" of a Soviet Union that was im-
perially, rather than ideologically, motivated. It may be that our post-Cold War

foreign policy will one day be seen to have had its beginnings in an even bolder and more detailed piece of written analysis: one that appeared in the journal *International Security.* The article, published in the fall of 1991 by Thomas Fraser Homer-Dixon, who is the head of the Peace and Conflict Studies Program at the University of Toronto, was titled "On the Threshold: Environmental Changes as Causes of Acute Conflict." Homer-Dixon has, more successfully than other analysts, integrated two hitherto separate fields—military-conflict studies and the study of the physical environment.

In Homer-Dixon's view, future wars and civil violence will often arise from scarcities of resources such as water, cropland, forests, and fish. Just as there will be environmentally driven wars and refugee flows, there will be environmentally induced praetorian regimes—or, as he puts it, "hard regimes." Countries with the highest probability of acquiring hard regimes, according to Homer-Dixon, are those that are threatened by a declining resource base yet also have "a history of state [read 'military'] strength." Candidates include Indonesia, Brazil, and, of course, Nigeria. Though each of these nations has exhibited democratizing tendencies of late, Homer-Dixon argues that such tendencies are likely to be superficial "epiphenomena" having nothing to do with long-term processes that include soaring populations and shrinking raw materials. Democracy is problematic; scarcity is more certain.

Indeed, the Saddam Husseins of the future will have more, not fewer, opportunities. In addition to engendering tribal strife, scarcer resources will place a great strain on many peoples who never had much of a democratic or institutional tradition to begin with. Over the next fifty years the earth's population will soar from 5.5 billion to more than nine billion. Though optimists have hopes for new resource technologies and free-market development in the global village, they fail to note that, as the National Academy of Sciences has pointed out, 95 percent of the population increase will be in the poorest regions of the world, where governments now—just look at Africa—show little ability to function, let alone to implement even marginal improvements. Homer-Dixon writes, ominously, "Neo-Malthusians may underestimate human adaptability in *today's* environmental-social system, but as time passes their analysis may become ever more compelling."

While a minority of the human population will be, as Francis Fukuyama would put it, sufficiently sheltered so as to enter a "post-historical" realm, living in cities and suburbs in which the environment has been mastered and ethnic animosities have been quilled by bourgeois prosperity, an increasingly large number of people will be stuck in history, living in shantytowns where attempts to rise above poverty, cultural dysfunction, and ethnic strife will be doomed by a lack of water to drink, soil to till, and space to survive in. In the developing world environmental stress will present people with a choice that is increasingly among totalitarianism (as in Iraq), fascist-tending mini-states (as in Serb-held Bosnia), and road-warrior cultures (as in Somalia). Homer-Dixon concludes that "as environmental degradation proceeds, the size of the potential social disruption will increase." ...

THE PAST IS DEAD

Built on steep, muddy hills, the shantytowns of Ankara, the Turkish capital, exude visual drama. Altindag, or "Golden Mountain," is a pyramid of dreams, fashioned from cinder blocks and corrugated iron, rising as though each shack were built on top of another, all reaching awkwardly and painfully toward heaven—the heaven of wealthier Turks who live elsewhere in the city. Nowhere else on the planet have I found such a poignant architectural symbol of man's striving, with gaps in house walls plugged with rusted cans, and leeks and onions growing on verandas assembled from planks of rotting wood. For reasons that I will explain, the Turkish shacktown is a psychological universe away from the African one.

To see the twenty-first century truly, one's eyes must learn a different set of aesthetics. One must reject the overly stylized images of travel magazines, with their inviting photographs of exotic villages and glamorous downtowns. There are far too many millions whose dreams are more vulgar, more real—whose raw energies and desires will overwhelm the visions of the elites, remaking the future into something frighteningly new. But in Turkey I learned that shantytowns are not all bad.

Slum quarters in Abidjan terrify and repel the outsider. In Turkey it is the opposite. The closer I got to Golden Mountain the better it looked, and the safer I felt. I had $1,500 worth of Turkish lira in one pocket and $1,000 in traveler's checks in the other, yet I felt no fear. Golden Mountain was a real neighborhood. The inside of one house told the story: The architectural bedlam of cinder block and sheet metal and cardboard walls was deceiving. Inside was a *home*—order, that is, bespeaking dignity. I saw a working refrigerator, a television, a wall cabinet with a few books and lots of family pictures, a few plants by a window, and a stove. Though the streets become rivers of mud when it rains, the floors inside this house were spotless.

Other houses were like this too. Schoolchildren ran along with briefcases strapped to their backs, trucks delivered cooking gas, a few men sat inside a café sipping tea. One man sipped beer. Alcohol is easy to obtain in Turkey, a secular state where 99 percent of the population is Muslim. Yet there is little problem of alcoholism. Crime against persons is infinitesimal. Poverty and illiteracy are watered-down versions of what obtains in Algeria and Egypt (to say nothing of West Africa), making it that much harder for religious extremists to gain a foothold.

My point in bringing up a rather wholesome, crime-free slum is this: its existence demonstrates how formidable is the fabric of which Turkish Muslim culture is made. A culture this strong has the potential to dominate the Middle East once again. Slums are litmus tests for innate cultural strengths and weaknesses. Those peoples whose cultures can harbor extensive slum life without decomposing will be, relatively speaking, the future's winners. Those whose cultures cannot will be the future's victims. Slums—in the sociological sense—do not exist in Turkish cities. The mortar between people and family groups is stronger here than in Africa....

To appreciate fully the political and cartographic implications of postmodernism—an epoch of themeless juxtapositions, in which the classificatory grid of nation-states is going to be replaced by a jagged-glass pattern of city-states, shanty-states, nebulous and anarchic regionalisms—it is necessary to consider, finally, the whole question of war.

... [W]ar-making entities will no longer be restricted to a specific territory. Loose and shadowy organisms such as Islamic terrorist organizations suggest why borders will mean increasingly little and sedimentary layers of tribalistic identity and control will mean more. "From the vantage point of the present, there appears every prospect that religious ... fanaticisms will play a larger role in the motivation of armed conflict" in the West than at any time "for the last 300 years," [military historian Martin] Van Creveld writes. This is why analysts like Michael Vlahos are closely monitoring religious cults. Vlahos says, "An ideology that challenges us may not take familiar form, like the old Nazis or Commies. It may not even engage us initially in ways that fit old threat markings." Van Creveld concludes, "Armed conflict will be waged by men on earth, not robots in space. It will have more in common with the struggles of primitive tribes than with large-scale conventional war." While another military historian, John Keegan, in his new book *A History of Warfare,* draws a more benign portrait of primitive man, it is important to point out that what Van Creveld really means is *re-primitivized* man: warrior societies operating at a time of unprecedented resource scarcity and planetary overcrowding.

Van Creveld's pre-Westphalian vision of worldwide low-intensity conflict is not a superficial "back to the future" scenario. First of all, technology will be used toward primitive ends. In Liberia the guerrilla leader Prince Johnson didn't just cut off the ears of President Samuel Doe before Doe was tortured to death in 1990—Johnson made a video of it, which has circulated throughout West Africa. In December of 1992, when plotters of a failed coup against the Strasser regime in Sierra Leone had their ears cut off at Freetown's Hamilton Beach prior to being killed, it was seen by many to be a copycat execution. Considering, as I've explained earlier, that the Strasser regime is not really a government and that Sierra Leone is not really a nation-state, listen closely to Van Creveld: "Once the legal monopoly of armed force, long claimed by the state, is wrested out of its hands, existing distinctions between war and crime will break down much as is already the case today in ... Lebanon, Sri Lanka, El Salvador, Peru, or Columbia."

If crime and war become indistinguishable, then "national defense" may in the future be viewed as a local concept. As crime continues to grow in our cities and the ability of state governments and criminal-justice systems to protect their citizens diminishes, urban crime may, according to Van Creveld, "develop into low-intensity conflict by coalescing along racial, religious, social, and political lines." As small-scale violence multiplies at home and abroad, state armies will continue to shrink, being gradually replaced by a booming private security business, as in West Africa, and by urban mafias, especially in the former communist world, who may be better equipped than municipal police forces to grant physical protection to local inhabitants.

Future wars will be those of communal survival, aggravated or, in many cases, caused by environmental scarcity. These wars will be subnational, meaning that it will be hard for states and local governments to protect their own citizens physically. This is how many states will ultimately die. As state power fades—and with it the state's ability to help weaker groups within society, not to mention other states—peoples and cultures around the world will be thrown back upon their own strengths and weaknesses, with fewer equalizing mechanisms to protect them. Whereas the distant future will probably see the emergence of a racially hybrid, globalized man, the coming decades will see us more aware of our differences than of our similarities.

14.2 BILL McKIBBEN

A Special Moment in History

According to the estimates of demographers, in the next 50 years the world's population will just about double again before stabilizing around 10 or 11 billion people. In the face of these estimates, young people just entering their 20s may be the crucial generation in history, according to Bill McKibben in the selection that follows. This generation is important because it will determine the fate of the planet through its technological, lifestyle, and population choices. McKibben asserts that human population is butting up against environmental and resource limits. There is much evidence to support this view, but there are also many uncertainties. Humans depend mainly on four biosystems: croplands, grasslands, forests, and the oceans. Each of these biosystems have been deteriorating for several decades. Croplands are no longer expanding, and they are losing soil around the world at worrisome rates. Total grassland acreage is declining as overgrazing turns ever more land into wastelands and deserts. Forest acreage is declining as forests are converted to cropland and pasture. And the majority of the world fisheries are in serious decline. McKibben believes that the world is on an unsustainable path and that a near-doubling of its population could seriously overexploit the environment, with frightening consequences. He provides numerous reasons why we should be concerned, and he emphasizes that the current college generation will be the one that makes the decisions that "will decide how strong and healthy the planet will be for centuries to come."

McKibben is a former staff writer for *The New Yorker* and a frequent contributor to *The New York Review of Books*. His books include *The End of Nature* (Random House, 1989), *The Age of Missing Information* (Random House, 1992), *The Comforting Whirlwind* (William B. Eerdmans, 1994), and *Hope, Human and Wild: True Stories of Living Lightly on the Earth* (Hungry Mind Press, 1997). The following selection is from "A Special Moment in History," *The Atlantic Monthly* (May 1998).

Key Concept: environmental limits

We may live in the strangest, most thoroughly different moment since human beings took up farming, 10,000 years ago, and time more or less commenced. Since then time has flowed in one direction—toward *more*, which we

337

have taken to be progress. At first the momentum was gradual, almost imperceptible, checked by wars and the Dark Ages and plagues and taboos; but in recent centuries it has accelerated, the curve of every graph steepening like the Himalayas rising from the Asian steppe....

But now—now may be the special time. So special that in the Western world we might each of us consider, among many other things, having only one child—that is, reproducing at a rate as low as that at which human beings have ever voluntarily reproduced. Is this really necessary? Are we finally running up against some limits?

To try to answer this question, we need to ask another: *How many of us will there be in the near future?* Here is a piece of news that may alter the way we see the planet—an indication that we live at a special moment. At least at first blush the news is hopeful. *New demographic evidence shows that it is at least possible that a child born today will live long enough to see the peak of human population.*

Around the world people are choosing to have fewer and fewer children —not just in China, where the government forces it on them, but in almost every nation outside the poorest parts of Africa.... If this keeps up, the population of the world will not quite double again; United Nations analysts offer as their mid-range projection that it will top out at 10 to 11 billion, up from just under six billion at the moment....

The good news is that we won't grow forever. The bad news is that there are six billion of us already, a number the world strains to support. One more near-doubling—four or five billion more people—will nearly double that strain. Will these be the five billion straws that break the camel's back?...

LOOKING AT LIMITS

The case that the next doubling, the one we're now experiencing, might be the difficult one can begin as readily with the Stanford biologist Peter Vitousek as with anyone else. In 1986 Vitousek decided to calculate how much of the earth's "primary productivity" went to support human beings. He added together the grain we ate, the corn we fed our cows, and the forests we cut for timber and paper; he added the losses in food as we overgrazed grassland and turned it into desert. And when he was finished adding, the number he came up with was 38.8 percent. We use 38.8 percent of everything the world's plants don't need to keep themselves alive; directly or indirectly, we consume 38.8 percent of what it is possible to eat. "That's a relatively large number," Vitousek says. "It should give pause to people who think we are far from any limits." Though he never drops the measured tone of an academic, Vitousek speaks with considerable emphasis: "There's a sense among some economists that we're *so* far from any biophysical limits. I think that's not supported by the evidence."

For another antidote to the good cheer of someone like Julian Simon, sit down with the Cornell biologist David Pimentel. He believes that we're in big trouble. Odd facts stud his conversation—for example, a nice head of iceberg lettuce is 95 percent water and contains just fifty calories of energy, but it takes

400 calories of energy to grow that head of lettuce in California's Central Valley, and another 1,800 to ship it east. ("There's practically no nutrition in the damn stuff anyway," Pimentel says. "Cabbage is a lot better, and we can grow it in upstate New York.") Pimentel has devoted the past three decades to tracking the planet's capacity, and he believes that we're already too crowded—that the earth can support only two billion people over the long run at a middle-class standard of living, and that trying to support more is doing damage. He has spent considerable time studying soil erosion, for instance. Every raindrop that hits exposed ground is like a small explosion, launching soil particles into the air. On a slope, more than half of the soil contained in those splashes is carried downhill. If crop residue—cornstalks, say—is left in the field after harvest, it helps to shield the soil: the raindrop doesn't hit hard. But in the developing world, where firewood is scarce, peasants burn those cornstalks for cooking fuel. About 60 percent of crop residues in China and 90 percent in Bangladesh are removed and burned, Pimentel says. When planting season comes, dry soils simply blow away. "Our measuring stations pick up African soils in the wind when they start to plough."

The very things that made the Green Revolution so stunning—that made the last doubling possible—now cause trouble. Irrigation ditches, for instance, water 27 percent of all arable land and help to produce a third of all crops. But when flooded soils are baked by the sun, the water evaporates and the minerals in the irrigation water are deposited on the land. A hectare (2.47 acres) can accumulate two to five tons of salt annually, and eventually plants won't grow there. Maybe 10 percent of all irrigated land is affected.

... [F]ood production grew even faster than population after the Second World War. Year after year the yield of wheat and corn and rice rocketed up about three percent annually. It's a favorite statistic of the eternal optimists. In Julian Simon's book *The Ultimate Resource* (1981) charts show just how fast the growth was, and how it continually cut the cost of food. Simon wrote, "The obvious implication of this historical trend toward cheaper food—a trend that probably extends back to the beginning of agriculture—is that real prices for food will continue to drop.... It is a fact that portends more drops in price and even less scarcity in the future."

A few years after Simon's book was published, however, the data curve began to change. That rocketing growth in grain production ceased; now the gains were coming in tiny increments, too small to keep pace with population growth. The world reaped its largest harvest of grain per capita in 1984; since then the amount of corn and wheat and rice per person has fallen by six percent. Grain stockpiles have shrunk to less than two months' supply.

No one knows quite why. The collapse of the Soviet Union contributed to the trend—cooperative farms suddenly found the fertilizer supply shut off and spare parts for the tractor hard to come by. But there were other causes, too, all around the world—the salinization of irrigated fields, the erosion of top-soil, and all the other things that environmentalists had been warning about for years. It's possible that we'll still turn production around and start it rock-eting again. Charles C. Mann, writing in *Science*, quotes experts who believe that in the future a "gigantic, multi-year, multi-billion-dollar scientific effort, a kind of agricultural 'person-on the-moon project,'" might do the trick. The next great hope of the optimists is genetic engineering, and scientists have indeed managed to induce resistance to pests and disease in some plants. To get more yield, though, a cornstalk must be made to put out another ear, and conventional breeding may have exhausted the possibilities. There's a sense that we're running into walls.

... What we are running out of is what the scientists call "sinks"—places to put the by-products of our large appetites. Not garbage dumps (we could go on using Pampers till the end of time and still have empty space left to toss them away) but the atmospheric equivalent of garbage dumps.

It wasn't hard to figure out that there were limits on how much coal smoke we could pour into the air of a single city. It took a while longer to figure out that building ever higher smokestacks merely lofted the haze farther afield, raining down acid on whatever mountain range lay to the east. Even that, however, we are slowly fixing, with scrubbers and different mixtures of fuel. We can't so easily repair the new kinds of pollution. These do not come from something going wrong—some engine without a catalytic converter, some waste-water pipe without a filter, some smokestack without a scrubber. New kinds of pollution come instead from things going as they're supposed to go—but at such a high volume that they overwhelm the planet. They come from normal human life—but there are so many of us living those normal lives that something abnormal is happening. And that something is different from the old forms of pollution that it confuses the issue even to use the word.

Consider nitrogen, for instance. But before plants can absorb it, it must become "fixed"—bonded with carbon, hydrogen, or oxygen. Nature does this trick with certain kinds of algae and soil bacteria, and with lightning. Before human beings began to alter the nitrogen cycle, these mechanisms provided 90–150 million metric tons of nitrogen a year. Now human activity adds 130–150 million more tons. Nitrogen isn't pollution—it's essential. And we are using more of it all the time. Half the industrial nitrogen fertilizer used in human history has been applied since 1984. As a result, coastal waters and estuaries bloom with toxic algae while oxygen concentrations dwindle, killing fish; as a result, nitrous oxide traps solar heat. And once the gas is in the air, it stays there for a century or more.

Or consider methane, which comes out of the back of a cow or the top of a termite mound or the bottom of a rice paddy. As a result of our determination to raise more cattle, cut down more tropical forest (thereby causing termite populations to explode), and grow more rice, methane concentrations in the atmosphere are more than twice as high as they have been for most of the past 160,000 years. And methane traps heat—very efficiently.

Or consider carbon dioxide. In fact, concentrate on carbon dioxide. If we had to pick one problem to obsess about over the next fifty years, we'd do well to make it CO_2—which is not pollution either. Carbon *mon*oxide is pollution: it kills you if you breathe enough of it. But carbon *di*oxide, carbon with two oxygen atoms, can't do a blessed thing to you. If you're reading this indoors, you're breathing more CO_2 than you'll ever get outside. For generations, in fact, engineers said that an engine burned clean if it produced only water vapor and carbon dioxide.

Here's the catch: that engine produces a *lot* of CO_2. A gallon of gas weighs about eight pounds. When it's burned in a car, about five and a half pounds of carbon, in the form of carbon dioxide, come spewing out the back. It doesn't matter if the car is a 1958 Chevy or a 1998 Saab. And no filter can reduce that flow—it's an inevitable by-product of fossil-fuel combustion, which is why CO_2 has been piling up in the atmosphere ever since the Industrial Revolution. Before we started burning oil and coal and gas, the atmosphere contained about 280 parts CO_2 per million. Now the figure is about 360. Unless we do everything we can think of to eliminate fossil fuels from our diet, the air will test out at more than 500 parts per million fifty or sixty years from now, whether it's sampled in the South Bronx or at the South Pole.

This matters because, as we all know by now, the molecular structure of this clean, natural, common element that we are adding to every cubic foot of the atmosphere surrounding us traps heat that would otherwise radiate back out to space. Far more than even methane and nitrous oxide, CO_2 causes global warming—the greenhouse effect—and climate change. Far more than any other single factor, it is turning the earth we were born on into a new planet.

... For ten years, with heavy funding from governments around the world, scientists launched satellites, monitored weather balloons, studied clouds. Their work culminated in a long-awaited report from the UN's Intergovernmental Panel on Climate Change, released in the fall of 1995. The panel's 2,000 scientists, from every corner of the globe, summed up their findings in this dry but historic bit of understatement: "The balance of evidence suggests that there is a discernible human influence on global climate." That is to say, we are heating up the planet—substantially. If we don't reduce emissions of carbon dioxide and other gases, the panel warned, temperatures will probably rise 3.6° Fahrenheit by 2100, and perhaps as much as 6.3°.

You may think you've already heard a lot about global warming. But most of our sense of the problem is behind the curve. Here's the current news: the changes are already well under way. When politicians and businessmen talk about "future risks," their rhetoric is outdated. This is not a problem for the distant future, or even for the near future. The planet has already heated up by a degree or more. We are perhaps a quarter of the way into the greenhouse era, and the effects are already being felt. From a new heaven, filled with nitrogen, methane, and carbon, a new earth is being born. If some alien astronomer is watching us, she's doubtless puzzled. This is the most obvious effect of our numbers and our appetites, and the key to understanding why the size of our population suddenly poses such a risk.

STORMY AND WARM

What does this new world feel like? For one thing, it's stormier than the old one. Data analyzed last year by Thomas Karl, of the National Oceanic and Atmospheric Administration, showed that total winter precipitation in the United States has increased by 10 percent since 1900 and that "extreme precipitation events"—rainstorms that dumped more than two inches of water in twenty-four hours and blizzards—had increased by 20 percent. That's because warmer air holds more water vapor than the colder atmosphere of the old earth; more water evaporates from the ocean, meaning more clouds, more rain, more snow. Engineers designing storm sewers, bridges, and culverts used to plan for what they called the "hundred-year storm." That is, they built to withstand the worst flooding or wind that history led them to expect in the course of a century. Since that history no longer applies, Karl says, "there isn't really a hundred-year event anymore... we seem to be getting these storms of the century every couple of years." When Grand Forks, North Dakota, disappeared beneath the Red River in the spring of last year, some meteorologists referred to it as "a 500-year flood"—meaning, essentially, that all bets are off. Meaning that these aren't acts of God. "If you look out your window, part of what you see in terms of weather is produced by ourselves," Karl says. "If you look out the window fifty years from now, we're going to be responsible for more of it."

Twenty percent more bad storms, 10 percent more winter precipitation—these are enormous numbers. It's like opening the newspaper to read that the average American is smarter by 30 IQ points. And the same data showed increases in drought, too. With more water in the atmosphere, there's less in the soil, according to Kevin Trenberth, of the National Center for Atmospheric Research. Those parts of the continent that are normally dry—the eastern sides of mountains, the plains and deserts—are even drier, as the higher average temperatures evaporate more of what rain does fall. "You get wilting plants and eventually drought faster than you would otherwise," Trenberth says. And when the rain does come, it's often so intense that much of it runs off before it can soak into the soil.

So—wetter and drier. *Different....*

The effects of... warming can be found in the largest phenomena. The oceans that cover most of the planet's surface are clearly rising, both because of melting glaciers and because water expands as it warms. As a result, low-lying Pacific islands already report surges of water washing across the atolls. "It's nice weather and all of a sudden water is pouring into your living room," one Marshall Islands resident told a newspaper reporter. "It's very clear that something is happening in the Pacific, and these islands are feeling it." Global warming will be like a much more powerful version of El Niño that covers the entire globe and lasts forever, or at least until the next big asteroid strikes.

If you want to scare yourself with guesses about what might happen in the near future, there's no shortage of possibilities. Scientists have already observed large-scale shifts in the duration of the El Niño ocean warming, for instance. The Arctic tundra has warmed so much that in some places it now gives off more carbon dioxide than it absorbs—a switch that could trigger a potent feedback loop, making warming ever worse. And researchers studying glacial cores from the Greenland Ice Sheet recently concluded that local climate shifts have occurred with incredible rapidity in the past—18° in one three-year stretch. Other scientists worry that such a shift might be enough to flood the oceans with fresh water and reroute or shut off currents like the Gulf Stream and the North Atlantic, which keep Europe far warmer than it would otherwise be. (See "The Great Climate Flip-flop," by William H. Calvin, January *Atlantic*.) In the words of Wallace Broecker, of Columbia University, a pioneer in the field, "Climate is an angry beast, and we are poking it with sticks."

But we don't need worst-case scenarios: best-case scenarios make the point. The population of the earth is going to nearly double one more time. That will bring it to a level that even the reliable old earth we were born on would be hard-pressed to support. Just at the moment when we need everything to be working as smoothly as possible, we find ourselves inhabiting a new planet, whose carrying capacity we cannot conceivably estimate. We have no idea how much wheat this planet can grow. We don't know what its politics will be like: not if there are going to be heat waves like the one that killed more than 700 Chicagoans in 1995; not if rising sea levels and other effects of climate change create tens of millions of environmental refugees; not if a 1.5° jump in India's temperature could reduce the country's wheat crop by 10 percent or divert its monsoons....

We have gotten very large and very powerful, and for the foreseeable future we're stuck with the results. The glaciers won't grow back again anytime soon; the oceans won't drop. We've already done deep and systemic damage. To use a human analogy, we've already said the angry and unforgivable words that will haunt our marriage till its end. And yet we can't simply walk out the door. There's no place to go. We have to salvage what we can of our relationship with the earth, to keep things from getting any worse than they have to be.

If we can bring our various emissions quickly and sharply under control, we *can* limit the damage, reduce dramatically the chance of horrible surprises, preserve more of the biology we were born into. But do not underestimate the task. The UN's Intergovernmental Panel on Climate Change projects that an immediate 60 percent reduction in fossil-fuel use is necessary just to stabilize climate at the current level of disruption. Nature may still meet us halfway, but halfway is a long way from where we are now. What's more, we can't delay. If we wait a few decades to get started, we may as well not even begin. It's not like poverty, a concern that's always there for civilizations to address. This is a timed test, like the SAT: two or three decades, and we lay our pencils down. It's *the* test for our generations, and population is a part of the answer....

The numbers are so daunting that they're almost unimaginable. Say, just for argument's sake, that we decided to cut world fossil-fuel use by 60 percent—the amount that the UN panel says would stabilize world climate. And then say that we shared the remaining fossil fuel equally. Each human being would get to produce 1.69 metric tons of carbon dioxide annually—which would allow you to drive an average American car nine miles a day. By the time the population increased to 8.5 billion, in about 2025, you'd be down to six miles a day. If you carpooled, you'd have about three pounds of CO_2 left in your daily ration —enough to run a highly efficient refrigerator. Forget your computer, your TV, your stereo, your stove, your dishwasher, your water heater, your microwave, your water pump, your clock. Forget your light bulbs, compact fluorescent or not.

I'm not trying to say that conservation, efficiency, and new technology won't help. They will—but the help will be slow and expensive. The tremendous momentum of growth will work against it. Say that someone invented a new furnace tomorrow that used half as much oil as old furnaces. How many years would it be before a substantial number of American homes had the new device? And what if it cost more? And if oil stays cheaper per gallon than bottled water? Changing basic fuels—to hydrogen, say—would be even more expensive. It's not like running out of white wine and switching to red. Yes, we'll get new technologies. One day last fall *The New York Times* ran a special section on energy, featuring many up-and-coming improvements: solar shingles, basement fuel cells. But the same day, on the front page, William K. Stevens reported that international negotiators had all but given up on preventing a doubling of the atmospheric concentration of CO_2. The momentum of growth was so great, the negotiators said, that making the changes required to slow global warming significantly would be like "trying to turn a supertanker in a sea of syrup."

There are no silver bullets to take care of a problem like this. Electric cars won't by themselves save us, though they would help. We simply won't live efficiently enough soon enough to solve the problem. Vegetarianism won't cure our ills, though it would help. We simply won't live simply enough soon enough to solve the problem.

Reducing the birth rate won't end all our troubles either. That, too, is no silver bullet. But it would help. There's no more practical decision than how many children to have. (And no more mystical decision, either.)

The bottom-line argument goes like this: The next fifty years are a special time. They will decide how strong and healthy the planet will be for centuries to come. Between now and 2050 we'll see the zenith, or very nearly, of human population. With luck we'll never see any greater production of carbon dioxide or toxic chemicals. We'll never see more species extinction or soil erosion. Greenpeace recently announced a campaign to phase out fossil fuels entirely by mid-century, which sounds utterly quixotic but could—if everything went just right—happen.

So it's the task of those of us alive right now to deal with this special phase, to squeeze us through these next fifty years. That's not fair—any more than it was fair that earlier generations had to deal with the Second World War or the Civil War or the Revolution or the Depression or slavery. It's just reality. We need in these fifty years to be working simultaneously on all parts of the equation—on our ways of life, on our technologies, and on our population.

As Gregg Easterbrook pointed out in his book *A Moment on the Earth* (1995), if the planet does manage to reduce its fertility, "the period in which human numbers threaten the biosphere on a general scale will turn out to have been much, much more brief" than periods of natural threats like the Ice Ages. True enough. But the period in question happens to be our time. That's what makes this moment special, and what makes this moment hard.

CHAPTER 15 Social Movements and Collective Behavior

15.1 MANCUR OLSON, JR.

The Logic of Collective Action

Mancur Olson, Jr. (1932–1998) was a professor of economics at the University of Maryland and a consultant to the RAND Corporation in Santa Monica, California, and to the Institute of Defense Analysis in Washington, D.C. His publications include *The Rise and Decline of Nations: Economic Growth, Stagflation, and Social Rigidities* (Yale University Press, 1982) and *The Logic of Collective Action: Public Goods and the Theory of Groups* (Harvard University Press, 1971), which is excerpted here.

It is often assumed that members of a group with a common interest would naturally act collectively to pursue that interest. In the selection that follows, however, Olson shows that this assumption is false. It is very difficult for most people to act collectively in their own behalf. The reason is that it is usually rational for individuals not to contribute any effort or money to the pursuit of their collective goal but to let others carry the load, since the noncontributors and contributors share equally in the gains. There are conditions, however, under which collective action is much more likely, and Olson spells them out. Unfortunately for democratic ideals, these conditions

346

Chapter 15
Social
Movements
and Collective
Behavior

make it easier for small elite groups to organize for their interests than it is for large disadvantaged groups.

Key Concept: rational self-interest

*I*t is often taken for granted, at least where economic objectives are involved, that groups of individuals with common interests usually attempt to further those common interests. Groups of individuals with common interests are expected to act on behalf of their common interests much as single individuals are often expected to act on behalf of their personal interests. This opinion about group behavior is frequently found not only in popular discussions but also in scholarly writings. Many economists of diverse methodological and ideological traditions have implicitly or explicitly accepted it. This view has, for example, been important in many theories of labor unions, in Marxian theories of class action, in concepts of "countervailing power," and in various discussions of economic institutions. It has, in addition, occupied a prominent place in political science, at least in the United States, where the study of pressure groups has been dominated by a celebrated "group theory" based on the idea that groups will act when necessary to further their common or group goals. Finally, it has played a significant role in many well-known sociological studies....

But it is *not* in fact true that the idea that groups will act in their self-interest follows logically from the premise of rational and self-interested behavior.... Indeed, unless the number of individuals in a group is quite small, or unless there is coercion or some other special device to make individuals act in their common interest, *rational, self-interested individuals will not act to achieve their common or group interests.* In other words, even if all of the individuals in a large group are rational and self-interested, and would gain if, as a group, they acted to achieve their common interest or objective, they will still not voluntarily act to achieve that common or group interest. The notion that groups of individuals will act to achieve their common or group interests, far from being a logical implication of the assumption that the individuals in a group will rationally further their individual interests, is in fact inconsistent with that assumption....

If the members of a large group rationally seek to maximize their personal welfare, they will *not* act to advance their common or group objectives unless there is coercion to force them to do so, or unless some separate incentive, distinct from the achievement of the common or group interest, is offered to the members of the group individually on the condition that they help bear the costs or burdens involved in the achievement of the group objectives. Nor will such large groups form organizations to further their common goals in the absence of the coercion or the separate incentives just mentioned. These points hold true even when there is unanimous agreement in a group about the common good and the methods of achieving it....

None of the statements made above fully applies to small groups, for the situation in small groups is much more complicated. In small groups there may very well be some voluntary action in support of the common purposes of the individuals in the group, but in most cases this action will cease before it reaches the optimal level for the members of the group as a whole. In the sharing of the costs of efforts to achieve a common goal in small groups, there is however a surprising tendency for the "exploitation" of the *great* by the *small*....

THE PURPOSE OF ORGANIZATION

... The kinds of organizations that are the focus of this study are *expected* to further the interests of their members. Labor unions are expected to strive for higher wages and better working conditions for their members; farm organizations are expected to strive for favorable legislation for their members; cartels are expected to strive for higher prices for participating firms; the corporation is expected to further the interests of its stockholders; and the state is expected to further the common interests of its citizens (though in this nationalistic age the state often has interests and ambitions apart from those of its citizens)....

Just as those who belong to an organization or a group can be presumed to have a common interest, so they obviously also have purely individual interests, different from those of the others in the organization or group. All of the members of a labor union, for example, have a common interest in higher wages, but at the same time each worker has a unique interest in his personal income, which depends not only on the rate of wages but also on the length of time that he works.

PUBLIC GOODS AND LARGE GROUPS

The combination of individual interests and common interests in an organization suggests an analogy with a competitive market. The firms in a perfectly competitive industry, for example, have a common interest in a higher price for the industry's product. Since a uniform price must prevail in such a market, a firm cannot expect a higher price for itself unless all of the other firms in the industry also have this higher price. But a firm in a competitive market also has an interest in selling as much as it can, until the cost of producing another unit exceeds the price of that unit. In this there is no common interest; each firm's interest is directly opposed to that of every other firm, for the more other firms sell, the lower the price and income for any given firm. In short, while all firms have a common interest in a higher price, they have antagonistic interests where output is concerned. This can be illustrated with a simple supply-and-demand model. For the sake of a simple argument, assume that a perfectly competitive industry is momentarily in a disequilibrium position, with price exceeding marginal cost for all firms at their present output. Suppose, too, that all of the adjustments will be made by the firms already in the industry rather than by new entrants, and that the industry is on an inelastic portion of its demand curve. Since price exceeds marginal cost for all firms,

348

Chapter 15
Social
Movements
and Collective
Behavior

output will increase. But as all firms increase production, the price falls; indeed, since the industry demand curve is by assumption inelastic, the total revenue of the industry will decline. Apparently each firm finds that with price exceeding marginal cost, it pays to increase its output, but the result is that each firm gets a smaller profit. Some economists in an earlier day may have questioned this result, but the fact that profit-maximizing firms in a perfectly competitive industry can act contrary to their interests as a group is now widely understood and accepted. A group of profit-maximizing firms can act to reduce their aggregate profits because in perfect competition each firm is, by definition, so small that it can ignore the effect of its output on price. Each firm finds it to its advantage to increase output to the point where marginal cost equals price and to ignore the effects of its extra output on the position of the industry. It is true that the net result is that all firms are worse off, but this does not mean that every firm has not maximized its profits. If a firm, foreseeing the fall in price resulting from the increase in industry output, were to restrict its own output, it would lose more than ever, for its price would fall quite as much in any case and it would have a smaller output as well. A firm in a perfectly competitive market gets only a small part of the benefit (or a small share of the industry's extra revenue) resulting from a reduction in that firm's output.

For these reasons it is now generally understood that if the firms in an industry are maximizing profits, the profits for the industry as a whole will be less than they might otherwise be. And almost everyone would agree that this theoretical conclusion fits the facts for markets characterized by pure competition. The important point is that this is true because, though all the firms have a common interest in a higher price for the industry's product, it is in the interest of each firm that the other firms pay the cost—in terms of the necessary reduction in output—needed to obtain a higher price.

About the only thing that keeps prices from falling in accordance with the process just described in perfectly competitive markets is outside intervention. Government price supports, tariffs, cartel agreements, and the like may keep the firms in a competitive market from acting contrary to their interests. Such aid or intervention is quite common. It is then important to ask how it comes about. How does a competitive industry obtain government assistance in maintaining the price of its product?

Consider a hypothetical, competitive industry, and suppose that most of the producers in that industry desire a tariff, a price-support program, or some other government intervention to increase the price for their product. To obtain any such assistance from the government, the producers in this industry will presumably have to organize a lobbying organization; they will have to become an active pressure group. This lobbying organization may have to conduct a considerable campaign. If significant resistance is encountered, a great amount of money will be required. Public relations experts will be needed to influence the newspapers, and some advertising may be necessary. Professional organizers will probably be needed to organize "spontaneous grass roots" meetings among the distressed producers in the industry, and to get those in the industry to write letters to their congressmen. The campaign for the government assistance will take the time of some of the producers in the industry, as well as their money.

There is a striking parallel between the problem the perfectly competitive industry faces as it strives to obtain government assistance, and the problem it faces in the marketplace when the firms increase output and bring about a fall in price. *Just as it was not rational for a particular producer to restrict his output in order that there might be a higher price for the product of his industry, so it would not be rational for him to sacrifice his time and money to support a lobbying organization to obtain government assistance for the industry. In neither case would it be in the interest of the individual producer to assume any of the costs himself. A lobbying organization, or indeed a labor union or any other organization, working in the interest of a large group of firms or workers in some industry, would get no assistance from the rational, self-interested individuals in that industry.* This would be true even if everyone in the industry were absolutely convinced that the proposed program was in their interest (though in fact some might think otherwise and make the organization's task yet more difficult).

Although the lobbying organization is only one example of the logical analogy between the organization and the market, it is of some practical importance. There are many powerful and well-financed lobbies with mass support in existence now, but these lobbying organizations do not get that support because of their legislative achievements. The most powerful lobbying organizations now obtain their funds and their following for other reasons, as later parts of this study will show....

Almost any government is economically beneficial to its citizens, in that the law and order it provides is a prerequisite of all civilized economic activity. But despite the force of patriotism, the appeal of the national ideology, the bond of a common culture, and the indispensability of the system of law and order, no major state in modern history has been able to support itself through voluntary dues or contributions. Philanthropic contributions are not even a significant source of revenue for most countries. Taxes, *compulsory* payments by definition, are needed. Indeed, as the old saying indicates, their necessity is as certain as death itself.

If the state, with all of the emotional resources at its command, cannot finance its most basic and vital activities without resort to compulsion, it would seem that large private organizations might also have difficulty in getting the individuals in the groups whose interests they attempt to advance to make the necessary contributions voluntarily.

The reason the state cannot survive on voluntary dues or payments, but must rely on taxation, is that the most fundamental services a nation-state provides are, in one important respect, like the higher price in a competitive market: they must be available to everyone if they are available to anyone. The basic and most elementary goods or services provided by government, like defense and police protection, and the system of law and order generally, are such that they go to everyone or practically everyone in the nation. It would obviously not be feasible, if indeed it were possible, to deny the protection provided by the military services, the police, and the courts to those who did not voluntarily pay their share of the costs of government, and taxation is accordingly necessary. The common or collective benefits provided by governments are usually called "public goods" by economists, and the concept of public goods is one of the oldest and most important ideas in the study of public finance. A common,

350

*Chapter 15
Social
Movements
and Collective
Behavior*

collective, or public good is here defined as any good such that, if any person X_4 in a group, $X_1, \ldots, X_4, \ldots, X_{98}$ consumes it, it cannot feasibly be withheld from the others in that group. In other words, those who do not purchase or pay for any of the public or collective good cannot be excluded or kept from sharing in the consumption of the good, as they can where noncollective goods are concerned.

Students of public finance have, however, neglected the fact that *the achievement of any common goal or the satisfaction of any common interest means that a public or collective good has been provided for that group.* The very fact that a goal or purpose is *common* to a group means that no one in the group is excluded from the benefit or satisfaction brought about by its achievement.... It is of the essence of an organization that it provides an inseparable, generalized benefit. It follows that the provision of public or collective goods is the fundamental function of organizations generally. A state is first of all an organization that provides public goods for its members, the citizens; and other types of organizations similarly provide collective goods for their members.

And just as a state cannot support itself by voluntary contributions, or by selling its basic services on the market, neither can other large organizations support themselves without providing some sanction, or some attraction distinct from the public good itself, that will lead individuals to help bear the burdens of maintaining the organization. The individual member of the typical large organization is in a position analogous to that of the firm in a perfectly competitive market, or the taxpayer in the state: his own efforts will not have a noticeable effect on the situation of his organization, and he can enjoy any improvements brought about by others whether or not he has worked in support of his organization.

There is no suggestion here that states or other organizations provide *only* public or collective goods. Governments often provide noncollective goods like electric power, for example, and they usually sell such goods on the market much as private firms would do. Moreover, as later parts of this study will argue, large organizations that are not able to make membership compulsory *must also* provide some noncollective goods in order to give potential members an incentive to join. Still, collective goods are the characteristic organization goods, for ordinary noncollective goods can always be provided by individual action, and only where common purposes or collective goods are concerned is organization or group action ever indispensable....

[C]ertain small groups can provide themselves with collective goods without relying on coercion or any positive inducements apart from the collective good itself. This is because in some small groups each of the members, or at least one of them, will find that his personal gain from having the collective good exceeds the total cost of providing some amount of that collective good; there are members who would be better off if the collective good were provided, even if they had to pay the entire cost of providing it themselves, than they would be if it were not provided. In such situations there is a presumption that the collective good will be provided. Such a situation will exist only when the benefit to the group from having the collective good exceeds the total cost by more than it exceeds the gain to one or more individuals in the group. Thus, in a very small group, where each member gets a substantial proportion of the total gain simply because there are few others in the group, a collective good can often be provided by the voluntary, self-interested action of the members of the group. In smaller groups marked by considerable degrees of inequality—that is, in groups of members of unequal "size" or extent of interest in the collective good—there is the greatest likelihood that a collective good will be provided; for the greater the interest in the collective good of any single member, the greater the likelihood that that member will get such a significant proportion of the total benefit from the collective good that he will gain from seeing that the good is provided, even if he has to pay all of the cost himself.

Even in the smallest groups, however, the collective good will not ordinarily be provided on an optimal scale. That is to say, the members of the group will not provide as much of the good as it would be in their common interest to provide. Only certain special institutional arrangements will give the individual members an incentive to purchase the amounts of the collective good that would add up to the amount that would be in the best interest of the group as a whole. This tendency toward suboptimality is due to the fact that a collective good is, by definition, such that other individuals in the group cannot be kept from consuming it once any individual in the group has provided it for himself. Since an individual member thus gets only part of the benefit of any expenditure he makes to obtain more of the collective good, he will discontinue his purchase of the collective good before the optimal amount for the group as a whole has been obtained. In addition, the amounts of the collective good that a member of the group receives free from other members will further reduce his incentive to provide more of that good at his own expense. Accordingly, *the larger the group, the farther it will fall short of providing an optimal amount of a collective good.*

This suboptimality or inefficiency will be somewhat less serious in groups composed of members of greatly different size or interest in the collective good. In such unequal groups, on the other hand, there is a tendency toward an arbitrary sharing of the burden of providing the collective good. The largest member, the member who would on his own provide the largest amount of the collective good, bears a disproportionate share of the burden of providing the collective good. The smaller member by definition gets a smaller fraction of the benefit of any amount of the collective good he provides than a larger member, and therefore has less incentive to provide additional amounts of the collective good. Once a smaller member has the amount of the collective good he gets free from the largest member, he has more than he would have purchased for himself, and has no incentive to obtain any of the collective good at his own expense. In small groups with common interests there is accordingly *a surprising tendency for the "exploitations" of the great by the small. . . .*

The most important single point about small groups in the present context, however, is that they may very well be able to provide themselves with a collective good simply because of the attraction of the collective good to the individual members. In this, small groups differ from larger ones. The larger a group is, the farther it will fall short of obtaining an optimal supply of any collective good, and the less likely that it will act to obtain even a minimal amount of such a good. In short, the larger the group, the less it will further its common interests. . . .

352

*Chapter 15
Social
Movements
and Collective
Behavior*

The analog to atomistic competition in the nonmarket situation is the very large group, which will here be called the "latent" group. It is distinguished by the fact that, if one member does or does not help provide the collective good, no other one member will be significantly affected and therefore none has any reason to react. Thus an individual in a "latent" group, by definition, cannot make a noticeable contribution to any group effort, and since no one in the group will react if he makes no contribution, he has no incentive to contribute. Accordingly, large or "latent" groups have no incentive to act to obtain a collective good because, however valuable the collective good might be to the group as a whole, it does not offer the individual any incentive to pay dues to any organization working in the latent group's interest, or to bear in any other way any of the costs of the necessary collective action.

Only a *separate and "selective" incentive* will stimulate a rational individual in a latent group to act in a group-oriented way. In such circumstances group action can be obtained only through an incentive that operates, not indiscriminately, like the collective good, upon the group as a whole, but rather *selectively* toward the individuals in the group. The incentive must be "selective" so that those who do not join the organization working for the group's interest, or in other ways contribute to the attainment of the group's interest, can be treated differently from those who do. These "selective incentives" can be either negative or positive, in that they can either coerce by punishing those who fail to bear an allocated share of the costs of the group action, or they can be positive inducements offered to those who act in the group interest. A latent group that has been led to act in its group interest, either because of coercion of the individuals in the group or because of positive rewards to those individuals, will here be called a "mobilized" latent group. Large groups are thus called "latent" groups because they have a latent power or capacity for action, but that potential power can be realized or "mobilized" only with the aid of "selective incentives." ...

SOCIAL INCENTIVES AND RATIONAL BEHAVIOR

Economic incentives are not, to be sure, the only incentives; people are sometimes also motivated by a desire to win prestige, respect, friendship, and other social and psychological objectives. Though the phrase "socio-economic status" often used in discussions of status suggests that there may be a correlation between economic position and social position, there is no doubt that the two are sometimes different. The possibility that, in a case where there was no economic incentive for an individual to contribute to the achievement of a group interest, there might nonetheless be a social incentive for him to make such a contribution, must therefore be considered. And it is obvious that this is a possibility. If a small group of people who had an interest in a collective good happened also to be personal friends, or belonged to the same social club, and some of the group left the burden of providing that collective good on others, they might, even if they gained economically by this course of action, lose socially by it, and the social loss might outweigh the economic gain. Their friends might use "social pressure" to encourage them to do their part toward achieving the group goal, or the social club might exclude them, and such steps might be effective, for everyday observation reveals that most people value the fellowship of their friends and associates, and value social status, personal prestige, and self-esteem.

The existence of these social incentives to group-oriented action does not, however, contradict or weaken the analysis of this study. If anything, it strengthens it, *for social status and social acceptance are individual, noncollective goods.* Social sanctions and social rewards are "selective incentives"; that is, they are among the kinds of incentives that may be used to mobilize a latent group. It is in the nature of social incentives that they can distinguish among individuals: the recalcitrant individual can be ostracized, and the cooperative individual can be invited into the center of the charmed circle....

THE "BY-PRODUCT" THEORY
OF LARGE PRESSURE GROUPS

If the individuals in a large group have no incentive to organize a lobby to obtain a collective benefit, how can the fact that some large groups are organized be explained? Though many groups with common interests, like the consumers, the white-collar workers, and the migrant agricultural workers, are not organized, other large groups, like the union laborers, the farmers, and the doctors have at least some degree of organization. The fact that there are many groups which, despite their needs, are not organized would seem to contradict the "group theory" of the analytical pluralists; but on the other hand the fact that other large groups have been organized would seem to contradict the theory of "latent groups" offered in this study.

But the large economic groups that are organized do have one common characteristic which distinguishes them from those large economic groups that are not, and which at the same time tends to support the theory of latent groups offered in this work. This common characteristic will, however, require an elaboration or addition to the theory of groups developed in this study.

The common characteristic which distinguishes all of the large economic groups with significant lobbying organizations is that these groups are also organized for some *other* purpose. The large and powerful economic lobbies are in fact the by-products of organizations that obtain their strength and support because they perform some function in addition to lobbying for collective goods.

The lobbies of the large economic groups are the by-products of organizations that have the capacity to "mobilize" a latent group with "selective incentives." The only organizations that have the "selective incentives" available are those that (1) have the authority and capacity to be coercive, or (2) have a source of positive inducements that they can offer the individuals in a latent group.

A purely political organization—an organization that has no function apart from its lobbying function—obviously cannot legally coerce individuals

354

*Chapter 15
Social
Movements
and Collective
Behavior*

into becoming members. A political party, or any purely political organization, with a captive or compulsory membership would be quite unusual in a democratic political system. But if for some nonpolitical reason, if because of some other function it performs, an organization has a justification for having a compulsory membership, or if through this other function it has obtained the power needed to make membership in it compulsory, that organization may then be able to get the resources needed to support a lobby. The lobby is then a by-product of whatever function this organization performs that enables it to have a captive membership.

An organization that did nothing except lobby to obtain a collective good for some large group would not have a source of rewards or positive selective incentives it could offer potential members. Only an organization that also sold private or noncollective products, or provided social or recreational benefits to individual members, would have a source of these positive inducements. Only such an organization could make a joint offering or "tied sale" of a collective and a noncollective good that could stimulate a rational individual in a large group to bear part of the cost of obtaining a collective good. There are for this reason many organizations that have both lobbying functions and economic functions, or lobbying functions and social functions, or even all three of these types of functions at once. Therefore, in addition to the large group lobbies that depend on coercion, there are those that are associated with organizations that provide noncollective or private benefits which can be offered to any potential supporter who will bear his share of the cost of the lobbying for the collective good....

THE "SPECIAL INTEREST" THEORY AND BUSINESS LOBBIES

The segment of society that has the largest number of lobbies working on its behalf is the business community. The *Lobby Index*, an index of organizations and individuals filing reports under the Lobbying Act of 1946 and 1949, reveals that (when Indian tribes are excluded), 825 out of a total of 1,247 organizations represented business. Similarly, a glance at the table of contents of the *Encyclopedia of Associations* shows that the "Trade, Business, and Commercial Organizations" and the "Chambers of Commerce" together take up more than ten times as many pages as the "Social Welfare Organizations," for example. Most of the books on the subject agree on this point. "The business character of the pressure system," according to [political scientist E. E.] Schattschneider, "is shown by almost every list available." This high degree of organization among businessmen, Schattschneider thinks, is particularly important in view of the fact that most other groups are so poorly organized: "only a chemical trace" of the nation's Negroes are members of the National Association for the Advancement of Colored People; "only one sixteen hundredths of 1 per cent of the consumers" have joined the National Consumers' League; "only 6 per cent of American automobile drivers" are members of the American Automobile Association, and only "about 15 per cent of the veterans" belong to the

American Legion. Another scholarly observer believes that "of the many organized groups maintaining offices in the capital, there are no interests more fully, more comprehensively, and more efficiently represented than those of American industry." [James MacGregor] Burns and [Jack Walter] Peltason say in their text that "businessmen's 'unions' are the most varied and numerous of all." V. O. Key points out that "almost every line of industrial and commercial activity has its association." Key also expresses surprise at the extent of the power of organized business in American democracy: "The power wielded by business in American politics may puzzle the person of democratic predilections: a comparatively small minority exercises enormous power."

The number and power of the lobbying organizations representing American business is indeed surprising in a democracy operating according to the majority rule. The power that the various segments of the business community wield in this democratic system, despite the smallness of their numbers, has not been adequately explained. There have been many rather vague, and even mystical, generalizations about the power of the business and propertied interests, but these generalizations normally do not *explain why* business groups have the influence that they have in democracies; they merely assert that they always have such an influence, as though it were self-evident that this should be so. "In the absence of military force," said Charles A. Beard, paraphrasing Daniel Webster, "political power naturally and necessarily goes into the hands which hold the property." But why? Why is it "natural" and "necessary," in democracies based on the rule of the majority, that the political power should fall into the hands of those who hold the property? Bold statements of this kind may tell us something about the ideological bias of the writer, but they do not help us understand reality.

The high degree of organization of business interests, and the power of these business interests, must be due in large part to the fact that the business community is divided into a series of (generally oligopolistic) "industries," each of which contains only a fairly small number of firms. Because the number of firms in each industry is often no more than would comprise a "privileged" group, and seldom more than would comprise an "intermediate" group, it follows that these industries will normally be small enough to organize voluntarily to provide themselves with an active lobby—with the political power that "naturally and necessarily" flows to those that control the business and property of the country. Whereas almost every occupational group involves thousands of workers, and whereas almost any subdivision of agriculture also involves thousands of people, the business interests of the country normally are congregated in oligopoly-sized groups or industries. It follows that the laboring, professional, and agricultural interests of the country make up large, latent groups that can organize and act effectively only when their latent power is crystallized by some organization which can provide political power as a by-product; and by contrast the business interests generally can voluntarily and directly organize and act to further their common interests without any such adventitious assistance. The multitude of workers, consumers, white-collar workers, farmers, and so on are organized only in special circumstances, but business interests are organized as a general rule.

The Decline of the 1960s Social Movements

In 1968 some thought that social movements were escalating to the point that they might precipitate a revolution in the United States. A few years later, the possibility of a revolution had passed. In the following selection, Anthony Oberschall analyzes the factors that brought about the demise of these social movements and the contributions the movements made to social change in American society. He suggests that internal weaknesses—including a loose organizational structure, annual changes in the leadership, a proliferation of social movements that were at times at cross-purposes with each other, factionalism, and an absence of grassroots membership—contributed to their demise. In addition, the social control agencies were very active in opposing these American social movements. Large staffs and abundant resources were employed in the effort to repress them. But repression, argues Oberschall, was only marginally effective. On the other hand, Oberschall finds that success of the movements was strongly associated with their demise. The antiwar movement achieved many of its goals and melted away. The civil rights and black power movements were highly successful in ensuring full citizenship to an excluded minority, and then they faded. Oberschall believes that these movements did not radically change the system but that they did make it more responsive to new groups.

Oberschall is a professor of sociology at the University of North Carolina at Chapel Hill. His earlier book on social movements, *Social Conflict and Social Movements* (Prentice-Hall, 1973), is considered a classic. His recent book *Social Movements: Ideologies, Interests, and Identities* (Transaction, 1993), from which this selection was taken, may become one also.

Key Concept: social movements

INTRODUCTION

The decline of the 1960s movements in the United States—the civil rights, black power, antiwar, and student movements sometimes collectively referred to as The Movement—in the late 1960s and early 1970s has not been satisfactorily explained. In 1967 and 1968, many commentators thought the United States in the throes of a revolution. Five years later few people remained apprehensive.

Yet the decline of The Movement was one of the most important and dramatic developments of the post–World War II cultural and political scene. Surely why and how it happened ought to tell us something important about American society, politics, and culture....

I will analyze the organizational structure, resource base, leadership and membership, ideology, tactics, and important activities of the major and vanguard social movement organizations such as the Student Nonviolent Coordinating Committee (SNCC), the Black Panther Party (BPP), Students for a Democratic Society (SDS) and its Weatherman offshoot, and the New Mobilization Committee to End the War in Vietnam (Mobe). I will also analyze the organization tactics and effectiveness of the social control agencies that were opposed to the movements (FBI, CIA, Justice Department). I will assess the part that the mass media, in particular television, played in the movements' rise and decline, as well as the complex links between the movements and the counterculture or youth culture of the middle and late sixties and early seventies....

MOVEMENT STRUCTURE AND MOBILIZATION

Though they were its most important pacesetting elements, the SMOs [Social Movement Organizations] were but the most organized and visible manifestations of the participatory explosion, popular unrest, protest activity, and civil disorders of the 1960s. The movements themselves were embedded in a complex cultural revolution (usually referred to as the counterculture and the black revolution) that they at once shaped and were shaped by, whose most political and politicized embodiment they became, but that to some extent ran its own autonomous course, propelled by its own inner logic. The social movements of the 1960s also ran parallel with, and interacted in complex ways with, institutionalized politics, presidential and congressional politics, electoral and pressure group politics. By no means did all incumbent and challenger elites see the social movements only as opponents.

Social movement growth and decline can be understood from a resource mobilization perspective. At the core of the 1960s American social movements was a relatively small number of full-time *activists* ... including fifty or so leaders that the mass media and political elite singled out for special attention, more so for ability to innovate in symbol production and manipulation than for organization skills. Their actions and pronouncements became especially newsworthy and were interpreted as reflecting the grievances and aspirations of a large constituency whose voice they became but with which they had but tenuous organizational ties.

Many collective actions, from marches and demonstrations to campus building occupations and ghetto riots, were composed of *transitory teams* in which activists were but a small minority. Transitory teams were strategically placed for contributing their own time and labor, at their own expense, in brief, but repeated spurts of activity. They swelled the numbers of petitioners, marchers, demonstrators, and rioters into the hundreds of thousands during major events.

358

*Chapter 15
Social
Movements
and Collective
Behavior*

The frequent resort to mass rallies, petitions, marches and other forms of visible aggregation—what I have called identification moves—are an important part in the overall strategy of social movements. Movement leaders often are not able to demonstrate their strength by means of the electoral process geared to party politics and the quadrennial cycle of presidential elections. They need proof that their views and demands have widespread support and thus merit recognition by the target group (usually the authorities). They have to instill confidence, hope of success, and a sense of safety resulting from large numbers among their followers and sympathizers. And in the absence of strong organization, collective events are shapers of a collective identity and are a means of political and ideological education and of pulse taking.

Lastly, the 1960s movement had many sympathizers who, although not contributing their labor and their bodies, sent financial contributions to movement organizations, provided broad public opinion support, and often also important skills for legal defense and organization. In addition to scattered individuals, sympathizers included organized entities such as civic associations, churches and foundations, and leaders who had the means to commit association funds and programs in support of movement activity. These social units and association leaders have been referred to as the *conscience constituency*. It should be noted that movement participants—activists, transitory teams, and the conscience constituency—were not necessarily members of groups who were the principal intended beneficiaries of movement goals. This was also true in the civil rights movement where white liberal backing played a key role in overcoming southern resistance and federal government inertia. In a broader sense, participants do anticipate some personal benefits, which might include relief from guilt, moral outrage, career advancement, and making the United States a "better" country, in terms of their preferences.

The three components of the 1960s movement played specialized roles in overall movement organization. Activists supplied ideologies, symbols, organization, and leadership; transitory teams supplied much of the "labor"; and the conscience constituency provided financial support. But some mechanism had to exist or had to be created to maintain these often very diverse sets of people in a collaborative working relationship for supplying their contributions jointly to some collective goal. The most common means of doing so relies on organizations and a shared political culture. . . .

The 1960s movements never achieved an overarching ideological, organizational, or tactical unity. Dave Dellinger remarked that when Dr. Martin Luther King, Jr. was moving toward a close alliance of the civil rights movement with the antiwar movement shortly before his assassination, "For a brief time it seemed that everything might come together in one powerful movement: the struggle for civil rights, the struggle against the war, and the struggle for economic justice."

But this was not to be. The movement actually never became one, but instead remained a loose congeries of parts broadly in agreement on their condemnation of social evils and in their opposition to the "system." Groups coalesced for particular goals but frequently competed for the same limited resource base and jockeyed to achieve a dominant position for their ideological and tactical agenda. . . .

The content of the news media was not purposely biased against the administration, as Vice President Agnew repeatedly charged. Content analysis of television news coverage of the student movement and of race issues between September 1968 and April 1970, found no systematic "denigration of political authority."

Both the government and its opponents managed to manipulate the news media quite successfully on occasion. Since they had no other means of influencing their potential constituency and frequently also of communicating with their supporters, it is not surprising that movement leaders were trying to manipulate the media and gear movement strategy to the media. They sought attention through newsworthy innovative tactics and ideological pronouncements and through confrontations designed to draw a repressive response in the full glare of publicity. . . .

Beyond intentional movement building through media visibility, a massive collective action capability by opposition groups was helped by a media created "star system," by media-disseminated focal symbols and stimuli, and by a media-provided instant communications system which stimulated bandwagon effects and a pacesetter-follower dynamic. These effects were neither intended nor anticipated. They followed from media organizational constraints and imperatives. And they provided, for a time, an effective substitute for movement organization structure. The 1960s movements caught the government, the citizenry, the media, opinion shapers, and the academic establishment intellectually and organizationally unprepared. This was particularly constraining on the news media. Under pressure for providing instant coverage, analysis, and commentary in the context of the highly competitive communications industry, news reporters, columnists, and anchormen turned to police chiefs, district attorneys, politicians, and law enforcement and administration officials on the one hand, and the movement leaders and political entrepreneurs on the other. . . .

For a time, . . . movement building through the media rather than through grassroots organizing worked effectively. Leaders used the media to communicate with transitory teams needed for backing up their pronouncements with action. Television especially provided a learning opportunity on how to organize and stage events, how to phrase "nonnegotiable" demands addressed to the authorities, and what roles to assume in confrontations with various target groups. Much information to movement participants and sympathizers about the movement) leader's ideologies, symbols, programs of action, etc.) and about the targets (the Pentagon, the CIA, university administrations, etc.) was disseminated free of cost to social movement organizations.

Yet neglect of grassroots organization and of an internally controlled communications system for information transfers and political education left the 1960s movements in a vulnerable position when media attention shifted to other issues. . . .

SOCIAL CONTROL

As a result of the Watergate affair and the reassertion of the Congress' role in making the executive branch accountable, volumes of information on the government's social control activities in the 1960s and 1970s have been released from numerous government sources and supplement the enormous material already published in newspapers and magazines. A preliminary examination of these documents provides as little cheer to civil libertarians as it does to taxpayers concerned with efficient spending of their tax dollars.

At first sight the magnitude and comprehensive nature of the social control effort is mind-boggling. The amounts of money spent, the size of the staffs involved, the number of agencies activated, the number of different programs and operations mounted, the number of investigations conducted, the number of files kept, the pieces of mail opened and telegrams examined, the paid informers, the agents provocateurs, the illegal break-ins, the scrutiny of federal income tax returns, the dirty tricks and harassment, the red squads of local police departments, the illegal wiretaps, the deliberate encouragement of violence by passing explosives to opposition groups, media manipulation, the centrally computerized information systems and technologically sophisticated surveillance techniques, the systematic evasion of the occasional and unsystematic attempts to limit and control these activities, and much else as well, must surely warm the hearts of citizens fearful of revolution. If one looks at output rather than input, a different picture emerges altogether. The summary of the Church committee report on domestic intelligence activities states among other things that

> Between 1960 and 1974, the FBI conducted over 500,000 separate investigations of persons and groups under the "subversive" category, predicated on the possibility that they might be likely to overthrow the Government of the United States. Yet not a single individual or group has been prosecuted since 1957 under the laws which prohibit planning or advocating action to overthrow the Government and which are the main alleged statutory basis for such FBI investigations (*New York Times*, April 29, 1976).

... The dirty tricks and provocations and informers probably had some weakening effect on the 1960s movement, but hardly as much as factionalism and organizational weaknesses. As with intelligence operations, dirty tricks were probably more effective in disrupting routinized enterprises such as the 1972 Muskie campaign than student and antiwar activities....

SUCCESS AND DECLINE

Repression of the 1960s movements was only marginally effective in precipitating movement decline. Internal weaknesses were quite important. In this section, the relationship between success of the 1960s movement and their decline will be examined. It is my contention that this relationship was quite strong and that their successes are considerable and lasting.

The survival of social movements and of social movement organizations is evidence of neither success nor failure. Movements might cease to exist because their goals have been successfully accomplished, or on the contrary because they have failed and their adherents became discouraged or intimidated. Social movements may also become institutionalized as pressure groups, political parties, and public agencies with a stable constituency and a routinized resource base....

Success can be measured by the extent to which the publicly proclaimed goals of social movements have been realized. Success and failure also have other aspects. When individuals and groups whose concerns have been ignored force public decision makers to recognize their needs and to commit institutional resources to implementing them, social movements can be said to be successful. Concretely, this means that the costs of pursuing the goals sought by the movement are shifted from movement adherent to the polity at large. This does not mean that movement goals will be promptly and effectively realized. It means that the interests and preferences of ignored groups has become a routinized input into the political process and will be dealt with by those in authority positions in the same manner as the concerns of other recognized groups and constituencies. Lastly, assessment of success and failure also depends on whether the social movements generate a novel realignment of political forces (coalitions, backlashes) making it easier or more difficult to implement concerns and goals similar to those advocated by the movements.

The principal goals of the antiwar movement was termination of American involvement in the Indochina War. The principal goals of the civil rights and black power movements were full citizenship rights and equality for blacks. The student movement subscribed to these goals as well, and beyond them sought the termination of the draft, more democratic governance for universities and colleges, and greater responsiveness to student needs. All three movements were partially successful in achieving their stated goals, in mobilizing powerful allies, in obtaining institutional recognition, and in avoiding a backlash that would in the longer run undermine their gains. Having said this, it is still true that the combined power of the three movements and the counterculture did not result in a major redistribution of power in the United States as was hoped by some activists.

The antiwar movement was a partial success. The Indochina War did end. American involvement in the war did not end as rapidly and as completely as the movement sought, but it did progressively scale down, from over a half million ground combat troops at the end of 1968 to virtually zero by the time the Ford administration was put into office. And although the bombing campaign in Indochina expanded under the Nixon administration, the pressures for signing a peace agreement and for ending the bombing were so powerful that by the 1972 election campaign the Nixon-Kissinger policy on Indochina had shifted from winning to face-saving exit.

Both the troop reduction and the exit policy resulted from forces generated by the antiwar movement. It succeeded in mobilizing public opinion and Congressional (especially Senate) opposition to the war. The Congress then forced the administration into reverse gear through the institutional political process.

362

*Chapter 15
Social
Movements
and Collective
Behavior*

It is difficult to assign causal priority to one or another set of factors for the crucial reversals of American Vietnam policy. Without the antiwar movement, the realization that the United States was boxing itself into a no-win strategy, with costs in lives, material resources, and domestic unrest far exceeding any possible benefits from victory, would not have penetrated so deeply into the Congress and powerful establishment groups. These the President of the United States could not in the end ignore. As the burden of maintaining pressure for war de-escalation and extrication from Vietnam shifted from antiwar movement to the Congress and other groups, the movement itself demobilized.

Together with Watergate and the forces it mobilized, the antiwar movement succeeded for the first time since World War II in checking the "imperial presidency" and the national security bureaucracy in the area of the president's war-making powers, executive privilege, secrecy, and lack of the accountability in foreign affairs. That was no mean feat. No backlash, domestic or international, has materialized as a result of the Indochina fiasco.

The success of the civil rights and black power movements in the area of full citizenship rights and of black political power have been impressive and well documented. In the domain of economic advance, the results so far have been more problematic. Nevertheless, as a result of the black movements of the 1950s and 1960s, race relations and race policies in the United States have dramatically shifted from an essentially "South African" pattern to one that shows promise of absorbing blacks into the mainstream of American life.

The civil rights and black power movement have become successfully institutionalized as the politics of black ethnicity. Much of the burden for enforcing equality of opportunity and for promoting equality in fact have been shifted from the movements to the courts, to executive departments of the federal and state governments, and to routine politics. No backlash of substantial proportions has resulted from black gains.

As for the student movement, it had some success in giving students greater rights and more voice in university governance, at least in many institutions of higher education. The draft was terminated. More importantly, the three movements under review have enabled other minorities and exploited groups —from Indians and Chicanos to women and homosexuals—to obtain a hearing for their concerns and provide a legitimate input into public decisions on matters of interest to them. The movements have fostered an intense examination and critical look at American society which produced new concerns for the environment, quality of life and rights of all minorities. Dave Dellinger wrote that "gradually other issues won new adherents from the several million people who were energized and activated by the anti-war struggle." The very existence of these new concerns and movements has siphoned off some of the activists and financial contributors of the original social movements, thereby contributing to their decline. Yet in a broader sense the decline from these losses can be seen as more victory than failure, for it helped those forces that favor changes in the United States consonant with the kinds of changes championed by the 1960s social movements.

The 1960s movements declined then for a number of reasons. Increased radicalism scared off the conscience constituency. The Democratic administration's erratic reformism that fueled the civil rights and black power movements gave way to the Nixon administration's consistent opposition to all dissent. Although repression was only mildly effective, it terminated the direct sponsorship by the government of opposition to itself. A weakening national economy forced transitory teams to worry about jobs and careers, to shift from attacking authority to coming to terms with it. The size of the movements could not be sustained after factionalism, partial success, and progressive disillusionment curtailed the steady recruitment stream needed to replenish the high turnover membership base. Internal weaknesses stemming from the absence of a grassroots organization structure and from reliance on the media for recruitment, communication, and political education destroyed the mobilizing capabilities of the pacesetter leaders and movement organizations when media attention shifted away from movement concerns and coverage. Activists drifted away into new movements, into nonpolitical countercultural pursuits, into jobs, and into institutional politics and reform.

Exit from movement activism into attractive alternative careers was possible for even the top movement leaders and media stars. Because the United States lacks an organized left and the 1960s movements failed to create one, the activists and leaders scattered into a wide spectrum of institutions and positions from which a concerted radical thrust is not possible. Yet the 1960s movements turned out surprisingly successful, in large part because institutional elites and organizations pressured and challenged by them took up the burden of implementing some of their goals just as the movements were disintegrating. . . .

Reform works because those influential groups who engineer it manage to pass its costs down to other social classes and groups, as they have indeed managed to do consistently with the tax burden. The liberal, white upper middle class who in the end swung the balance of forces around to desegregation and integration do not live in integrated neighborhoods and do not send their children to integrated schools. Reform expands the bureaucracies and industries that the most talented individuals from less privileged groups end up using as their mobility escalator. And thus the system is strengthened.

CHAPTER 16 Global Social Change

16.1 DANIEL CHIROT

The Modern Era

The major issue that the founding fathers of sociology analyzed was how societies change. Emile Durkheim described how societies changed from traditional simple (Durkheim's term was *mechanical*) to modern complex (*organic*) societies. Karl Marx developed a dialectical theory of history that emphasized technological change, the way that production is organized, the stratification system, and class conflict. Max Weber studied the rise of capitalism and the larger process of the increasingly rational organization of society. These three intellectual traditions combine into a theory of modernization that provides the foundation for modern theories of social change, including that of sociologist Daniel Chirot. In the selection that follows, which is from *How Societies Change* (Pine Forge Press, 1994), Chirot applies his theory in exploring how modern society evolved.

For Chirot the process of modernization starts with industrialization, which greatly increases production and standards of living but which also irrevocably alters society's culture and social systems, including family, education, religion, and government. Chirot asserts that "most people are better off than their ancestors," even though "the rapidity of change has had a wrenching effect on all the societies affected." Chirot's story of Western industrialization features five technological waves, or cycles, built around (1) textiles; (2) railroads; (3) chemicals; (4) automobiles and mass consumer goods; and (5) electronics, computers, and biomedical products. A major thesis of Chirot's theory of history is that "the transition from one cycle to another produces great international [and national] stress" and a great potential for civil unrest and war. His other major thesis is that industrialization in the long run increases education, professional occupations, and the middle class on the one hand and increases democracy (the periodic legal displacement of elites) on the other hand.

Chirot is a professor of sociology in the Henry M. Jackson School of International Studies at the University of Washington. He has performed research in Austria and Indonesia, and he has been a visiting professor in Taiwan and a consultant in Romania and Africa. In addition to *How Societies Change,* he is the author of *Modern Tyrants: The Power and Prevalence of Evil in Our Age* (Free Press, 1994) and *Social Change in the Modern Era* (Harcourt Brace Jovanovich, 1986).

Key Concept: industrial cycles and their internal and international social consequences

The quantitative changes in human societies produced by the advent of the modern industrial age are staggering....

In 1800 well over 90 percent of the human population lived in rural villages or very small towns, and most of these people were peasants. On the whole, whether in Europe or elsewhere, they worked hard, were not free to move as they pleased or to dispose of their goods as they wished, paid high taxes to their lords, were illiterate, and had no foreseeable way of improving their lives. They had many children, but one third to one half, or in bad times even more, died before they reached the age of five.

By the late twentieth century in Europe, North America, Australia, Japan, and the other most advanced societies of East Asia, the vast majority of people live in cities or their adjacent suburbs. Almost all adults are literate. They have far fewer children, but almost all of them survive into adulthood. They pay an even higher portion of what they make in taxes than their peasant ancestors, but disposable income has gone up so much that the average inhabitant in these advanced societies has large amounts of money left over after paying for taxes and necessities. Much of the income of modern people is spent on what would have been considered unbelievable luxuries in the past: private cars, holiday trips, well-heated, clean, and spacious housing, durable and well-tailored clothing, immense varieties of healthy food available at low prices, and medical care that allows most people to live comfortably and productively into their sixties and seventies. It is a natural human propensity to complain and to claim that the present is worse than the past. But no one who has actually lived in an authentic, vermin-infested, socially and politically oppressive agrarian village and compared this to life in a modern society can have many doubts about which one most people would prefer....

The modernization that began in western Europe has now spread throughout most of the world and irrevocably changed societies. This is because West European societies evolved a way of life that produces stronger and better adapted societies than those that existed before. This hardly means that other societies are on their way to being physically exterminated by the Europeans, but that their cultures and social systems are being irrevocably altered.

It would be possible to give production statistics that underlie the vast progress made during the modern era: steel production, tons of coal mined, square meters of cloth manufactured, numbers of automobiles that have come off assembly lines, and so on. As far as most of us are concerned, however, it is not such production figures that matter but how our lives and the perception of our lives have changed.

Emphasizing the purely material aspects of change in the modern era can be misleading. If most people are better off than their ancestors, this does not mean that there are no problems associated with modernization. On the contrary, the rapidity of change has had a wrenching effect on all the societies affected. Even in the most advanced parts of Europe these changes have occurred only in the past six to eight generations, and throughout most of the world, only in the past two to four generations. Thus human societies have not yet had time to absorb the consequences of all these transformations or to find workable solutions to all the problems they have produced. After all, it took two thousand years for agrarian-state societies to work out religious and ideological solutions to the moral problems raised by the changes they brought about. It will take at least a few centuries for modern industrial social systems to do the same.

Furthermore, the intellectual, religious, and political elites who produce the ideas through which human societies interpret their world have been far from universally happy about modernization. Many have devoted their lives over the past two hundred years to resisting modernization, denigrating it, and proposing ways of reorganizing societies to nullify the effects of capitalism, markets, and industrialization. If material progress throughout the modern era had always been smooth, without periodic crises, and if it had been evenly distributed, so that all parts of every society had gained at an equal rate, these intellectuals would have had few listeners. But social change in the modern era has been anything but smooth and evenly distributed.

It is to the problems raised by modernization that we must now turn in order to better understand social and cultural change in the past two centuries.

INDUSTRIAL CYCLES

The Industrial Revolution is usually thought to have begun in England in about 1780. Though no economic change can be dated precisely, it is certain that between 1760 and 1800 a major change took place. Wool and linen cloth manufacturing were vastly surpassed by the production of manufactured cotton cloth, and this cotton cloth started to be made in factories that were more mechanized than any large-scale manufacturing process had ever been before. In the 1750s to 1770s, England, which can grow no cotton because it is too cold, imported an average of one to three thousand metric tons of cotton per year, mostly from India. By 1790 that shot up to 14,000 tons per year, by 1800 to 24,000, by 1810 to 56,000, and by 1840 to 208,000 tons. By that time, the South in the United States had become the world's major producer of cotton. The spectacular inventiveness of entrepreneurs in England yielded a long set of mechanical improvements that allowed cloth to be made faster, better, and more cheaply than ever before in human history, so that English cloth exports gained markets all over the world.

... The progress of capitalism did not cease with the growing of the textile-led economy. A new "high-tech" product was invented, the railroad, that became, literally as well as figuratively, the engine of an enormous new burst of growth. The railroad, unlike the mechanical loom, was an invention that was out in the open for everyone to see, and it was a marvel of modern engineering. It made cheap and rapid land transportation available for the first time in human history. It brought remote regions into contact with the rest of the world. It greatly lowered the cost of transporting people and bulk goods. Thus it revolutionized all aspects of the economy and brought modernization everywhere it went. . . .

But the passing of the second industrial cycle in the 1870s only heralded the start of a third phase. This time, the leading "high-tech" products were organic chemicals (used at first to produce dyes for textiles), steel (which replaced iron), and, in the 1880s, electrical machinery.

Just as railroads had seemed a fantastic product of high technology—so did the new discoveries bring about more wonders. This time, however, there was something new. Textile manufacturing had used not advanced science but inspired tinkering and clever entrepreneurship to make its advances. Railroads were much closer to being a product of genuine scientific progress, but even there, the actual scientific knowledge required to make such machines, if not yet the engineering, had been available for many decades. But with the advent of organic chemistry as a vital component of industry, pure scientific research came into its own. It required advanced scientists to keep up with what was going on, and the first society to actively finance research into this area through its universities, Germany, gained a huge advantage. From the last part of the nineteenth century on, the relationship between science and technology became much more direct, and only those societies willing and able to finance scientific research could hope to keep up. This meant that scientific research now received much more financing than ever before from both governments and private firms eager to find new processes and products.

The third industrial cycle also saw something else. Contrary to the expectations of Karl Marx and other foes of capitalism, the most advanced industries no longer needed just masses of poorly paid unskilled laborers. Growing technological sophistication required a better educated work force.

It is not surprising, therefore, that the two Western societies that invested the most in the late nineteenth century in research universities and in giving a larger proportion of their population a sound secondary education, the United States and Germany, moved ahead of England. England did not lose ground in any absolute sense, but it grew more slowly and lost its primary position in the world economy.

... [T]he First World War, ... which went from 1914 to 1918, marked the end of the third industrial cycle, and again produced widespread belief that capitalism and its attendant political innovations, democracy and greater respect for individual freedom, were now obsolete. Yet once again, despite the difficulty of adjusting to a new industrial cycle, capitalism did not end. In the

1920s and 1930s there began the fourth period, the age of automobiles, petro-chemicals, and mass-produced mechanical consumer goods. This started in the United States and was marked by an enormous increase in the availability of high-technology popular goods such as refrigerators, cars, and radios. World War II, fought from 1939 to 1945, interrupted this cycle, but it resumed again in the 1950s and spread its benefits to large parts of the world. Rapid advances in airplane technology made very rapid transportation throughout the world possible. In this period the world economy was dominated by the United States.

By about 1970, however, new signs of trouble began to appear. Competitors in Japan and western Europe were gaining ground on the United States. Throughout the formerly most advanced industrial parts of the world, obsolete plants with highly paid workers were starting to lose money. New factories and entire new industries sprang up, making the industrial giants of the previous industrial cycles vulnerable. Just as the textile manufacturing heartland of England had suffered at the time of the end of the first industrial cycle, so now the Middle West in the United States, the industrial cities of Great Britain, of northern France, of Belgium, and in the Ruhr Valley of Germany faced declining employment, intense pressure to lower high wages, and a string of bankruptcies of venerable old firms. Within the United States new industrial regions in the West and South prospered while old centers declined. In Germany it was Bavaria that made gains against the older industrial centers. But because of the crisis in the old centers of industrial production there was again a sense that capitalism was on the verge of failure. As always at the end of one industrial cycle and the start of another, uncertainty produced growing social unrest in the 1960s and 1970s. This period also saw the high point of Marxism.

Marxist revolutionaries had taken power in Russia in 1917, in Eastern Europe after 1945, in China in 1949, in North Vietnam in 1954, in Cuba in 1959, and in South Vietnam, Laos, and Cambodia after a long war against the United States in 1975. It began to seem that Marxist socialism was the inevitable future of the world and that capitalism was doomed to decline in crisis and internal unrest. But this was no more the case in the 1970s than it had been in the 1920s and 1930s, in the 1870s and 1880s, or in the 1830s and 1840s.

Instead the 1970s saw the start of the fifth industrial cycle. This one, in which we still live, has been dominated by electronics, and as it progresses the highest of "high-tech" products will be biomedical. The basis of these changes was, first of all the transistor and then the silicon computer chip. As in past industrial cycles, innovations in one area spread quickly to others. Automobile, machine tool, and textile manufacturing were all revolutionized by the new technologies. Computers have made communications fantastically faster than ever before and have made it possible to store and manipulate giant amounts of information. This in turn has changed business practices as well as accelerated scientific research.

But the most momentous changes of the fifth industrial cycle are still to happen. Advances in fundamental theoretical biology in the 1950s, the discovery of how genes work, has led in the 1980s and 1990s to the start of a whole new branch of the economy. Biomedical manufacturing is just beginning, but it will revolutionize agriculture as well as other aspects of economic life. It will also begin to produce miracle medical products as dramatic as those that came in the first half of the twentieth century when a variety of infectious diseases were brought under control. Whereas the world demand for certain goods such as food, textiles, televisions, or cars may soon reach an upper limit, the demand for greater health and longevity is unlikely to be sated at any time soon. Those who believed in the past that capitalism was doomed because of overproduction and sated demand will be proved as wrong this time as in the past. Each new industrial cycle brings enormous new demand in previously unanticipated sectors, as well as new jobs, new opportunities for profit, and a thorough renewal as old, seemingly all-powerful firms lose ground to more innovative little enterprises....

The only certainty is that education and scientific research will continue to play an ever increasing role in determining economic success. And those societies that apply this lesson best will dominate the future even more surely than England did in most of the nineteenth century and the United States in most of the twentieth.

INTERNAL AND INTERNATIONAL SOCIAL CONSEQUENCES OF MODERNIZATION AND INDUSTRIAL CYCLES

The social consequences of the Industrial Revolution were enormous. Some have already been mentioned: urbanization, very rapid population growth, a much higher level of education for the average person, the transformation of old solidarities in favor of a more individualistic, market-driven type of behavior, and great improvements in material well-being. There were many others. Families became smaller. They had fewer children, and because of much greater physical mobility, fewer close relatives continued living near each other. Monetary calculations became a much more important part of daily life because virtually all economic life was monetized; that is, whereas in the past peasants directly raised much of their own food and made many of the goods they needed, modern workers are paid in money and buy what they need. Almost no family still produces a significant proportion of the necessities it needs to live....

Though it took a long time to produce the conditions that led to World War I, it can be shown that the fundamental problem was failure by the Europeans to adjust to the third industrial cycle or to understand its implications.

Similarly, the aftermath of World War I was bad enough, but the coincident shift from the third to the fourth industrial period compounded the problem. In the fourth industrial age, research and education assumed an ever greater importance, but so did something quite new. Automobiles and the spread of electrical consumer appliances demanded a rapidly broadening mass consumer base. The Great Depression of the 1930s was primarily a failure of demand to keep up with increasing productivity. What would have been required was a highly stimulating macroeconomic policy on the part of the main industrial powers, chiefly the United States, the only country able to go through the transformation of the fourth industrial age in the 1920s. But the United States did not follow such a policy, particularly abroad, and this made it virtually impossible for the world economy to adjust to the changes occurring.

In contrast to this, the United States after World War II refloated the world economy and created the conditions for the greatest economic boom in history. During that time, the fourth industrial age flourished; its benefits spread throughout the advanced Western countries and Japan and even began to spread beyond that into formerly poor countries. But now that age has ended, and the United States is losing the hegemonic preponderance it once had. The transition to the fifth industrial age, though unlikely to be as rocky as some of the past transitions, will not be without its problems. That is what much of the discussion about the decline of the United States in the 1980s and 1990s has been about.

There is no question that the transition from one cycle to another produces great international stress. Nationalism, an invention of the modern era, intensifies. Competition seems to take on a particularly bitter edge because of the fear that a temporary downturn is really the beginning of a final collapse. And those who are gaining at the expense of others demand greater power and privilege in the world political system, while the old hegemons try to keep their power intact. The possibility of conflict between major advanced countries is therefore greatest during the shift from one industrial age to another....

Thus the social tensions of modernization, exacerbated by the industrial cycles that have caused disruptions even in the most advanced economies, have led to a variety of political protest movements within advanced societies and internationally.

CLASS, STATUS, AND POWER
IN MODERN SOCIETIES

Just as the invention of agriculture and the state drastically changed the pattern of social stratification, the distribution of power and privilege in human societies, so did the Industrial Revolution. Peasants gradually disappeared. This most numerous of classes, which included the vast majority of human beings who lived between the third millennium B.C. and the twentieth century A.D., virtually vanished in less than 150 years in the advanced societies of the world. The old nobilities who had controlled the land and been a military elite in most agrarian societies vanished at about the same time. Almost all of the princes, kings, and emperors who had ruled agrarian societies lost their powers or were eliminated entirely. Though cities grew enormously the old urban merchant and artisan classes were transformed beyond recognition.

The new economic classes that replaced the old ones were, at the top, owners and controllers of capital: entrepreneurs, financiers, and top managers of businesses. Immediately below them there developed a class of specialized professionals—doctors, lawyers, engineers, researchers and educators, journalists—whose advanced education and skills were necessary to keep ever more complex economies and societies functioning smoothly. Below them there grew a large new class of people who were neither owners of businesses nor highly qualified specialists, but bureaucratic, low-level managers. These kinds of white-collar occupations also proliferated in government machines that became increasingly bureaucratic and intrusive as modernization advanced and the powers of the state to administer society grew. Yet one more level below them were another growing class, clerical workers, who formed a kind of lower middle class with higher aspirations. Finally, those who provided most of the labor during the first century and a half of the Industrial Revolution were the growing working class. There remained those in agriculture, but these now metamorphosed from peasants into farmers: business managers and entrepreneurs on the land following the dictates of the market rather than of tradition or community restrictions.

The multiplication of special professions and the continual changes in technology over the life of the five industrial cycles have continued to change class structures in modern societies.

In England in about 1870 about 4 to 5 percent of all households were in what could be considered the "middle class," that is, what used to be called the "bourgeoisie" (which comes from the French term for townsmen). These were the owners and managers of enterprises and the new professionals. Above them there still remained the old aristocracy, and below them were the clerks in the lower middle class and the workers who were in the new urban lower class. Only a very small number of the new bourgeoisie was rich or owned much property. Most owners of enterprises had small businesses rather than very large ones, and most of the new bourgeoisie worked for others instead of for their own businesses. But even so, this class was of growing importance. By the early twentieth century the bourgeoisie included close to 10 percent of the households in England and slightly more than that in the United States. If the lower middle class, the clerical workers who aspired to being bourgeois, is included, the middle class as a whole included about 20 percent of the households in the most advanced Western societies of the early twentieth century.

Nothing quite like it had ever existed before. The number of people between the princes and nobles on one hand and the peasants on the other had always been quite small in agrarian societies. Now there were not only many of them, but they were educated and politically aware, and they demanded privileges and rights that underlings had never had before. They also found important and powerful allies in the upper bourgeoisie, the most successful entrepreneurs, financiers, owners, and managers who controlled the productive resources of modern societies. All were interested in reducing the powers of the old aristocracies, in promoting government action to keep markets free, and in allowing political representation of the middle class. They shared a common ideology of nationalism and distrust of the lower classes.

Not only did the bourgeoisie as a whole become politically more powerful as it took over the main roles in the economy, but the way in which its members lived set the standards for society as a whole. They were utilitarian, business oriented, and practical. They believed in hard work, thrift, and sexual self-control. Their families were the primary focus of their social lives and economic calculations. Their cultural tastes and habits have been named after the Queen of England who reigned from 1837 to 1901, "Victorian."

"Victorian bourgeois" values have been derided by intellectuals and by opponents of capitalism, especially its British and American forms, from the late nineteenth century until the present. Yet these repressed, disciplined, striving people were actually carrying forward the old values of the rational townspeople who had begun the transformation of the European economy and made modernization possible. Bourgeois culture was highly adaptive and successful in modern societies. Not only did it make individual families successful, but the spread of these habits throughout other social classes, particularly into the working class, created the self-restraint, discipline, and order necessary to make industrial systems work.

It turns out that in the late twentieth century the most dynamic societies in the world, those of East Asia, are dominated by a growing middle class whose hard work, thrift, desire for education, ambitions for their children, and self-control closely approximate the Victorian bourgeois culture of western Europe and the United States in the late nineteenth and early twentieth century.

By the late twentieth century, in the most advanced societies, the middle class makes up close to 30 percent of the population, and the lower middle class, another 25 percent. These two classes now make up the majority of the population of advanced societies, though in the West their values and habits have become much more lax than when they were still "Victorian."...

Neither class nor status structure is sufficient to account for the distribution of power in modern societies. To be sure, the rising middle class took a larger share of power in the nineteenth and twentieth centuries, and the richest owners of businesses gained a disproportionate share of that power. Older and fading elites used their high status to hold on to some power well into the twentieth century in Europe, and they continue to be important in many poorer countries. But modern societies also have professional politicians and government officials who pursue power for its own sake, not to defend any particular class or interest group....

Government officials have become a class in and of themselves. Though they do not own their means of production, they have a vested interest in keeping their jobs and expanding their privileges. The only check on their tendency to expand their power and privilege is the existence of elected officials who set their budgets and are supposed to be responsive to the will of the general population. In dictatorships where such officials do not exist—for example, in the communist states that disintegrated in the late 1980s and early 1990s—top bureaucrats became the ruling class. Like the Confucian officials in classical China, they stifled innovation, took too much power, and caused their societies to stagnate.

In capitalist societies, where private ownership of the means of production and elected officials keep control over the bureaucracy, the situation is much better. Yet elected officials themselves can easily become a distinct class, using their power to accumulate personal wealth and putting aside the interests of their constituents in order to preserve their own. If they work too closely with the bureaucrats they are meant to oversee, it can be difficult to get society's larger interests represented....

The main political difference between the most successful modern societies of the twentieth century and agrarian societies is that a mechanism for the renewal of power through the periodic displacement of elites is available. That is the chief function of democracy: not to represent all the various interests in a modern society perfectly, which is impossible, but to limit the tenure and power of the professional power seekers and to keep some control over corruption.

Despite all the potential for concentration of power in ever more powerful governments, modern societies cannot maintain the highly unequal structure of reward that characterized agrarian societies. An industrial economy needs too many educated people who demand a greater share of the rewards available. High education and concentration of people in urban areas makes political organization easier, and interest groups resist the imposition of policies that hurt them. In this respect, Marx was correct. Not only the middle classes, but the working class and other groups have been able to organize far more successfully than nonelites ever could in agrarian societies, and this has placed a limit on how great a share of the surplus wealth small elites can take.

The Clash of Civilizations?

The end of the cold war spawned the hope for a more peaceful world. The outline of the emerging world order is still unclear, but perhaps the most discussed analysis of it to date is Samuel P. Huntington's vision of conflict between civilizations as presented in the following selection from "The Clash of Civilizations?" *Foreign Affairs* (Summer 1993).

The future, according to Huntington, will be full of conflict. Nation-states will be divided by and struggle over differences in history, language, culture, tradition, and religion. Huntington believes it is religion that defines the relationship between people and the concept of God, individual and group, citizen and state, parents and children, husband and wife, rights and responsibilities, and equality and hierarchy. Huntington is concerned about the deadly conflicts that these differences are likely to produce. Author Robert D. Kaplan's recent observations and predictions about a "coming anarchy" in many Third World nations are equally frightening and differ only on the level of the dividing lines. Huntington predicts clashes of civilizations, while Kaplan predicts clashes of ethnic, national, religious, and tribal groups. Both versions of the future see war, not peace, reigning.

Huntington is the Eaton Professor of the Science of Government and the director of the John M. Olin Institute for Strategic Studies at Harvard University. His books include *No Easy Choice: Political Participation in Developing Countries* (Harvard University Press, 1976), coauthored with Joan M. Nelson, and *The Third Wave: Democratization in the Late Twentieth Century* (University of Oklahoma Press, 1991).

Key Concept: clashing civilizations

THE NEXT PATTERN OF CONFLICT

World politics is entering a new phase, and intellectuals have not hesitated to proliferate visions of what it will be—the end of history, the return of traditional rivalries between nation states, and the decline of the nation state from the conflicting pulls of tribalism and globalism, among others. Each of these visions catches aspects of the emerging reality. Yet they all miss a crucial, indeed a central, aspect of what global politics is likely to be in the coming years.

It is my hypothesis that the fundamental source of conflict in this new world will not be primarily ideological or primarily economic. The great divisions among humankind and the dominating source of conflict will be cultural.

Nation states will remain the most powerful actors in world affairs, but the principal conflicts of global politics will occur between nations and groups of different civilizations. The clash of civilizations will dominate global politics. The fault lines between civilizations will be the battle lines of the future.

Samuel P. Huntington

Conflict between civilizations will be the latest phase in the evolution of conflict in the modern world. For a century and a half after the emergence of the modern international system with the Peace of Westphalia, the conflicts of the Western world were largely among princes—emperors, absolute monarchs and constitutional monarchs attempting to expand their bureaucracies, their armies, their mercantilist economic strength and, most important, the territory they ruled. In the process they created nation states, and beginning with the French Revolution the principal lines of conflict were between nations rather than princes. In 1793, as R. R. Palmer put it, "The wars of kings were over; the wars of peoples had begun." This nineteenth-century pattern lasted until the end of World War I. Then, as a result of the Russian Revolution and the reaction against it, the conflict of nations yielded to the conflict of ideologies, first among communism, fascism-Nazism and liberal democracy, and then between communism and liberal democracy. During the Cold War, this latter conflict became embodied in the struggle between the two superpowers, neither of which was a nation state in the classical European sense and each of which defined its identity in terms of its ideology.

These conflicts between princes, nation states and ideologies were primarily conflicts within Western civilization, "Western civil wars," as William Lind has labeled them. This was as true of the Cold War as it was of the world wars and the earlier wars of the seventeenth, eighteenth and nineteenth centuries. With the end of the Cold War, international politics moves out of its Western phase, and its centerpiece becomes the interaction between the West and Non-Western civilizations and among non-Western civilizations. In the politics of civilizations, the peoples and governments of non-Western civilizations no longer remain the objects of history as targets of Western colonialism but join the West as movers and shapers of history.

THE NATURE OF CIVILIZATIONS

During the cold war the world was divided into the First, Second and Third Worlds. Those divisions are no longer relevant. It is far more meaningful now to group countries not in terms of their political or economic systems or in terms of their level of economic development but rather in terms of their culture and civilization.

What do we mean when we talk of a civilization? A civilization is a cultural entity. Villages, regions, ethnic groups, nationalities, religious groups, all have distinct cultures at different levels of cultural heterogeneity. The culture of a village in southern Italy may be different from that of a village in northern Italy, but both will share in a common Italian culture that distinguishes them from German villages. European communities, in turn, will share cultural features that distinguish them from Arab or Chinese communities. Arabs,

Chinese and Westerners, however, are not part of any broader cultural entity. They constitute civilizations. A civilization is thus the highest cultural grouping of people and the broadest level of cultural identity people have short of that which distinguishes humans from other species. It is defined both by common objective elements, such as language, history, religion, customs, institutions, and by the subjective self-identification of people. People have levels of identity: a resident of Rome may define himself with varying degrees of intensity as a Roman, an Italian, a Catholic, a Christian, a European, a Westerner. The civilization to which he belongs is the broadest level of identification with which he intensely identifies. People can and do redefine their identities and, as a result, the composition and boundaries of civilizations change.

Civilizations may involve a large number of people, as with China ("a civilization pretending to be a state," as Lucian Pye put it), or a very small number of people, such as the Anglophone Caribbean. A civilization may include several nation states, as is the case with Western, Latin American and Arab civilizations, or only one, as is the case with Japanese civilization. Civilizations obviously blend and overlap, and may include subcivilizations. Western civilization has two major variants, European and North American, and Islam has its Arab, Turkic and Malay subdivisions. Civilizations are nonetheless meaningful entities, and while the lines between them are seldom sharp, they are real. Civilizations are dynamic; they rise and fall; they divide and merge. And, as any student of history knows, civilizations disappear and are buried in the sands of time.

Westerners tend to think of nation states as the principal actors in global affairs. They have been that, however, for only a few centuries. The broader reaches of human history have been the history of civilizations. In *A Study of History*, Arnold Toynbee identified 21 major civilizations; only six of them exist in the contemporary world.

WHY CIVILIZATIONS WILL CLASH

Civilization identity will be increasingly important in the future, and the world will be shaped in large measure by the interactions among seven or eight major civilizations. These include Western, Confucian, Japanese, Islamic, Hindu, Slavic-Orthodox, Latin American and possibly African civilization. The most important conflicts of the future will occur along the cultural fault lines separating these civilizations from one another.

Why will this be the case?

First, differences among civilizations are not only real; they are basic. Civilizations are differentiated from each other by history, language, culture, tradition and, most important, religion. The people of different civilizations have different views on the relations between God and man, the individual and the group, the citizen and the state, parents and children, husband and wife, as well as differing views of the relative importance of rights and responsibilities, liberty and authority, equality and hierarchy. These differences are the product of centuries. They will not soon disappear. They are far more fundamental than differences among political ideologies and political regimes. Differences do not necessarily mean conflict, and conflict does not necessarily mean violence. Over the centuries, however, differences among civilizations have generated the most prolonged and the most violent conflicts.

Second, the world is becoming a smaller place. The interactions between peoples of different civilizations are increasing; these increasing interactions intensify civilization consciousness and awareness of differences between civilizations and commonalities within civilizations. North African immigration to France generates hostility among Frenchmen and at the same time increased receptivity to immigration by "good" European Catholic Poles. Americans react far more negatively to Japanese investment than to larger investments from Canada and European countries. Similarly, as Donald Horowitz has pointed out, "An Ibo may be... an Owerri Ibo or an Onitsha Ibo in what was the Eastern region of Nigeria. In Lagos, he is simply an Ibo. In London, he is a Nigerian. In New York, he is an African." The interactions among peoples of difference civilizations enhance the civilization-consciousness of people that, in turn, invigorates differences and animosities stretching or thought to stretch back deep into history.

Third, the processes of economic modernization and social change throughout the world are separating people from longstanding local identities. They also weaken the nation state as a source of identity. In much of the world religion has moved in to fill this gap, often in the form of movements that are labeled "fundamentalist." Such movements are found in Western Christianity, Judaism, Buddhism and Hinduism, as well as in Islam. In most countries and most religions the people active in fundamentalist movements are young, college-educated, middle-class technicians, professionals and business persons. The "unsecularization of the world," George Weigel has remarked, "is one of the dominant social facts of life in the late twentieth century." The revival of religion, "la revanche de Dieu," as Gilles Kepel labeled it, provides a basis for identity and commitment that transcends national boundaries and unites civilizations.

Fourth, the growth of civilization-consciousness is enhanced by the dual role of the West. On the one hand, the West is at a peak of power. At the same time, however, and perhaps as a result, a return to the roots phenomenon is occurring among non-Western civilizations. Increasingly one hears references to trends toward a turning inward and "Asianization" in Japan, the end of the Nehru legacy and the "Hinduization" of India, the failure of Western ideas of socialism and nationalism and hence "re-Islamization" of the Middle East, and now a debate over Westernization versus Russianization in Boris Yeltsin's country. A West at the peak of its power confronts non-Wests that increasingly have the desire, the will and the resources to shape the world in non-Western ways.

In the past, the elites of non-Western societies were usually the people who were most involved with the West, had been educated at Oxford, the Sorbonne or Sandhurst, and had absorbed Western attitudes and values. At the same time, the populace in non-Western countries often remained deeply imbued with the indigenous culture. Now, however, these relationships are being reversed. A de-Westernization and indigenization of elites is occurring in many non-Western countries at the same time that Western, usually American, cultures, styles and habits become more popular among the mass of the people.

Fifth, cultural characteristics and differences are less mutable and hence less easily compromised and resolved than political and economic ones. In the former Soviet Union, communists can become democrats, the rich can become poor and the poor rich, but Russians cannot become Estonians and Azeris cannot become Armenians. In class and ideological conflicts, the key question was "Which side are you on?" and people could and did choose sides and change sides. In conflicts between civilizations, the question is "What are you?" That is a given that cannot be changed. And as we know, from Bosnia to the Caucasus to the Sudan, the wrong answer to that question can mean a bullet in the head. Even more than ethnicity, religion discriminates sharply and exclusively among people. A person can be half-French and half-Arab and simultaneously even a citizen of two countries. It is more difficult to be half-Catholic and half-Muslim.

Finally, economic regionalism is increasing. The proportions of total trade that were intraregional rose between 1980 and 1989 from 51 percent to 59 percent in Europe, 33 percent to 37 percent in East Asia, and 32 percent to 36 percent in North America. The importance of regional economic blocs is likely to continue to increase in the future. On the one hand, successful economic regionalism will reinforce civilization-consciousness. On the other hand, economic regionalism may succeed only when it is rooted in a common civilization. The European Community rests on the shared foundation of European culture and Western Christianity. The success of the North American Free Trade Area depends on the convergence now underway of Mexican, Canadian and American cultures. Japan, in contrast, faces difficulties in creating a comparable economic entity in East Asia because Japan is a society and civilization unique to itself. However strong the trade and investment links Japan may develop with other East Asian countries, its cultural differences with those countries inhibit and perhaps preclude its promoting regional economic integration like that in Europe and North America.

Common culture, in contrast, is clearly facilitating the rapid expansion of the economic relations between the People's Republic of China and Hong Kong, Taiwan, Singapore and the overseas Chinese communities in other Asian countries. With the Cold War over, cultural commonalities increasingly overcome ideological differences, and mainland China and Taiwan move closer together. If cultural commonality is a prerequisite for economic integration, the principal East Asian economic bloc of the future is likely to be centered on China. This bloc is, in fact, already coming into existence. As Murray Weidenbaum has observed,

> Despite the current Japanese dominance of the region, the Chinese-based economy of Asia is rapidly emerging as a new epicenter for industry, commerce and finance. This strategic area contains substantial amounts of technology and manufacturing capability (Taiwan), outstanding entrepreneurial, marketing and services acumen (Hong Kong), a fine communications network (Singapore), a tremendous pool of financial capital (all three), and very large endowments of land, resources and labor (mainland China).... From Guangzhou to Singapore, from Kuala Lumpur to Manila, this influential network—often based on extensions of the traditional clans—has been described as the backbone of the East Asian economy.[1]

Culture and religion also form the basis of the Economic Cooperation Organization, which brings together ten non-Arab Muslim countries: Iran, Pakistan, Turkey, Azerbaijan, Kazakhstan, Kyrgyzstan, Turkmenistan, Tadjikistan, Uzbekistan and Afghanistan. One impetus to the revival and expansion of this organization, founded originally in the 1960s by Turkey, Pakistan and Iran, is the realization by the leaders of several of these countries that they had no chance of admission to the European Community. Similarly, Caricom, the Central American Common Market and Mercosur rest on common cultural foundations. Efforts to build a broader Caribbean-Central American economic entity bridging the Anglo-Latin divide, however, have to date failed.

As people define their identity in ethnic and religious terms, they are likely to see an "us" versus "them" relation existing between themselves and people of different ethnicity or religion. The end of ideologically defined states in Eastern Europe and the former Soviet Union permits traditional ethnic identities and animosities to come to the fore. Differences in culture and religion create differences over policy issues, ranging from human rights to immigration to trade and commerce to the environment. Geographical propinquity gives rise to conflicting territorial claims from Bosnia to Mindanao. Most important, the efforts of the West to promote its values of democracy and liberalism as universal values, to maintain its military predominance and to advance its economic interests engender countering responses from other civilizations. Decreasingly able to mobilize support and form coalitions on the basis of ideology, governments and groups will increasingly attempt to mobilize support by appealing to common religion and civilization identity.

The clash of civilizations thus occurs at two levels. At the micro-level, adjacent groups along the fault lines between civilizations struggle, often violently, over the control of territory and each other. At the macro-level, states from different civilizations compete for relative military and economic power, struggle over the control of international institutions and third parties, and competitively promote their particular political and religious values.

THE FAULT LINES BETWEEN CIVILIZATIONS

The fault lines between civilizations are replacing the political and ideological boundaries of the Cold War as the flash points for crisis and bloodshed. The Cold War began when the Iron Curtain divided Europe politically and ideologically. The Cold War ended with the end of the Iron Curtain. As the ideological division of Europe has disappeared, the cultural division of Europe between Western Christianity, on the one hand, and Orthodox Christianity and Islam, on the other, has reemerged....

Conflict along the fault line between Western and Islamic civilizations has been going on for 1,300 years.

... This centuries-old military interaction between the West and Islam is unlikely to decline. It could become more virulent. The Gulf War left some Arabs feeling proud that Saddam Hussein had attacked Israel and stood up to the West. It also left many feeling humiliated and resentful of the West's military presence in the Persian Gulf, the West's overwhelming military dominance, and their apparent inability to shape their own destiny. Many Arab countries, in addition to the oil exporters, are reaching levels of economic and social development where autocratic forms of government become inappropriate and efforts to introduce democracy become stronger. Some openings in Arab political systems have already occurred. The principal beneficiaries of these openings have been Islamist movements. In the Arab world, in short, Western democracy strengthens anti-Western political forces. This may be a passing phenomenon, but it surely complicates relations between Islamic countries and the West....

On both sides the interaction between Islam and the West is seen as a clash of civilizations. The West's "next confrontation," observes M. J. Akbar, an Indian Muslim author, "is definitely going to come from the Muslim world. It is in the sweep of the Islamic nations from the Maghreb to Pakistan that the struggle for a new world order will begin."...

Historically, the other great antagonistic interaction of Arab Islamic civilization has been with the pagan, animist, and now increasingly Christian black peoples to the south. In the past, this antagonism was epitomized in the image of Arab slave dealers and black slaves. It has been reflected in the on-going civil war in the Sudan between Arabs and blacks, the fighting in Chad between Libyan-supported insurgents and the government, the tensions between Orthodox Christians and Muslims in the Horn of Africa, and the political conflicts, recurring riots and communal violence between Muslims and Christians in Nigeria. The modernization of Africa and the spread of Christianity are likely to enhance the probability of violence along this fault line....

The conflict of civilizations is deeply rooted elsewhere in Asia. The historic clash between Muslim and Hindu in the subcontinent manifests itself now not only in the rivalry between Pakistan and India but also in intensifying religious strife within India between increasingly militant Hindu groups and India's substantial Muslim minority. The destruction of the Ayodhya mosque in December 1992 brought to the fore the issue of whether India will remain a secular democratic state or become a Hindu one....

The interactions between civilizations vary greatly in the extent to which they are likely to be characterized by violence. Economic competition clearly predominates between the American and European subcivilizations of the West and between both of them and Japan. On the Eurasian continent, however, the proliferation of ethnic conflict, epitomized at the extreme in "ethnic cleansing," has not been totally random. It has been most frequent and most violent between groups belonging to different civilizations. In Eurasia the great historic fault lines between civilizations are once more aflame. This is particularly true along the boundaries of the crescent-shaped Islamic bloc of nations from the bulge of Africa to central Asia. Violence also occurs between Muslims, on the one hand, and Orthodox Serbs in the Balkans, Jews in Israel, Hindus in India, Buddhists in Burma and Catholics in the Philippines. Islam has bloody borders.

CIVILIZATION RALLYING: THE KIN-COUNTRY SYNDROME

Groups or states belonging to one civilization that become involved in war with people from a different civilization naturally try to rally support from other members of their own civilization. As the post–Cold War world evolves, civilization commonality, what H. D. S. Greenway has termed the "kin-country" syndrome, is replacing political ideology and traditional balance of power considerations as the principal basis for cooperation and coalitions. It can be seen gradually emerging in the post–Cold War conflicts in the Persian Gulf, the Caucasus and Bosnia. None of these was a full-scale war between civilizations, but each involved some elements of civilizational rallying, which seemed to become more important as the conflict continued and which may provide a foretaste of the future. . . .

Civilization rallying to date has been limited, but it has been growing, and it clearly has the potential to spread much further. As the conflicts in the Persian Gulf, the Caucasus and Bosnia continued, the positions of nations and the cleavages between them increasingly were along civilizational lines. Populist politicians, religious leaders and the media have found it a potent means of arousing mass support and of pressuring hesitant governments. In the coming years, the local conflicts most likely to escalate into major wars will be those, as in Bosnia and the Caucasus, along the fault lines between civilizations. The next world war, if there is one, will be a war between civilizations. . . .

IMPLICATIONS FOR THE WEST

This article does not argue that civilization identities will replace all other identities, that nation states will disappear, that each civilization will become a single coherent political entity, that groups within a civilization will not conflict with and even fight each other. This paper does set forth the hypotheses that differences between civilizations are real and important; civilization-consciousness is increasing; conflict between civilizations will supplant ideological and other forms of conflict as the dominant global form of conflict; international relations, historically a game played out within Western civilization, will increasingly be de-Westernized and become a game in which non-Western civilizations are actors and not simply objects; successful political, security and economic international institutions are more likely to develop within civilizations than across civilizations; conflicts between groups in the same civilization; violent conflicts between groups in different civilizations will be more frequent, more sustained and more violent than conflicts between groups in different civilizations are the most likely and most dangerous source of escalation that could lead to global wars; the paramount axis of world politics will be the relations between "the West and the Rest"; the elites in some torn non-Western countries will try to make their countries part of the West, but in most cases face major obstacles to accomplishing this; a central focus of conflict for the immediate future will be between the West and several Islamic-Confucian states.

NOTES

1. Murray Weidenbaum, *Greater China: The Next Economic Superpower?*, St. Louis: Washington University Center for the Study of American Business, Contemporary Issues, Series 57, February 1993, pp. 2–3.

ACKNOWLEDGMENTS

1.1   From Peter L. Berger, *Invitation to Sociology: A Humanistic Perspective* (Anchor Books, 1963). Copyright © 1963 by Peter L. Berger. Reprinted by permission of Doubleday, a division of Bantam Doubleday Dell Publishing Group, Inc.

1.2   Excerpted from *The Sociological Imagination* by C. Wright Mills (Oxford University Press, 1959). Copyright © 1959 by Oxford University Press, Inc.; renewed 1987 by Yaraslava Mills. Reprinted by permission of Oxford University Press, Inc.

2.1   From Clyde Kluckhohn, *Mirror for Man: The Relation of Anthropology to Modern Life* (McGraw-Hill, 1949). Copyright © 1949 by George E. Taylor. Reprinted by permission.

2.2   From Horace Miner, "Body Ritual Among the Nacirema," *American Anthropologist,* vol. 58, no. 3 (June 1956). Copyright © 1956 by The American Anthropological Association. Reprinted by permission. Not for further reproduction.

2.3   From Colin M. Turnbull, *The Mountain People* (Simon & Schuster, 1972). Copyright © 1972 by Colin M. Turnbull. Reprinted by permission of Simon & Schuster, Inc.

2.4   From Elijah Anderson, "The Code of the Streets," *The Atlantic Monthly,* vol. 273, no. 5 (May 1994), pp. 81–94. Adapted from Elijah Anderson, *The Code of the Streets* (W. W. Norton, 1994). Copyright © 1994 by Elijah Anderson. Reprinted by permission of the author and W. W. Norton and Company, Inc.

2.5   From Deborah Tannen, *You Just Don't Understand: Women and Men in Conversation* (William Morrow, 1990). Copyright © 1990 by Deborah Tannen. Reprinted by permission of William Morrow and Company, Inc.

3.1   From George Herbert Mead, *Mind, Self and Society* (University of Chicago Press, 1934). Copyright © 1934 by University of Chicago Press. Reprinted by permission. Notes omitted.

3.2   From Margaret L. Andersen, *Thinking About Women: Sociological Perspectives on Sex and Gender,* 4th ed. (Allyn & Bacon, 1997). Copyright © 1997 by Allyn & Bacon. Reprinted by permission. References omitted.

3.3   From Herbert Blumer, "Society as Symbolic Interaction," in Arnold M. Rose, ed., *Human Behavior and Social Processes* (Houghton Mifflin, 1962). Copyright © 1962 by Houghton Mifflin Company. Reprinted by permission.

4.1   From Peter L. Berger, *Invitation to Sociology: A Humanistic Perspective* (Anchor Books, 1963). Copyright © 1963 by Peter L. Berger. Reprinted by permission of Doubleday, a division of Bantam Doubleday Dell Publishing Group, Inc.

4.2   From Erving Goffman, *The Presentation of Self in Everyday Life* (Anchor Books, 1959). Copyright © 1959 by Erving Goffman. Reprinted by permission of Doubleday, a division of Bantam Doubleday Dell Publishing Group, Inc. Some notes omitted.

5.1   From Daniel Patrick Moynihan, "Defining Deviancy Down," *The American Scholar,* vol. 62, no. 1 (Winter 1993). Copyright © 1992 by Daniel Patrick Moynihan. Reprinted by permission of *The American Scholar.*

5.2   From Stanley Milgram, "Some Conditions of Obedience and Disobedience to Authority," *Human Relations,* vol. 18, no. 1 (1965). Copyright © 1965 by Stanley Milgram. Reprinted by permission of Alexandra Milgram, literary executor. Notes omitted.

5.3   From Herbert C. Kelman and V. Lee Hamilton, *Crimes of Obedience: Toward A Social Psychology of Authority and Responsibility* (Yale University Press, 1989). Copyright © 1989 by Yale University Press. Reprinted by permission. Notes and some references omitted.

5.4   From James Q. Wilson, "What to Do About Crime," *Commentary* (September 1994). Copyright © 1994 by The American Jewish Committee. Reprinted by permission. Notes omitted.

6.1   From Charles Horton Cooley, *Social Organization* (Charles Scribner's Sons, 1909). Copyright © 1909 by Charles Scribner's Sons; renewed 1937 by Elsie Jones Cooley.

6.2   From Robert D. Putnam, "The Prosperous Community: Social Capital and Public Life," *The American Prospect* (Spring 1993). Copyright © 1993 by New Prospect, Inc. Reprinted by permission.

384

Acknowledgments

6.3 From Louis Wirth, "Urbanism as a Way of Life," *American Journal of Sociology*, vol. 44, no. 7 (July 1938). Copyright © 1938 by University of Chicago Press. Reprinted by permission. Notes omitted.

6.4 From Max Weber, "Bureaucracy," in H. H. Gerth and C. Wright Mills, eds. and trans., *From Max Weber: Essays in Sociology* (Oxford University Press, 1958). Copyright © 1946, 1958 by H. H. Gerth and C. Wright Mills. Reprinted by permission of Oxford University Press, Inc.

7.1 From Karl Marx and Friedrich Engels, *The Communist Manifesto* (1848). Reprint, International Publishers, 1983. Reprinted by permission of International Publishers Company, Inc. Some notes omitted.

7.2 From Kingsley Davis and Wilbert E. Moore, "Some Principles of Stratification," *American Sociological Review*, vol. 10, no. 2 (1945). References omitted.

7.3 From Barry Bluestone, "The Inequality Express," in Robert Kuttner, ed., *Ticking Time Bombs* (New Press, 1996). Copyright © 1996 by *The American Prospect*. Reprinted by permission.

7.4 From Daniel D. Huff, "Upside-Down Welfare," *Public Welfare* (Winter 1992). Copyright © 1992 by The American Public Human Services Association. Reprinted by permission. Notes omitted.

8.1 Excerpted from *The Inner Circle: Large Corporations and the Rise of Business Political Activity in the U.S. and U.K.* by Michael Useem (Oxford University Press, 1984). Copyright © 1984 by Oxford University Press. Reprinted by permission. Notes omitted.

8.2 From Jonathan Kozol, "Poverty's Children: Growing Up in the South Bronx," *The Progressive* (October 1995). Copyright © 1995 by The Progressive, Inc. Adapted from *Amazing Grace: The Lives of Children and the Conscience of a Nation* (Crown, 1995). Reprinted by permission of The Progressive, Inc.

9.1 From Andrew Hacker, *Two Nations: Black and White, Separate, Hostile, Unequal* (Ballantine Books, 1995). Copyright © 1995 by Andrew Hacker. Reprinted by permission of Scribner, a division of Simon & Schuster, Inc.

9.2 From William Julius Wilson, *The Truly Disadvantaged: The Inner City, the Underclass, and Public Policy* (University of Chicago Press, 1987). Copyright © 1987 by University of Chicago Press. Reprinted by permission. Notes omitted.

9.3 From Judith Lorber, *Paradoxes of Gender* (Yale University Press, 1994). Copyright © 1994 by Yale University. Reprinted by permission of Yale University Press. Notes and references omitted.

9.4 From Toni Nelson, "Violence Against Women," *World Watch* (July/August 1996). Copyright © 1996 by The Worldwatch Institute. Reprinted by permission.

10.1 From G. William Domhoff, *Who Rules America? Power and Politics in the Year 2000*, 3rd ed. (Mayfield, 1998). Copyright © 1998 by Mayfield Publishing Company. Reprinted by permission. Notes omitted.

10.2 From Marvin J. Cetron and Owen Davies, "The Future Face of Terrorism," *The Futurist* (November/December 1994). Copyright © 1994 by The World Future Society, Bethesda, MD. Reprinted by permission.

11.1 From Rosabeth Moss Kanter, Barry A. Stein, and Todd D. Jick, *The Challenge of Organizational Change: How Companies Experience It and Leaders Guide It* (Free Press, 1994). Copyright © 1994 by Rosabeth Moss Kanter, Barry A. Stein, and Todd D. Jick. Reprinted by permission of The Free Press, an imprint of Simon & Schuster, Inc. References omitted.

11.2 From Mark Dowie, "Pinto Madness," *Mother Jones*, vol. 2, no. 8 (September/October 1977). Copyright © 1977 by Mark Dowie. Reprinted by permission.

11.3 From George Ritzer, *The McDonaldization of Society: An Investigation into the Changing Character of Contemporary Social Life*, rev. ed. (Pine Forge Press, 1996). Copyright © 1996 by Pine Forge Press. Reprinted by permission. Notes omitted.

12.1 From Stephanie Coontz, *The Way We Really Are: Coming to Terms With America's Changing Families* (Basic Books, 1997). Copyright © 1997 by Basic Books, a division of HarperCollins Publishers, Inc. Reprinted by permission of Basic Books, a subsidiary of Perseus Books Group, LLC. Notes omitted.

12.2 From Kathleen Gerson, "Coping With Commitment: Dilemmas and Conflicts of Family Life," in Alan Wolfe, ed., *America at Century's End* (University of California Press, 1991).

Copyright © 1991 by the Regents of the University of California. Reprinted by permission. Notes omitted.

12.3   From Peter L. Berger and Hansfried Kellner, "Marriage and the Construction of Reality," *Diogenes,* vol. 45 (Summer 1964). Copyright © 1964 by Casalini Libri, Fiesole. Reprinted by permission. Notes omitted.

13.1   From Robert Wuthnow, "How Small Groups Are Transforming Our Lives," *Christianity Today* (February 7, 1994). Adapted from *Sharing the Journey: Support Groups and America's New Quest for Community* (Free Press, 1994). Copyright © 1994 by Robert Wuthnow. Reprinted by permission of *Christianity Today* and The Free Press, a division of Simon & Schuster.

13.2   From D. L. Rosenhan, "On Being Sane in Insane Places," *Science,* vol. 179 (January 19, 1973), pp. 250–258. Copyright © 1973 by The American Association for the Advancement of Science. Reprinted by permission. Some notes omitted.

14.1   From Robert D. Kaplan, "The Coming Anarchy," *The Atlantic Monthly* (February 1994). Copyright © 1994 by Robert D. Kaplan. Reprinted by permission.

14.2   From Bill McKibben, "A Special Moment in History," *The Atlantic Monthly* (May 1998). Copyright © 1998 by Bill McKibben. Reprinted by permission of the author.

15.1   From Mancur Olson, Jr., *The Logic of Collective Action: Public Goods and the Theory of Groups* (Harvard University Press, 1971). Copyright © 1965, 1971 by the President and Fellows of Harvard College. Reprinted by permission of Harvard University Press. Notes omitted.

15.2   From Anthony Oberschall, *Social Movements: Ideologies, Interests, and Identities* (Transaction, 1993). Copyright © 1993 by Transaction Publishers. Reprinted by permission. Notes and references omitted.

16.1   From Daniel Chirot, *How Societies Change* (Pine Forge Press, 1994). Copyright © 1994 by Pine Forge Press. Reprinted by permission.

16.2   From Samuel P. Huntington, "The Clash of Civilizations?" *Foreign Affairs* (Summer 1993). Copyright © 1993 by The Council on Foreign Relations, Inc. Reprinted by permission.

Index